Psychodrama: Advances in Theory and Practice provides a comprehensive overview of developments in the theory and practice of psychodrama, integrating different psychodramatic schools of thought.

Psychodrama is one of the pioneering approaches of psychotherapy and is practised by thousands of practitioners and in most countries of the world. The editors of this volume bring together contributions from eight European countries, South America, Australia, Israel and the USA to explain and explore recent innovations. They look at how psychodrama has contributed to the development of psychotherapy, introducing concepts that have had a profound influence on other therapies. These include concepts such as role theory, the encounter, the co-unconscious, the social atom, sociometry, action research, group psychotherapy, the cycle of spontaneity and creativity, role play, the significance of the moment in the here-and-now and many related concepts and techniques.

This book will be of great interest to all students, practitioners and trainers in the field of psychodrama. It will also appeal to professionals and students in the related fields of psychotherapy, counselling, psychology and psychiatry.

Clark Baim is a psychodrama trainer based in the UK and is Co-Director of the Birmingham Institute for Psychodrama. He has written and co-edited a number of books, journal articles and chapters. He was the founding director of Geese Theatre UK, a company focusing on rehabilitative drama with offenders.

Jorge Burmeister became the President Elect of the International Association of Group Psychotherapy in 2006. He is a founding member of the Federation of European Psychodrama Training Organizations (FEPTO) and has worked as a psychodrama trainer and supervisor in several European countries.

Manuela Maciel is currently chairperson of the International Psychodrama Section of the IAGP (International Association of Group Psychotherapy). She has been a Psychodrama Practitioner for 20 years and is a psychodrama trainer and supervisor in her native Portugal.

Advancing Theory in Therapy
Series Editor: Keith Tudor

Most books covering individual therapeutic approaches are aimed at the trainee/student market. This series, however, is concerned with *advanced* and *advancing* theory, offering the reader comparative and comparable coverage of a number of therapeutic approaches.

Aimed at professionals and postgraduates, *Advancing Theory in Therapy* will cover an impressive range of theories. With full reference to case studies throughout, each title will

- present cutting-edge research findings
- locate each theory and its application within cultural context
- develop a critical view of theory and practice.

Titles in the series

Body Psychotherapy
Edited by Tree Staunton

Transactional Analysis: A Relational Perspective
Helena Hargaden and Charlotte Sills

Adlerian Psychotherapy: An Advanced Approach to Individual Psychology
Ursula E. Oberst and Alan E. Stewart

Rational Emotive Behaviour Therapy: Theoretical Developments
Edited by Windy Dryden

Co-Counselling: The Theory and Practice of Re-evaluation Counselling
Katie Kauffman and Caroline New

Analytical Psychology
Edited by Joe Cambray and Linda Carter

Person-Centred Therapy: A Clinical Philosophy
Keith Tudor and Mike Worrall

Psychodrama

Advances in Theory and Practice

Edited by Clark Baim, Jorge Burmeister and Manuela Maciel

 Routledge
Taylor & Francis Group

LONDON AND NEW YORK

First published 2007 by Routledge
27 Church Road, Hove, East Sussex BN3 2FA

Simultaneously published in the USA and Canada
by Taylor & Francis Inc
270 Madison Avenue, New York, NY 10016

Routledge is an imprint of the Taylor & Francis Group, an Informa Business

Typeset in Times by Garfield Morgan, Swansea, West Glamorgan
Printed and bound in Great Britain by TJ International Ltd, Padstow, Cornwall
Paperback cover design by Sandra Heath

This publication has been produced with paper manufactured to strict
environmental standards and with pulp derived from sustainable forests.

British Library Cataloguing in Publication Data
A catalogue record for this book is available from the British Library

Library of Congress Cataloging-in-Publication Data
Psychodrama : advances in theory and practice / edited by Clark Baim, Jorge
Burmeister, and Manuela Maciel.
     p. ; cm. – (Advancing theory in therapy)
  Includes bibliographical references and index.
  ISBN-13: 978-0-415-41913-0 (hbk.)
  ISBN-10: 0-415-41913-1 (hbk.)
  ISBN-13: 978-0-415-41914-7 (pbk.)
  ISBN-10: 0-415-41914-X (pbk.)
  1. Drama–Therapeutic use. I. Baim, Clark. II. Burmeister, Jorge. III. Maciel,
Manuela. IV. Series.
  [DNLM: 1. Psychodrama. 2. Psychological Theory. WM 430.5.P8 P973
2007]
  RC489.P7P7594 2007
  616.89'1523–dc22

                                                                2006036741

ISBN 978-0-415-41913-0 hbk
ISBN 978-0-415-41914-7 pbk

'It is a great pleasure to invite the reader to an encounter with the thoughts and experiences of twenty-five outstanding psychodramatists from twelve different countries. Their collaboration in this book represents the first global project in psychodramatic literature in the 21st century.

The outstanding benefits of psychodrama, sociometry and group psychotherapy have spread across the globe. All of the human sciences are increasingly benefiting from approaches that have grown out of the introduction of the psychodramatic stage and its related healing techniques. One of the great strengths of the psychodramatic approach is its adjustability to the demands of different realms of life (e.g. internal, interpersonal, spiritual, and across cultures and sub-cultures) as well as its inherent emphasis on human creativity. All of this is reflected in psychodrama's various styles of application and modes of interpretation, of which the present book is an excellent example. What joy to give this miraculous product of human creativity into the reader's care.'

Grete A. Leutz, MD, Founder of the Moreno Institute for Psychodrama, Sociometry and Group Psychotherapy, Überlingen, Germany; Fellow of the International Association of Group Psychotherapy and the American Society of Group Psychotherapy and Psychodrama; Recipient of the J. L. Moreno Award for lifelong outstanding contributions in the field of psychodrama.

'This volume pays homage to the genius of J. L. Moreno, who has inspired us all. When he and I met in 1941, his name was already well established in the social sciences, although he had not yet succeeded in having his ideas accepted, especially his ideas about what psychotherapy should be and what psychodrama, sociometry and group psychotherapy meant to the field of psychotherapy in general.

We, his heirs, should be conscious of the historic facts underlying Moreno's philosophical and practical ideas of changing society, and our relationship to the Godhead, which makes us all responsible for one another and thus co-creators of the universe. It is particularly the latter idea – with which he was imbued as a mystic – which found such hard resistance, even neglect and ridicule, in the psychiatric community. Nevertheless, Moreno never entertained doubts about his vision. The element that is basic to all of the instruments he gave us is that of The Encounter: eye-to-eye, face to face, nothing standing between us.

Recently, the members of the Federation of European Psychodrama Training Organizations (FEPTO) found a significant indication of how well Moreno is remembered when they discovered that there is a street named "Dr. Moreno Strasse" in a village where Moreno was physician in the Children's Hospital during the First World War from 1917–1918. His medical position made it possible for him not only to directly observe children in their development, but also inspired the idea of sociometry to right the wrongs he observed in the community, which was then an internment village. The Moreno Strasse (whose existence he did not know about in his lifetime) can be seen as a permanent record of his activities in Mitterndorf, activities which, if officially viewed as Quixotic, underscore the need for all of us to continue to join him in his endeavor to enable The Encounter. May this book be part of that endeavor.'

Zerka Moreno, Author, *The Quintessential Zerka*, writings by *Zerka Toeman Moreno on Psychodrama, Sociometry and Group Psychotherapy*

Contents

Contributors

Anne Ancelin Schützenberger, PhD is a psychodramatist, TEP, University Professor of clinical and social psychology emeritus (Nice, France), co-founder of the IAGP, international group leader, trainer, trainer of trainers and consultant for health, psychodrama, family therapy, psychodrama and transgenerational psychotherapy and group psychotherapy. She also works for industry and organizations. Professor Schützenberger organized the first international congress of psychodrama in Paris in 1964, and she is a former consultant and trainer for the United Nations. She has trained and lectured on five continents and has bestselling books on psychodrama, J. L. Moreno and transgenerational links which have been translated into nine languages. Born in 1919, Professor Schützenberger is still working, teaching, lecturing and appearing on television and radio programs (website: http://perso.orange.fr/a.ancelin. schutzenberger/toc.htm).

Clark Baim, MEd, is a registered psychodrama trainer with more than 20 years of experience in group facilitation and supervising in prisons, probation and mental health settings. He is Co-Director, with Susie Taylor, of the Birmingham Institute for Psychodrama. He has worked as a group facilitator and for the National Probation Service as a Lead National Trainer. He has also worked as a psychodramatist in HM Prison Grendon Underwood, and in the 1980s was the founder and first director of Geese Theatre UK, a company specializing in rehabilitative drama with offenders. In recent years, Clark has focused on attachment theory as it relates to offending behavior. A native of Chicago, based in the UK, Clark has written and co-edited a number of books, journal articles and chapters related to psychodrama, applied theatre and offender rehabilitation (email: cbaim@hotmail.com).

Anne Bannister, PhD, is a psychodramatist, dramatherapist and former social worker who has specialized in working with traumatized children. She is the author of six books, the most recent being *Creative Therapies* *with Traumatised Children* (2003) and, with co-editor Annie Huntington, *Communicating with Children and Adolescents* (2002). She has also contributed chapters to several books, including *The Handbook of Psychodrama*, edited by Marcia Karp, Paul Holmes and Kate Bradshaw Tauvon, and also *Psychodrama with Trauma Survivors*, edited by Peter Felix Kellermann and M.K. Hudgins.

Adam Blatner, MD, TEP, is board certified in both adult and child/ adolescent psychiatry; author of three widely used books in psychodrama (*Acting In*; *Foundations of Psychodrama*; *The Art of Play*) and many chapters and journal articles. He received the J. L. Moreno Award for Lifetime Contributions and the David Kipper Award for Scholarship. Adam is a writer and teacher living in Texas. (For numerous papers on psychodrama and related topics see website: www.blatner.com/ adam/)

Dr Jorge Burmeister is a certified trainer and supervisor in psychodrama and CBT, and is a specialist in Psychiatry and Psychotherapy in Switzerland and Spain. He is a past president of the German Association of Group Psychotherapy and Group Dynamics and a founding member of the Federation of European Psychodrama Training Organizations. In 2006 he became President Elect of the International Association of Group Psychotherapy. He is a lecturer in Group Psychotherapy and Psychodrama at universities in Zurich, Milan, Valencia, Granada and Innsbruck. He is also the Dean of the International Summer Academy for Groups in Granada and co-director of the International Training Center 'Jacob L. and Zerka T. Moreno' in Granada (email: bulmonte21 @bluewin.ch; website: www.centromoreno.com).

John Casson, PhD is a dramatherapist, psychodrama psychotherapist, senior trainer and supervisor in private practice near Manchester, UK. He has 22 years of experience as a therapist, 11 of which were in the NHS. He is a founder member of the Northern School of Psychodrama. His book *Drama, Psychotherapy and Psychosis: Dramatherapy and Psychodrama with People Who Hear Voices* is published by Routledge. He has written a play, *Voices and Visions*, based on his research (email: drjohncasson@gmail.com; website: www.creativepsychotherapy.info).

Rosa Cukier is a psychologist in São Paulo, Brazil, with over 30 years of clinical experience doing psychodrama, psychoanalysis and teaching and supervising at two of the psychodrama institutes there. She is the author of three books on psychodrama as well as chapters and articles.

Sue Daniel lives and works in Melbourne as a psychotherapist in private practice with individuals, couples and families. She travels in many countries conducting workshops and seminars in psychodrama and its application. She is a trainer, educator, practitioner and supervisor and the director of the Psychodrama Institute of Melbourne. She founded the Moreno Psychodrama Society. She is the chairperson of the Australian Advisory and Assessment Board of Psychodrama and was chair of the Psychodrama Section of the International Association of Group Psychotherapy from 2000–2003 (website: www.psychodrama-institute-melbourne.com).

Maurizio Gasseau is a Jungian analyst, group analyst, and psychodramatist in Italy as well as a leader of training groups all over the world. His main interest is researching dreams in psychodrama. He developed the Jungian Psychodrama method and theory, and other credits include: Vice President of the Federation of European Psychodrama Training Organisations, board member of the International Association of Group Psychotherapy, President of the Mediterranean Association of Psychodrama, and Professor of Theory and Techniques of Group Dynamics at the University of Turin.

Jaime Guerrero, MA is a PhD student in the College of Education's Counseling Psychology Program at the University of Kentucky. He received his Master of Arts Degree in Counseling Psychology at the University of Denver in 1999 and his Bachelor of Science Degree in Psychology from Santa Clara University in 1997. His research interests include studying the effects of using psychodrama with a variety of populations including as a method for training future counselors.

M. Katherine Hudgins, PhD, TEP is an American clinical psychologist and board-certified psychodrama trainer. Dr Hudgins is a well-known international expert on post-traumatic stress disorder and has worked with torture and trauma survivors using clinical psychodrama for more than 20 years, developing the Therapeutic Spiral Model™ with valued colleagues, students and people seeking to heal from the effects of violence. She has brought her model to more than a dozen countries, and currently spends over six months per year teaching in Asia. From 1990 to 2000, Dr Hudgins ran the Center for Experiential Learning. In 2000, she founded Therapeutic Spiral International (a non-profit foundation) in Charlottesville, Virginia, for which she currently acts as Training Director. In 2001 she received the Innovator's Award from the American Society for Group Psychotherapy and Psychodrama (ASGPP) in recognition of her work in developing the Therapeutic Spiral Model. Dr Hudgins' most recent publication is *Experiential Treatment for PTSD: The Therapeutic Spiral Model* (2002). In 2000, she co-edited *Psychodrama with Trauma Survivors: Acting Out Your Pain* with Peter Felix Kellermann.

Edward Hug retired from a 35-year career as a research engineer in the early 1990s, promptly finishing his qualifications as a psychodrama director, then adapting psychodrama methods in his work with chronically mentally ill people. He is currently an active researcher and writer in the realms of psychodrama, psychosynthesis, neurobiology and the neuroscience foundations of psychodrama. He lives in central Massachusetts and can be contacted by email (edwhug@hotmail.com).

Peter Felix Kellermann, PhD is a clinical psychologist and an international trainer of psychodrama and sociodrama. He is a fellow of the ASGPP (Zerka T. Moreno Award 1993) and was the elected chair of the psychodrama section of the IAGP, 1998–2000. He was born in Stockholm, Sweden, but has lived in Jerusalem with his family since 1980. He is the author of *Focus on Psychodrama* (1992), *Sociodrama and Collective Trauma* (2007) and a co-editor (2000) of *Psychodrama with Trauma Survivors* (email: natank@netmedia.net.il).

David A. Kipper, PhD, ABPP, CGP, TEP is Research Professor of Psychology at Roosevelt University, Chicago, a diplomate in Group Psychology, a TEP and the current President of the American Academy of Group Psychology. He is a past President of the American Society of Group Psychotherapy and Psychodrama, past President of APA Division 49, past board member of the IAGP and the first chair and co-founder of its international psychodrama section. A past co-executive editor of the *Journal of Group Psychotherapy, Psychodrama and Sociometry*, he is widely published, an international presenter of master classes, and the recipient of the J. L. Moreno Award.

Anna Maria Knobel is a Brazilian psychologist and psychodramatist specializing in clinical work. She has a Masters in Clinical Psychology and is a supervisor/teacher within the Brazilian Psychodrama Federation (FEBRAP). In 2003 she published *Moreno em Ato* [*Moreno in Action*], in which she applies structural text analysis to J. L. Moreno's work. Anna has also published several articles about groups, focusing on sociometry, and she is a sociometry professor at the Sedes Sapientiae Institute.

Manuela Maciel studied clinical psychology at the University of Lisbon and did postgraduate studies in Social Psychology and in Health Psychology. She has been a psychodrama director for 20 years, consistently running groups during that time. She is now running four clinical groups per week and also two supervision groups on Psychodrama and Sociodrama. She is the Chairperson of the Psychodrama Section of the International Association of Group Psychotherapy and is a member of the board and a teacher and supervisor in the Portuguese Psychodrama Association. She is also the Co-Director of the International Institute of Souldrama. Manuela has presented psychodrama workshops in Australia, Brazil,

Spain, Portugal, Angola, Greece, United States, Israel, Turkey, Finland and England and has developed a model of working with transgenerational psychodrama and historydrama (email: manuelamaciel@sapo.pt).

Connie Miller, NCC, PAT developed Souldrama® in 1997 and trademarked it in 1999 as a therapeutic tool created for use as an adjunct to psychodrama designed to move clients from co-dependency to co-creativity. Her article, 'The Technique of Souldrama® and its Applications,' was published in the *International Journal of Action Methods* (Winter 2000). She has created the International Institute of Souldrama® to further teach this technique for spiritual growth and recovery (website: www.souldrama.com).

Renée Oudijk, TEP, ECP, MA has been a psychodramatist, trainer and educator for more than 25 years. Twenty years ago she started her own practice and founded the School of Psychodrama in the Netherlands. Since that time, she has trained 40 elementary groups and 20 advanced groups in psychodrama. She is co-founder of the Dutch Association of Psychodrama, the Federation of European Psychodrama Training Organisations and the Dutch Belgian Board of Examiners in Psychodrama (website: www.psychodrama.nl).

José Luís Pio-Abreu, MD, PhD is a Psychiatrist at Coimbra University Hospital, Portugal, and Professor of Psychiatry and Communication at the Medical School. He is also a psychodramatist and was the President of the Fourth Ibero-American Congress of Psychodrama, April 2001. He has undertaken and supervised research in the field of biological psychiatry and psychotherapies. He has written several books, one of them – *How to Get a Mental Disorder* – now translated into four European languages.

Rory Remer received his PhD in counseling and research methodology from the University of Colorado in 1972. Professor Remer has taught Counseling Psychology at the University of Kentucky for more than 30 years. An ABE-TEP, Fellow of ASGPP, licensed psychologist, and ABPP in Family Psychology, his research interests include interpersonal communication modeling, multicultural perceptions and interactions, rape prevention, gerontology, and dynamical family systems research methodology. Dr Remer won a Fulbright Scholarship to study in Taiwan during 2002–2003.

Ruth Riding-Malon is a doctoral candidate in Counseling Psychology at the University of Kentucky. She received her Masters in Counseling Psychology in 2002 and an Education Specialist degree in Counseling Psychology from the University of Kentucky in 2005. She is currently Assistant Director of the CPS Center, an outpatient university-based mental health clinic in Lexington. Her research interests are in trauma therapy and multicultural, immigrant and refugee issues as well as in effective pedagogy and its measures.

Marta Risques is a psychologist working with the systemic psychotherapeutic model in a protective commission for children and young people at risk. This is within the Social Security Institute in Lisbon, Portugal. She was trained in psychodrama theory within the Portuguese Psychodrama Association. She has experience of directing psychodrama groups in therapeutic communities and she has presented psychodrama workshops at conferences and universities.

Wilma Scategni is a medical doctor and psychiatrist. Her current and past credits include: Editor of *FEPTO News*; Founding Member of FEPTO; Member of the FEPTO Council; Accredited Analyst, International Association for Analytical Psychology; President, Group Analytical Association for Jungian Analytical Psychology and Psychodrama; individual and group analyst; Director of Psychodrama Institute of Training since 1989; Editor of the review *Anamorphosis: Groups, Analytical Psychology and Psychodrama*. She has written books, essays and articles published in many different countries.

Michael Schacht, PhD is a psychologist and psychodramatist working as a psychotherapist in private practice. As a trainer in group therapy and psychodrama, he is especially interested in the theory of psychodrama. He is a member of the editorial committee of the German 'Zeitschrift für Psychodrama und Soziometrie.' He has published several articles on spontaneity-creativity as well as a book on the psychodramatic theory of development.

Leni Verhofstadt-Denève is a psychodrama trainer (TEP) and a professor in theoretical and clinical developmental psychology at the University of Ghent, Belgium. She is founder of the School for Experiential-Dialectical Psychodrama, Ghent, Belgium and a Member of the Royal Flemish Academy of Belgium for Science and the Arts (email: leni.deneve@ugent.be).

Fernando Vieira works as a psychiatrist in Miguel Bombarda Hospital and in the National Institute of Legal Medicine in Lisbon, Portugal. He has a psychotherapeutic background and education within the cognitive-behavioural model and also family therapy. He started psychodrama training in 1998 as a member of the Portuguese Psychodrama Association. In this association he has served on the board of directors, the educational committee and from 2002–2004 he was President of the association. He has presented psychodrama workshops and papers at conferences in Portugal and internationally, and has also directed psychodrama groups in mental hospitals, therapeutic communities and private practice.

Cristina Villares-Oliveira MD, PhD is Auxiliary Professor of Psychiatry at the Medical School of the University of Coimbra, Portugal. She is an adolescent psychiatrist, psychodramatist and family therapist. She is the current President of the Portuguese Psychodrama Association. She has conducted research projects in sociometry and psychopathology in adolescents, as well as in psychotherapeutic approaches to eating disorders (email: cristinv@netcabo.pt).

Michael Wieser is a doctor of philosophy, assistant professor at Alpen Adria Universitaet Klagenfurt, psychologist and psychodrama psychotherapist and trainer. His current and past credits include: Coordinator of psychodrama research in the Austrian Association of Group Therapy and Group Dynamics and in the IAGP; Chairperson of the research committee and co-chairperson of the European affairs committee in the Federation of European Psychodrama Training Organisations; Project member of a Moreno museum near Vienna; Member of the editorial board for *Psychotherapy Forum* (email: michael.wieser@ uni-klu.ac.at; website: http://www.uni-klu.ac.at/~mwieser).

Series preface

This series focuses on advanced and advancing theory in psychotherapy. Its aims are: to present theory and practice within a specific theoretical orientation or approach at an advanced, postgraduate level; to advance theory by presenting and evaluating new ideas and their relation to the approach; to locate the orientation and its applications within cultural contexts both historically in terms of the origins of the approach, and contemporarily in terms of current debates about philosophy, theory, society and therapy; and, finally, to present and develop a critical view of theory and practice, especially in the context of debates about power, organization and the increasing professionalization of therapy.

Psychodrama is one of the early, pioneering approaches in the field of psychotherapy and, with its emphasis on movement, action and social context, both complemented and supplemented the early developments in psychoanalysis. Psychodrama has contributed to our understanding of the social world, and has promoted the view that psychotherapy and psychotherapists should impact in and on community and society. From Moreno's early work with children in hospital, in an internment village and later in child guidance clinics, through his establishment of the Theatre of Spontaneity, through Boal's experimentation with new forms of theatre, culminating in the Theatre of the Oppressed, through other developments in practice represented in this book, to its application in working with intercultural conflict, psychodrama and sociodrama have, in many ways, led the field in bringing together the personal and the political.

I am especially gratified that this is such an international volume, which reflects the spread and influence of psychodrama across many countries in the world. The spread or width of the book is matched by the depth of its coverage. The 20 chapters cover a range of applications and developments in the field, including: interdisciplinary and integrative perspectives on psychodrama and experiential therapy, existential-dialectic psychodrama, and Jungian psychodrama; developments in psychodrama theory with regard to spontaneity, role, mirroring, the co-unconscious and the social atom, and the Therapeutic Spiral Model; and other chapters which examine the relationship of psychodrama to current debates in philosophy, theory and practice such as chaos theory, postmodernism, spirituality, neuroscience, child development, psychopathology and research. This book certainly fulfils the brief of the series to advance the approach and I am grateful to the international team of editors for their organization and editing, and for bringing this particular volume to the stage.

Keith Tudor

Introduction

This has been an exciting and fascinating project to be a part of. Twenty-five authors from twelve countries have contributed their views on theoretical and practical applications of psychodrama that advance the field as a whole. Their ideas expand the range of concepts developed by J. L. and Zerka Moreno and their collaborators and take them in new directions.

Like any of the psychotherapeutic approaches, psychodrama should be informed by strong underlying theory as well as technique, and backed up by research. To this end, the contributions in this book include theory, practice and research about psychodrama's effectiveness. The contributions provide many insights into the range of applications of this powerful approach to both therapeutic and social intervention.

Taken as a whole, the book offers a contribution to the ever-expanding application of psychodrama in more than a hundred countries (and counting) across the world. Psychodrama is one of the pioneering approaches of psychotherapy. It has contributed to the development of psychotherapy by introducing such concepts and techniques as group psychotherapy, sociometry, role theory, role play, sociodrama, role reversal, the double, action research, dramatic improvisation, perspective-taking, the primacy of interpersonal relationships in therapy, the encounter, co-consciousness and the co-unconscious, the cycle of spontaneity and creativity, and projective methods such as 'the empty chair'. Many of these concepts and techniques have had a wide influence and have led to the development of new approaches in fields such as psychotherapy, counselling, applied drama, organizational development and community work, to name just a few.

J. L. Moreno had a vision of using psychodrama and sociodrama for the therapy of society, an approach he called 'sociatry'. Many psychodramatists take inspiration from the opening words of Moreno's *Who Shall Survive?*: 'A truly therapeutic procedure cannot have less an objective than the whole of mankind.' Moreno's methods are indeed being used all over the world in the contexts of social intervention, education, community work, conflict resolution, health, management, organizations and politics. In our world of many global changes, threats, conflicts and inequities, there is an ever-growing need for 'sociatry'. In recent decades there has been a greater acceptance throughout the world of the vast possibilities contained within Moreno's holistic approach to human beings in their interpersonal relations. There are associations, training institutions, many thousands of practitioners, and conferences of psychodrama in many countries. In a growing number of countries, psychodrama is fully recognized as a method of psychotherapy by government departments of health.

Psychodrama is very well suited to the interdisciplinary approach. A number of alternative approaches to psychodrama have developed over the years, such as psychoanalytic psychodrama, Rogerian psychodrama, Jungian psychodrama and others. One might observe that a transdisciplinary approach fits perfectly with psychodrama's theoretical foundations, since psychodrama is a deeply holistic intervention, integrating the person's body, mind and emotions in action and often in situ.

This book deepens the theoretical and scientific foundation and the key concepts of psychodrama, in both its therapeutic and non-therapeutic applications. In doing so, the book also works toward the integration of different psychodramatic schools of thought. This book presents a diverse overview of the developments within psychodramatic theory and also the basic concepts of modern psychodrama. It is meant to stimulate the dialogue with colleagues from within the psychodrama profession and from colleagues in other approaches.

The chapters in Part I – New Perspectives on Psychodramatic Theory – address psychodrama's underlying theories and relate these to a range of modern theories which have influenced the field of psychotherapy. These chapters also describe how psychodrama's modern applications develop from a solid theoretical foundation. In these chapters, specific psychodrama concepts such as role theory, spontaneity, the matrix of identity, the cultural atom and mirroring are analysed, elaborated upon and compared with other theories. The chapters in Part I also illustrate how related theoretical perspectives can be integrated with well-known theoretical concepts within psychodrama.

The chapters in Part II – Developments in Psychodrama Practice and Research – cover new and emerging approaches to psychodramatic practice and also describe how recent discoveries in neurobiology, trauma work, attachment, psychopathology, child development and psychotherapy research can help to inform practice. These chapters focus on the special benefits of psychodrama and also its limitations. Taken together, they offer a strong case for the continuing application and adaptation of psychodrama as a treatment of choice for addressing a wide range of mental health disorders. In keeping with Moreno's deepest sources of inspiration for psychodrama, the importance of spirituality to psychodramatic healing is also included in Part II. The final chapter gives an overview of state-of-the-art research into the effectiveness of psychodrama in treating mental health disorders, and indicates the eminent place the method deserves in the realm of scientific approaches.

We also include a useful appendix by Adam Blatner and Rosa Cukier, which helpfully describes many of Moreno's basic concepts.

Of course, there are many other avenues we could have explored in this book, and many other authors we could have included. We wish this book could have been much bigger and included many more of the excellent theorists and practitioners who offered to contribute.

Acknowledgements

We acknowledge and thank the many fine authors who have written for this book. We also acknowledge and thank our colleagues and friends at Routledge, most particularly Joanne Forshaw, Jane Harris, Kathryn Russel, Sarah Gibson, Penelope Allport and Claire Lipscomb. We also thank the Series Editor, Keith Tudor, for his enthusiastic wish to include psychodrama as part of this series, for his invitation to us to edit this book, and for his patient guidance through the editing process. We thank the American Society for Group Psychotherapy and Psychodrama (www.asgpp.org) for their kind permission to reprint passages from the work of J. L. Moreno. We thank Anne Ancelin Schützenberger, Kate Bradshaw Tauvon, Adam Blatner, Grete Leutz and Zerka Moreno, who gave special forms of support in the early and production phases of this book.

Manuela thanks her children, Sara and António, and her mother, Irene, and father, Salvador, for all their personal support. She also thanks Adam Blatner, Sue Daniel, Anne Ancelin Schützenberger, Connie Miller and Zerka Moreno for being important models and opening the doors to the psychodrama world for her.

Jorge would like to thank his dear wife Natacha and his family for all their love, hope and confidence in him. He gives special thanks to Grete Leutz for bringing the spirit of psychodrama to him.

Clark thanks and acknowledges the encouragement of his dear family, friends and colleagues, who have shown so much support. He also extends thanks to long-time colleagues Sally Brookes, Alun Mountford, Mary Leyland, David Middleton and Tony Morrison, and his psychodrama trainers, Susie Taylor and Peter Haworth, who showed the way.

Clark Baim, UK/USA
Jorge Burmeister, Switzerland/Spain
Manuela Maciel, Portugal

January 2007

Part I

New perspectives on psychodramatic theory

The chapters in Part I bring new perspectives to psychodramatic theory developed by J. L. Moreno and Zerka Moreno more than half a century ago. These chapters reflect the wide diversity among practitioners in different parts of the world concerning theoretical progress in psychodrama. The authors formulate new concepts and address some of the assumptions and cultural conserves of the psychodramatic method. The rich theoretical explorations in this section enlarge and enhance psychodramatic theory while stimulating new thoughts and new paths of inquiry for us, the co-creators of its theory.

For example, in Chapter 1, 'Meta-Theoretical Perspectives on Psychodrama', Adam Blatner explains the need for an adequate theory of mind-in-society-in-culture and welcomes the presence of many component theories that may interconnect. In his eyes, psychodrama not only does not need to have its own single comprehensive theory, but in fact it will never be able to achieve it. Blatner argues that psychodrama can be used effectively within other structures because of the innate flexibility of the method. He observes that Moreno's role theory offers a unifying language that can serve as a framework for different theories.

Michael Schacht offers a fascinating model for understanding the process of change in Chapter 2, 'Spontaneity–Creativity: The Psychodramatic Concept of Change'. Schacht links the concepts of spontaneity–creativity, human will and the process of change. He suggests a new way of viewing and analysing the psychodramatic process, evaluating each intervention and consequence in the light of his reformulated concept of spontaneity and change.

The chapter by Schacht links well with David Kipper's reformulation of psychodrama in Chapter 3, 'Experiential Reintegration Action Therapy (ERAT)', which offers a deeper understanding of why psychodrama is an effective approach to psychological healing. Kipper describes nine directorial strategies of ERAT and draws on major psychological theories and findings, including neurobiology. As a variant of the experiential group therapy approach, ERAT provides a psychological rationale and empirical foundation for a group therapy intervention that examines, alters, and enriches group members' experiential repertoire. It brings to the surface experiences both traumatic and pleasant and reprocesses and restructures them. ERAT connects present experiences to a past that is given meaning.

In Chapter 4, 'The Role of the Meta-Role: An Integrative Element in Psychology', Adam Blatner takes as his starting place the Morenian concept of role theory and goes on to describe the concept of the meta-role. The meta-role encompasses a complex of psychological functions or capacities and may serve as a kind of inner director, the part of the mind that consciously reflects on, interviews, decides, and engages in other executive acts. This makes it uniquely both Morenean and also integrative. The meta-role may therefore be a key focus for therapy and education, and also a key in integrating different methods of psychology and psychotherapy.

Sue Daniel further develops the theme of role theory in Chapter 5, 'Psychodrama, Role Theory and the Cultural Atom: New Developments in Role Theory'. Daniel presents an innovative framework for understanding and applying role theory. She discusses role theory's advantages for individual and group psychotherapy, and also points out the value of role theory as applied in a variety of settings, including the teaching and learning of psychodrama. She demonstrates how role theory may open up new ways of thinking systemically about a person in relation to others and their environment.

Peter Felix Kellermann focuses on one particular psychodrama technique in Chapter 6, 'Let's Face It: Mirroring in Psychodrama'. In this chapter, Kellermann discusses the psychodramatic mirror technique with references to social psychology, object relations theory and self-psychology. He suggests a differentiation between three kinds of mirroring: idealizing, validating and subjective mirroring. These three kinds of mirroring represent a process of interpersonal growth in which a person moves from a primitive and egocentric state to a more mature and social level of self-development. While these three kinds of mirroring represent a possible pattern of growth for clients, they also may be seen as a combined perspective that might help to integrate psychoanalytic and psychodramatic theory.

In Chapter 7, 'A Chaos Theory Perspective on Psychodrama: Reinterpreting Moreno', by Rory Remer, Jaime Guerrero and Ruth Riding-Malon, Chaos Theory (ChT) is applied to Morenean theory, challenging the classic scientific view of cause and effect and offering new ways to understand what we are doing when we direct (or participate in) a psychodrama. After a brief review of the basics of ChT, the authors explain some of what they see as links and parallels between ChT and Morenean theory. They show that, with the lens of ChT, the unpredictability of a psychodramatic session does not necessarily provide more freedom for the director but might instead necessitate more sensitivity in order to focus on the core issue of spontaneity.

Continuing to explore psychodrama's links with other theories, in Chapter 8, 'Existential-Dialectic Psychodrama: The Theory behind Practice', Leni Verhofstadt-Denève illustrates her existential-dialectic model of personality and how this may inform psychodrama theory. Using six basic questions centered on the concept of 'I and Me', she explains her view of the dialectic dynamic of human development. With reference to her model, psychodrama constitutes one of the ideal agents for human development: Its techniques favour the dialectic processes of self-reflection and self-clarification, and frequently address existential issues which encourage reflection on the fundamental issues of human development across the lifespan.

In Chapter 9, 'How Does Psychodrama Work?: How Theory is Embedded in the Psychodramatic Method', José Luís Pio-Abreu and Cristina Villares-Oliveira explain their understanding of a working model of psychodrama. They discuss how psychodrama obeys certain consistent rules, techniques and designations. Underlying this, there are ideas about the human psychic life and human development and psychopathology. The authors explore some of the central ideas within psychodrama and demonstrate how these ideas are put to practical use. For example, some of psychodrama's core techniques correlate with children's natural activities (e.g. spontaneous role play). Related to this, concepts such as human encounter, spontaneity, role and tele lead to an outward-driven rather than an inward-driven psychology. The authors suggest that psychodrama can be characterized as an open, client-centred therapy. They explain that this is concordant with psychodrama's humanistic tradition, and is in line with newer scientific contributions (for example, the discovery of mirror neurons in the brain).

Renée Oudijk, in Chapter 10, 'A Postmodern Approach to Psychodrama Theory', neatly draws together many of the ideas in Part I with her highly integrative and universal conceptualization of psychodrama. Oudijk observes that the human capacity to give meaning to life experiences is universal and all-important. This meaning-giving manifests in psychodrama as an experiential and social learning process of construction, deconstruction and reconstruction of reality. Oudijk explains that there are three cornerstones defining the theoretical essence of psychodrama: the concept of spontaneity and creativity; the theory and practice of action research; and the triadic structure of psychodrama. As Oudijk explains, psychodrama fits especially well with postmodern thinking, as it crosses the borders of scientific approaches and disciplines in highly integrative ways.

Chapter 1

Meta-theoretical perspectives on psychodrama

Adam Blatner

Introduction

This chapter offers a meta-theoretical consideration of psychodrama's place within the wider contexts of psychotherapy, psychology and culture. Meta-theory addresses issues such as the purpose and importance of theory, whether theory should be closely woven or loose, how theory can operate at multiple levels, and how one theory can be integrated with other theories. There have been some unspoken beliefs about the theory of psychodrama as a form of psychotherapy that need to be articulated clearly, critiqued, and alternative approaches considered.

In the early twentieth century, Freud introduced a contaminating sensibility by treating those who would modify and expand his approaches – innovators such as Adler, Jung and Rank – as deviationists. Freud disqualified their ideas because he interpreted them as being motivated by envy and competition with a father figure. He thus made his approach less scientific and more like a religion, with orthodox believers and those who were more on the edge of revision.

In the mid-century, there were a number of schools of psychotherapeutic thought that were compartmentalized, and, as with religions, professionals tended to be 'adherents' of one or the other. Eclecticism seemed 'shallow' and was not a respectable alternative. By the late twentieth century, even as approaches to psychotherapy and theories of personality had proliferated, a corresponding movement towards intelligent eclecticism and the search for integrating principles had begun.

Several developments have fostered this movement towards a rethinking about theory, including:

- dramatic improvements in many conditions caused by appropriate medications
- research in neuroscience
- research about the effectiveness of different psychotherapies as applied to different psychological problems

- a greater appreciation of the pervasiveness and depth of the influence of trauma and the pathogenic power of addictions
- the potential of a more positive approach to psychology.

As a result, it is becoming less tenable to claim to be a 'follower' of only one approach.

As psychotherapy has expanded its scope, its methods are being applied increasingly with clients who are less psychologically minded, often less voluntary, and with a broader range of basic ego skills. People who Freud would have dismissed as 'unanalyzable' are being worked with using different approaches. From a meta-theoretic viewpoint, we should then recognize that psychotherapy may involve processes that operate differently according to the relative activity of two variables:

- One variable involves the client's awareness that a therapeutic process is going on, and a conscious joining with the goals of that process. This is not always present when working with children, delinquent adolescents and selected other populations.
- A second variable involves an extension of the first. This variable considers to what extent the client can actively join in learning and intentionally utilizing some of the operations of therapy such as self-observation, detachment of identity from overinvolvement in the perspectives of a role, and the drawing in of more current values and aspirations. Some approaches to therapy, such as the hypnotherapy of Milton Erickson or some kinds of play therapy, require relatively little in the way of conscious, self-reflective collaboration, and there are some patients for whom this may be most effective.

In this regard, psychodrama should be recognized as a complex of methods associated with a variety of theoretical principles, but not so tightly organized that it cannot be modified and applied in a wide range of contexts. The lack of a certain ambition within the psychodrama field to explain all psychopathology within a coherent system is actually an advantage – it gives the method greater flexibility.

Theory has multiple levels

We should recognize that the understanding of the workings of a complex system may occur at many levels within the system (see Chapter 7 by Remer et al.). Regarding the mind, there are theoretical concepts that address the function of the chemicals and the nerve cells in the brain, relating to molecular shape, permeability of membranes, and the like. At a higher level, there are other theories that deal with whole structures within the brain, and higher, the interaction of brain and body, hormones, stress, and so forth. Higher still are the ways the mind operates largely beyond the physical-material realm, in its 'intrapsychic' dynamics, the various defense mechanisms or coping mental maneuvers, and inner conflicts and their compromises and resolutions.

Moreno was one of the first to remind psychotherapists that both difficulties and healing can be influenced by the interpersonal field as much as individual psychodynamics. He also extended this to social networks, families and groups, recognizing the power of interaction, feelings of belonging or alienation, and so forth. In developing the methods of socio-drama and axiodrama, Moreno further acknowledged the power of social role conflicts and cultural definitions of ideals to be significantly influential in sickness and health.

The point here is that different dynamics may be noted as operative at each of the more complex organismic and social levels, and different theories are continuously deserving of development, refinement, and further revision in light of the advance of knowledge. Developments in parallel fields – linguistics, anthropology, cultural history, child development, neuroscience and so forth – all suggest the need for that valuing of creativity and its implications, and the struggle to counter tendencies towards theory becoming rigid.

In addition to its various body, mind, and collective levels, psychodrama also juggles a variety of frames of reference, including political, economic, social, philosophical, spiritual, aesthetic (including poetic, musical, dance-gesture, drama, the visual arts, and other integrations), humorous and playful, and irreverent and boundary testing (the archetype of the trickster). From this viewpoint, psychodrama is not only a subset of psychology – the exploration of how the mind-body-in-social-settings operates – but at times psychodrama's functions may be appreciated theoretically within other contexts such as education, sociology, politics, anthropology, religion, recreation, and everyday life (Blatner 2003). From a meta-theoretic stand-point, the understanding of how psychodrama operates is influenced by the context it is in or its mode of application in the same way as, for example, the understanding of a person may shift depending on their being viewed as a worker, a consumer, a sexual or romantic person, a family person or as a soul on a life journey.

Different contexts of psychodrama

Psychodrama is often defined as a method of group psychotherapy, and that has been its more classical mode of application. However, for those more acquainted with Moreno's work and the scope of his interests, the term 'psychodrama' also has a broader meaning, acting as a metonymic key word for a greater field of which its own method is just one more widely known representative. The wider field of psychodrama encompasses aspects of role theory, the theory of creativity, and the methods of sociodrama, sociometry, improvisational drama, and their applications in and beyond psychotherapy, including in education, business, community building and so forth. It also may be viewed as extending to and/or overlapping with the use of experiential methods in therapy and organizational development, action techniques, role playing and other forms of simulation, and applications of psychodramatic techniques in modified form in therapy with families, couples or individuals (Moreno 2006).

From a meta-theoretical perspective, it is important to note that the theory of how psychodrama works varies to some degree according to the context in which it is applied. This present book, for example, emphasizes psychodrama's theory in the context of psychotherapy. Other books might be needed to more fully explicate how psychodrama's principles and methods operate in other settings, such as in education (or pedagogy).

In addition to situating psychodrama within broader categories, we should recognize that the method itself involves a number of subtheories. For example, the theories involved in working with group dynamics overlap with, yet are somewhat different from the theories involved in helping patients (or, as they're frequently referred to by non-medical counselors, 'clients') deal with, for example, the effects of trauma.

Why theory?

The need for formulation

Some people may find this question unnecessary because they already agree with the pioneer of psychology Kurt Lewin, who in 1951 (p. 169), probably drawing from Wilhelm Dilthey, wrote: 'There is nothing so practical as a good theory.' Yet there are numerous therapists and some psychodramatists who abjure theory and instead foolishly trust the overly simplistic phrase 'Trust the method.' While there are moments in the process when this maxim has some usefulness, especially regarding the willingness to let the group dynamics proceed and the various group members help each other, the maxim should not interfere with the recognition of the director's responsibility for diagnosis and formulation.

Good therapists need to spend time assessing the client's situation, and from this develop working hypotheses and rationally derived strategies. These formulations need not be held rigidly – there is room for ongoing revision and refinement. A theory is a kind of figurative 'map' for making sense out of the information obtained in the diagnostic process. The ideal of spontaneity should not interfere with this attitude, because Moreno's definition of spontaneity includes the *aim of being effective*.

Because a powerful method can do harm as well as good, the role of the director should be recognized as including the component of *assessment*, so as to identify the protagonist's key dynamics and his or her relationship to the group (Blatner 2004). In simpler terms, I think therapists should be able to answer the implicit question 'Why are you doing what you are doing with this patient?' or 'What is the purpose of this maneuver?'

Implications of a multileveled theory

Theory, to be useful, must be flexible enough to adapt itself to helping to explain a wide range of phenomena. Because of its many levels and frames of reference, an adequate theory of mind-in-society-in-culture should be flexible. The meta-theoretical point here is that we should abandon the effort of creating a grand unified theory, and instead welcome the presence of many component theories. It is, of course, desirable that some coordination and coherence be found among the various theories, but lacking a clear consensus at this point should not serve as an obstacle to appreciating the usefulness of these component theories.

Applying this perspective, we should recognize that psychodrama entails a number of theoretical concepts that operate at different levels (this is also explored in other chapters of this volume). For example, we shouldn't assume – as have some orthodox psychoanalysts – that an adequate psychosocial theory of early childhood development should also apply to the challenges of middle or later life. The issues are so different. This doesn't mean that early life experiences don't affect later life, but so many later experiences and variables intervene that the degree to which early experience is in fact relevant may be minimal.

As we expand our theories of psychopathology, we notice that not only are more obvious factors at work, such as trauma, but also more subtle factors, embedded in the society. What was once taken as normalcy – such as the constraints and indignities imposed on women – has now become recognized as pathogenic, and reflecting a society that is itself pathological. Feminism and other approaches challenge the assumption that mere normalcy is healthy and as good as can ever be hoped for. Normalcy is now being viewed as an intermediate stage, a compromise, getting by, but yet far from ideally healthy. (Moreno's formulation of sociatry anticipated this postmodern social critique.) In turn, our theories must then include more general ideas about health and illness, and how these states are defined – often by a sociolinguistic matrix that itself may be biased and not ideally healthy.

Another way to view this is to recognize that a great deal of the literature in psychiatry and psychology has been predicated on the assumption that the general population had little insight and was not terribly psychologically minded. This is still so in the main, but a growing number of people are integrating the insights developed by the field of psychology in the last century, and working with these people shifts the nature of the work significantly. They can collaborate far more as equals, and this needs to be built into the methods being used.

Similarly, within the theories of treatment, we should recognize something noted 2400 years ago by Hippocrates, the first known writer who commented in depth on the art of medicine. He noted that healing involved both directly seeking to reverse pathological processes, and, equally important – if not more so – indirectly promoting the overall health of the patient so as to evoke natural healing forces. The recognition of these two different types of approaches is an important example of the opening of meta-theory to a number of complementary explanations, instead of seeking to find an overly simplistic and unified formula.

In this regard, psychotherapy should be recognized as only one type of treatment. Many patients are helped as much if not more by medicines, opportunities to be in the controlled environment of a hospital, or help with generating a richer matrix of socio-economic resources. Within the realm of therapy, there are theories that deal more with talking and others with doing – not just action or experiential therapies, but practical ones, like vocational guidance or spiritual comfort.

Psychodrama is interesting because it may be conducted in different forms. The classical exploratory procedure is a protagonist-centered process, usually in a group setting, and generally requiring an hour or more for its full effectiveness. However, psychodramatic methods are used far more frequently, adapted as an aid in group counseling (Corey 2007), in family or couple therapy, or in individual therapy (sometimes called 'bi-personal' psychodrama or 'psychodrama à deux') (Corsini 2005: xi). Each context to some degree draws on different theories.

So, to restate, no single theory can or should be expected to explain all these dynamics. This is true in psychotherapy no less than it is so in medicine (Blatner 2000: 129). This point is being made in order to challenge the residual belief that there should be a unified general theory. For many decades in the middle of the last century, and continuing today to a fair degree, there have been 'schools of thought' that seem to claim that their approach is valid and comprehensive, and imply that other approaches are lacking. This should be recognized as a sentimental and simplistic illusion, a residue, a cultural conserve. While each approach might offer certain insights, no single theory can encompass the breadth of psychology (how the mind works), psychopathology (how it becomes dysfunctional) and psychotherapy or psychiatry (what approaches seem to help). In other words, from a meta-theoretical perspective, I am suggesting as a first principle that many theories can coexist and operate within their own domain, all being useful in different ways.

When there seem to be disagreements among different systems, part of the challenge of meta-theory is to articulate these and seek to determine in what ways each might have some valid insights and how the best points might then be resynthesized. Such new syntheses can add clarity, new insights, suggest subtheoretical adjustments, and yet they should not be thought of as eliminating the need for many other subtheories. (An example of a more effective and integrative theory is mentioned briefly at the end of this chapter and also in Chapter 4 on the concept of the meta-role.)

Are Moreno's writings sufficient?

Some practitioners believe that their work is sufficiently explained by the general cultural conserve of Moreno's writings. The problem with this is that Moreno, in spite of being a brilliant and seminal thinker, an innovator and promoter, nevertheless failed to develop his ideas in an intellectually systematic fashion. Nor do his writings constitute a comprehensive system of psychology, psychopathology, and healing. There are many other approaches and ideas that are also needed. The point here is to refuse to make a single contributor – i.e., Moreno – the sole source of input. Rather, we should treat this body of concepts and techniques as tools that can mix with contributions from other innovators in psychotherapy. Also, Moreno's work, the work of his successors, and the work of those in other fields all invite continued re-evaluation and revision, in the spirit of Moreno's rejection of a reliance on any cultural conserve and valuing of the deeper spirit of creativity.

Does psychodrama need its own theory?

I believe that Moreno has offered a number of valuable concepts that help construct a more vigorous integrated theory of psychology and psycho-therapy. Nevertheless, I do not think that his writings in themselves suffice, as mentioned above. Nor does any other single theory suffice. The vast phenomena investigated by psychology do not require only one theory that is true and the others less so. It is possible to view the complexities of human experience from a number of viewpoints.

Psychodrama, too, can be in part explained in Morenean terms, but it should be noted that a number of psychodramatists find it useful to ground their work to varying degrees in theories other than those developed by Moreno (see other chapters in this volume). Other authors not in this book have used psychodrama within the context of Glasser's reality therapy (Greenberg and Bassin 1976), Berne's transactional analysis (Jacobs 1977), psychoanalytic object relations theory (Powell 1986), or Adler's individual psychology (Starr 1977). Meta-theoretically, then, we should note that Moreno's methods can be used effectively apart from his own theoretical structures. These adaptations speak to the innate flexibility of the methodology. This is especially important, because the associated theoretical rationale also guides the way the techniques are applied.

Increasingly, psychotherapists are becoming eclectic, integrating the best insights and also techniques from a variety of sources. Thus, many therapists who are not particularly identified with psychodrama nevertheless apply a variety of psychodramatic methods. (The analogy here is that many family physicians, while not specializing in surgery, nevertheless use selected surgical *techniques* for minor office procedures.) Ideally, these clinicians avoid the depth of exploration and full power of classical psychodrama, but instead apply selected principles and techniques as needed to catalyze certain experiences (Corey 2007; Corsini 2005).

Nevertheless, there are a number of principles introduced or emphasized by Moreno that are powerful additions to other approaches, such as valuing creativity, developing the intentional use of improvisation (spontaneity), utilizing the dynamics of warming up, rapport (tele), promoting self-expression, empathy with others, and so forth (Blatner 2005a).

A meta-theoretical question then: Does psychodrama need to have its own theory? Because I question that any single theory should be asked to address all of the complexities of life, but rather a complex of theories would better be applied at different levels in different situations, my point is that using psychodramatic methods or any other group of techniques should not be predicated on those techniques having a single comprehensive theory. More, Moreno and his successors have come up with a number of ideas, and have refined these ideas, constituting significant contributions to the overall enterprise of psychotherapy.

Related fields

Many fields of study would benefit from learning about and appreciating Moreno's ideas or their extensions and further developments by later innovators, such as those who have written for this book. Some of these related fields include: creativity studies; the academic study of play; play therapy; drama therapy; drama in education; theatre arts; performance studies; philosophy and theology; and so forth. Interestingly, Moreno addressed applications in many of these fields, but his writing style was such that the gems of insight are often obscured by a lack of systematization.

In turn, psychodramatists are often ignorant of the significant developments in those other fields that are fairly relevant to its practice, such as drama therapy, the other creative arts therapies and other active or experiential therapies. Certainly, some psychodramatists creatively combine approaches, but I am here referring to a broader appreciation of the theoretical foundation involved.

The meta-theoretical point here is again to turn away from the general intellectual world view that believed a single theory was possible. Here I am suggesting that not only many theories from different approaches be distilled and developed, but also links be created with other fields. For example, in medical practice, a continuing effort must be exerted to help physicians integrate the best insights of psychology so they can work effectively at the mind–body interface. More, in the last decade or so, an increasing effort is being exerted to include also spiritual concerns. This applies in psychiatry as well as medical practice.

In the last two decades, there have been many shifts in psychology. One is the move towards 'positive psychology,' emphasizing the amplification of strengths, rather than the earlier tendency to focus on the details of the problem. Solution-focused brief therapy also aligns with this approach.

Another trend has been a focus on skill building and competencies, such as may be found in Marcia Linehan's 'dialectical behavior therapy.' The underlying paradigm of thinking in terms of separate functions has been challenged by some innovators who note that the underlying nature of the mind works not only as gestalts but also as a story-making process. Role theory and its roots in the dramaturgical metaphor, and metaphor in general, tend to build from this basis.

Psychodrama is only one component

Psychodrama should not be viewed as the only component of therapy. In the course of treatment, there may be many elements that consist of talking, making arrangements with the family, setting up a more congenial environment, and so forth, and these can often be as helpful – if not more so – than the action components.

Indeed, I think there are many cases in which psychodrama is contra-indicated. The clients are just not ready for this modality. Sometimes I think of 'classical' psychodrama as being analogous to the place of surgery within medical practice – an important element, more relevant in some cases, but not useful in others. This kind of understanding again positions psychodrama within a broader context.

Increasingly, psychodramatists have integrated more 'distanced' forms of role playing, incorporating a principle from the related field of drama therapy: Some people cannot tolerate the sense of personal responsibility that comes with playing oneself in an enactment. Instead, they can play the role of a fictional character, 'someone else,' who perhaps shares certain concerns or predicaments, and through this enactment, they can benefit quasi-vicariously. Of course, children do this naturally in play therapy or in the self-healing of make-believe play, which incidentally has come to be called 'sociodramatic' play by those who study the dynamics of play in childhood (Smilansky 1968).

Intercultural applications of psychodrama

It is also important to note that psychodrama as an integral method transcends cultural boundaries, which is why it is used in Asia, Europe, the Middle East, the Americas, Australia and New Zealand, and so forth. Certain cultures do require some mild modifications. For example, I have found that subtle group pressure in Japan supports a more extended sharing: once one person starts, the others seem to feel called upon to join in, so extra time should be built in by the director to allow this to unfold at its own pace.

In some situations where people are using a language different from the one they were raised with, it is often useful to encourage protagonists to speak in their native language, even if the director and most group members can't understand them. Often the voice tones, expressions, and gestures are vivid enough so that the deeper meaning is communicated, and actually understanding the details is less important than the protagonists having a more authentic catharsis. Some directors make use of simultaneous translators, and this can be useful too.

Because of the way psychodrama can shift into a consideration of cultural norms and more sociodramatic scenes, questions about intercultural dynamics can be more explicitly raised and evaluated. It is not necessary for the director or the group to determine these norms, beyond the basic requirements of non-violence. This allows for an examination of themes that may arise (for example) for refugees or immigrants, and the inter-mixing of people with very different cultural, racial, religious, political or social-economic backgrounds and varied lifestyles – people from all walks of life.

Applying modalities separately

A controversial idea put forth here is that although psychodrama, socio-metry, and applied role theory are integrated in mainstream psychodrama, these approaches can be and not infrequently are applied separately. In European and other countries, they often have a non-clinical track for pedagogic or sociometric applications, and these are usually applied in the non-clinic setting.

Sociometry, for example, preceded psychodrama, and at times Moreno suggested that psychodrama was an offshoot or extension of his ideas about sociometry. Certainly, many sociometric ideas and techniques could be applied beyond the psychotherapeutic context. For example, sociometry became well known in sociology in the 1950s and 1960s, and in 1956, Moreno's journal, *Sociometry*, was given over to the American Sociological Association. (However, the use of sociometry has declined in popularity since the mid-1960s, and many texts on sociology or social psychology no longer mention it. Nevertheless, these ideas have great potential.)

Narrative and postmodernism

A major shift in psychotherapy theory has occurred in the last few decades. Instead of attempting to determine the actual 'source' of a problem in order to produce authentic insight as an avenue to healing, there has been a shift to simply retelling the story. The problem of interminable analysis that Freud wrote about in part is due to the way memories are images that often function as a 'screen' for other associated memories. Thorough investigation, attempting to separate reality from fantasy becomes mired in an unending series of associations and images. This realization has been facilitated by recent developments in chaos theory and the nature of fractals in mathematics: it is quite possible to have patterns lead to variations unendingly (see Chapter 7 by Remer *et al.*). Another boost to this revision of theory is the growing research literature on the suggestibility of memory.

Arising from innovations in strategic individual and family therapy, an alternative idea has emerged, that of thinking of the mind as not simply a process of reacting to fixed memories, but rather as a dynamically active process of continuously retelling that inner story, the 'narrative,' selecting memories and attributing various sets of associated meanings to these images. Such complexes of memories and meanings often operate primitively, offering symbolic protection, much as a child may compulsively replay a stressful or traumatic experience, yet they inhibit mature adaptation. Patients may be thought of as often telling themselves self-defeating stories, laced with guilt, remorse, denial, excuses, 'if-onlys,' doubt and self-reproach.

Building on the critique of language by postmodernist thinkers, therapists using narrative approaches give their patients the freedom to retell their story in a more positive, constructive fashion. This loosening of cultural assumptions about the need for 'objective' truth thus allows for explorations of more dynamic approaches to healing.

Interestingly, psychodrama may be seen in retrospect as having utilized a similar dynamic from its inception, decades before narrative became more mainstream. More than merely telling the story, or entertaining more constructive images, protagonists are helped to also enjoy the kinesthetic, relational and non-verbal dimensions of a reparative experience when, following the enactment of a stressful event, they are allowed to replay it with a more positive outcome. Perhaps the other person behaves more supportively, rather than antagonistically, or perhaps the protagonist in the replay is able to assert and affirm themselves more forcefully.

This shift in the basic inner experience is a core dynamic explaining other therapeutic approaches that have similarities with psychodrama, from Hellinger's family constellation therapy and Pesso and Boyden's psycho-motor therapy, to shamanistic healing – the key theme being the re-experiencing of a negative event redone so that it is worked out in a more life-affirming fashion.

Integrating theory

Other theoretical concerns include the search for a common language, a way of talking about psychological and social interactions that is relatively understandable to people who are coming from different theoretical backgrounds and professional disciplines, and also to patients and their family members. A modified form of role theory, such as the role dynamics approach I have developed, may apply here (Blatner 2005b and Chapter 4 on the meta-role).

Another meta-theoretical challenge is the integration of the seeming diversity in the field of psychotherapy. Again, a variety of role theory may apply here. It is arguable that most if not all the main types of therapy have in common the implicit development of a healthier, more flexible ego, that part of the mind which manages and modifies the way the various roles are played. (The problem with the word 'ego' is that it is often confused with mere vanity, but in this sense we are referring to the capacity to relatively autonomously coordinate and modulate the psychological functions, and this was what was meant by the 'ego psychology' approach in psycho-dynamic psychology in the 1950s.) Another metaphor that makes this abstract concept more understandable again may be drawn from psycho-drama: the client is invited to identify with and develop their own inner 'director' as a type of 'meta-role.' These theoretical developments deserve to be tested and explored further.

Beyond the context of psychotherapy

Although the emphasis of this book is on the applications of psychodrama in psychotherapy, the reality is that many psychodrama techniques and concepts may have as much if not more application in non-clinical contexts, in business, education, organizational development, professional training, law, politics, religion, the arts and even in everyday life (Blatner 2003). Moreno (1934: 3) began his magnum opus on sociometry, *Who Shall Survive?*, with the line: 'A truly therapeutic procedure cannot have less an objective than the whole of mankind.' As I interpret it, his meaning is that, first, therapy is meant in the broadest sense as anything that expands consciousness; second, the complex of tools associated with his work – sociometry, role theory, role training, sociodrama as well as psychodrama – are all available for multiple uses in the service of humanity's advance.

Moreno also coined the term 'sociatry' as a play on the word psychiatry, and used it as the title of the first two years of the journal that later became *Group Psychotherapy*. The basic idea is that Morenean methods also may be used for critiquing society (via sociodrama, for example) and advancing overall cultural progress (Blatner 2007).

The point from a meta-theoretical perspective is that each context requires its own theoretical foundation. While there might be some overlap of principles in different contexts, such as between education and therapy, there would also be rather different associated relevant theories. For example, if a management trainer wants to train staff in better interpersonal skills, and in the course of the role-playing exercises one of the group members hints at having personal problems related to the skill in question, it would be inappropriate to pursue this in the work context. In the past, practitioners who slipped into such quasi-therapeutic explorations often left the participants feeling that a contract had been breached. They hadn't attended to get 'therapy.' Similar problems occurred in some school settings, and created a general misunderstanding about the nature of role playing as a tool for skill development (Blatner 2006a, 2006b).

Therefore, different contexts require a balanced assessment as to the effects and ethical dimensions of their application. Extensions of psychodrama or Morenean approaches, including sociometry, systems analysis, sociodrama and so forth, must each be considered within its own social framework. Regarding those parallel fields, it should be recognized that while there is a ready synergy among them, role theory, sociometry, group psychotherapy and psychodrama can each be practiced separately.

Worth debating is the activity of open psychodramas, which Moreno conducted regularly for decades in New York City, and which a number of psychodramatists continue in various settings around the world. However, some practitioners (and other observers) are doubtful about the ethics of this kind of personal exploration in front of strangers, with no arrangements for follow-up should a particularly upsetting issue be raised. I think there should be some carefully reasoned debate in some journal, and this also translated into other languages.

Kellermann (1992: 35) notes that psychodrama has a number of elements that are a bit closer to the systematic approaches of science. On the other hand, when approached as a general exercise of life exploration, away from a clinical context, psychodrama is a bit closer to art or the creation of meaning. Thus, this meta-theoretical approach recognizes that when psychodramatic methods are applied in their non-classical form, as role playing or sociodrama, they should be evaluated in terms of the theoretical considerations associated with that context. For example, in using a method my wife and I devised called 'The Art of Play' – a creative drama approach for adults that includes a variety of psychodramatic techniques that help the character (in role) expand and deepen that role experience – the theoretical foundations partake of theories of drama in education and theories of recreation (Blatner and Blatner 1997).

Summary

Meta-theory invites us to view psychodrama from a variety of standpoints and to evaluate its assumptions from these diverse perspectives. We must allow for the synergistic operation of a wide number of theoretical constructs – both from Moreno and other psychodramatists, and also from associated and distant fields – without having to reduce them all to a single formulation. There is a coherence of theme among these concepts, and yet they can often be applied separately in time or context. Moreno's role theory, developed as role dynamics, further offers a generally unifying language and broad theoretical construct that can serve as a framework within which numerous subtheories can be organized, depending on the circumstances of the work involved.

References

Blatner, A. (2000) *Foundations of Psychodrama: History, Theory, and Practice* (4th edn), New York: Springer.
—— (2003) 'Applications of psychodramatic methods in everyday life', in J. Gershoni (ed.) *Psychodrama in the 21st Century: Clinical and Educational Applications*, New York: Springer.
—— (2004) *The art of case formulation*. Online. Available <http://www.blatner.com/adam/psyntbk/formulation.html> (accessed June 2005).
—— (2005a) 'Psychodrama', in R. J. Corsini and D. Wedding (eds) *Current psychotherapies* (7th edn), Belmont, CA: Thomson Brooks/Cole. An updated version may be downloaded at www.thomsonedu.com/counselling/corsini.
—— (2005b) 'Beyond psychodrama', *New Therapist*, 36: 14–21.
—— (2006a) 'Enacting the new academy: Sociodrama as a powerful tool in higher education,' *ReVision: A Journal of Consciousness & Transformation*, 29, 3: 30–35.
—— (2006b) 'Current trends in psychodrama', *International Journal of Psychotherapy*, 10, 3: 43–53.
—— (2007) Blatner, A. (with D. J. Weiner) (eds) *Interactive and Improvisational Drama: Varieties of Applied Theatre and Performance*, Lincoln, NE: iUniverse.
Blatner, A. and Blatner, A. R. (1997) *The Art of Play: Helping Adults Reclaim Imagination and Spontaneity*, New York: Brunner/Routledge.
Corey, G. (2007) 'Psychodrama', in G. Corey (ed.) *Theory and Practice of Group Counseling* (7th edn), Belmont, CA: Brooks/Cole-Thomson Learning.
Corsini, R. J. (2005) 'Preface', in R. J. Corsini and D. Wedding (eds) *Current Psychotherapies* (7th edn), Belmont, CA: Thomson/Brooks/Cole.
Greenberg, I. and Bassin, A. (1976) 'Reality therapy and psychodrama', in

A. Bassin, T. Bratter and R. Rachin (eds) *The Reality Therapy Reader*, New York: Harper and Row.

Jacobs, A. (1977) 'Psychodrama and TA', in M. James (ed.) *Techniques in Transactional Analysis*, Reading, MA: Addison-Wesley.

Kellermann, P. F. (1992) *Focus on Psychodrama: The Therapeutic Aspects of Psychodrama*, London: Jessica Kingsley.

Lewin, K. (1951) *Field Theory in Social Science: Selected Theoretical Papers*, D. Cartwright (ed.), New York: Harper & Row.

Moreno, J. L. (1934) *Who Shall Survive? A New Approach to the Problem of Human Interrelations*, Washington, DC: Nervous & Mental Disease Publishing. Revised edition 1953, Beacon, NY: Beacon House.

Moreno, Z. T. (2006) *The Quintessential Zerka: Writings by Zerka Toeman Moreno on Psychodrama, Sociometry and Group Psychotherapy* (compiled and edited by Toni Horvatin and Edward Schreiber), New York: Routledge.

Powell, A. (1986) 'Object relations in the psychodramatic group', *Group Analysis*, 19: 125–138.

Starr, A. (1977) *Rehearsal For Living: Psychodrama*, Chicago: Nelson Hall.

Smilansky, S. (1968) *The Effects of Sociodramatic Play on Disadvantaged Preschool Children*, New York: Wiley.

Chapter 2

Spontaneity–creativity

The psychodramatic concept of change

Michael Schacht

Overview

Moreno's concept of spontaneity–creativity is a cornerstone of psychodramatic and action theory. Using the concepts of action theory and relating them to pragmatic philosophy (Schacht 2003), we see that action should not be confused simply with activity. In the tradition of pragmatism, action includes activity as well as sensitivity, peacefulness or humility – a way of being in the world. Action is conceptualized as an ongoing, more or less spontaneous and creative process of problem solving.

In general, we are able to manage everyday life using well-established habits – Moreno's 'role conserves.' Only when we face a problem, an interruption in our routine, are we forced to act intentionally. The inhibition functions as the starter for a warming-up process. We have to search for a solution to our problem. It is necessary to find a new response to an old situation or an adequate response to a new situation. In many cases the 'stereotype' variety of spontaneity will suffice (Moreno 1956: 129). As psychodramatists, we are usually not interested in this type of spontaneity. Most of the time we work with people who have to deal with problems that require warming up to truly creative spontaneity. These are people who want to act in a specific manner but find themselves unable to do so: 'I know I am depressed but I don't know what to do about it.'

Warming up to creative solutions includes letting go of old role conserves. These conserves might have inhibited change, but they have also supplied a sense of stability and certainty. In order to enter new territory, the person must be able to tolerate uncertainty and ambiguity (Moreno 1980). The spontaneity state is neither disturbed by self-reflection nor by the intrusion of reason into emotion (Moreno 1970). Only subsequently is it possible to consciously add rational meaning to the immediate experience.

The beginning of a transition from old to new may come about as consciously intended and planned or via a spontaneity state. In the first case, the person makes a conscious deliberate choice. In the second case, the person chooses unconsciously (spontaneous choice). I use Moreno's notion of 'status nascendi' as a generic term for both processes. The status nascendi marks the very beginning of a transition. In order to really solve a problem, there still is a long way to go. For example, the strongly felt commitment to quit substance abuse has to be put to the proof again and again in order to become sober. The new intention to hold one's ground requires further training of necessary social skills if the person wants to improve his or her self-assertion. Since this is the time when new roles and new realities are created in a narrower sense, I call this the creative phase of the process.

Gradually, the individual acquires more and more experience with their new role. They learn about its possibilities and limitations. Slowly, they take it for granted. The formerly new role has become a readily available role conserve, which can be defined as an habitual action routine. Another cycle of spontaneity–creativity might be necessary if the person once more encounters a problem that calls for a creative solution.

Moreno closely connects his concept of spontaneity–creativity with the idea of human will. Spontaneity is understood as action 'sua sponte' – of free will. It is experienced as 'autonomous and free' (Moreno 1980: 111). In order to incorporate the notion of human will into the concept of spontaneity–creativity, I refer to Heinz Heckhausen's so-called 'Rubicon' model (Heckhausen 1989).

The Rubicon model

Briefly, this model postulates a sequence of four action phases – the pre-decisional, the pre-actional, the action, and the post-action phase. During the pre-decisional phase, the individual weighs up a number of motifs (e.g. wishes or needs) against each other. How important are they? How are the expectations to realize them? This process may take place without deliber-ate thought on an emotional level. The pre-actional phase starts when the individual makes a choice. Like Caesar crossing the Rubicon on his march to Rome, the person commits himself or herself to realize one of the motifs. Wishing has shifted to willing. They have set a goal. But this intention is still very general. It is not clear when and how they will take action. During the pre-actional phase, this is specified. Eventually, the person makes an action plan which is realized in the following action phase. Finally, in the post-actional phase, the action is evaluated. Perhaps the goal has been achieved or some other option has to be tried.

I think it is helpful to conceptualize the warming-up process in terms of Heckhausen's pre-decisional phase. As psychodramatists we look at the problems that our protagonists present from an action theory perspective. With their actions, they pursue conscious and unconscious intentions. These intentions are themselves part of the problem. For example, someone who has difficulties with self-assertion may unconsciously pursue the goal

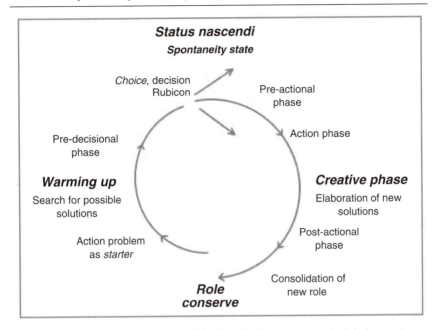

Figure 2.1 Model of spontaneity–creativity (psychodramatic terms in *italics*)

of avoiding any kind of rejection. His action to avoid annoying other people can thereby cause his lack of self-assertion. If the goals that people have set for themselves are part of the problem, then they have to be redefined. This is precisely the objective of the pre-decisional phase. Later, I will elaborate this idea in further detail.

Making a choice can be understood as the onset of the status nascendi. In the case of conscious, deliberate decisions, the status nascendi goes along with Heckhausen's pre-actional phase. The following creative phase can be understood as the action per se. In the course of a spontaneity state, decision and action are one and the same. Heckhausen's post-actional phase can be interpreted as part of the creative phase. The individual via emotional or cognitive feedback verifies that he was effective in meeting his goals and motifs, and continually modifies the new role towards a more efficient action. The creative phase leads gradually into the phase of role conserve. Finally, the new role bears all the hallmarks of an habitual routine. Figure 2.1 illustrates the model of spontaneity–creativity as it has been outlined so far.

Change does not occur with one phase neatly lined up after the other. With respect to different issues, people may be in different phases of the process. The recently sober alcoholic may be in the creative phase with regard to stopping drinking. But at the same time, he may be warming up to face conflicts with his wife due to his growing self-confidence. One of my patients was warmed up to deal with his anxiety but he didn't want to accept that his impulsiveness caused him vocational problems, i.e. he avoided the respective warm-up with the consequence that he lost his job.

The key point is that the efficiency of our psychodramatic interventions increases if we take into consideration which phase of the spontaneous–creative process our protagonist is going through at the moment. It makes a big difference whether I interpret the increasing complaints of my patient as an indication that he has not changed yet and more warming up has to be done, or that he is in the middle of a spontaneity state without realizing this. In the first case, I might be tempted to start a new round of biographical work, thereby strengthening the patient's belief that things are getting worse. In the latter case, I will motivate him to look for any clues that things are changing without him having noticed it.

In order to be able to match interventions to the status of change concerning a specific issue, it is important to first review this status on a regular basis on a macroscopic level. From a microscopic perspective it can be useful to do this several times during one single session. In the following sections I will develop some ideas concerning psychodramatic work with regard to the phases of the spontaneous–creative change process. First I will describe some aspects of the warming-up process.

Before this, I want to introduce still one other model that will be helpful during the following discussions. This concerns the 'transtheoretical' model that was developed by James Prochaska and Carlo DiClemente. I had been occupied with many of the ideas that are outlined in this article for a long time when I recently stumbled over the transtheoretical model. I was intrigued immediately because I realized many parallels between my ideas and this model. More than that, I am convinced that the psychodramatic model of spontaneity–creativity can profit a lot from this approach.

The transtheoretical model

Prochaska and his collaborators conducted empirical studies examining the process of change. First they investigated what happened when smokers stopped smoking. Later they examined other populations, e.g. alcoholics on their way to recovery. They came up with a sequence of five typical stages of change (Connors *et al.* 2001; DiClemente and Velasquez 2002; Prochaska *et al.* 2002).

The first stage is pre-contemplation. In the beginning, people usually don't want to change. This may be because they are either unaware of their problem or unwilling to change. They might also be demoralized after several futile attempts. If confronted with their problem, pre-contemplators are usually defensive and try to avoid learning about their problems.

The next stage is contemplation. Contemplators acknowledge that they have a problem and begin to think seriously about solving it. This might take quite a while, often several years. People in contemplation often feel stuck. Almost all people in this stage are eager to talk about themselves and their problems. If they begin to focus on solutions rather than on their problems, to think more about the future than about the past, then the transition to the stage of preparation is near.

People in the stage of preparation make or have made a decision to change. They plan to take action within the next month, making final adjustments before they begin to change their behavior. Often this is a time of anticipation, anxiety, and excitement.

The stage of action is most obviously the one in which change seems to happen. In fact, there is the danger to equate action with change.

For research purposes, Prochaska and collaborators determined that the last stage – maintenance – starts six months after the first successful action like the last cigarette or the last drink. Maintenance is the stage where it is important to keep up the commitment to continue with the new behavior in order to prevent relapse.

Comparing the models

The similarities between the model of spontaneity–creativity and the trans-theoretical model seem to be obvious, although it is not a one-to-one relationship. This is true with respect to the Rubicon model also. The model of spontaneity–creativity claims to encompass action in general. The Rubicon model tries to outline the typical course of one single action. The transtheoretical model concerns changes of behavioral problems like addictive behaviors. In spite of these differences, all three models try to describe similar processes. Figure 2.2 points out some of the parallels. Some important differences should be noted.

First of all, the transtheoretical model as well as the Rubicon model refer to conscious deliberate decisions. This is why it makes sense in both to identify pre-action phases (preparation in one, and pre-actional in the other). The psychodramatic model stresses the importance of the spon-taneity state with choice and action going hand in hand without separate preparation. Next, as Figure 2.2 depicts, there is no clear-cut distinction between warming up and pre-contemplation. Finally, the same is true for the stage of maintenance and the phase of conserve.

Warming up

Moreno's true second time

With his quotation 'Every true second time is the liberation from the first' (Moreno 1980: 28), Moreno outlines a rationale for psychodramatic work. He points out that the objective of the psychodramatic enactment is to

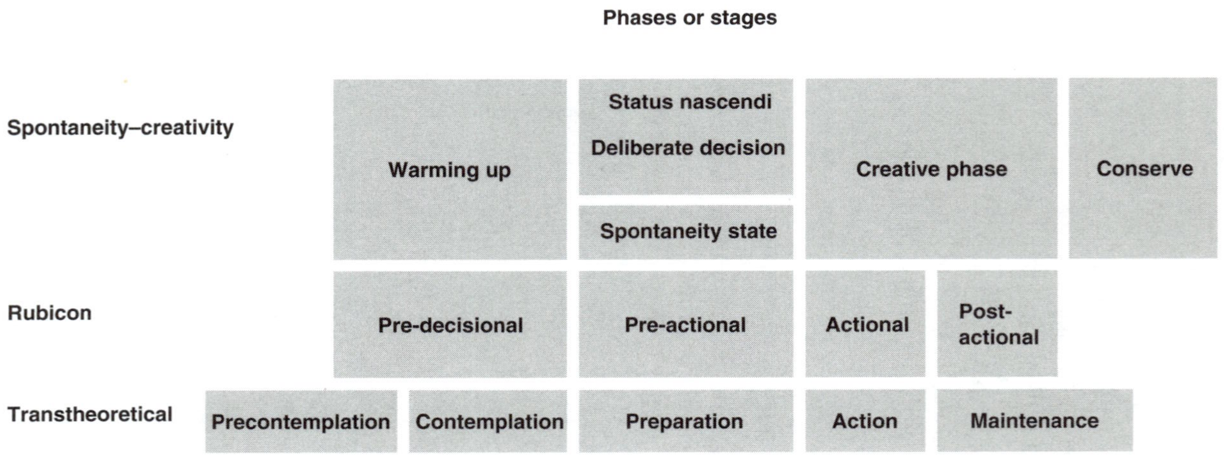

Phases or stages

Spontaneity–creativity	Warming up	Status nascendi / Deliberate decision	Creative phase	Conserve
		Spontaneity state		
Rubicon	Pre-decisional	Pre-actional	Actional	Post-actional
Transtheoretical	Precontemplation / Contemplation	Preparation	Action	Maintenance

Figure 2.2 Comparison of the three models of change

enable the protagonist to realize that they create their own suffering. The protagonist is supposed to gain 'towards his own life, towards all one has done and does, the point of view of the creator.' The protagonist experiences 'that his existence in chains has been the deed of his own free will' (1980: 29). People do suffer because they have become victims of other people; just think of trauma therapy or acts of violence from domestic to international war. Nevertheless, in general, people are not only victims but also active agents. Moreno highlights this side of the polarity.

The experience of a status nascendi often goes along with uncertainty and ambiguity. This is the reason why Moreno states that human beings are afraid of spontaneity (1978). In the German version of *Who Shall Survive?* Moreno (1974) distinguishes followers of the truly imperfect, who are spontaneous and creative people, from followers of the truly perfect, who avoid spontaneity. I believe that, consciously or unconsciously, the latter try to achieve illusionary, 'perfect' goals such as, 'I will never be ashamed again, never be rejected again.' As a result of their childhood experiences, it might be understandable that they pursue such objectives, but as a consequence of these illusionary goals they create their own suffering.

I want to point out that we are talking here about role conserves with their typical habitual qualities. The person who unconsciously wants to avoid any rejection will avoid taking those risks that are indispensable in order to live a spontaneous and creative life. From the view of physical and/ or emotional childhood injuries, this intention may be comprehensible. But almost inevitably, the consequence will be that the person unintentionally also avoids the experience of being loved, being accepted, appreciated or respected. Even if people close to this person offer love, acceptance, appreciation or respect, the person will not be able to be really receptive because this would also require being vulnerable.

My view is that the psychodramatic enactment of the 'true second time' does not have to take place within one session. Usually it is a process that may cover several sessions. Regardless of circumstances and technical procedures, the basic idea is that the protagonist experiences, as vividly as possible, that he or she pursues illusionary intentions, thereby causing their pain. In order to prevent the protagonist from feeling ashamed, it may first be necessary to work with the biography in order to understand why as a child they had good reasons to establish goals that from an adult perspective appear illusionary.

This procedure starts a process of warming up insofar as the protagonist inevitably begins to weigh the pros and cons of their present conduct. It is significant to point out to the protagonist that they should not try immediately to change their behavior. The reason being that change would probably be premature and based solely on a rational decision without emotional foundation. In the course of several sessions – perhaps in the course of months – I help the protagonist to examine daily episodes in order to learn about advantages and disadvantages of their old role conserve. This way the process of weighing up pros and cons involves emotions as well as intellect.

When the protagonist chooses to try something new, thereby reaching a status nascendi (perhaps a spontaneity state if they made the choice unconsciously), their motifs are clear and unequivocal.

The goal of this procedure is insight into intrapsychic processes. However, some people with structural deficits usually are not able to benefit from this kind of work. Here the objective should be to promote insight in concrete, practical terms: These are my actions. These are the consequences that I have neglected up to now. 'If I continue to drink or consume drugs, then I will have to go through . . . .' This starts a pre-decisional phase of weighing up advantages and disadvantages in terms of concrete behavior. It is the same basic idea as with more structured people, but the level of self-reflection is different. In either case it seems important to keep a neutral stance with respect to the future decision of the protagonist. Otherwise they might feel obliged to change in order to please the psychodramatist.

There are other concepts that resemble Moreno's 'true second time.' For example, Donald Meichenbaum's (1977) cognitive behavioral approach comprises a sequence of steps that are similar to the procedure described above. Motivational interviewing is a client-centered method 'for enhancing intrinsic motivation to change by exploring and resolving ambivalence' (Miller and Rollnick 2002: 25). What seems to be unique to the psychodramatic approach is its emphasis on spontaneous, unplanned change, whereas cognitive behavioral approaches as well as motivational interviewing focus on conscious, deliberate attempts to change.

Warming up visualized with the 'diamond of opposites'

Psychodramatists usually know the diamond of opposites as a sociometric concept (Carlson-Sabelli et al. 1992). But according to Hector Sabelli (1989), his concepts are especially important in understanding the processes of change. These can be described in terms of interacting opposites. I have applied his ideas to visualize the process of warming up (Schacht 1994).

Think of the opposites that were mentioned earlier in talking about illusionary, perfect goals. 'I will never be rejected again.' We can think of the perceived positive aspects of this intention as one side of a polarity. As the goal is 'perfect,' the intensity of this pole is extremely high. On the other hand, there is usually little awareness of the negative consequences that go along with this intention. The intensity of this second pole is low. The interplay between both opposites can be depicted in a diamond of opposites as shown in Figure 2.3. I call this mode of interaction number three. (In my 1994 article I describe five modes of interaction. Due to limitations in space I discuss only three of them in this chapter. I will not mention modes of interaction two and five.)

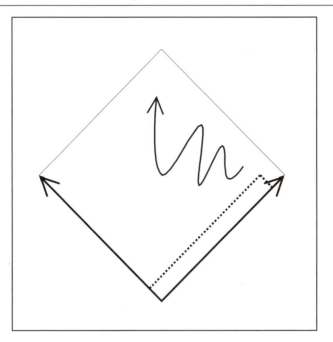

Figure 2.3 Mode of interaction 'number three'

Whenever polarities (in this case the perceived positive and negative consequences of an intention) interact like this, the individual experiences tension and perhaps even anxiety and suffering. They are aware of a problem trying to find a solution. Yet the warming up doesn't lead to a status nascendi, because one pole of the union of opposites is repressed. In many cases mode number three characterizes people early in the contemplation stage (transtheoretical model). 'I have no problem with drinking at all' vs 'Perhaps sometimes I drink a little bit too much.' Or the other way round: people are very aware of why they should not do some behavior like drinking (high intensity of the negative consequences), but they cannot change their behavior because they are not as aware of how this behavior does help them to meet their 'perfect' goals (low intensity of the positive consequences).

The wavy line in Figure 2.3 marks a possible pathway for the warming-up process. In order to reach a status nascendi, the intensity of both opposites has to be quite high. The general principle of stimulating a warm-up process goes as follows: Intensify the weak pole and make the pole that is too strong more relative to the weaker.

Table 2.1 shows related opposites that play an important role in motivational interviewing. I like this table because it presents a good general impression of issues that are relevant when it comes to stimulate the process

Table 2.1 Four aspects relevant for decisional balancing

Considerations for change	Considerations against change
Negatives of the behavior	Positives of the behavior
Positives of the change	Negatives of the change

(Connors, Donovan and DiClemente 2001)

of warming up. One basic idea of motivational interviewing is similar to the principle described above. It is the attempt to raise the level of ambivalence that a person experiences in respect to change (Miller and Rollnick 2002).

Often mode of interaction number three is relevant for people who are already in the middle of a warming-up process. They might be stuck but they are already dealing with questions of change. This is different from mode number one. This mode of interaction is characterized by low intensities of both poles. The person does not experience ambivalence; the opposites neutralize each other – a more or less static situation. A lot of daily routines can be characterized by this mode of interaction (Figure 2.4).

If as psychodramatists we work with someone who deals with certain issues in mode number one, the first thing we have to pay attention to is our patience. Other people might think that it is important for our protagonist to change. For them it isn't even an issue. At least subjectively, they don't have a problem that might start a warm-up. Change is not important to

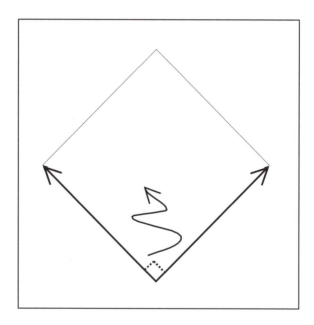

Figure 2.4 Mode of interaction 'number one'

them at this stage. This is 'a normal stage in the process of change' (Miller and Rollnick 2002: 10).

The overall principle for stimulating a warming-up process is as follows: intensify mutually all relevant opposites. This helps to enhance the perceived importance of change. With this mode, warming up is a matter of small steps. In the language of the transtheoretical model, people functioning in mode number one are 'precontemplators.' Connors *et al.* (2001: 106) point out that within every client who does not want to consider their problem, there lies a reservoir of doubt: 'The challenge is to tap into that reservoir of doubt so that the doubt can be turned into serious consideration of change.' But that does not mean to exert pressure. More pressure does not produce more change: 'Nowhere is this less true than with precontemplators. More intensity will often produce fewer results with this group' (DiClemente and Velasquez 2002: 208).

As such, all strategies that focus directly on behavior change requiring activity and commitment on the part of the client are not useful for precontemplators and contemplators. This will be different when the client reaches a status nascendi.

Status nascendi – crossing the Rubicon

The status nascendi can be characterized as the interaction of opposites with high intensity. Figure 2.5 depicts the respective area in the diamond. Mode of interaction number four produces novelty. The status nascendi is a time of tension, uncertainty, disorientation, ambiguity, and perhaps even anxiety. The causal nexus is broken, the potential future is open. Even in the case of deliberate decisions with clear intentions, e.g. to stop smoking, it is not yet determined whether the future will be successful. The person has to risk making mistakes (Blatner 2000). They must also deal with their ambivalence. They made a choice, but this choice is not set for once and for all. The overall principle for this phase is: Give your client or patient support so that the tension can be tolerated. More than in any other phase does the protagonist now need his psychodramatist as an auxiliary ego. This principle is especially noteworthy if a client or patient reaches a spontaneity state, which may be experienced as an anxiety-provoking crisis. But the principle also makes sense if a certain choice is deliberately made.

I will first comment on status nascendi that involve deliberate decisions and eventually detailed preparation and planning as it is described by the transtheoretical as well as the Rubicon model. According to the latter, during the pre-decisional phase the individual uses a motivational orientation, weighing up the pros and cons, looking at the issue from different perspectives in order to get the full picture. Crossing the Rubicon, the mental set shifts to a so-called volitional orientation. From now on the individual

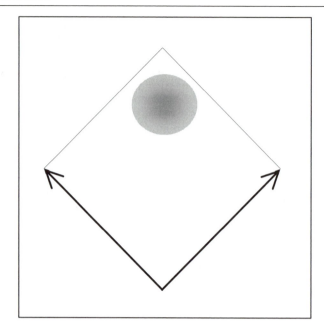

Figure 2.5 Mode of interaction 'number four'

favors positive outlooks on forthcoming actions. Such an optimistic stance strengthens the commitment to act.

The transtheoretical model points in the same direction. After reaching the stage of preparation, it is helpful to focus on the future and the new self. A positive vision of one's own future strengthens the commitment to change. The focus of treatment with a client in the preparation stage is planning and commitment enhancement. Planning should specify what he needs to do in order to change his problem behavior. For example, how to handle different days of the week and different situations that could be dangerous in terms of falling back into old behaviors. The plan should deal with questions like: Who could help? or What could go wrong? In order to do this it might be useful to check prior attempts to change. One of the therapist's tasks during the status nascendi is to give encouragement and feedback.

Before I continue with the dynamics of the spontaneity state, let me develop an idea concerning the question regarding under which circumstances change proceeds either via deliberate choice with preparation and planning or 'sua sponte' via spontaneity states. Status nascendi, as a deliberate decision with planning and preparation, differs from the spontaneity state insofar as different levels of functioning are dominant. Here, competences of the sociodramatic role level like rational thought, self-reflection, and verbal self-instructions are up front. These competences develop rather late in middle childhood and youth. Basic competences of the psychosomatic role level (developing in infancy) and of the psychodramatic role level (developing up to age 4–6) are not as important. It is the other way round with spontaneity states. Here, the basic role levels come to the fore. Affect, imagination, and fantasy – to name only three aspects – take over. Rational thought and self-reflection, though available in general, stand back for a while. According to Moreno, the spontaneity state is neither disturbed by self-reflection nor by the intrusion of reason into emotion. Only afterwards is it possible to give rational meaning to the immediate experience.

Since in the course of a spontaneity state, rational sociodramatic competencies shift to the background, the person's psychosomatic and psychodramatic competences have to be well developed. It would be disorienting to rely on these role levels if they were severely disturbed. Therefore I argue that in the course of counseling or therapy, spontaneity states will occur in general with more mature, relatively structured protagonists. At least when it comes to far-reaching change processes as they are intended in psychotherapies, the regulation mechanisms of people with structural disorders would be overtaxed in the course of spontaneity states. This does not mean that people with this kind of disorder cannot experience spontaneity states. It just makes a whole lot of difference if we talk about a spontaneity state, e.g. in sports or the arts on the one hand or when it comes to self-transformation on the other. When self-transformation is asked for – and this is what change is all about in psychotherapy – deliberate choices with preparation and planning seem to be appropriate for people with structural deficits. This is just one aspect of the general principle that therapies with structural disordered clients usually need to be more structured.

Spontaneity states between flow and crisis

Most of the time, our consciousness is dominated by competencies on the sociodramatic role level. This goes so far that we usually identify ourselves with the rational self. In the course of spontaneity states, the basic competencies of the psychosomatic and psychodramatic role level are dominant. The sociodramatic competencies are present but they are not at the center of our experience. All role levels are functioning together harmoniously. Think of one of those special moments when you finally get the creative insight you've been looking for for quite a while. Suddenly everything seems to make sense, whereas before you were confused and couldn't see the light at the end of the tunnel. Now everything seems to fall into place without effort. In moments like this our attention is focused. We are totally involved. Nothing else matters. Action is intrinsically motivated. Rewards don't matter – at this moment. Action and consciousness are one. The person 'is entirely absorbed by a role, no part of his ego is free to watch it' (Moreno 1937: 46). There is no space for self-reflection, but the person experiences a sense of competence and control. Everything just feels right. Only in the course of spontaneity states do we feel so alive, so powerful, so full of confidence. This is how I understand Moreno's thesis: 'The locus of the self is spontaneity. . . . When spontaneity grows, the self expands' (Moreno 1947: 9). This extraordinary, rich sense of self comes about without consciously having to think about it. As a matter of fact, if we start thinking about it, we might lose the feeling. The spontaneity state is in continuous flow. We can't hold on to it.

Indeed it makes sense to interpret spontaneity states with respect to Csikszentmihalyi and Csikszentmihalyi's (1988) concept of 'flow.' According-ing to the Csikszentmihalyis, people potentially experience flow when they engage in some kind of action that they know they are able to master, while at the same time the task is difficult enough to require all available com-petencies. There is no flow when the task is too easy or too difficult. We really have to face a problem, i.e. a situation that requires engagement beyond the habitual role conserve. In addition, in order to experience flow the situation needs to be clearly structured. It is necessary to receive direct feedback on whether the person makes progress or not.

Moreno's subtype of spontaneity, called 'originality,' is not identical with the Csikszentmihalyis' flow, but it hints at a similar direction. Originality, according to Moreno, is 'that free flow of expression which . . . does not reveal any contribution significant enough to call it creativity, but which . . . is a unique expansion or variation from the cultural conserve as a model' (Moreno 1980: 92). It is also possible to experience truly creative spontaneity with all the hallmarks of the Csikszentmihalyis' flow. But spontaneity states can have all characteristics of crises as well. This is especially true for self-transformations in the course of psychotherapies.

There are two characteristics of spontaneity states that are closely related to possible crises. First, the individual often doesn't know whether they will be able to master the challenge. Usually, flow occurs in situations that are clearly structured and contained. In the case of creative self-transformations, this is not the case. And yet the person has to take a risk. In order to be creative, a choice has to be made – often unconsciously – without knowing where the journey goes. The more a person is afraid of the risk, the more they try to avoid ambiguity, the more the spontaneity state will bear the hallmarks of a crisis. Or there will be no spontaneity state at all.

The second characteristic in question is closely related to the first. Often we think that it is necessary first to know in order to be able to decide afterwards. Insight comes first, then it is time for action. This is not true for spontaneity states. As psychodramatists, we talk about 'action insight' (Moreno 1965; Kellermann 1992). We gain insight while we are acting. First of all, this is a sensory process (psychosomatic role level) accompanied by imagery (psychodramatic role level). If everything seems to fall into place, this might not be a problem. But it may be a problem if the person experiences 'something' without being able to grasp the newness and meaning of their own actions. This happens quite often. In such an instance, the individual might get the subjective impression of crisis. By definition, in the course of a spontaneity state the person does something new without deliberate intention. That's why people often don't notice the importance of the alterations. It is up to the psychodramatist to help the client realize that something special is happening and that they, the client, are the agent of the change.

I think of the spontaneity state as a continuum that ranges from flow to crisis. Whether it is experienced as flow or as crisis depends on situational as well as on personal characteristics. We have already talked about situational aspects. Personal qualities are, for instance, experience and confidence. A well-structured person, who has successfully mastered many self-transformations, thereby passing many spontaneity states, might be able to even experience the spontaneity state of a far-reaching personal transformation as flow. An insecure, anxious individual might experience the same spontaneity state as a distressing crisis, perhaps compelling them to hold on to old role conserves, thereby interrupting the spontaneity state prematurely.

There are patients who feel worse than before when they enter a spontaneity state. They complain that their anxiety, insecurity or depression has become stronger. Confronted with ambiguity in the course of change, people often interpret the situation in terms of their old role conserves, i.e. in terms of their symptoms. If the therapist doesn't pay attention to subtle cues for change, a spontaneity state is interrupted prematurely. Instead of progress, the old conserves are solidified.

Another aspect of the director's role as an auxiliary ego in the course of a protagonist's spontaneity state is to give support concerning the regulation of tensions and affects. Spontaneity states are characterized by mode of interaction number four: the individual goes through a lot of tension. Pain and sorrow may have been repressed for a lifetime. Now the person gets ready to let go. This can be frightening. I often assure my patients of the fact that the tears will stop eventually, that they will be able to regain control. The protagonist will feel supported if he or she realizes that the psychodramatist knows about their anxieties.

The regulation of tension and affect may be important for the therapist himself or herself. If a protagonist enters a spontaneity state, the situation might be intense and ambiguous for the psychodramatist as well. It is necessary to tolerate tension and ambiguity without prematurely making up one's mind what is going on. A lot of spontaneity states occur in the context of the patient—therapist relationship. In this case, I am concerned directly. I myself might not know what I am feeling right now, but still I must act somehow. Otherwise it is me who interrupts the progress of the interpersonal spontaneity state.

Another aspect of being an auxiliary ego concerns the fact that sometimes people don't know the words for an affect that they are experiencing. Affects as felt-sense impressions exist prior to words and verbal meaning. As a double, it might be necessary for the therapist to suggest the meaning of an affect. Just think of somebody who doesn't know what anger or sorrow feels like. In the course of a spontaneity state, he might experience 'something worrying.' Only from the outside might it be possible to realize which kind of feeling this could be.

There is no clear line between the passage of a spontaneity state and the following creative phase. Slowly the person is more and more able to reflect on their own process while they are deliberately acting in a manner that first appeared without conscious intention. In the case of a status nascendi of the deliberate choice type, the line between the pre-actional phase (preparation in the transtheoretical model) and action is easier to define. It is when action finally takes place.

Creative phase

Consolidation of new roles

The model of spontaneity–creativity by itself doesn't have a lot to offer concerning this phase of the process. It is helpful to interpret the creative phase as action and post-actional evaluation (Rubicon model) or as action and maintenance (transtheoretical model).

Think of a status nascendi with a deliberate decision and careful planning to stop drinking. Early in the action stage, the need for commitment is paramount. What is true in the case of a spontaneity state is true in this situation. People need encouragement and support for reaffirming their decisions and taking responsibility for their actions during the post-actional (Rubicon model) evaluation.

This also applies for more structured patients after their passage through a spontaneity state. They definitely need reinforcement with respect to their progress. Without action plans that specify the intended behaviors, it is more difficult for the individual to evaluate their own behavior.

The transtheoretical model stresses that the action plan needs to be reviewed regularly in order to be changed as needed (verification and validation feedback). In general, the model postulates a shift concerning the kind of interventions that are regarded as helpful. During the stages of pre-contemplation and contemplation, cognitive and experiential interventions are important that are typical for psychodynamic and humanistic approaches. Starting with the action stage, the model favors interventions typical for behavioral therapy. With some restrictions, I agree with this assumption, keeping in mind that psychodrama offers a number of options to work according to this line of thought.

In contrast to the assumptions of the transtheoretical model, I believe that biographical work with an emphasis on consciousness raising and emotional relief can be quite appropriate during the creative phase. But it goes along with a shift of direction. During the warming up, it is aimed at building motivation to change. Now it is directed towards consolidation of changes that have already taken place. It takes a certain distance to perceive something clearly. As a person develops new roles in the course of the creative phase, they often get a new look at their own history. Now certain issues that have been obscure before become clear and emotionally relevant.

According to the transtheoretical model, during the stage of maintenance two factors are fundamental: sustained long-term effort and a revised lifestyle. The danger is a possible erosion of commitment. It needs patience and persistence to continue with the process of change. There are three common internal challenges: overconfidence, daily temptations, and self-blame. To me, overconfidence seems to be relevant especially in the case of addictions. Daily temptations as well as self-blame appear to be relevant in most psychotherapies. A person suffering from panic attacks, hypochondria or depression will encounter daily temptations to fall back into old role conserves. Whenever this happens they will almost certainly be afflicted with self-blame along with decreased self-esteem, doubts and perhaps even guilt.

In order to prepare my patients for possible lapses, in the course of the spontaneity state and creative phase I usually tell them several times that there will probably be more difficult situations ahead to overcome. I like the metaphor of a hurdle race with hurdles that are increasingly higher. Each hurdle is an opportunity to strengthen the new capacities. Whenever one hurdle is overcome there will be a period of smooth functioning. But sooner or later a higher hurdle is waiting that is too much for one's capacities to 'jump.'

In this way, I try to familiarize my patients with the idea that they will probably have to cycle through the phases of the spontaneous–creative process a couple of times unless their new roles are stable enough. It is not easy to define when a new role is stable enough so that we can talk of the phase of role conserve. In many cases, a person will always have to put considerable energy into maintaining a certain role. This might never be habituated enough to be taken for granted. So it might be appropriate to think of the dividing line between creative phase and conserve, respectively maintenance and conserve, as open.

Acknowledgement

I want to thank Mark Baker, PhD for editing this text and for his helpful comments on many issues.

References

Blatner, A. (2000) *Foundations of Psychodrama: History, Theory, and Practice* (4th edn), New York: Springer.

Carlson-Sabelli, L., Sabelli, H., Patel, M. and Holm, K. (1992) 'The union of opposites in sociometry', *Journal of Group Psychotherapy, Psychodrama and Sociometry*, 44, 4: 147–171.

Connors, G. J., Donovan, D. M. and DiClemente, C. C. (2001) *Substance Abuse Treatment and the Stages of Change: Selecting and Planning Interventions*, New York: Guilford Press.

Csikszentmihalyi M. and Csikszentmihalyi, I. S. (eds) (1988) *Optimal Experience – Psychological Studies of Flow in Consciousness*, Cambridge: Cambridge University Press.

DiClemente, C. C. and Velasquez, M. W. (2002) 'Motivational interviewing and the stages of change', in W. Miller and S. Rollnick *Motivational Interviewing: Preparing People for Change*, New York: Guilford Press.

Heckhausen, H. (1989) *Motivation und Handeln* [*Motivation and Action*], Berlin: Springer.

Kellermann, P. F. (1992) *Focus on Psychodrama*, London: Jessica Kingsley.

Meichenbaum, D. (1977) *Cognitive Behavior Modification: An Integrative Approach*, New York: Plenum Press.

Miller, W. R. and Rollnick, S. (2002) *Motivational Interviewing: Preparing People for Change*, New York: Guilford Press.

Moreno, J. L. (1937) 'Inter-personal therapy and the psychopathology of inter-personal relations', *Sociometry*, 1: 9–76.

—— (1947) 'The future of man's world', *Psychodrama Monographs* 21, Beacon, NY: Beacon House.

—— (1956) 'System of spontaneity–creativity–conserve', in J. L. Moreno (ed.) *Sociometry and the Science of Man*, Beacon, NY: Beacon House.

—— (1970) *Das Stegreiftheater* [*Theatre of Spontaneity*], Beacon, NY: Beacon House.

—— (1974) *Die Grundlagen der Soziometrie* [German version of *Who Shall Survive?*], Opladen: Westdeutscher Verlag.

—— (1978) *Who Shall Survive? Foundations of Sociometry, Group Psychotherapy and Sociodrama* (2nd edn), Beacon, NY: Beacon House.

—— (1980) *Psychodrama, Volume One*, Beacon, NY: Beacon House. (Originally published 1946.)

Moreno, Z. T. (1965) 'Psychodramatic rules, techniques, and adjunctive methods', *Group Psychotherapy*, 18: 73–86.

Prochaska, J. O., Norcross, J. C. and DiClemente, C. C. (2002) *Changing for Good*, New York: Quill.

Sabelli, H. (1989) *Union of Opposites: A Comprehensive Theory of Natural and Human Processes*, Lawrenceville, VA: Brunswick.

Schacht, M. (1994) 'Besser, schöner, schneller, weiter – nicht immer. Erwärmung im Selbstorganisationsmodell der Spontaneität-Kreativität' [Better, more beautiful, faster – not always. Warming up according to the model of spontaneity-creativity as self-organization], *Psychodrama*, 7: 17–53.

—— (2003) *Spontaneität und Begegnung: Zur Persönlichkeitsentwicklung aus der Sicht des Psychodramas* [*Spontaneity and Encounter: A Psychodramatic View on the Development of the Person*], München: Inscenario.

Chapter 3

Reformulating psychodrama as an experiential reintegration action therapy (ERAT)

The corrective emotional approach

David A. Kipper

Introduction

Experiential reintegration action therapy (ERAT) is a new conceptual formulation for the method of classical psychodrama and the various therapeutic procedures that have sprung from it. The ERAT approach provides a psychological rationale and a system of directorial strategies for a practice that applies the structure and techniques of psychodrama as well as action method interventions. ERAT offers a theoretical system for a group psychotherapy that focuses on examining, replacing, altering, correcting and enriching group members' existing experiential repertoire.

Historically, the method of psychodrama grew out of Moreno's theoretical ideas (Moreno 1953, 1964). Naturally, the clinical practice and its underlying rationale were well integrated and for a long time thought to be inseparable. However, in the early 1980s a new trend evolved in psychodrama theory. Its central message was that making psychodrama more congruent with other psychological theories might expand the applicability of the method. To achieve this aim, several psychodrama scholars and practitioners offered innovative models that added to Moreno's classical one, only this time their approaches were based on the separation between the psychodrama *method* and its *original theoretical* foundation (see, for example, Kipper 1986; Holmes 1992; Garfield 2000; Razza and Tomasulo 2005). The new thinking has been that the compatibility with other mainstream psychotherapeutic approaches represents an enhancement of the value of psychodrama. The ERAT approach that I have developed (Kipper 2005) is in keeping with the above-mentioned trend and provides another illustration of it.

In day-to-day clinical practice, the difference between classical psychodrama and the experiential reintegration action therapy (ERAT) approach boils down to the focus of the intervention. Classical psychodrama emphasizes helping clients to become more spontaneous. ERAT emphasizes reshaping and correcting, hence reorganizing, the client's *pool of significant experiences*. To be clear, the ERAT position does not dispute the hypothesis that spontaneity (Moreno 1953) and 'setting clients free' (May 1981) might well be the overall aim of existential psychotherapy (see, for example, Greenberg *et al.* 1998; Schneider 1998). The experiential reintegration approach operates under the assumption that spontaneity and the freedom to be or to act are the *automatic byproduct* of the changes that occur in the composition of the clients' pool of significant experiences caused by the experiential reintegration action therapy.

There are significant advantages to the ERAT formulation. First, the proposed theoretical concepts of ERAT are well embedded in contemporary psychological literature. Second, the position of the ERAT approach is that it can augment verbal group therapies. It represents a compatible rather than a competing approach. Third, the original theory of psychodrama did not lend itself to an impressive body of scientific research regarding its validity and clinical effectiveness. Indeed, for a long time several reviewers pointed to the paucity of such research and recommended various approaches to remedy this situation (for example, D'Amato and Dean 1988; Rawlinson 2000; Kipper and Hundal 2003). In contrast, it is believed that the ERAT reformulation is easily amenable to empirical, qualitative and narrative research (Kipper and Ritchie 2003). Finally, classical psychodrama promoted one basic format for therapeutic intervention that appears to be indicated for every problem. In contrast, the ERAT formulation offers multiple directorial strategies that are to be implemented differently, depending on the kind of experience under treatment. Therefore, the structure of the session or the way it is conducted may vary depending on the type of experience under treatment.

Rationale for experiential reintegration action therapy (ERAT)

The theoretical cornerstone of the ERAT approach is a position agreed by all major theories of personality development. It holds that human behavior, adaptive as well as maladaptive, is formed through the aggregate effect of experiences accumulated during one's lifetime. Maladaptive behavior may also develop as the result of single or repeated extreme traumatic event(s). Studies have shown that the process of absorbing and the subsequent coding (learning) of all experiences in the brain is a physiological, chemical and neurological phenomenon that follows a consistent pattern (van der Kolk *et al.* 1996). However, the interpretation of the *meaning* of the recorded experiences is a *psychological product*, the outcome again of physiological, chemical and neurological processes. Meaning manifests itself in the form of inferences that become attitudes, philosophical outlooks and guidance to future conduct. The ERAT addresses this psychological component of the experience by changing the experience itself.

For instance, one may remember an unpleasant childhood event, for example, laughing responses from family members to the sharing of an embarrassing situation. These reactions might have been interpreted by the child to mean that he or she was inadequate. In reality, however, the laughing was a reaction to the situation itself, which was funny. The recorded event, the *memory* of the experience, may not be easy to erase. However, the *psychological meaning* ascribed to it can be altered in psychotherapy.

Basic concepts

The following are the key concepts associated with ERAT:

- an experience
- a significant experience
- context
- emotional reactions
- reintegration.

An experience

An experience is defined as the storage in memory of the emotional reactions and/or the cognitive inferences of an event that involve interactions between an individual and a situation. Human experiences are innumerable and obviously only relatively few might be subjected to therapeutic scrutiny and subsequent intervention. Hence, the ERAT approach addresses only experiences that require attention because they produce dysfunctional outcomes. The presence of such difficulties may be determined by the client's stated issues, the client's presenting problems and/or the observation of the client's responses by other people or by the therapist.

A significant experience

This refers to an experience that, when it occurred, involved strong positive or negative emotional reactions. The experiences that are addressed in the course of psychotherapy fall under this category and practically all involve intense negative emotional reactions, such as fear, anger or tears. Sometimes, the memory of such an intense experience is never forgotten or discarded. Sometimes, a significant negative experience is remembered but disowned. Sometimes it is so painful and overwhelming that it is suppressed, relegated to the unconscious or the pre-awareness levels. Like other forms of psychotherapy, the ERAT approach explores the deleterious effect of negative experiences. However, it also advocates that a considerable part of the psychotherapeutic repair work will involve strengthening positive significant experiences.

The context

Human experiences occur in contexts that remain integral parts of the subsequent memory of the experiences. The context can be a real, concrete situation or an imagined one, for example, a dream or a fantasy. In the vast majority of cases, the context involves the presence of other people. However, many experiences do not. Examples of situations that do not necessarily involve interactions with other human beings are reactions to natural events (e.g., thunder, an earthquake), interactions with animals (e.g., a pet, falling off a horse) or with inanimate objects (e.g., losing a ring, a car accident). Because the interaction with the situation is inextricably bound up with the experience, reliving past experiences may be greatly facilitated by re-creating, and simulating, their original contexts as accurately as possible.

Emotional reactions

An emotional reaction is a basic biologically adaptive system that operates by evaluating situations in relation to one's well-being. Most contemporary theoreticians who write about emotions agree that the expression of emotion is the result of synchronization of a number of systems including physiological, readiness to act, and cognitive appraisals (Lyons 1998). Cognition, which affects the systems directly, 'may be particularly important for triggering the onset of the emotional process' (Flack et al. 1998: 324). Scott and Ingram (1998: 201–202) described the central role of evaluative-cognitive appraisals in the evocation of an emotion. Such appraisals refer to 'the assessment of meaning that an individual constructs of a person–environment relationship that may have harmful or beneficial consequence for the individual's well-being.' The process is described as follows. Cognitive appraisals evoke changes in the physiological arousal. Then the alteration in the arousal pattern is expressed as a state of action readiness: a tendency to respond in a certain manner. Finally, the (emotional) response is communicated by means of expressive behavioral patterns.

Reintegration

Reintegration is the cognitive reappraisal of the meaning of new or altered experiences. This is the natural outcome of the processes involved in going through an emotional experience and combining this with cognitive appraisal. There are two main factors that can enhance the successful completion of the reintegration. One is the potency of the newly offered experience and the other is normalizing its outcome. The former requires that the newly offered experience will have a high-impact capability with sufficient emotional intensity to eradicate or substantially alter the old ones.

The latter depends on the supportive feedback and affirmation given by the group members and the therapist.

Classification of significant experiences

To be clear, the ERAT does not address every experience clients may have had. As a psychotherapeutic modality, it is concerned only with experiences that appear to cause psychological pain and/or other dysfunction. There are four major categories that include the kind of experiences that become the subject of the psychotherapy. They are the combination of two dimensions that represent two basic therapeutic principles. One is whether or not the experience in question had already occurred, namely is it an encapsulated or an unrealized experience. The second dimension is whether or not the experience was a rewarding one – that is, *satisfying* (*positive*) or *unsatisfying* (*negative*). Figure 3.1 shows these categories and the various directorial strategies associated with each of the categories.

The first category includes three directorial strategies (1, 2 and 3) shown in the upper left quadrant of Figure 3.1 titled *unsatisfying* and *encapsulated* experiences. Encapsulated experiences refer to events that actually occurred in the past. For the well-adjusted person, the majority of encapsulated experiences are positive and satisfying. Negative experiences are fewer by comparison and cause only minor difficulties. However, for the person with adjustment difficulties, certain unsatisfying past experiences may be remembered as painful, dangerous or devastating events, and typically are associated with anger, hurt, failure, guilt, fear, shame and trauma.

The second category (the lower left quadrant of the figure) includes *satisfying* and *encapsulated* experiences marked as directorial strategies 4, 5 and 6. Here one finds significant *rewarding* experiences that occurred in the past. They represent positive past experiences that, in the context of psychotherapy, are evoked to counter, diffuse or diminish the effect of the unsatisfying experiences. More about this will be described below.

The third category includes *unsatisfactory* and *unrealized* experiences (the upper right quadrant of the figure). Unlike encapsulated experiences, the *unrealized* ones address events that have not occurred yet. They are regarded as important experiences because in the mind of the client they are *likely* to occur (or are *already occurring* in the fantasy) and the effect of the anticipation associated with them might be considerable. The upper right category addresses unrealized experiences that have a *negative* outcome, such as anxiety and fear. The expectation is for *the worst*.

The fourth category (the lower right quadrant of the figure) is also concerned with unrealized experiences, but in contrast it refers to anticipated *positive*, satisfying experiences, for example, dreams, fantasies and wishes. The manner in which such experiences might be brought into the therapeutic process, and their potential contribution to it, will be explained below.

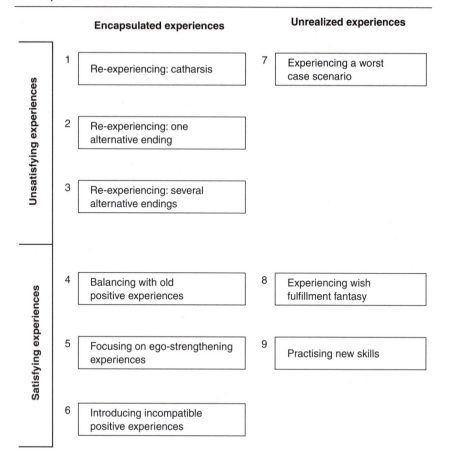

Figure 3.1 Classification of significant experiences and directorial strategies

Directorial strategies for different experiences

The foregoing four categories suggest nine directorial strategies, that is procedures the psychodrama therapist can adopt depending of the kind of experience that is being treated. These are described below, and their respective number corresponds to the number of the boxes shown in Figure 3.1.

Encapsulated experiences (left column)

1 Changing the effect of the painful experience through cathartic reaction

Some experiences are so painful that they are untouchable unless the hurt is first reduced or eliminated. In such instances, protagonists will show resistance to appropriately address the difficult issue involved in the experience as long as the pain has not been expiated or reduced considerably. This first directorial strategy calls for such an intervention, aimed at reducing the pain. One of the most effective treatments in such a situation is helping the protagonist to reach a cathartic experience. The therapeutic session moves slowly, moving 'from the periphery to the center.' The protagonist re-enacts past scenes associated with the painful experience, starting with more benign ones, progressing gradually until they are ready to face the traumatic experience(s) that constitute the core of their difficulties.

The conduct of such a session follows the traditional *classical psychodrama* model. Briefly, the first enacted scene features the presentation of the protagonist's problem, a situation where it manifested itself. The plot and the level of involvement progress in a gradual fashion with the peak (point of catharsis) attained after four or six scenes (see Kipper 1986; Hollander 2002). The action portion ends with one last, post-catharsis scene that brings closure. This strategy is often used with a highly traumatic past experience. The application of this first directorial strategy as well as the next one in cases of PTSD and physical and sexual abuse must proceed with extreme caution lest the treatment cause retraumatization (Hudgins 2002).

2 Changing the painful effect of the experience with one new positive ending

In traumatic past experiences, the painful memories of the event are often the result of the manner in which the experience ended. An alternative way of eliminating the hurt may not require a cathartic experience that unleashes repressed intense anger, fear, guilt or jealousy. Instead, the directorial strategy would be to re-enact the original event and the issues surrounding it but to end it in an alternative, *positive* manner, thus replacing the old painful one. This way, protagonists get a chance to end the old painful experience differently and hence shift the memory associated with it from an adverse to a better one. The psychodrama session progresses along the *classical* model except that (a) it need *not* culminate with catharsis; (b) the enactment culminates in role playing a positive ending *suggested by the protagonist*. This strategy is used either in conjunction with the previous one or on its own.

3 Changing the painful effect of the experience with several positive alternative endings

This directorial strategy is similar to that described in the previous strategy (2) and differs only in that the ending is not suggested by the protagonist but by group members and/or the director. As this directorial strategy calls for enacting several alternative positive endings, the session does not allow time to explore, in depth, many past experiences. Instead, for the most part, the enacted scenes in the session focus on *here-and-now* situations. Protagonists portray a number of alternative endings, and then select the one that they feel suits them best. This strategy is used in cases when the deleterious effects of the past experience are not as painful as the ones displayed in the two previous situations (1 and 2).

4 A balancing act: reducing the painful effect of the experience by putting it in a proper perspective

Sometimes, people exaggerate the significance of an unsatisfying experience they have had. This happens not so much by remembering the experience as more painful but rather by ascribing undue importance to it. In such instances, the recommended directorial strategy is to attempt to focus the therapeutic intervention on the protagonist's repertoire of positive experiences. The rationale behind this strategy is to help protagonists realize that the perception of the problem they thought they had is now changed and seen in a different light. With this strategy, the session will comprise the enactment of positive experiences that puts the old unsatisfying experience in an otherwise generally positive context.

5 Focusing on ego-strengthening experiences

This is another directorial strategy that focuses on the enactment of positive experience. However, unlike the previous strategy, it does not address a specific negative past experience. Instead, it concerns the accumulative effect of many unsatisfying effects a protagonist has had in the course of his or her life. In particular, it addresses the outcome of many past negative experiences that resulted in low self-esteem, self-deprecation and low self-image. The directorial strategy calls for re-enacting positive past experiences that emphasize the skills and talents protagonists already possess but tend to downgrade.

6 Changing the effect of the experience by introducing a special positive experience that is incompatible with the painful one

This directorial strategy aims at changing the undesirable effect of an old experience by confronting it with either an old or new incompatible, positive experience. The strategy operates under the principle that two incompatible experiences cannot coexist. The therapeutic intervention causes cognitive dissonance aimed at steering the protagonist away from the old memory and adopting the new positive one. Left with a choice between retaining the painful memory of the old experience and choosing the new desirable one, it is highly probable that the protagonist will choose the latter. The critical key to the success of this directorial strategy is that the selected positive experience must be so potent and highly intense that it overrides the effect of the old, undesirable experience.

Unrealized experiences (right column)

The next three directorial strategies concern experiences that have not yet occurred in reality. They are experiences made in fantasy or ones that are completely new to the protagonists. These too are classified into the unsatisfying and satisfying categories.

7 Changing the effect of the experience by enacting a 'worst case' scenario

This directorial strategy is recommended in treating a relatively milder adverse impact of a past experience. Like other strategies, it too follows the rationale that placing past events in a different perspective tends to reduce (or eliminate) their deleterious effects. One strategy of accomplishing this was described above (4) and it focused on reframing the significance of the painful experience in the context of the many positive ones the protagonist has already had in the past. The present strategy calls for an opposite approach. It proposes the enactment of the 'worst case' scenario. It aims at changing the protagonist's appraisal of the effect of the old undesirable experience by re-enacting it with a different, much worse ending. The realization that there could have been a much worse outcome often changes the protagonist's view of the meaning of the experience. Often it greatly diminishes its adverse memory. This directorial strategy is one of the less frequently used. It should be applied with caution and only in instances when it is determined that the protagonist's ego is strong enough to prevent unintended harm.

8 Missed or untried experiences: the fulfillment of a wish or a fantasy

Certain experiences that often affect present behavior fall under the category of missed and untested experiences. Missed experiences are those that people would like to have had in the past, for example, a protective parent, a sister or a better teacher. The untested experiences are those that people would like to have in the future, for example, a dream, or a wish fulfillment. The directorial strategy used in this type of experience offers protagonists the opportunity to experience their wishes and pleasant fantasies by enacting them as if they were occurring in the present. With this strategy, the role-playing session differs from the one used in classical psychodrama in that it is designed by the director consistent with the manner in which such events occur in reality. Consequently, the auxiliaries are not asked to offer clues. More than in any other directorial strategy, the present one is 'dictated' by the director together with the protagonist. Typically the plot is spread over five to six scenes and culminates in the fulfillment of the wish enacted in the last scene in the session, ending the session on a highly satisfying note.

9 Practicing new skills

This directorial strategy is used when the protagonist displays a lack of coping skills. Role-playing enactment and psychodrama procedures are particularly helpful in training and practicing such skills which include, among others, social and intimacy skills, problem-solving skills, reducing shyness and loneliness, increasing assertiveness, and anger control skills. The session is based on creating situations that require appropriate responses. These may be generated by the director or, as is typically the case, by other group members who demonstrate such responses that are then copied and practiced by the protagonist.

Concluding comments

It is not surprising that the majority of the nine directorial strategies of the ERAT approach address unsatisfactory experiences of the past. After all, the ERAT formulation maintains that significant past experiences are implicated in the present psychological dysfunction. This position is shared by all major group psychotherapy approaches (Yalom 1995; DeLucia-Waack et al. 2004). Some of the strategies described above address a past experience directly (e.g., strategies 1 through 5). Other strategies address the past more indirectly (e.g., 6 and 7). In contrast, strategies 8 and 9 focus entirely on the present and the future. Together with the fifth strategy, they address the healthy parts of the protagonist, a position consistent with the ERAT philosophy.

Many psychodrama practitioners already apply most of the above strategies. The fact that the ERAT approach explicitly spells out a system of classification for directorial strategies should help the therapist's decision regarding which strategy to adopt in a given case. It is also hoped that such a system might facilitate studies of treatment efficacy.

Finally, the case for the usefulness of any theory of psychotherapy rests upon its ability to generate empirical research to support its premises, hypotheses and predictions. This holds true for the ERAT approach as well. One of the questions that arises from the proposed classification of directorial strategies is: What are the clinical considerations that guide the practitioner's decision as to which of the above strategies would be the best in a given situation? While the ERAT approach may provide theoretical guidance in that regard, in the final analysis the answer depends on the results of future research.

References

D'Amato, R. C. and Dean, R. S. (1988) 'Psychodrama research: therapy and theory: a critical analysis of an arrested modality', *Psychology in the Schools*, 25: 305–314.

DeLucia-Waack, J. L., Gerrity, D. A., Kalodner, C. R. and Riva, M. T. (2004) *Handbook of Group Counseling and Group Psychotherapy*, Thousand Oaks, CA: Sage.

Flack, W. F., Laird, J. D., Cavallaro, L. A. and Miller, D. R. (1998) 'Emotional expression and experience', in W. F. Flack and J. D. Laird (eds) (1998) *Emotions in Psychopathology: Theory and Research*, New York: Oxford University Press.

Garfield, S. (2000) 'Transference in analytic psychodrama', *International Forum of Group Psychotherapy*, 8: 14–18.

Greenberg, J. C., Watson., J. C. and Lietaer, G. (eds) (1998) *Handbook of Experiential Psychotherapy*, New York: Guilford Press.

Hollander, C. E. (2002) 'A process for psychodrama training: the Hollander psychodrama curve', *International Journal of Action Methods: Psychodrama, Skill Training, and Role Playing*, 54: 147–157.

Holmes, P. (1992) *The Inner World Outside: Object-relations Theory and Psychodrama*, London: Tavistock/Routledge.

Hudgins, M. K. (2002) *Experiential Treatment for PTSD*, New York: Springer.

Kipper, D. A. (1986) *Psychotherapy through Clinical Role Playing*, New York: Brunner/Mazel.

—— (2005) 'Psychodrama in a new light: the corrective experiential approach', *Group Psychologist*, 15: 17–18.

Kipper, D. A. and Hundal, J. (2003) 'A survey of clinical reports on the application of psychodrama', *Journal of Group Psychotherapy, Psychodrama and Sociometry*, 55: 141–157.

Kipper, D. A. and Ritchie, T. D. (2003) 'The effectiveness of psychodrama techniques: a meta-analysis', *Group Dynamics: Theory, Research and Practice*, 7: 13–25.

Lyons, W. (1998) 'Philosophy, the emotions, and psychopathology', in W. F. Flack and J. D. Laird (eds) (1998) *Emotions in Psychopathology: Theory and Research*, New York: Oxford University Press.

May, R. (1981) *Freedom and Destiny*, New York: Norton.

Moreno, J. L. (1953) *Who Shall Survive? Foundations of Sociometry, Group Psychotherapy and Sociodrama* (2nd edn), Beacon, NY: Beacon House.

—— (1964) *Psychodrama, Volume One*, Beacon NY: Beacon House. (Originally published 1946.)

Rawlinson, J. W. (2000) 'Does psychodrama work? A review of the literature', *British Journal of Psychodrama and Sociodrama*, 15: 67–101.

Razza, N. J. and Tomasulo, D. J. (2005) *Healing Trauma: The Power of Group Treatment for People with Intellectual Disabilities*, Washington, DC: American Psychological Association.

Schneider, K. J. (1998) 'Existential process', in L. S. Greenberg, J. C. Watson and G. Lietaer (eds) (1998) *Handbook of Experiential Psychotherapy*, New York: Guilford Press.

Scott, W. D. and Ingram, R. E. (1998) 'Affective influences in depression', in W. F.

Flack and J. D. Laird (eds) (1998) *Emotions in Psychopathology: Theory and Research*, New York: Oxford University Press.

van der Kolk, B. A., McFarlane, A. C. and Weisaeth, L. (eds) (1996) *Traumatic Stress: The Effects of Overwhelming Experience on Mind, Body, and Society*, New York: Guilford Press.

Yalom, I. D. (1995) *The Theory and Practice of Group Psychotherapy* (4th edn), New York: Basic Books.

Chapter 4

The role of the meta-role

An integrative element in psychology

Adam Blatner

Moreno's role theory implies a pluralistic model of the mind – the idea that a person plays many roles – and combines this concept with the notion that it is possible to identify these roles, name them, re-evaluate their definitions and modulate the way they are played (Moreno 1946). Moreno did not develop or fully articulate the theoretical implications of the ability of one part of the mind to modulate the other parts that are involved in roles. Nevertheless, it is this part – the 'meta-role' complex of functions – with which the director in psychodrama generates the treatment alliance, and it is this part of the mind that joins with the director and the group as a kind of inner co-director, a part that analyzes and decides how the various roles should be played.

I call this part the 'meta-role' because it carries certain elements of a role while also transcending the other roles being played. The meta-role thus operates at a level beyond the other roles – hence the Greek prefix meaning 'beyond': 'meta.' With clients, I may use this word or some others, such as 'your inner manager.' Other terms that sometimes help include the 'inner chief executive officer,' the 'conductor of your inner orchestra,' the 'choosing self,' 'inner audience/director' and so forth.

While role theory is an established part of psychodrama – and my systematic development of applied role theory as 'role dynamics' (Blatner 1985, 1991) might itself be an advancement in its theory – a key point of this chapter is the recognition that when we form a treatment alliance with our client we engage with their meta-role. Many approaches to therapy may have as a common denominator the implicit development of various meta-role functions. (A number of these functions will be described further on.) Role dynamics proposes that this whole operation be made *explicit* and that the meta-role be named in whatever terms the client finds useful. In this approach, the therapist can address the client in this role, redirecting the complexes of identifications from their role-based motivations to a broader motivational idea, that of coordinating and balancing all motivations, needs, and goals within a more meaningful life plan.

Identification: a key dynamic

Identification involves the association of the sense of self with certain symbols, ideas, role elements, and so forth. In terms derived from George Herbert Mead's philosophy in the 1930s, it is useful to differentiate between a role-free pure subjectivity, the 'I,' and the object of that inner observation, those qualities that in their aggregate constitute the 'Me' (Mead 1934; also Chapter 8 of this volume). Thus, when a person says 'I am Italian, I'm a man, I am middle-aged, I am a Republican, I am a Catholic, I am a husband and a father, I am a dentist' and so forth, all those qualities are parts of the various roles that for this person lend him his identity, but they are all part of the 'Me' – who the man thinks he is. He may deny that he is a 'cheater,' for example, rationalizing some of his marginal moral actions. (That role, then, would be part of what Carl Jung calls the 'shadow' complex, and also might be called the 'not-me.')

This man could also be imagined to say 'I am a being who plays all of the aforementioned roles, but I am more than all those roles. Thus, I can change some of those roles, or certain elements in those roles. I can change how I weight them in terms of priority and significance, and I can rethink and negotiate what assumptions I bring to how I define them. I can say, "Just because I'm Catholic doesn't mean I have to follow all their rules," or, "Just because I'm Italian doesn't mean I have to like spaghetti."'

Put another way, role dynamics promotes a lifting of the identity away from the tendencies and habits of thinking of one's self as 'being' the specific roles in a person's role repertoire. Role dynamics also promotes a shift that allows that identity to be the one who can reflect on the big picture and choose to re-evaluate, rebalance and re-create one's own life plan and identity. One begins to say things like 'I'm a spiritual being having a physical experience,' or 'I'm the manager of my life plan.'

Incidentally, being the manager or executive of one's life need not presume that one is in full control. There can be many events that are beyond personal control. Nevertheless, a person can become more effectively and intentionally responsible for how they interpret the events that happen in life and how they react to those events. In other words, a person can accept the role component of being in charge to some degree even while accepting the reality that often one isn't in control. Indeed, being 'mature' involves learning to cope sensibly with those events that are out of one's control, such as the illness or death of loved ones, and ultimately one's own illness and dying.

Background

Moreno was one of the pioneers of role theory (Biddle and Thomas 1966). Many of the social psychologists and sociologists active in the field found in role theory and its associated dramaturgical approach a useful way of describing the complexities of the dynamic interaction among the levels within the mind, in the interpersonal field, the various group affiliations and the culture (Blatner 2006a). Moreno's approach was more oriented to *practical* applications of role theory. Many of his methods may be viewed as ways of identifying and working with the roles we play, and in turn his role theory may be thought of as providing a language for his methods of psychodrama, sociodrama, group psychotherapy and sociometry, as well as others such as impromptu theatre.

Moreno's ideas about role theory are scattered throughout his many writings, but lack a clear systematic explication. I attempted such a systematization, calling the approach 'role dynamics' (Blatner 1985, 1991). A little later, continuing to work with Moreno's seminal contributions, I suggested that role dynamics might offer a 'user-friendly' language for psychology, a way that people from many disciplines, as well as patients, could speak about their problems in a way that was more understandable by all concerned. In addition, I found that this way of looking at psychology offered a host of positive benefits (Blatner 1991, 2000a, 2003).

Meanwhile, other workers in psychodrama have also developed role theory, and major contributions have been made regarding the naming, categorizing and ways of working with roles, especially by leaders in the psychodrama community in Australia and New Zealand (for example, see Chapter 5 by Sue Daniel).

More recently, I have continued to develop the idea of the meta-role as a complex that, when identified explicitly, can be addressed as the focus of therapy and education. Not only can clients or protagonists be helped to shift their identity beyond their roles to their meta-role or inner director, but they can also be helped as part of the therapy to consciously and intentionally develop and practice the many skills and functions of the meta-role (to be described further on).

The meta-role in child development

The maturation of the meta-role continues throughout a person's life, although for most people this process unfolds implicitly rather than explicitly. By naming the function, it may be possible to help people utilize this capacity more consciously and effectively. As soon as a baby is able to play 'peek-a-boo' it is beginning to develop the meta-role function. Some events become recognized as being of a different cognitive type – i.e., 'play,' – in which the consequences of behavior are not the same as what happens in the domain of 'seriousness.' At first, the awareness of the play context is signaled with a look, a smile and the juxtaposition of that which is expected with a small but tolerable degree of the unexpected.

By late infancy, babies begin to tease back, for example, by offering something, then pulling it away. They are aware that this mixed message –

'Look, a gift! Ha, ha! No, it's not!' – can be a 'game.' It is accompanied by giggles and nervous laughter. Within a year, babies begin to know how to signal when actions are more or less playful, and by age four children have learned verbal signals such as 'time out' (or, in my culture, the words, 'King's X'). Calling 'time out' breaks the flow of play with the complex message that, if spelled out, would say: 'Look, I'm going to have to take a break from this action. Please let's continue when I come back (from going to the bathroom, or my mother is calling me for lunch, etc.) as if there had been no break in the play.' Sometimes, the time out will be just to comment on or adjust the play: 'Hey, you're pushing too hard.' 'Okay, now you be the baby and I'll be the mommy' (Blatner and Blatner 1997).

In the early years of childhood, words and phrases such as 'pretend' and 'make believe' are more commonly used to describe this mode of play. Many cultures (including the culture I grew up in) are such, though, that imaginative domains are marginalized, treated as second-class, inconsequential, not worthy of notice. In the teen years, this domain may be resurrected in skits and the controlled methods of formal theatre, with other people writing the scripts and improvisation minimized. The point here is that the activities of the director and playwright, the roles that incorporated a measure of audience reaction and critic, all were part of those early modes of improvised play. The child was both in role and exercising the meta-role actively. Play in the early-mid-childhood years is a very active process of social renegotiation of roles, rules and modes. We need to continue to cultivate that skill building.

Alas, what happens in traditional western education is the imposed domination of an attitude that relies on the authority of the cultural conserve. Obedience and passive learning become important elements in child development, and the meta-role functions remain somewhat neglected. Ideally, around the ages of 8 through 18, youngsters should be helped to recognize the meta-role function, the choosing self, or inner director, and to cultivate its skills by asking questions such as: 'Wait. Now stand back from this situation. How else might you handle it? You are able to rethink how you want to be.' Furthermore, such questions should be asked in settings where the situations are social and political, not just technical. A mode for achieving this would be that of integrating sociodrama into the curriculum (Blatner 2006b).

In neuroscience, Ramachandran (2004) describes the function in humans of the capacity for not just representation, but 'meta-representation.' In role talk, there are then the two levels: the role, and the broader range of when and how that role may be played. At first, there is little variability. This is what Moreno meant by 'role taking.' A child playing a fireman has a few stock phrases and general actions, based mainly on imitation. This is true also for an adult learning a new role. As the role is learned, one begins to become a bit more flexible and creative, at which point it might better be described as role *playing*. With more self-awareness, though, one advances to role *creating*, and more actively using meta-role functions. This might involve the person modifying his or her behavior in a variety of ways by asking questions such as:

- Which role should be played here?
- How involved do I choose to be in this role?
- How explicitly conscious am I that I am playing this role, or balancing more than one role?
- How am I being perceived in this role? How effective am I in this role?
- Do I notice that there might be a conflict between two or more of the roles I'm playing?
- What might need to change in order that I might perform this role more successfully?
- Am I also aware that I could play this role differently? Should I play this role more strongly, loudly, with greater intensity – or more lightly, softer?

And so forth.

A new language of psychological literacy

The shift of identity to the meta-role also reflects a general cultural trend in which psychology is becoming a mainstream skill. Until the waning of the twentieth century, psychology was still generally a marginal field, mainly associated with mental illness or the cartoon image of a self-indulgent neurotic lying on a couch. However, managers began to recognize that mental flexibility and self-modulation were important in business, organizational development and the promotion of teamwork and creativity. Good psychological mindedness, communications skills, problem-solving skills and self-awareness became recognized as being essential to success in business and other organizational tasks (Goleman *et al.* 2002).

Part of this move has involved the shift to new types of language. The jargon of psychoanalysis was too oriented to intimations of pathology and too much associated with obscure and counter-intuitive concepts. What was needed was a more neutral language, and role dynamics offers this as a more familiar and acceptable way of describing complex psychosocial situations. The meta-role concept is a congenial one for this new trend towards psychological literacy. The ideal manager, or better, a chief executive officer, suggests a shift in focus from merely addressing the task at hand to a more interdisciplinary approach – the bigger picture. This new focus may include a re-evaluation as to whether the task at hand really should have priority. Sometimes the task must be put on hold so that the social domain can be reinforced, injured feelings repaired, 'fences mended,' recognition given, morale lifted, apologies made and forgiveness granted – all elements of 'team building.' Good management becomes more holistic.

In turn, these shifts have also influenced our thinking about psychotherapy. Patients or clients are being viewed as needing more 'empowerment,' and that includes their role in the process of therapy itself. In psychodrama, for example, I talk to the protagonist as if we are not only going to address and analyze the problem at hand, but equally important, the protagonist is going to learn the ways that we approached the situation so as to be able to implement these skills in addressing future challenges. As the Chinese proverb says: 'If you give a man a fish, you feed him for a day. If you teach a man to fish, you feed him for the rest of his life.' In other words, attention is given to the naming and recognition of the meta-role, helping the client to identify with that meta-role more than with the component social and intrapsychic roles. The idea is that the client will develop a high level of skill in using the various meta-role functions in self-management.

The meta-role functions

Just as the psychodrama director may be imagined to play a number of component roles, so, too, might all people learn to think of themselves as the director of the range of roles in their own role repertoire (Blatner 2005a). Here I offer an overview of some of the key functions of the meta-role.

Self-observation

The first role is related to the concept in psychoanalysis called the 'observing ego.' Part of becoming more 'psychologically minded' involves developing a capacity for self-reflection. The meta-role acts as a director watching the actors in rehearsal. This role observes as if watching from a small distance, witnessing, taking an imagined video of an interaction and playing it back, reflecting on what is seen and heard. With practice, one learns to notice tendencies to interpret situations in certain ways and how they're based on previously unexamined assumptions. Indeed, this whole process may be taken to yet another level of meta-meta-role! One also asks 'How well am I performing my various meta-role skills?'

Investigating

Merely observing is not enough; it is too passive an activity. One needs to learn the meta-role skills of going beyond observing, becoming one of the investigators. This includes interviewing, listening, double-checking for inconsistencies, acting a bit like a detective, checking for coherence, accuracy and asking penetrating questions.

Questioning

An attitude that analyzes at a deeper level needs to be cultivated. The challenge here isn't just to figure out ways of getting around obstacles – of just being more clever – but rather learning to call into question all elements, beliefs and relationships, especially anything that has become accepted and subconsciously fixed, which might possibly include non-adaptive attitudes. Fritz Perls, one of the founders of Gestalt therapy, was said to have observed that most patients don't want to stop being neurotic; they just want to be better at it. It is often the goals themselves that need to be reconsidered, expanded from more selfish and short-term objectives. This will help our goals to become more value laden, with a greater sensitivity towards other people and the community (Adler 1979).

Becoming a student

The meta-role recognizes that the learning of these skills and learning in general is a lifelong, never-ending process. It takes on this learning willingly and with curiosity. Thus, conflicts, problems and troubles all become occasions for learning self-leadership (Schwartz 1995). (This is not the same as 'self-control.' A good leader recognizes the need to find ways of self-expression, allowing emotions to become aids in human relationships. Self-leadership isn't merely being inhibited or repressed.)

Inner interviewing

There is an interesting skill in exploring one's own inner role repertoire. In the theatre, a good director might draw out an actor, coach them, help the deeper feelings in the role to come forth. These insights into the role are not immediately accessible; a process is needed to warm up and soften up the defensively compartmentalized complexes. This 'inner interviewing' role component also includes elements of communicating sympathy and offering reassurance.

Inner support

In addition to taking on a role of reassuring one's self, there are still more skills that need to be learned. These skills include being supportive of complexes, roles such as the 'inner child,' who may be shy, almost hidden, afraid of admitting deeper needs or vulnerabilities. This supportiveness also needs to recognize the presence of other complexes that react to vulnerability with harsh judgments, so as to counteract those negative voices. This firmness is then mixed with the learning of skills of encouraging, self-forgiveness and learning how to make supportive self-affirmations. A powerful maxim is: Don't put patients in touch with their negative voices until you have first grounded them in their positive voices. This will help to remind the vulnerable parts of the self of positive values, strengths, and achievements. Not only is this a good concept for therapists, it also applies in working constructively with one's self.

Reframing

This term, drawn from constructivist approaches in family therapy, involves the development of meta-role skills in working with the interpretations of events – becoming a bit of a 'spin doctor.' Situations that have in the past simply evoked shame or overwhelming guilt need to be placed in perspective so that constructive action can move forward. This involves the skills of weighing positive elements properly and identifying helpful talents, achievements and other elements that can be built on in creating a more positive future.

Diagnosing

This involves more than merely putting a label on a complex of feelings or symptoms. The word 'diagnosis' really means seeing through, penetrating and understanding the deeper dynamics. This weaves together many of the previously mentioned skills: observing, investigating, inner interviewing and so forth. The point is to create the kind of formulation that can guide the envisioning of a variety of remedies, solutions and treatments.

Analyzing

This involves including additional knowledge from all other areas of learning, so that the highest degrees of rational thought can be brought to bear on a situation.

Choosing

The meta-role also shifts from the role of investigator to the role of chooser and decision-maker. This role weaves into all of the aforementioned functions the growing awareness that certain behaviors must be recognized as choices, with alternatives. The choosing function can then decide on and follow through with those choices.

Patient revisiting

Although one might wish it were easier, in fact deep learning usually involves an ongoing practice of unlearning and relearning, addressing often fairly entrenched habits. The meta-role needs to be vigilant towards relapse into such habits of feeling, thinking, and reactive behavior, and be prepared to recognize and counter these for as long as they recur.

Similarly, whether it is a therapist working with patients, a director with actors or a person taking a more conscious role of self-leadership with their own various subroles, the process often operates like a gradually rising spiral. Old themes come around, and once again need to be both investigated and supported as they are helped to move forward.

Generating enthusiasm

A skilled meta-role is aware that when it is decided what is needed, a bit of salesmanship is called for! The process includes getting in touch with wants, warming up latent desires, developing interests. This also needs to be balanced with another part that checks to see that one isn't just rationalizing, talking one's self into a foolish behavior.

Letting go

The opposite skill is also needed. Sometimes what becomes clear is that a certain desired complex is not good for one in the long run, and both the meta-role and the involved subrole need to practice warming down, detaching and letting go of certain wants and 'needs.' (Some needs are not really needed, they just feel that way.)

Balancing

The meta-role recognizes that self-leadership involves the coordinating of a large number of roles that are jockeying for satisfaction, expression and protection, and this in turn requires a fair amount of balancing, harmonizing, integrating, synthesizing and taking turns.

Creativity

As the world changes, it becomes clear that in many or most cases, a situation does not have a simple 'right answer,' packaged by someone in the past (i.e., a piece of the creative conserve). Even if certain principles are built upon, in most cases the problem at hand requires skill in creative thinking, imagining and opening up novel alternatives, in the service of the aforementioned and other functions. This function is sometimes called going 'outside the box.' There are many books on creative thinking, and this skill especially can take many years to develop.

Modulating

Often what is needed isn't so much a change in strategy as a shift in style, simply varying the intensity of some behavior or emotional interaction, tuning up or tuning down. Sometimes one needs to be more forceful, other times more gentle; perhaps more serious, or on the other hand more playful.

Remembering

A good meta-role function takes into consideration the past and investigates the history of both the person and the group in which the person is situated. Part of this history includes an analysis of many frames of reference, biases, backgrounds that have to do with economic factors, power and status gradients, gender and so forth. This skill also includes a healthy awareness of – and coping techniques to counter – the temptation to fall into the regressive mental maneuver called denial.

Anticipating

The challenge of self-leadership also includes what Moreno called 'daring to dream again' and 'dreaming new dreams' (Marineau 1989: 30). Many people inhibit their capacity to envision the future lest they be disappointed, and so the future becomes as repressed as some past memories. With a bit of encouragement and guidance, one can learn to practice imagining a positive future. From this, more goal-directed planning can proceed, which includes acknowledging certain concerns that must be taken into account.

Higher leadership

This meta-role function is what differentiates a mere manager who is caught up in the system from a true executive officer. The individual developing this skill takes on the responsibility of weaving in the highest ideals. That is what makes a leader. This skill includes opening up to higher guidance, intuition, the influence of 'the muses,' poetic 'lateral thinking,' imagination and inspiration, all of which are crucial elements in creative thinking. Moreno hinted at these higher dimensions of spirituality, which transcend both roles and meta-roles (Blatner 2005b).

Philosopher

Related to the function of higher leadership is the function of the philosopher. The challenge is to cultivate one's value system. Developing a philosophy of life need not be a scholarly enterprise, but may simply involve some attempt to coordinate one's values and behavior, purpose and sense of belonging.

Cherishing the creative child complex

The meta-role recognizes the vitality and inspiration that comes through this innocent complex in the mind. One needs to learn to open up to feelings and dreams while also critically assessing them a bit. In Morenian terms, it involves learning to be spontaneous without lapsing into pathological spontaneity. This skill actively recognizes and values one's own childlike qualities. The wise meta-role is willing also to sympathize to some degree with the vulnerability of the inner child, acknowledging the experience of difficulty or of feeling overwhelmed, the traumas and victimizations. To some degree, we should learn to forgive our past self at the same time as we reaffirm new intentions in the present.

Celebrate life

Many dimensions of life transcend rational problem solving and partake of a cultivation of the aesthetic sensibility. The skilled meta-role also learns to receive, appreciate, thank, recognize, celebrate and enjoy. To this end, some engagement in one or several types of art may be added to or strengthened in one's role repertoire (Blatner 2000b).

Discussion

In summary, the meta-role becomes the 'locus of control,' the 'I' who chooses, shifting one's identity to self-managing the big picture. With meta-role functioning more explicitly, a woman may cease thinking about herself only as a wife, mother, daughter, worker and so forth, but instead as one who orchestrates all the roles and reflects on how they are played. From this standpoint, the meta-role can learn to become increasingly skillful, seeking:

1 To become more alert and self-aware.
2 To engage with problems and intend to learn, assert and move forward.
3 To balance not only elements of one's role repertoire, but also the aforementioned meta-role skills.
4 To optimize the 'flow' or 'spontaneity' in a process.
5 To balance responsibility with love and faith.

Add to this list if you need to. These various skills apply to the management of most adult roles, even the ones learned or practiced in playing with children or otherwise indulging in 'silliness.' Indeed, one definition of wisdom might be that, in order to be wise, we must operate at a more integrated and higher skill level of meta-role development (Blatner 2005a).

Conclusion

The central 'meta-role' should become the core of identity, instead of any other social or otherwise ordinary role. Furthermore, this central 'I' should in turn be recognized as being the nexus of 'response-ability' – the role that plays out all those functions just mentioned. This role serves the wider nexus of archetypal influences that make up the higher individuated self – the soul – and express the many dimensions of the 'spirit' (Blatner 2005b).

Many of the various forms of psychotherapy and personal development may be understood as implicitly fostering the meta-role functions – the ability to manage the welter of inner conflicts and complex adaptative strategies. Let us make this meta-role more explicit by naming it. The meta-role concept is a contribution to a high-level, inclusive, integrative approach to a theory of psychology and psychotherapy. It is a refinement of Moreno's role theory, taking his ideas and making them more explicit, systematizing them and adding my own ideas. The meta-role concept also offers a user-friendly language that can speak to and integrate many different therapies. Although other approaches do not use the term 'meta-role,' most psychotherapies involve activities that strengthen the function of the meta-role as a conscious center of primary identity and a skilled modifier of behavior. It is what Freud meant when he said, 'Where id was, there shall ego be.' Other psychotherapists speak of cultivating the 'observing ego' or the 'adult ego state' (Berne 1976).

Relatively free of most social qualities, the meta-role is concerned only with being effective, and is more or less skilled. The richness of this meta-role is that there are a score or more functions which can be developed, and many of these involve in turn a number of component functions. The meta-role, when awakened to its own identity, begins to be the inner 'leader' or – drawing from the metaphor 'all the world's a stage' – the inner director/playwright of the ongoing improvised play, with the actors being the various roles we play.

References

Adler, A. (1979) *Superiority and Social Interest: A Collection of Later Writings* (H. L. Ansbacher and R. R. Ansbacher), eds, New York: Norton.
Berne, E. (1976) *Beyond Games and Scripts*, New York: Grove Press.

Biddle, B. J. and Thomas, E. J. (eds) (1966) *Role Theory: Concepts and Research*, New York: Wiley.

Blatner, A. (1985) 'Role dynamics: an integrated psychosocial theory', in *Foundations of Psychodrama*, San Marcos, TX: Self-published.

—— (1991) 'Role dynamics: a comprehensive theory of psychology', *Journal of Group Psychotherapy, Psychodrama and Sociometry*, 44, 1: 33–40.

—— (2000a) *Foundations of Psychodrama: History, Theory and Practice*, New York: Springer.

—— (2000b) 'A new role for psychodramatists: master of ceremonies', *International Journal of Action Methods*, 53, 2: 86–93.

—— (2003) 'Not mere players: psychodrama applications in everyday life', in J. Gershoni (ed.) *Psychodrama in the 21st Century*, New York: Springer.

—— (2005a) 'Perspectives on wisdom-ing', *ReVision: A Journal of Consciousness and Transformation*, 28, 1: 29–33.

—— (2005b) 'Role theory, archetypes and Moreno's philosophy illuminated by the Kabbalistic Tree of Life', *Journal of Group Psychotherapy, Psychodrama and Sociometry*, 58, 1: 3–13.

—— (2006a) *Bibliography on role theory*. Online. Available HTTP: <http://www.blatner.com/adam/psyntbk/rlthbibliog.html> (accessed January 2006).

—— (2006b) 'Enacting the new academy: sociodrama as a powerful tool in higher education', *ReVision: A Journal of Consciousness & Transformation*, 29, 3: 30–35.

Blatner, A. and Blatner, A. (1997) *The Art of Play*, New York: Brunner/Routledge.

Goleman, D., Boyatzis, R. and McKee, A. (2002) *Primal Leadership: Realizing the Power of Emotional Intelligence*, Boston: Harvard Business School Press.

Marineau, R. (1989) *Jacob Levy Moreno 1889–1974: Father of Psychodrama, Sociometry and Group Psychotherapy*, New York: Tavistock/Routledge.

Mead, G. H. (1934) *Mind, Self, and Society*, Chicago: University of Chicago Press.

Moreno, J. L. (1946) *Psychodrama, Volume One*, Beacon, NY: Beacon House.

Ramachandran V. S. (2004) *A Brief Tour of Human Consciousness*, New York: PI Press.

Schwartz, R. A. (1995) *Internal Family Systems Therapy*, New York: Guilford Press.

Chapter 5

Psychodrama, role theory and the cultural atom

New Developments in Role Theory

Sue Daniel

What are we without our relationships? It is through our interactions with others and the world around us that we make sense of the world and ourselves. We know others and ourselves through this living experience. If we are mirrored adequately when young we have the chance to develop a sense of ourselves, who we are, what we do and don't like. If the mirroring we receive is distorted, we may end up with a sense of ourselves that is not true but rather reflective of others.

In this chapter I present a role theory framework (Daniel 2004) focusing on the concept of the cultural atom, the idea of relationship as a third entity and introduce a new subcategory within the role chart. The work illustrates an expansion of role theory as it is practiced today. I demonstrate the effect of small yet timely interventions and the advantages of a role theory and role training approach in individual and group psychotherapy, touching on the teaching and learning of role theory. Certain viewpoints of Gregory Bateson, Konrad Lorenz, Jacob Moreno and Zerka Moreno are illustrated in relation to the concept of role and role relationships.

Relationship is the essential stuff of role theory. This idea may be familiar to the psychodramatist who understands the twin canon of the social and cultural atom – the social atom being the people in our lives and the tele that flows between us, and the cultural atom being our roles and the relationship between these roles. The core paradigm of role theory is mutuality, imbued by tele. Tele, taken from the Greek, meaning 'at' or 'to a distance,' is a two-way relationship of sense across space. Like the wave and the particle in physics, the social and cultural atom is inextricably entwined. It is a fact of life and a living process.

The social and cultural atom

The essential components of role theory are the roles and the role relationship that exist in any given moment that arises between two or more people. To illustrate this, let's look at a mother and a child, Alice and Bella. The first entity is Alice and the second entity is Bella. The third entity is

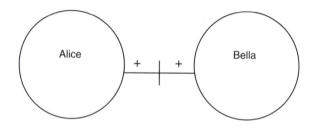

Figure 5.1 The social atom of Alice (mother) and Bella (child): the tele is mutually positive

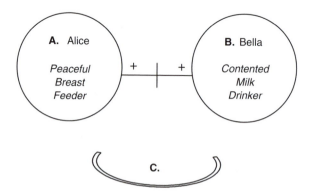

C. Warm, generous relationship of mutual partaking in life

Figure 5.2 The cultural atom of Alice (entity A) and Bella (entity B). Alice and Bella are in a reciprocal positive role relationship: the Peaceful Breast Feeder and the Contented Milk Drinker. The tele relationship between the two roles is mutually positive and reciprocal. At this point in Alice and Bella's relationship, the role relationship (entity C) is warm and close

their relationship, which manifests through their respective role interactions at any time or place (Figures 5.1 and 5.2).

Role theory and the interactional space

The space *between* people is highly significant because it is here that they can encounter one another and their relationship comes into existence. Take a look at the trees outside, the leaves, the branches, and now look at the spaces between them, the sky or the shadows. These spaces have shape. Just as the breeze changes the shape of the space between the leaves and branches of a tree, so does a change of role affect our relationships. Everything is in relation to something else. Artists and architects know about this space and recognize it as an essential component in their work. When an artist paints a picture or a photographer takes a photograph, the spaces are always considered and have equal importance with the objects in the scene. The finished painting or photograph shows the whole, an entire picture captured in a moment. Perhaps this is why Jackson Pollock was considered so revolutionary in the beginning, because he didn't define space in the usual way. However, there is spatial definition in his paintings because of the color and its trajectory.

The role of the artist

The psychodramatic role of the artist is useful in the role repertoire of the psychodrama practitioner, since it transcends the limits of knowledge and brings in the faculty of imagination. While words and actions also inform what is seen, a receptive imagination is essential for the knowledge and practice of role theory. Seeing what is in front of you rather than making an interpretation of what you see means seeing what someone is expressing and how the other is receiving it: to see relationship as it is in any given moment. This view of people and the world means that new things can be created for the personality and the world of relationship. Contrary to popular belief, the personality is not set by the ages of five or seven; it is, and has the opportunity, to always be in creation through the development of new roles and the linking and integration of these roles.

The creator of role theory

The creator of role theory and the father of psychodrama, sociometry and group psychotherapy was Jacob Moreno MD (Moreno 1934, 1946). Together with his primary collaborator and wife, Zerka Moreno, he inspired a generation of psychodramatists and others in the field of social sciences (for example, Kurt Lewin and Ron Lippitt, two of the founders of the National Training Laboratories in Bethel, Maine, and Fritz Perls in his development of the Gestalt method) to think and use role theory, sociometry, sociodrama and psychodrama (Moreno and Moreno 1959, 1969). Psychodrama has permeated the field of mental health and human services in our community with the result that Moreno's ideas on group psychotherapy, group method and the concept of role are widely applied and known throughout the world, even though many people may not know where these ideas originated.

Role theory is as significant for humanity now as it was in the first quarter of the twentieth century. It has opened up a whole new way of thinking about human beings in relation to themselves and other entities. This has an immense impact on people and their environment because it proposes that we are always connected to something through our spontaneity and creativity. Even in situations where our values seem to have no relevance or value to another, our spontaneity and creativity can serve us to come up with new and adequate responses, thus opening a path for new paradigms and healthy progressive relationships.

The role theory framework

The role theory framework is a simple and useful perspective and can be applied in one-to-one counselling and psychotherapy, working with couples and families, in business and organisations, teaching the psychodramatic method and in everyday living. It provides an opportunity for insight and invites us to live in the here and now. Whether we talk of the past or the future, we can only be in the here and now.

The role concept

Role theory is at the heart of sociometry and psychodrama. It encompasses the whole person matrix by including the faculties of thinking, feeling and action. Behaviour is part of the role theory matrix yet role theory is not behavioural. Moreno talked of the operational links between the roles and the roles clusters forming a partial self (Moreno 1946). According to him, 'a role is a unit of function and organisation. It is a form of phenomena, more than behaviour, observable in a particular situation in relation to other phenomena' (Moreno 1946: iii). Roles can be psychosomatic (physiological), psychodramatic (psychological) or social and they may overlap.

The three components of a role

A role is comprised of thinking, feeling and action. When thinking, feeling and action are in harmony, the role is described as congruent. Sometimes there are blocks in a role, which can be observed and described as incongruent. A person's thinking and feeling may be synchronised but, even so, the person is unable to act. A person may have the feeling and action in harmony yet no thinking is involved, or, thinking and action are in accord but the feeling component is missing or underdeveloped (Figure 5.3).

The role chart

A role map or chart is used to assess and work with role systems, of the person (intra-role relations) or groups (inter-role relations) with an aim to serve relationship, development and progress. It is divided into three sections:

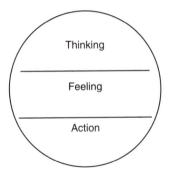

Figure 5.3 The components of a role

- the progressive roles that are reflective of unity and quality of life
- the coping roles that reflect the optimal means of survival in family and social systems
- the retrogressive roles that can contain fragmented aspects of the personality, not linked to the here and now.

I have further expanded the role framework (Clayton 1982; Daniel 1992, 2004) I have used for over 20 years to include the new subcategory of 'freezing' within the coping role category. The framework is a map that is used to look at what is going on in a drama or session at any point of time. All roles are seen in relation to other roles and can only be adequately identified through the use of a role system approach.

The role categories

The progressive role category is divided into two sections: 'well developed' and 'developing.' The coping or survival roles are divided into three sections: 'going towards,' 'going away' (withdrawing), 'going against' (fighting) and the new category of 'freezing.' Retrogressive roles are divided into two sections: 'diminishing' and 'fixed' (see Table 5.3).

These are the terms that I use in my teaching and practice (Daniel 2001). Any of the basic types of roles (psychosomatic, psychodramatic or social) may be placed within these categories depending on the situation. For example, social roles: *warm teacher, appreciative pupil*; psychodramatic roles: *lover of life, doomsday prophet*; somatic roles: *secret crier, warm hugger*. However, it is important to understand that 'a role is just a role' (Moreno 1989). It is not until a role is looked at in a context, taking into consideration time and place and its anchoring in the role relationship, that we can adequately name it.

Complementary and symmetrical role relationships

Gregory Bateson (1979) coined the terms 'complementary and symmetrical role relationships.' Complementary roles are best described as having difference, for example, parent/child, lover/fighter, whilst symmetrical roles are those that are similar, parent/parent, fighter/fighter. In some situations, the deliberate taking up of either a complementary or symmetrical role – depending on the situation – can assist people and nations in building relationships, even if they do not like one another, and may serve to break conflicts and stalemates. There are no right or wrong or weak or strong roles; it is a matter of the *adequacy* of the roles in a given context. Establishing whether a role relationship is complementary or symmetrical can be very useful, especially when relationships are bogged down, conflictual or competitive.

The application of role theory in group psychotherapy

In this section, role training with one protagonist illustrates the use of role theory and includes the new role category that I call 'freezing.' Relevant implications for practitioners can be found within the discussion sections.

John is the protagonist. The role training is almost complete. In the first scene he confronted and literally stood over his son-in-law, Sam, in a hotel dining-room. Sam and his wife Rachel (John's daughter) had been having breakfast together. There was a short verbal fight, which ended with Sam getting up and leaving, hurriedly saying, 'I am not having any of this therapy crap.' John had chased Sam and begged him to listen (Figure 5.4).

John's actions were robotic and his body was very tight. He was angry with Sam because he had violated John's values. John felt impotent and was very critical of himself. The role training process had provided some 'time out' of the drama for John. It gave him an opportunity to see himself in relation to Sam and observe their relationship from the mirror position. He was able to see himself as others saw him in relation to Sam, through their mirroring, and then experience several group members as they modeled different roles. I noticed that he was extremely attentive and

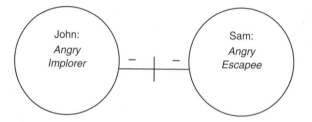

Figure 5.4 The initial role system of John

Table 5.1 John and Sam's relationship of antagonism

Coping (survival) role category			
Going toward	Going away	Going against	Freezing
	(b) Angry Escapee (Sam)	(a) Angry Implorer (John)	

(a and b is a complementary role relationship. The tele is mutually negative.)

thoughtful throughout this process. Table 5.1 illustrates roles mapped in the coping role category, one of three sections that make up the role chart seen in Table 5.3 (p. 75).

The development of a new role

In the next scene, John walked up to Sam and Rachel and said, 'Rachel, could I talk with Sam please.' This was new. In the role reversal with Rachel, she (he) said, 'Sure.' She left, and he sat down opposite Sam. Several role reversals between John and Sam took place during the role test. This time John (as Sam) didn't leave the table, despite being very tense. (Table 5.2 illustrates the change in roles.) Through the role training, John developed new roles in relation to Sam and Rachel.

John realized, for the first time, that Sam was very frightened of him. Back in his own role, he became very tense and red in the face. 'John,' I said. 'Let yourself breathe.' He expelled a big breath of air. I asked him to do it twice more, thus maximizing the role. He realized that he had been frightened. John became calm and thoughtful with this new insight. His body softened. The realization that Sam was frightened of him was very important to him. Celebrating this new knowledge was the next step. The fear that he had felt previously had put him in a role state that he had been unable to shift from. The fear of losing people so precious to him had been intense, so in the moment that he froze he stopped breathing. Slowing down the action and gently coaching John to breathe had served to bring him in

Table 5.2 The new roles

Coping (survival) roles			
Going toward	Going away	Going against	Freezing
(a) Clear Communicator (John, a and b)	(b) Warm Acceptor (Rachel)	(c) Tense Negotiator (John) and (d) Frightened Defender (Sam, c and d)	(e) Frightened Robot (John, b and c)

(a and b, c and d and e and d are all complementary role relationships.)

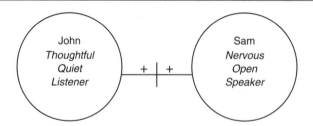

Figure 5.5 John takes a complementary role to Sam – the tele is mutually positive

touch with himself. He was then able to role reverse with Sam and in so doing discovered Sam in all his otherness as himself, as human, in a real encounter (Figure 5.5).

Recognizing and celebrating the new

There is much value in recognizing something not previously seen or known and then celebrating this recognition. We can't know what we weren't aware of so it makes good sense to celebrate the new awareness. This maintains the new role, confirms the here and now reality of the protagonist and assists a person to look forward. It can also stop him or her from unraveling their work or doing themselves in, especially if the person was prone to being critical of themselves. Once a person becomes clear, much of the therapeutic work is done. John had at first been imploring Sam to listen to him. However, now he realized that it was he who had to listen to Sam. In the final stage of the drama, he sat quietly and listened, moving toward his son-in-law with heart and mind. The complementary role of 'thoughtful, quiet listener' enabled him to listen to Sam (see Figure 5.5). The freeing of the breath allowed John's fear to evaporate and his spontaneity to emerge, with the result that his response to Sam was new and adequate. Slowing everything down and encouraging a protagonist to breathe can be very productive when the protagonist is very tense or full of feeling. In the role of Sam, John was more open to talking about his feelings. This was new for both of them, spontaneity begetting spontaneity (see Table 5.3).

Discussion

It is useful to look closely to see how a person is breathing. Sometimes, fear can be a warm cloak – an old familiar role, which a person may not be ready to give up. So to breathe, and get in touch with feelings, can some-times be frightening. This may mean that many psychodramas are neces-sary until new progressive roles have developed, or new operational links between roles or role clusters have crystallized, before a person is ready to work on the fearful role. I am not talking about any fear, fear of snakes and

Table 5.3 The role relationship of John and Sam at the end of the role training

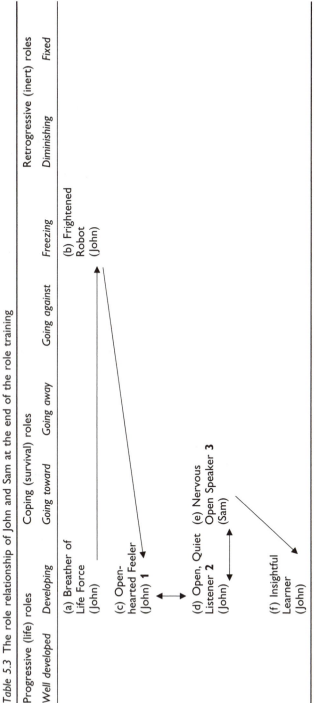

Progressive (life) roles			Coping (survival) roles				Retrogressive (inert) roles	
Well developed	*Developing*		*Going toward*	*Going away*	*Going against*	*Freezing*	*Diminishing*	*Fixed*
	(a) Breather of Life Force (John)					(b) Frightened Robot (John)		
	(c) Open-hearted Feeler (John) **1**							
	(d) Open, Quiet Listener **2** (John)	(e) Nervous Open Speaker **3** (Sam)						
	(f) Insightful Learner (John)							

(a and b, b and c, c and d, d and e and e and f are all complementary role relationships. 1 and 2 and 2 and 3 are mutually positive role relationships.)
Legend: The lines with one-way arrowheads indicate the progress of the roles and the operational links between roles, while the two-way arrowheads indicate reciprocal and mutually positive tele.

so forth but rather a particular kind of fear, which is close to, if not actually, terror, where an aspect of the self has frozen because the person has perceived danger or felt unsafe.

The new category of freezing

Tables 5.2 and 5.3 reveal the role categories that include the new fourth category of 'freezing' within the coping roles category. The creation of this new category came about through the practice of using the role map over a period of time and finding that certain roles didn't fit in any of the categories. The 'frightened robot' for example didn't fit in the going against (fighting), going away (withdrawing) or going toward categories in John's drama. Because he was seen as attempting to cope, I dismissed the possibility of the role being retrogressive. Whilst it could be described as retrogressive in another situation, in the former encounter I viewed it as coping. Practitioners working in sexual abuse and domestic violence situations frequently note the freezing response in their clients or patients. A freezing response can also occur in authoritarian systems and as a reaction to terror, when one's life, physically, psychologically or socially is at risk. Animals know this instinctively. The ethologist, Konrad Lorenz, watching fighting wolves, observed where, at a certain point in the fight, one gives way and becomes vulnerable to the other, through an inbuilt freezing response:

> A dog or wolf that offers its neck to an adversary in this way will never be bitten seriously. The other growls ands grumbles, snaps his teeth in the empty air and even carries out, without delivering so much as a bite, the movements of shaking something to death in empty air. However this strange inhibition from biting persists only as long as the defeated dog or wolf maintains his attitude of humility. Since the fight is stopped by this action, the victor frequently finds himself straddling his vanquished foe in anything but a comfortable position. So to remain with his muzzle applied to the neck of the 'under-dog' soon becomes tedious for the champion, and, seeing that he cannot bite anyway, he soon withdraws. Upon this, the understanding dog may hastily attempt to put distance between himself and his superior. But he is usually not successful in this, for, as soon as he abandons his rigid attitude of submission, the other falls upon him again like a thunderbolt and the victim must again freeze into his former posture.
>
> (Lorenz 1952: 188)

Using role theory to make interventions

The role of the clear seer (one who sees 'what is') was not present initially in John. His fear had prevented him from seeing Sam clearly, and, he did not know that he was frightened. It is sometimes the case that protagonists cannot reverse roles until they feel accepted with their feelings. In John's case, thinking and action were together but his frozen feeling of fear had become a block. The role training had assisted John in being seen and heard. As soon as he was able to reverse roles, he experienced a deep catharsis. It was from this experience that a catharsis of integration occurred; the roles became integrated and congruent and John felt at peace.

The use of role theory in individual psychotherapy

Role theory can be applied in individual psychotherapy, counseling, supervision, coaching and consulting. The practitioner is encouraged to see the minutiae and work with small movements or small changes of role, sometimes found in the way a person speaks or the words they use. There can be much potency working delicately and sensitively in seemingly small pieces of work. Being with a person, quietly yet actively listening, mirroring or putting yourself in their shoes through doubling or role reversing can all be very helpful. Shifts in roles or changes in role states can happen suddenly, so it is well if the practitioner is spontaneous and able go with the flow. Here is an example of a role theory approach applied in individual psychotherapy.

Jude

Jude sat down and said he had a lot on his mind. I got up, picked up a box of tissues from my desk and crossed the room to where he was sitting and gave it to him. As I sat down again, I said, 'Ok, how about you pull a tissue out and say, in your own mind, you don't need to tell me what that tissue is for, and the next one, and so on.' He grinned ruefully and said, 'Have you got enough tissues?' but after pulling the third one out, he turned pink in the face, and tears ran down his cheek. I gently asked him to breathe and just let his feelings, his life force, be there.

Discussion

This was a crucial turning point in Jude's therapy because up to this point he hadn't cried in front of anyone. His family of origin is particularly painful for him; one brother has schizophrenia and rings him many times a day, often verbally abusing him, a sister has a mental illness yet to be adequately diagnosed, and another brother has cerebral palsy. Jude used heroin regularly for ten years but had been free of this habit for two years prior to seeing me. He was still dealing drugs but not heroin. My relationship with Jude was quite strong so I felt reasonably sure that he would follow my instruction. He had been coming along once a week for a few months. However, I had not used any action up to this point. The element of surprise and the timing of this intervention were also important. Whilst Jude is no stranger to expressing anger, he was relieved and grateful to be able to get in touch with his sadness and to cry.

The use of role theory with couples

Introducing the couple to the idea that their relationship is a third entity can make a profound difference to how they see themselves in relationship. Some people think it is just 'you or me,' right or wrong, weak or strong. Yet in role theory there is no right and wrong or weak or strong; it's a matter of the adequacy of the roles and also the relationship between these roles. Asking the couple sociometric questions such as 'What kind of relationship do you have, right now?' can be useful since it gives them a picture of their relationship and an opportunity to see how the other perceives it. Sometimes I place a cushion between them, which serves to concretize their relationship as an entity. This is often very effective, as they may never have realized that the relationship is their creation. Once people think about what they might do or say, or take on a role to improve a relationship, choice and responsibility for self enters the picture: 'I can't change you yet I can change myself, which will affect us.' This can be a potent motto.

Role interrelatedness

When thinking about a person's role in relation to another, you can think about where it exists, what came before, what came after, what was the response from the other, and what is developing between the two people in the here and now. It's not enough to just put something out, it is important to see how it is being received. If we name a role without observance of the 'other,' and the situation we are in, all we are doing is labeling a person and acting as if this role does not require anchorage in another person's role. This borders on solipsism – the belief that the self is all that exists or can be known. It is wise to keep in mind the interconnected nature of our roles. Roles do not exist in isolation because we do not; we are always in relationship to something.

Teaching role theory

A collaborative involvement of the therapist with the client or the director with a group is advised when teaching role theory or assisting people to look at their role relationships. This is a very interactive process and it involves practitioners' timing and skill. Using a whiteboard or piece of paper, you can list the roles that you observe in your client in relation to his or her significant others. You can start with the general category of a role and then give it an adjective or the other way round. You can use your imagination and draw pictures on the whiteboard or your client may draw their own diagrams in a journal.

Naming roles is a form of spontaneity training

Naming the roles is not a labeling process but rather a form of spontaneity training. In a training group, directly after the sharing phase of a drama, and a teabreak, a trainer may engage the group in a role-processing phase. After the role chart is drawn on the board, the group members reflect on the drama and endeavor to name the roles that they observed in the drama. After this, the trainer generally invites the protagonist to make some comments, asking which role resonated most within them. Often one role is picked very quickly. Sometimes the trainer might ask the trainee to think of things that they might do to further develop that role, or ask the group members to put forward some ideas, for the protagonist to consider, to maintain the role. In these cases, the process becomes a kind of role training. The naming of roles is a mirroring process and the aim is to serve the spontaneity of the protagonist and the group.

The language of role theory across cultures

The different structure of languages impels us to be spontaneous and to use a certain amount of creativity when naming a role. In English, a role is often named by using one or more adjectives and a noun: big ball – big red ball – big, red, bouncing beach ball on white sand. With each additional adjective a new picture emerges, hence the usefulness of the imagination and the role of language. For example, a certain protagonist loves life, he sings as he rides his bicycle in the wind. In English, we might describe him as an 'openhearted lover of life.' In Russian or in Japanese, for example, we might describe him as 'the man who loved life with all of his heart' or 'the man who sings while he rides his bicycle.' It doesn't really matter, what is important is getting the essence of the role in its context. For example, 'Marco Polo' may be the role description of an adventurer about to leave home for the first time and venture out into the world. The use of the imagination is not bound by language differences.

Implications for practitioners and trainers

Directors could use the images that appear in their minds as they work with their protagonists. They often have an intuitive perception yet forego the formal charting of roles, valuing instead their warm-up and that of their protagonist or group. It is not always necessary to make role diagrams, even in training workshops, as this may create obstacles in your warm-up and bring in something extraneous to your relationship with your protagonist. What a role theory framework provides is a structure for looking at our roles and the relationship between them. A role or personality profile doesn't exist as an entity in its own right. The role diagram is a dynamic structure in charting social and cultural atoms and is relevant only to the here and now. It must be used wisely.

The real self

We can reframe words that people use to describe themselves through habit, or to correct distorted mirroring of the self, in role theory terms. This semantic flexibility is constructive because it avoids any trend towards pathologizing labels. New role descriptions can be an effective and specific therapeutic intervention. For example, if a child is told often enough that he is naughty (but in reality he is just a child with a lot of energy, climbing trees and generally being curious and inventive), he may develop an inaccurate and negative view of himself. New mirroring may reveal to the adult person that he was and is a 'bold adventurer' and full of life. Seeing oneself through accurate mirroring may enable a person to change how they see themselves and their world. When people are accurately mirrored, they are often more energized, spontaneous and in touch with their real self. They are then more likely to make new decisions or keep on with what they are already doing with greater confidence. According to Christopher Bollas, the true self is that which is able to be spontaneous: 'The true self listens to a Beethoven Sonata, goes for a walk, reads the sports section of a newspaper, plays basketball and daydreams about a holiday' (Bollas 1989: 21).

Conclusion

When we express ourselves through our roles and continually develop and maintain our role relationships, role theory becomes a living process. Only then can we really grasp what people are doing and get a sense of them as they are in relation to their world (and us). Role theory is refreshing because of its here and now nature and the fact that it addresses each person's creative potential. Anything is possible in this realm. New things emerge. This is what it is to be in the present. Let's use our creative inspirations and images as they appear. This is essential if we are to develop and sustain positive, mutual and life-affirming role relationships in our work and life.

Note

The names and details of the people in this chapter have been changed significantly to retain confidentiality.

References

Bateson, G. (1979) *Mind and Nature*, London: Wildwood House.

Bollas, C. (1989) *Forces of Destiny: Psychoanalysis and Human Idiom*, London: Free Association Books.

Clayton, L. (1982) 'The use of the cultural atom to record personality change in individual psychotherapy', *Journal of Group Psychotherapy, Psychodrama and Sociometry*, 35, 3: 111–117.

Daniel, S. (1992) *Building a Healthy Culture: A Psychodramatic Intervention*, unpublished thesis, Board of Examiners, Australia and New Zealand Psychodrama Association.

—— (2001) *Psychodrama Training Curriculum*, Melbourne: Psychodrama Institute of Melbourne.

—— (2004) 'Through the mirror: role theory expanded', *British Journal of Psychodrama and Sociodrama* 19, 2.

Lorenz, K. Z. (1952) *King Solomon's Ring*, London: Methuen.

Moreno, J. L. (1934) *Who Shall Survive? A New Approach to the Problem of Human Interrelations*, Washington, DC: Nervous & Mental Disease Publishing. Revised edition 1953, Beacon, NY: Beacon House.

—— (1946) *Psychodrama, Volume One*, Beacon, NY: Beacon House.

Moreno, J. L. and Moreno, Z. T. (1959) *Psychodrama, Volume Two: Foundations of Psychotherapy*, Beacon, NY: Beacon House.

—— (1969) *Psychodrama, Volume Three: Action Therapy and Principles of Practice*, Beacon, NY: Beacon House.

Moreno, Z. T. (1989) Training workshop, Holwell, UK.

Chapter 6

Let's face it

Mirroring in psychodrama

Peter Felix Kellermann

I was looking at myself in the mirror the other day and saw the face of an aged person – gray hair, wrinkles around tired eyes, dry aged skin – and asked, 'Who is this old man that is reflecting my image?' Realizing that this was still me, I wondered, 'Is this the same me as the one I have lived with for over 50 years?' There was no point in shutting my eyes for the truth. Sighing, I answered my own question with some resentment: 'Yes, I guess so. It seems I have grown old.' Facing the image of myself in the mirror, urged me to face myself.

Looking at ourselves in the mirror forces us to repeatedly come to terms with who we are, even though we continually change. This process of 'mirroring' is in fact a central and inherent part of 'being in the world,' since it helps us through life to synchronize the reciprocal interaction between the outer world and ourselves. But mirroring is not only a process in which we are watching reflections of ourselves in a 'looking-glass.' The term is also used as a description of the general process of parental responsiveness to their children, and it was chosen by J. L. Moreno (1946) to depict a central therapeutic technique within psychodrama. It is this latter aspect of 'mirroring' that will be the focus of this chapter. After a brief introduction of the classical practice and theory of mirroring in psychodrama, I will suggest a developmental theoretical perspective of three kinds of mirroring from the point of view of social psychology, object relations theory and self-psychology. It is my hope that this perspective will provide an advance in the integration of contemporary developments both in psychoanalytic and psychodramatic theory.

Practice

A 16-year old teenage girl joined an inpatient psychodrama group because she had developed symptoms of anorexia nervosa with a distorted body image. In one session, she enacted a scene in which she tried out for the cheerleading team, comparing herself to the other girls. Her image of a cheerleader was a thin, blonde, and chipper girl wearing a short skirt. Comparing herself to the other good-looking girls, she felt that she didn't have a chance to be accepted because she was too fat. Suddenly overwhelmed by despair, she ran right out of the gymnasium, deciding that she had to make a total change in her appearance. She went on a strict and exaggerated diet, which finally brought her to the hospital in a serious state of anorexia. After the enactment of this scene in the group, she started to cry silently and sat down on the floor. The director asked her to watch as another girl played her role in the original cheerleading competition. The girl went through the motions of the troubled teenager and made a point in emphasizing her sense of 'inadequate' body image. After the enactment, the anorexic girl said, 'But you are so beautiful! You would have been surely picked for the team.' The director urged her again to take her role within the scene and listen to her own words to herself: 'But you are so beautiful! You would have been surely picked for the team.' Hearing these words coming from herself, rather than from another person, made them so much more meaningful and effective. It was a definite sign of progress in her therapy. It was the first time anybody had heard her say something positive about herself.

The technique used by the director in this psychodrama is called 'mirroring.' In this technique, another person in the group (sometimes called the 'auxiliary ego') is asked to portray the role of the protagonist, who watches the enactment of himself or herself from outside as if looking into a mirror. Following the portrayal, the protagonist is usually encouraged to comment on what he or she has observed and/or to re-enter into the action (Hollander 1967).

Mirroring may depict a general portrayal of how the protagonist is coming across in a specific situation, providing an opportunity for the protagonist to get a more distant perspective of his or her behavior. Recently, a protagonist who was watching himself approaching his boss in a timid fashion, shouted, 'Stand up for yourself and tell him what you want! He is not your father, you know.' Seeing himself from outside made it easier to understand what was going on in the interaction and to let insight evolve from within himself, rather than from somebody else.

While care should be taken not to make a caricature mockery presentation of the protagonist that would hurt their feelings, the auxiliary ego may exaggerate one or more aspects of the protagonist's behavior. Depending on the purpose of the portrayal (and what the protagonist should be faced with), the auxiliary ego may be urged to exaggerate body language (e.g. posture and voice tone) to make the protagonist aware of discrepancies between verbal messages and physical expression. For example, a person may say that he is not angry while his entire body posture depicts anger (which he is unable to express).

Mirroring is also frequently used as a warm-up exercise within psychodrama groups. As such, it may focus on the outer signs of our inner state of mind and give an opportunity for some feedback. One such exercise is the simple mirroring in pairs. Two persons stand or sit facing each other, about one meter apart. One is himself or herself, the other is the 'mirror.' Moving only from the waist up, the person begins to make simple gestures or movements while the 'mirror' person duplicates the movements as best as possible. This exercise can also be made in a small or large group with multiple mirrors duplicating the words and movements of one of the group members at a time. Sometimes, real mirrors can be used to work on some or another part of our body image. This may be especially useful when there is a problem in this area and there is a tendency to shy away from mirrors. Participants may then be asked to really take a good look at themselves, and to describe their body and its parts (their height, weight, hair color and type, skin, hands, feet, etc.) and to share their feelings about these parts (Blatner and Blatner 1997).

Technically, the mirror is primarily a feedback method to let the protagonist see a reflection of himself or herself from outside. As in an instant video replay, an auxiliary ego repeats an event that the protagonist has just completed. The psychological distance allows a more realistic appraisal of oneself.

The interpersonal dynamics and psychological resonance of mirroring are not only manifested within classical psychodrama. The improvisational method of playback theatre seems also to be based on some mirroring principles. Someone tells a story or moment from their life, chooses actors to play the different roles, then watches as their story is immediately re-created and given artistic shape. Similarly, the behavioral technique of modeling includes certain mirroring aspects.

The mirroring concept

Pendergast (2003) shows how throughout its history *the mirror* has symbolized vanity, self-examination and the limits of human understanding. The mirroring concept is based on the simple fact that we are unable to really see ourselves from outside. We need someone or something from outside to reflect who we are.

In western culture, as illustrated in fairy tales and Greek mythology, the mirroring concept is an archetype for self-infatuation and idealization, as well as disillusionment and destruction. The stories commonly describe a person who first watches himself or herself with admiration in a mirror but who later is confronted with the fact that he or she is not the center of the universe. The most well-known examples are perhaps the idealized self-reflections of Narcissus and the stepmother of Snow White, who both end in misery.

In the story of Narcissus, the handsome son of a god discovers his own image in the fountain and immediately falls in love with himself. While feeling okay with oneself may be a prerequisite for feeling okay with others, Narcissus' exaggerated self-love becomes a curse, since it prevents him from also loving others. In fact, it became the model for what modern psychiatry has called a 'narcissistic personality disorder': a person who has a grandiose sense of self-importance but who is too self-centered and self-absorbed to have any empathy or concern for others. Such people have been found to be excessively prideful in order to compensate for their fragile self-esteem, and as a consequence, they are driven to constantly seek admiration and attention, but are unable to develop any meaningful interpersonal relations with others.

Similarly, in the story of Snow White, the stepmother stands in front of her magic looking-glass and asks, 'Mirror, mirror on the wall. Who is fairest of them all?', The mirror answers, 'You, O Queen, are the fairest of all!' Later in this story, however, the threatening image of Snow White is introduced by the mirror, who always tells the truth. Snow White evokes the envy of the Queen, and since the Queen is unable to develop a more realistic self-image that is devoid of outside comparison, she becomes consumed with hatred. In this story, mirroring not only represents the instrument for an idealized self-image, but also emphasizes the importance of realistic appraisal of a person.

In sum, both stories delineate a normative and universal two-stage process of idealization and confrontation that is involved in all mirroring. These are also the two main components of the use of the psychodramatic mirror technique. To paraphrase the Queen's question to the mirror in the story of Snow White, we yearn for the psychodrama group to provide us with first a positive and idealized picture of ourselves to gain strength and self-confidence, and also with a correct portrayal that will help us deal with ourselves in a more realistic and differentiated manner. In effect we are asking, 'Mirror, mirror on the wall, tell me who is the fairest of them all? Tell me if I am the fairest of all, or . . . if not . . . if I am just Me . . . if you will still love me, or if I can still love myself?' Facing our mirror image in such a manner may thus help us in the gradual process of facing ourselves.

Theory

From a theoretical perspective, the psychodramatic mirroring technique is based on universal interpersonal feedback processes that evolve during our entire lifespan to reinforce our sense of self. We continue to rely on the various more or less appreciative responses towards us all through life. But mirroring is not limited to the responses of other human beings towards us. There are an endless number of things and events that mirror us in every aspect of life.

The enthusiastic welcome of an affectionate pet will make us feel momentarily good, while the unconditional love of a mother will leave a permanent imprint. As one of the characters in the first of the bestselling Harry Potter books tells our young hero, 'A love as powerful as your mother's for you leaves its own mark. . . . to have been loved so deeply, even though the person who loved us is gone, will give us some protection forever. It is in your very skin' (Rowling 1997: 216).

But mirroring is an even more universal process. In addition to the sense of being either accepted or rejected by our intimate family, we may feel either included or excluded by society in general, or experience either a fortunate or catastrophic destiny by Mother Nature. All such extraneous events will in some way reflect upon how we interpret the way the world looks at us and how we, as a result, look at ourselves in the world. Even the weather may have an enormous mirroring influence on how we feel about ourselves, letting either the sun shine on us, or the rain pull us down. Similarly, the seasons of the year may infuse us with energies that are inspiring either growth or hibernation. Every environment is sending a subliminal mirroring message to us, indicating that we are either part of it or separated from it. People who are more aware of such messages may search in nature for the kinds of mirroring influences that they need at certain times in their lives – from the trees in the forest, the waves of the ocean, the open views at the mountain-top, the desolate silence of the desert or the bustle of urban locations. These are places where we might find some peace and balance within ourselves, and where we feel at home and can enjoy the environmental mirroring.

Finally, traumatic life events may also have a profound and long-lasting mirroring influence on us. Such tragic events may not only make us feel vulnerable, anxious and depressed, but will also affect the way we look at the world as more or less predictable and benevolent. In addition, if we have been abused, molested or tortured by other human beings, we may become suspicious of other people and later develop a sense of worth-lessness and inferiority that is clearly connected to the maltreatment which we endured. 'I was treated as an object,' said a woman who had been raped, 'and I still feel like one.' Her sense of self had been transformed from being a lovable person to one without value – from a 'you' to an 'it' – and she had internalized that sense of self.

Thus it seems that the self is comprised of a kind of mirroring, or reflected appraisal of the various responses we get from people in the social world, from environmental states and from the more or less traumatic events in our lives. However, the first sense of our 'self' seems to evolve as a result of the mirroring that we experienced during the first years of life.

Stages in the development of the self

Watching a person pass through the various stages of child development makes it possible to delineate a few universal stages of the development of the self. In his paper on the spontaneity theory of child development, Moreno (1944) described the following stages:

1   All-identity – the other person is a part of the infant.
2   The infant centering attention upon the other stranger part of himself.
3   The infant lifting the other part from the continuity of experience and leaving all other parts out, including himself.
4   The infant placing himself actively in the other part and acting its role.
5   The infant acting in the role of the other, towards someone else.

These five stages represent, according to Moreno, the psychological bases for all 'self–and' role processes: 'It is an image-building and co-action process' (p. 62). The five stages were later reformulated by Z. T. Moreno (1975) into three phases of child development:

- The first universe, or 'matrix of all-identity' (primary narcissism) in which 'I am the total universe.'
- The second universe of differentiated all-identity, in which other people are perceived as separate from one another, but the child is not yet aware that he or she does not control them. In psychoanalytic terminology, this would represent a kind of part-object, or partly separated self-object.
- The third universe of differentiation, in which there is a breach between fantasy and reality and a sense that 'I am not the world, there is another world outside me.'

These three stages are presented here, not as elaborate theories of psychological child development, but as historic forerunners of, and as a theoretical basis for, the use of the main psychodramatic techniques and the three kinds of mirroring presented below.

One of the advances in theory in psychodrama has been the writing that shows how all the central psychodramatic techniques that were developed by J. L. and Z. T. Moreno may be understood and explained within the framework of normative child development (Leutz 1974; Krüger 1997). These psychodramatic techniques and their association with stages of development may be summarized as follows:

1   *Soliloquy* (talking aloud in the role and associating freely) is based in the first phase of 'all identity' and primary narcissism (also known as the 'symbiotic' phase).
2   *Doubling* (the auxiliary is expressing the inner thoughts and feelings of the protagonist) is based on the second phase of partial differentiation, since the child does not yet experience the mother as a separate object.

3   *Mirroring* (the outside reflection) is also based on the second phase of
     partial differentiation, within the subphase of separation–individua-
     tion.
4   *Role reversal* (the protagonist reverses role with the auxiliary) is based
     on the third phase of differentiation between 'self' and 'other' or when
     object constancy (the sense that the other person exists even if he or she
     is out of sight) has been achieved.

Soliloquy, doubling, mirroring and role reversal are not only basic techniques in the process of psychodrama therapy for adults, but are also
essential for the adequate psychosocial growth of children. In other words,
people who are given the opportunity to express themselves freely, and who
are provided with adequate mirroring, doubling and role reversal, will
continue to develop and grow. All of these techniques are put in motion
with the active help of 'auxiliary egos,' the therapeutic assistants who help
the protagonist fill the various 'significant other' roles in the psychodrama
in the same way as children use their parents as natural untrained auxiliary
ego objects that help the infant get started in life (Moreno and Moreno
1959).

However, since the interpersonal theories of Moreno need to be
expanded, mirroring should be also understood from the point of view of
social psychology (G. H. Mead and C. H. Cooley), object relations theory
(M. Mahler and D. W. Winnicott) and self-psychology (H. Kohut), which
seem to be congruent with Morenian conceptions. From such an integrative
broad theoretical perspective, I suggest a differentiation between three
kinds of mirroring:

- idealizing mirroring
- validating mirroring
- evaluative mirroring.

These kinds of mirroring underscore our intrinsic (self-object) relationship
needs for merging with an idealized object, for alter-ego reflection and for
adversarial and subjective responses to ourselves. This gradual process of
self-development is schematically presented in Table 6.1.

Idealizing mirroring

'If I love myself as my mother loved me, I will be OK.'

Mirroring during the first phase of earliest childhood refers to the various
parental idealization responses to the child's first entrance upon the stage of
life. The parents admire everything about their newborn child: 'How sweet
he is! How wonderful and perfect she looks!' While the baby does not look

Table 6.1 Mirroring in psychodrama

Universe: (Moreno 1975)	First universe: 'All-identity'	Second universe: 'Differentiated all-identity'	Third universe: 'Differentiation'
Feedback	Idealization	Validation	Evaluative
Evaluation	Positive	Neutral reflection	Critical (subjective/ objective)
Phase of child development	Autistic	Separation- individuation	Self-object constancy
Self-differentiation	Symbiosis: Me	Part object: Me–I	Self
Theory of self	Self-psychology	Object relations	Social psychology

very different from other babies, parents view it as the most wonderful creature in the world and, in normal circumstances, they extend their unconditional love to the child in every possible manner. This first stage of mirroring is characterized by 'idealization' and helps the child to be accepted into the family of humankind.

This idealizing mirroring is congruent with Kohut and Goldberg's (1984) suggestion that healthy (narcissistic) self-development proceeds from adequate responsiveness of caregivers to the child's vital emotional needs, including:

- *alter-ego (or auxiliary ego) needs* – children need to be involved with others to develop
- *idealizing (or doubling) needs* – children need to feel attached to a loving caregiver who can hold them
- *mirroring needs* – children need to feel understood and appreciated.

If these needs are not met in childhood, and throughout the lifespan, psychological problems will occur. Neglectful parenting – either physical or emotional neglect or worse, abuse – can result in derailments of self development and impair the individual's ability to form healthy relationships (Stern 1985, 2004).

Feeling understood and appreciated seems to be a basic human desire all through life, and is a part of the regular attitude of successful therapists to their clients. Whether calling it 'unconditional positive regard' (Rogers 1957), 'adequate empathy' or 'idealized transference,' it seems to be a powerful curative factor in many interpersonal therapies. Such mirroring of a good object does not convey a 'realistic reflection' of a looking-glass mirror, but is a decidedly positive and appreciative reflection of the client. Some of J. L. Moreno's students have described that he often conveyed such a positive attitude towards them, which made them feel special. Some of them have quoted him saying, 'Yes!' loudly when they entered the room, as if he was affirming their very existence. Others (Marcia Karp, personal communication) remember him saying, 'You are a genius!' Such idealized mirroring surely was a boost for the self of these adult students.

Validating mirroring

When I look I am seen, so I exist.

(Winnicott 1971: 134)

As the child grows up, his or her mirroring needs will also change. Idealizing mirroring will leave place for a more neutral and validating, but still empathic, responsiveness of the parent to the developing child's separation–individuation needs. This kind of mirroring may be understood within object-relations theory, which emphasizes the importance of early self- and object relationships on our lives, and in which there is a gradual internalization of a reliable and stable mother image.

According to Mahler (1979), the child goes through a normal autistic and symbiotic phase before entering the important subphases of separation–individuation proper (including differentiation, practicing and rapprochement) to finally reach object constancy. During the first phase of symbiosis, affect mirroring is regarded as very important. An attuned parent would display empathic responses through eye contact, facial and vocal expression, touch, holding, movement, etc. Winnicott (1971) suggests that the precursor of the mirror is the mother's face, in which the baby sees him or herself. The mother's gaze upon her infant is thus a founding experience for the child's development of a sense of self as a loved and supported individual. The mirroring look establishes a template for the child's ego as a site for something good and wanted.

One of our most crucial needs in order to develop an authentic personality is to receive such 'validation' mirroring. As children, we needed to have our true feelings – our true self – mirrored, in order to help us develop trust in our own experiences. When this does not happen, painful wounds develop and we feel that we cannot be ourselves. However, when we receive empathic attunement (validating mirroring), this nurturing environment allows the blossoming of the true self of the child.

Being accurately understood by a non-judgmental other person can be very helpful. In psychodrama, the protagonist is encouraged to present his or her own truth in a completely subjective manner (no matter how distorted this may appear to the spectator). This affirmation by the psychodramatist of a protagonist's personal truth and unique experience of reality is called 'existential validation,' and it provides a formidable empowerment of the growth of an inner self (Kellermann 1992: 114). It is therefore understandable that most mirroring scenes within psychodrama constitute simple repetitions of the earlier action, in order for the protagonist to confirm that he or she has been seen and heard.

Evaluative mirroring

> *A group member to another*: When I meet you, I feel enriched. Because you look at me from another perspective.

Evaluative mirroring is not exclusively positive or neutral; it may contain other kinds of feedback as well, including friendly critique. It is a highly subjective view of the protagonist that brings in a new and sociometric perspective of the situation, which acknowledges the fact that people function as magnets. Like in energy fields with a positive and a negative pole, people can be either drawn to one another in sympathy, or be repulsed by one another in antipathy through the effect of interpersonal chemistry, or 'tele' as Moreno (1946) liked to call it. Positive expressions of delight in another person's activities signal that these are accepted as legitimate, while other expressions of dislike, may give a more critical message of disapproval. Such more differentiated mirroring responses promote socialization and reality testing and may correct biased perception of ourselves and of others.

For example, Bob presented a scene in which he quarreled with his wife. He stated his case and argued that she did not pay enough attention to him and neglected his needs. A woman in the role of his wife presented the other side of the story, throwing fuel on the already overheated marital conflict. And so it went on in what seemed to be an endless battle of words and accusations. The director used the mirror technique in an effort to break the deadlock. He asked Bob to step out of the scene and watch it all from outside (as if in a mirror), with another man playing the role of himself.

Watching the fight as a spectator, Bob listened carefully to both partners. The person playing Bob exaggerated the husband's 'child–parent' interaction, rather than the 'adult–adult' position (in terms used by Transactional Analysis, he was in a child ego state). At that point, the wife ended a sentence with 'but you are not my son, Bob. You are my husband!' Hearing and seeing this from outside the scene seemed to allow Bob to absorb his wife's message in a less defensive manner, and he started to laugh at himself, admitting to the group that it apparently had been a concealed and largely unconscious wish in him to be treated by his wife as a child, and that he would have to relinquish it if he wanted to save his marriage.

This kind of mirroring has its theoretical roots in social psychology. Cooley (1902) used the metaphor of the self as a mirror, or a 'looking-glass self,' to illustrate the idea that individuals' sense of self is primarily formed as a result of their perceptions of how others perceive them. That is, the appraisals of others act as mirror reflections that provide the information which individuals use to define their own sense of self. The view of mirroring within social psychology maintains that children develop in interaction with certain main caretakers who either stimulate or inhibit their emotional and cognitive growth as well as their sense of self. These significant others convey an outer social reality with which the child can identify. In the dialogue with this outer social reality, the child becomes an object for itself, thus developing a self as object ('Me'). The self as object, or the social self, is the first conception of a self and grows from the perceptions and responses of other people. Sooner or later, however, the child starts to question its view of outer social reality and the self as subject ('I') develops. This subjective part of the self responds from within, in the here and now, on the spur of the moment. While self as object is conventional, demanding socialization and conformity, the self as subject breaks out in spontaneous, uninhibited and sometimes impulsive actions. Mead pointed out that 'it is through taking the role of the other that a person is able to come back on himself and so direct his own process of communication' (Mead 1934). This is a process replayed in every psychodrama session.

Although the self is a product of socio-symbolic interaction, it is not merely a passive reflection of the generalized other. The individual's response to the social world is active: he or she *decides* what to do *in the light of* the attitudes of others. The conduct is not mechanically determined by such attitudinal structures. In psychodrama, and in many other forms of group psychotherapy, we are not only encouraged to take upon ourselves the attitudes of others towards ourselves, but also to express our own spontaneous and authentic responses to this outside influence. This continual struggle between the 'Me' and the 'I' within ourselves is highlighted in this third kind of psychodramatic mirroring, and is possibly a universal conflict in most human beings. At one point or another (as manifested in the normative adolescent separation–individuation and differentiation process) we will assert ourselves against the significant others.

Conclusion

Mirroring as a developmental process

Mirroring is a most pivotal concept in human growth. It involves the provision of outside feedback that can be positive, neutral or constructively critical. People seem to need positive affirmation and validation on a regular basis and few influences can have such a profound effect on a person's behavior as praise and affirmation. In addition, people need also to be confronted with areas that can be improved and, when presented in a constructive and caring fashion, they can make good use of information on how to improve shortcomings.

If the psychodrama group is sufficiently supportive, there is a potential for a powerful feedback cycle that can be set in motion within the psycho-dramatic mirroring technique. This will include reassurance, validation and subjective interpersonal feedback. At the first level of this feedback cycle, there will be only positive idealization. At the second level, there will be a simple and 'neutral' repetition of what was seen, without a value judgment. At the third level, however, there is clear value judgment that can either be accepted or rejected by the protagonist. This value judgment does not pretend to be objective or tell the 'truth' but is an expression of one or the other position that is held by the outside world. Such feedback gives the opportunity to enter into an inner dance between the parts of ourselves that prefer to play to the tunes of others and those that rather would play to the tunes of ourselves.

These three kinds of mirroring – the idealizing, validating and evaluative mirroring – clearly represent a process of interpersonal growth in which a person moves from a primitive and egocentric state to a more mature level of self-development. Protagonists who are suffering from the effects of earlier deprivation and interpersonal trauma may be more suspicious and distrustful towards others, and may therefore need a more extended period of holding, containing and idealizing mirroring. Others who have a more integrated sense of self, and a clear sense of separateness, autonomy and independence, may be able to enter into a more reciprocal relation in which subjective mirroring and honest interpersonal feedback are a part of the process.

All interpersonal approaches to psychotherapy, including psychodrama, provide clients with an opportunity to enhance their self-understanding through some of these kinds of mirroring responses. The mirroring tech-nique can thus help us to become more aware of ourselves. It can bring the unique gift of self-discovery. But mirroring also holds the key to something much more valuable: to discover who we want to be. Whatever we see in the mirror, we are not forced to accept all our present personal qualities. We have within ourselves the power to change and become someone that we might like better. Psychodramatic mirroring enables the protagonist to look at himself or herself and to objectively assess what he or she sees. The idea is to liberate ourselves from self-limiting conceptions and become the person we were intended to become.

References

Blatner, A. and Blatner, A. (1997) *The Art of Play: Helping Adults Reclaim Imagination and Spontaneity*, New York: Brunner/Mazel.

Cooley, C. H. (1902) *Human Nature and Social Order*, New York: Scribners (reprinted 1956, New York: Free Press).

Hollander, C. (1967) 'The mirror technique as a psychodramatic encounter', *Group Psychotherapy*, 20: 103–112.

Kellermann, P. F. (1992) *Focus on Psychodrama*, London: Jessica Kingsley Publishers.

Kohut, H. and Goldberg, A. (eds) (1984) *How Does Analysis Cure?*, Chicago: University of Chicago Press.

Krüger, R. T. (1997) *Kreative Interaktion* [*Creative Interaction*], Göttingen: Vandenhoeck and Ruprecht.

Leutz, G. L. (1974) *Psychodrama: Theorie und Praxis*, Berlin-Heidelberg: Springer Verlag.

Mahler, M. (1979) *Selected Papers of Margaret S. Mahler*, New York: Aronson.

Mead, G. H. (1934) *Mind, Self and Society*, Chicago: University of Chicago Press.

Moreno, J. L. (1944) 'Spontaneity theory of child development', *Sociometry*, 7 (reprinted in Moreno 1946).

—— (1946) *Psychodrama, Volume One*, Beacon, NY: Beacon House.

Moreno, J. L. and Moreno, Z. T. (1959) *Psychodrama, Volume Two: Foundations of Psychotherapy*, Beacon, NY: Beacon House.

Moreno, Z. T. (1975) 'The significance of doubling and role reversal for cosmic man', *Group Psychotherapy and Psychodrama*, 28: 55–59.

Pendergast, M. (2003) *Mirror Mirror: A History of the Human Love Affair with Reflection*, New York: Basic Books.

Rogers, C. (1957) 'The necessary and sufficient conditions of therapeutic personality change', *Journal of Consulting Psychology*, 21: 95–103.

Rowling, J. K. (1997) *Harry Potter and the Philosopher's Stone*, London: Bloomsbury.

Stern, D. (1985) *The Interpersonal World of the Infant: A View From Psychoanalysis and Developmental Psychology*, New York: Basic Books.

—— (2004) *The Present Moment in Psychotherapy and Everyday Life*, New York: Norton.

Winnicott, D. W. (1971) *Playing and Reality*, London: Tavistock.

Chapter 7

A chaos theory perspective on psychodrama

Reinterpreting Moreno

Rory Remer, Jaime Guerrero and Ruth Riding-Malon

Introduction

The purpose of this chapter is to look at Morenean theory through a chaos theory lens. Chaos theory has much to contribute to informing – both reinforcing and reformulating – Morenean thought, which includes both theory and philosophy. Chaos theory provides a bridge between the widely accepted 'logical positivist' view of the world and the postmodernist and constructivist philosophies entertained at present – and it does so using a mathematical basis.

J. L. Moreno had many brilliant insights. He produced a theoretical network of ideas, conceptualizations and constructs that still helps us recognize and address interpersonal and intrapsychic patterns which are integral to human existence – those of thoughts, feelings, behaviors and interactions. However, like other innovators within the zeitgeist of his time, he strove for universal laws and the unequivocal shared understanding/ meaning of phenomena. These goals (or beliefs in goals) influenced and colored his thinking.

Chaos theory – and related views such as dynamical systems theory, ecological theory, constructivist philosophical thought, non-linear/non-independent mathematical modeling – has demonstrated that these aims are unattainable. Psychological and social phenomena are at best short-term predictable and long-term not predictable. In light of this shift from the logical positivist paradigm, many of Moreno's interpretations, observations and suggested interventions could benefit from re-examination.

In this chapter, we show how patterns of interaction identified with Moreno's five subtheories – enactment (psychodrama), sociometry, role, spontaneity/encounter, and social atom – can be reinterpreted in light of the constructs and insights offered by chaos theory. For example, the work of Hudgins with trauma victims (Hudgins and Kiesler 1987; Hudgins 2000) using the containing double, Kipper's (2002) cognitive double, Tomasulo's (2000) and Remer and Remer's (in press) use of spontaneity theory (cultural conserves) with multicultural groups, and Blatner's objections to labeling the social atom a theory (Remer 2001a) can be viewed through the chaos theory lens with the goal of both shifting Moreno's ideas forward and showing how prescient he was, if not for exactly the correct rationales.

Examining all aspects (theory, constructs, techniques) of Morenean theory at various levels (psychodramatic enactment theory, the cultural conserve, role reversal, etc.) is a task far too extensive to address here. To provide both a pattern and a flavor for this process, we will choose one technique from enactment theory – doubling – on which to focus. First, a short overview of the Morenean subtheories is presented in order to supply the context and explanation for the function of the double. Then the chaos theory links to these theories will be supplied. Looking at Moreno's perspective on doubling and also the perspectives of other notable psychodramatists, we compare their insights with those offered by chaos theory. Our hope is not only to make an initial foray into reinterpreting Morenean thought by supplying an example, but also to inspire others to learn about chaos theory and what it has to offer not only for the conceptualization of Morenean theory specifically but 'the scientific' view of social science theory generally. Some of this work has been done already (e.g., Remer 2004, 2005). Essential parts are supplied here briefly. The reader is invited to consult the more extensive expositions for more complete coverage.

To anticipate a concern, one of the criticisms that has been levied at these manuscripts is that they seem 'just translations of Moreno's work into chaos theory terminology.' Even if they were 'just' a translation, they would still be beneficial in the sense that they challenge the reader to think differently and to 'make meaning' in a new way (Remer 2001b). Nor is this exercise examining Morenean thought for its 'meshing' with other theories like gestalt or cognitive-behavioral approaches. We believe this reinterpretation goes beyond simply converting to a 'different language.' Chaos theory looks at the dynamics of patterns – systems and processes – in a more basic way, allowing parallels and generalizability at a deeper level, perhaps offering more universal connections and insights.

Given the complexity of the task involved, let us prime the reader with the plan and structure of this chapter. First, we offer a very short introduction to chaos theory. To demonstrate both the approach and its implementation, we will then address one technique – doubling – in depth. During this exploration we will explore the interface between chaos theory and the essential theories of enactment, role, and spontaneity, which are essential to understanding doubling. Then selected, previously offered rationales supporting doubling are examined and juxtaposed with those from chaos theory. We hope that this exposition will suffice. Similar analyses can be done with all aspects of Morenean theory, from the most general constructs to the most specific applications.

The mathematical basis of chaos theory

$$X_{t+1} = k \, x_t \, (1 - x_t)$$

This equation, or model, is called a logistical map. It is recursive, meaning that it feeds values back into itself. The patterns it generates – its behavior – evidence all the essential characteristics of a chaotic, dynamical system, such as a group, a family or an individual. As to the x in the equation, it is just a typical algebraic variable. It can stand for 'the number of words spoken,' 'the number of rabbits in the population,' 'the amount of rain,' or anything else you want to predict at a later time (in this instance the next time period: $t+1$) based on what was observed at the present time (t). If k (called the tuning constant) is small, the patterns produced are stable and predictable (point or cyclical attractors). Once reached, they do not change under further iteration. For large values of k, patterns are chaotic. They are sensitive to initial conditions and are both short-term predictable and long-term unpredictable. Chaos is highly sensitive disorderly orderliness.

Application to group/social systems

Chaos theory deals with patterns and how they develop and change. These patterns may be related to phenomena at various levels of application or abstraction from various disciplines – physics, chemistry, biology, ecology, sociology, psychology, anthropology – wherever dynamical systems exist. In the case of psychodrama, these patterns apply to thoughts, feelings, behaviors, and interactions.

Due to its seemingly paradoxical nature (determined randomness or predictable unpredictability), chaos theory has important implications for how we approach the study of the structure, processes and patterns of such systems. As such, chaos theory can provide a fundamental basis – perhaps even universal – for comprehension of these pervasive phenomena, those of Morenean thought included. However, understanding and applying chaos theory requires a different mindset than the concrete, cause–effect view with which we have been inundated. To grasp chaos theory and what it implies, the reader will need a vocabulary for and understanding of at least ten of the most basic constructs:

1   *Phase spaces* – the conceptualization of the possible views of a system. By specifying different values of chosen variables, a mapping – the pattern produced – is obtained. Phase space conveys the idea that, at best, we see only a portion of 'reality' at one time – that part on which we choose to focus. Different theoretical perspectives define different phase spaces – different maps, simplifications – of the system reality.

2   *Strange attractors and their basins of attraction* – focal points for many, and the most challenging, patterns generated by dynamical, chaotic systems. Strange attractors are sets of attracting and repelling points making up and generating patterns. Their basins of attraction are the areas containing those patterns within their boundaries. Social systems, their members, and other sub and supra-systems are strange attractors. The crux lies in understanding how 'attraction' is understood. Mathematically *point* and *cyclical* attractors correspond more to the popular conceptions of attraction. In each case, patterns return exactly to points they have visited before, as if drawn to them. In the case of strange attractors, the patterns can approach a point already on the trajectory, and even come arbitrarily close, but never again reach that point. In fact, points that were attractors can switch valence from positive to negative so that patterns diverge drastically from what might be expected. Although the patterns remain somewhat predictably in a region, within the region their trajectories are virtually random (or seem random). Hence the label 'strange attractor.'

3   *Fractals* – measures/representations of complexity. Fractals convey two very important concepts: (a) what you see depends largely on your perspective; and (b) 'accuracy' of measurement often depends on the definition of the process. The structures and patterns of systems are fractal.

4   *Self-affinity* – denotes the tendency for recursive processes to evidence recurring patterns of various types. Patterns tend to repeat themselves, not exactly but still enough to be recognizable even on different levels and scales.

5   *Bifurcation (and bifurcation cascade)* – splitting in two. Bifurcation increases pattern complexity. 'Cascade' is when bifurcations happen at such a rate that no patterns seem discernible.

6   *Recursivity* – self-reflexiveness, the feeding of information from one's patterns back into the process of producing them. Mathematically, non-linearity and non-independence.

7   *Unpredictability* – the inability to say with certainty what the next state of a system will be or what its previous state was, given knowledge of its present state. The type most associated with chaos theory is sensitivity to initial conditions. This type – and others consistent with chaos theory – indicates that everything about a system cannot be known to absolute certainty and any attempt to assess a situation will affect it. This conveys a humbling, daunting yet realistic perspective on how little control we actually have over complex systems.

8   *Equilibrium* – the tendency (or inertia) of a system to resist change by staying near or returning to points of attraction (homeostasis). Patterns change significantly and most unpredictably in far-from-equilibrium

(chaotic) systems, those whose sensitivity (tuning constant) has exceeded a threshold of stability.

9 *Self-organization* – the inherent tendency for systems in a chaotic state to form new coherent patterns, to reorganize, based only on the interactions of their components.

10 *Resonance* – the synchronicity of constituent components of a system, leading to reciprocal influence and the production of patterns – chaos, reorganization and stagnation.

Applying these ideas to human society, we may observe that social systems, as 'strange attractors,' evidence continual disruptions (chaos) to various degrees and at different levels that can be examined, discussed and addressed using these ideas and structures. Violent, unanticipated and unanticipatable external impacts can cause severe disruptions in system patterns, e.g., social havoc. These pattern dissolutions should not be termed chaotic. However, an understanding of the chaotic properties of dynamical systems is required in order to address social havoc.

Although people addressing dynamical systems disagree about how to approach chaos, they do concur that without it change cannot occur. There is broad agreement that dynamical systems must be sensitive – in a ready state, and far from equilibrium. The readiness seems to rely on the tuning constant.

Applying chaos theory to doubling

Chaos – disruption – is a necessary and sufficient condition for change in social systems. It is not only part of the dynamics in evolution, but a coping mechanism for addressing havoc, drastic upheavals. Welcoming chaos – engendering, recognizing and using it – is incumbent on psychodramatists if they are to be effective. To see more specifically how and why, we will now turn to applying these constructs to doubling in the enactment process. As a necessary prelude, we first review the major components of Morenean theory involved in doubling – enactment, spontaneity/encounter theory and role theory.

Enactment theory

Enactment theory deals with what most people associate with the term psychodrama: the portrayal of scenes from life in order to work through problems. Of course, psychodramatic enactment has broader, more flexible goals than just resolving problems. In any case, enactment theory provides the terminology to talk about and implement all enactments.

Overview of the enactment of the double

Hollander (1969) provided one of the most informative, classic descriptions of enactment theory (or psychodramatic theory) via the 'Hollander Curve.' He integrates various other aspects of Morenean theory in explaining how the enactment emerges from group interaction during the warm-up phase, moving to the enactment proper, and culminates with re-entry into group dynamics in the closure. As the protagonist is chosen, representing the group theme, scenes are selected and portrayed on the stage using the protagonist's conserves but incorporating the energy and connected issues of the other group members and the director/leader as they serve as auxiliaries and audience. The act-hunger – potential energy – is transformed to kinetic energy and channeled into examining and disrupting the conserves, reaching a peak at the catharsis of abreaction. New, more functional conserves are tried out and assimilated as the energy is focused through the use of surplus reality during the catharsis of integration. The enactment ends and those engaged in the enactment return to group mode where sharing, and possibly processing, occurs.

As part of this process, auxiliaries are required to make it work. The auxiliaries (auxiliary egos) are the active parts of the structure provided, representing significant features of the conserved situation, the scene. They may be significant others or important aspects that are necessary for the release of blocked energy. A special type of auxiliary – the double – stands for the internal processes of the protagonist, specifically feelings and thoughts. In a sense, the audience members are also auxiliaries, providing a complementary perspective to that of the double. They have an external, removed view that can be incorporated into the action either directly by becoming active auxiliaries or indirectly through the director or other auxiliaries.

Chaos theory connections with the enactment of the double

Doubling, as a particular technique, demonstrates a specific aspect of the chaos theory connection. As the psychodrama session starts, each group member brings patterns of thoughts, feelings, behaviors and interactions to the session. In chaos theory terms, people are strange attractors whose patterns, while both self-affine and fractal, are contained in a basin of attraction, providing a degree of consistency. At the start of a group, people's patterns, individually and with each other, must shift slightly and into a 'working mode' (a different basin of attraction).

The warm-up promotes this shift to the enactment pattern. In this transition, the phase (enactment), action orientation, the scene and the stage act as embedded basins of attraction that constrain and influence the interaction patterns in certain desired directions. Through the warm-up and setting the scene, specifically choosing auxiliaries, engaging their energies and spontaneity, the combination of individual attractors' patterns are synergistically promoted via resonance. Their interaction also promotes recursive patterns.

The choices made – who and what to include, what to focus on – define the phase space to be examined. As each auxiliary modifies the pattern that the protagonist indicates during the scene setting, the patterns are bifurcated. The bifurcations continue to occur in the context of the recursivity of the interactions. These aspects produce chaos, the catharsis of abreaction, providing the system with the ability to change.

Again altering the patterns of interaction via the techniques of surplus reality, the strange attractors self-organize their interaction patterns producing new ones – both self-affine and fractal to the previously existing ones – integrating the components present, though in unpredictable ways. Once this catharsis of integration occurs, the pattern is again shifted to the larger basins of attraction, the group interaction and the outside world, where the new patterns not only of the protagonist, but also each of the other members influenced by the process, are enacted via the new conserves (strange attractor patterns) created.

The orchestration of these patterns, moving between and among different patterns and different pattern levels – basins – is influenced by the director. The director is also a strange attractor, but one who is more conscious not only of the various attractors, basins and levels involved, but also possibilities for influencing new pattern production.

Connections with psychodramatic practice

Chaos theory tends to reinforce many of the tenets that psychodramatists learn about fostering beneficial enactments. It does strongly suggest the need for an open, collaborative leadership/directorial style, but also one that is balanced with providing enough structure to define the basins of attraction and phase space. To be effective, the director must not only be able to recognize, but also to foster and tolerate the sense of confusion and disconcerting feelings that attend chaos. Otherwise change will be impossible and act-hunger will increase. Since the patterns dealt with are both self-affine and fractal, the director and auxiliaries must have enough familiarity with them (for example, when the group is having a hard time shifting into working mode, or someone has lost spontaneity) to recognize changes and to have possibilities available for intervening, although those conserves will have to be adapted (patterns bifurcated) to accommodate the situational demands.

On the other hand, chaos theory disavows overdirecting because any intervention will have a degree of unpredictability to it, especially in the long run. The director, auxiliaries and audience, as interacting strange attractors, must allow the process to unfold, both influencing and following almost simultaneously. This aim/skill calls for spontaneity – the willingness to explore possibilities (bifurcations) openly and creatively. 'Trusting in the process' means allowing self-organization (Remer 1998) and reliance on the system resonance where the system patterns break up, re-emerge, and cohere in what is most functional at the moment. Effective psychodramatic enactment calls for embracing chaos.

Spontaneity/encounter theory

Spontaneity/encounter theory is central to the Morenean system. It primarily addresses the phenomena that are essential to all the other sub-theories – bonding, trust and interactive energy. In particular it focuses on adaptability to interpersonal and other life situations.

Overview

These two areas of Morenean theory – spontaneity and encounter – have been united because they are central to the subtheory constellation, neces-sary to understanding and implementation of all the others. Given the essential interpersonal/social nature of all Morenean thought, they are inextricably linked. You cannot have effective encounter without spon-taneity and you cannot have spontaneity in interpersonal interactions without encounter.

Spontaneity is the ability to respond to new circumstances adequately or to react in 'old' situations creatively, energetically, and appropriately (Moreno 1993). To judge whether one is acting spontaneously, as indicated by the acronym PANIC, the action must be:

- within the *p*arameters of the situation
- *a*dequate to the demands of the situation
- *n*ovel, in order to generate energy to have an impact
- *i*mmediate, in the present moment
- *c*reative, modifying the established pattern from which the action arises in order to increase future adaptability (based on descriptions offered by Carl Hollander, personal communication, 28 January 1985; acronym structure devised by Remer 2005).

As indicated by the last criterion, spontaneity is grounded in a structure that has developed from previous experience, either personal experience or that of others.

In particular, when other people are involved, being spontaneous requires adjusting to demands injected by their needs, perceptions, and so forth as well as one's own (e.g., acting assertively). Assessing what these requirements might be (i.e., meeting the first two criteria) necessitates encounter – connecting with others in a congruent, honest, open manner. To engage in a productive encounter one must be able to recognize the basic structure of the interaction and adapt accordingly (i.e., respond spontaneously). To have functional encounter, one must be clear about one's own needs and perceptions and willing and able to see the situation from another's perspective. Furthermore, in taking another person's role, using role reversal, one must be able to convey an understanding of and respect for the other person's view. Otherwise the encounter will not be functional (Hale 1981; Remer and de Mesquita 1990).

Whether promoting a functional enactment, exploring and attending to role structures, examining and repairing social atom relationships, or dealing with the sociometry of a group, both encounter and spontaneity come into play. Spontaneity and encounter theories supply the terms and understandings to do so.

Chaos theory connections with spontaneity/enactment

Clearly, the spontaneity process is dynamical. Conserves are strange attractors and warm-ups release and focus the energy necessary for self-organization. Patterns of spontaneity, warm-up, creativity and act-hunger are self-affine and fractal over time, and in many ways with the patterns of other people. Although they are certainly within basins and short-term predictable, they can vary a great deal depending on situational influences.

The concept that spontaneity requires parameters means that a phase space is defined. The process is recursive, with conserves influencing warm-ups, warm-ups influencing spontaneity level, spontaneity influencing creativity and creativity influencing conserves. Both the process and its outcome, the modified conserve, is self-affine and fractal, which allows conserves to serve as the basis for action, which in turn requires adaptability. However, the flow is neither linear nor cyclical, but rather non-independent and interactive – unpredictable and complex. During the process, conserves are bifurcated, often to the point of cascade, particularly when other people (strange attractors) and their patterns are involved (Remer 1996).

Similarly, encounter is chaotic. As anyone who has engaged in the process can attest, the disconcerting reaction engendered by opening one's patterns to exploration (both a 'butterfly' effect and Heisenberg unpredictability phenomenon) is an experience of chaos, but one that is necessary for patterns to be influenced. The recursive interaction of strange attractors is a necessity, but is typically effective only if contained in the larger basin of attraction provided by the pattern of encounter (Hale 1981) and, usually, by a group setting (at least the presence of a third party).

Connections with psychodramatic practice

The parallels between Moreno's 'canon of creativity' and chaos theory reinforce the insights offered by Moreno (1993) about how spontaneity operates to allow continual adaptation and the necessity for being able to adapt. The unpredictability of dynamical system patterns points to the need for such adaptivity. The fractal and self-affine characteristics relate to important facets of the outcome, a revised conserve. The process of bifurcation indicates the how.

The constructs and interventions supplied by Morenean theory also provide a means to cope with the impact of dynamical human systems, areas not within the purview of chaos theory. Methods of spontaneity training, role training, sociometric analysis and enactment all help in promoting and containing chaotic patterns.

When encounter is examined, the image of two strange attractors interacting to generate new patterns within a larger basin of attraction suggests an approach and a goal for dealing with chaotic interaction patterns. Such an approach emphasizes and increases self-affinity; acknowledging and positively reframing fractal aspects. Similar to the observations on spontaneity just mentioned, role reversal, doubling and guidance offered by sociometry theory (e.g., the 'sociogenetic law' – the pairing of individuals to promote telic connections, thus shifting the phase space and operating within a different basin) again suggest direction. Trusting the process emphasizes the need to trust in the ability of such interacting systems to self-organize, finding functional patterns as the constituent systems define them.

The role of the double, from a chaos theory perspective

Doubling defined

Briefly, as background and to indicate points of contrast, here is how the role of the double has been viewed historically. Kipper cogently discusses doubling in some detail. Essentially, in the doubling technique:

> An auxiliary is assigned to portray a specialized role, one that duplicates the protagonist (client). The auxiliary plays this role simultaneously with the original protagonist and attempts to become his or her 'psychological twin,' to serve as the protagonist's inner voice and conscience, to reflect his or her feelings, to uncover concealed thoughts and concerns, and to assist the protagonist in expressing these fully and openly.
>
> (Kipper 1986: 152)

Moreno's view of doubling

As powerful a technique as doubling has proved to be, why does it have its effects? According to Moreno (1985), the double experience replicates an early childhood dynamic, where the young child looks into a mirror and sees another child, someone else who is exactly like himself.

Blatner's view of doubling

Blatner (1996) reiterates this role of the double when he describes the double as a specialized role where the auxiliary plays the part of the inner self of the protagonist. Blatner considers the double to be the most important technique in psychodrama, because it helps protagonists clarify and express a deeper level of emotion and pre-conscious ideation. He explains that doubling is also used by the therapist as a means of giving empathic feedback to the client.

Other authors on the use of the double

Other authors describe the double's functions in varying ways. The double is variously characterized as (a) a social investigator; (b) a support for the protagonist; (c) a co-therapist; (d) an extension of the director; (e) a cata-lyzer of spontaneity (Hollander 1979). As Kipper notes (personal communication, 10 May 2005), doubling can be examined and explained from a host of perspectives, some already mentioned. However, if and when rationales are offered, they generally still leave the question unanswered as to why doubling effects change (Toeman 1948).

For example, the notion that doubling creates a common understanding and promotes empathy and tele (Turner 2002; Michaels-Hollander 2003) does not explain why doing so is necessary and sufficient to promote change. Although many explanations are possible, few have been proffered. More hows have been suggested than whys, despite the need for the whys to direct the hows. An explanation at a more basic level would seem to offer more assurance, and be less regressive.

The role of the double through the chaos theory lens

When we consider the role of the double through the lens of chaos theory, we can observe that the double most obviously sets up a recursive inter-action, with protagonists encountering both themselves (their own words and demeanor) and the perspectives of other people (most notably the double, but also auxiliaries, audience and director) interactively and reflex-ively (on all parts). Thus, the non-linearity and non-independence of the interpersonal and intrapersonal dynamical systems are engaged. Most directly, the double affords the possibility of ratcheting up the system sensitivity via challenging through the co-therapist and director extension functions (other auxiliaries add energy as well).

Even in the description of the doubling functions, the potential strange attractor patterns of competing demands are epitomized and represented. The more resonant the patterns, the more likely their interactions will impact each other. Much of the infusion of energy comes where the patterns are most deeply entrenched, at the level of expectations and norms (Biddle 1979) or core beliefs (Kipper 2002) that are often unconsciously operating. The focus of the input of the double forces the protagonist to cycle the information at different most likely more conscious levels, also increasing the move of the system from equilibrium.

In addition, the bifurcation of meaning (Remer 2001b) and the tension enhanced by the interplay of either doubles of conflicting or competing demands (or between a double and another auxiliary) and by the interjection of patterns self-affine and fractal from other sources (the strange attractor patterns of the double) further provoke the pattern disruption.

As a function of the social investigator, the double explores the phase space, opening up possibilities of disruption in dimensions heretofore either not involved or even recognized. Similarly, the addition of other views and/or focusing on fewer perspectives addresses pattern aspects (e.g., the doubling of strong and/or contradictory emotions), expanding the phase space. The expansion, say through attention to multiple sensory modalities, provides more avenues for the injection of energy into the system, provoking increased sensitivity. This also allows a more comprehensive view of the disruption of the patterns.

The support function of the double can be viewed as attempting to limit the patterns to an acceptable basin of attraction. Thus the protagonist can experience the full effects of the chaos without being totally overwhelmed and self-organization can proceed during the surplus reality and integration phases of the enactment (see Hudgins 2000 and also Chapter 12 for more on her concept of the 'containing double'). Still, like all chaotic dynamics, only unpredictability can be assured (i.e., what type of input will be containing or provocative will only become apparent as the process proceeds), so the process must be spontaneously engaged, although self-organization will have to occur.

Summary and implications

The beauty of the chaos theory explanation is not only its simplicity, but also its basic nature. Establishing a recursive interaction, sensitizing the system to permit change, maneuvering to disrupt present patterns and introduce new aspects, are all that have to be done, and all that can be done predictably. This approach permits the use of other perspectives as means of conveying or framing these strategies, because it is at a more basic level that can support them as well.

The chaos theory perspective also provides support for more unusual applications of psychodrama, such as 'doubles' for other enactment roles. Interestingly, while the idea that all the roles in an enactment are protagonist projections contraindicates the use of doubles on other auxiliaries (Hollander 1979) – a projection of a projection makes little sense – this option is not precluded strictly from a chaos theory point of view where the disruption and confusion of the patterns (conserves) is essential if lasting change is to occur. Hence doubling for other roles is warranted in any useful way possible, thus increasing the flexibility for the application of the technique.

Conclusion

While just scratching the surface here, apparently the kind of explanations chaos theory leads to can direct our course of action in ways that other perspectives do not. The lessons offered may be disconcerting because they are inconsistent with the messages of the 'scientific' rationales with which we have been inculcated. Yet the chaos theory view of reality has mathematical support and experiential validity. Learning to use it allows for more spontaneous action, the only approach that seems adequate to the circumstances – as Moreno's original insights suggested.

References

Biddle, B. J. (1979) *Role Theory, Expectations, Identities, and Behaviors*, New York: Academic Press.

Blatner, A. (1996) *Acting-in: Practical Applications of Psychodramatic Methods* (3rd edn), New York: Springer.

Hale, A. E. (1981) *Conducting Clinical Sociometric Explorations: A Manual for Psychodramatists and Sociometrists*, Roanoke, VA: Royal.

Hollander, C. E. (1969) *A Process for Psychodrama Training: The Hollander Psychodrama Curve*, Denver, CO: Snow Lion Press.

—— (1979) *A Guide to Auxiliary Ego Development*, Denver, CO: Colorado Psychodrama Center.

Hudgins, M. K. (2000) 'The therapeutic spiral model: treating PTSD in action', in P. F. Kellerman and M. K. Hudgins (eds) *Psychodrama with Trauma Survivors: Acting Out your Pain*, London: Jessica Kingsley Publishers.

Hudgins, M. K. and Kiesler, D. J. (1987) 'Individual experiential psychotherapy: an analogue validation of the intervention module of psychodramatic doubling', *Psychotherapy*, 24: 245–255.

Kipper, D. A. (1986) *Psychotherapy through Clinical Role Playing*. New York: Brunner/Mazel.

——— (2002) 'The cognitive double: integrating cognitive and action techniques', *Journal of Group Psychotherapy, Psychodrama and Sociometry*, 55: 95–106.

Michaels-Hollander, E. (2003) 'Expanding consciousness through speech and spoken language', *Dissertation Abstracts International Section A: Humanities and Social Sciences*, 64, 1-A: 25.

Moreno, J. L. (1985) *Psychodrama, Volume One*, Beacon, NY: Beacon House. (Originally published 1946, 4th edn 1994, McLean, VA: American Society for Group Psychotherapy and Psychodrama.)

——— (1993) *Who Shall Survive? Foundations of Sociometry, Group Psychotherapy and Sociodrama* (2nd edn), Roanoke, VA: Royal Publishing Company.

Remer, R. (1996) 'Chaos theory and the canon of creativity', *Journal of Group Psychotherapy, Psychodrama and Sociometry*, 48: 145–155.

——— (1998) 'Chaos theory and the Hollander psychodrama curve: trusting the process', *International Journal of Action Methods: Psychodrama, Skill Training and Role-Playing*, 50: 51–70.

——— (2001a) 'Social atom theory revisited', *International Journal of Action Methods: Psychodrama, Skill Training, and Role-Playing*, 54: 74–83.

——— (2001b) 'The evolution of sociometric theory from a chaos perspective', *International Journal of Action Methods: Psychodrama, Skill Training, and Role-Playing*, 53: 17–32.

——— (2004) 'Chaos theory links to Morenean theory', unpublished manuscript, Lexington, KY.

——— (2005) 'An introduction to chaos theory for psychodramatists', *Journal of Group Psychotherapy, Psychodrama and Sociometry*, 58: 130–150.

Remer, R. and de Mesquita, P. J. (1990) 'Teaching and learning the skills of interpersonal confrontations', in D. D. Cahn (ed.) *Intimates in Conflict*, Hillsdale, NJ: Lawrence Erlbaum.

Remer, R. and Remer, P. (in press) 'The use of psychodramatic interventions and techniques to enhance multi-cultural interactions', in M. Carroll *et al.* (eds) *Praxis: Drama as Reflective Action for Social Transformation*.

Toeman, Z. (1948) 'The "double situation" in psychodrama', *Sociatry: The Journal of Group and Intergroup Therapy*, 1: 436–446.

Tomasulo, D. J. (2000) 'Culture in action: diversity training with a cultural double', *International Journal of Action Methods: Psychodrama, Skill Training, and Role-Playing*, 53: 51–65.

Turner, S. (2002) 'Facing Jerusalem – reflections on doubling', *ANZPA Journal*, 11: 15–19.

Chapter 8

Existential-dialectic psychodrama

The theory behind practice

Leni Verhofstadt-Denève

Introduction

This chapter consists of two sections. The first section considers how the human being can be seen as a person who is at the same time subject (*I*) and object (*Me*), where the *I* is capable of reflection on, and construction of, the *Me*. Within this viewpoint, six fundamental *I-questions* can be seen as the foundation of a therapeutically workable and living *personality model*. While *dialectic* movements can be considered as the motivational force behind the developmental process, it is *existential issues* which constitute a major content of the *I–Me* reflection. The second section outlines how existential-dialectic theory can inform a better theoretical understanding of psychodrama practice.

An existential-dialectic theory

The personality model

Viewing the human being as a person who is at the same time subject (*I*) and object (*Me*), the *I* is capable of reflection on, and construction of, the *Me*, i.e. the subjective phenomenological image of ourselves and the others (Verhofstadt-Denève 1988, 2000). This view can be compared with the scheme proposed by William James (1950), who splits the self into *I* ('the experiencing aspect of self as knower') and *me* ('the knowledge of self as object or self as known'). The distinction of *I* and *me* also reminds us of Sartre's thesis that human beings are simultaneously *consciousness*, 'pour soi' and *object*, 'en soi' (Sartre 1949: 33). Comparable notions are to be found in George Herbert Mead (1934) and in the narrative approach of Hermans (2003). See also Chapter 4 of this volume.

Through the process of the *I* reflecting on and constructing the *Me*, the *Me* is built up by the answers to some fundamental questions (see Figure 8.1):

a. Conscious aspirations
b. Unconscious aspirations
c. 'Unrealistic' aspirations
d. Totality of personal aspirations
e. Unknown aspects of ideal situations
f. Hypothetically 'ideal' situation

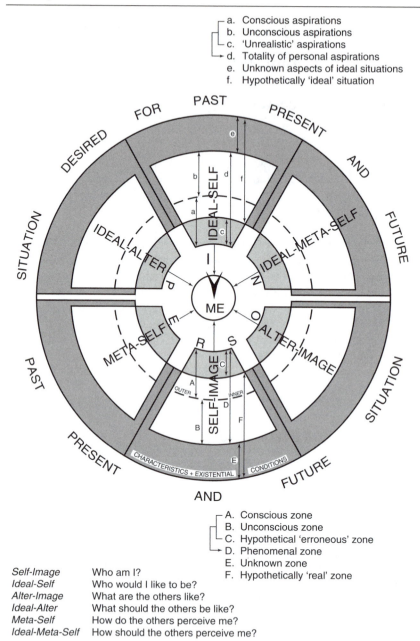

A. Conscious zone
B. Unconscious zone
C. Hypothetical 'erroneous' zone
D. Phenomenal zone
E. Unknown zone
F. Hypothetically 'real' zone

Self-Image   Who am I?
Ideal-Self   Who would I like to be?
Alter-Image   What are the others like?
Ideal-Alter   What should the others be like?
Meta-Self   How do the others perceive me?
Ideal-Meta-Self   How should the others perceive me?

Figure 8.1 Phenomenological-dialectic personality model

1 Who am I? (Self-Image.)
2 Who would I like to be and become? (Ideal-Self.)
3 What are the others like? (Alter-Image.)
4 What should the others be like? (Ideal-Alter.)
5 How do the others perceive me? (Meta-Self.)
6 How should the others perceive me? (Ideal-Meta-Self.)

These six I-questions constitute the foundation of a therapeutically workable and 'living' personality model. Accordingly, the model has six dimensions and proceeds on the assumption that every human constructs their
own unique subjective (phenomenological) interpretation of himself or
herself and the surrounding reality at different levels of consciousness and
behaviour.

Moreover, a distinction can be made, for each dimension, between an
external aspect (the way we behave externally, what we say, etc.) and an
internal aspect (what we think and feel). An adolescent might say to his
father 'You are a loser. You destroy everything in me.' Yet he might at the
same time be thinking 'How can I say this to him? After all, he means well'
(i.e. the external Alter-Image versus the internal Alter-Image/Self-Image).
In therapeutic sessions, there must be space for expression of such hidden
contents.

This personality model also makes allowance for the fact that these
constructions about ourselves and about the other people may show distortions, errors and omissions. Alternative interpretations are certainly
possible. Thus the belief that 'Father hates mother, he makes her unhappy'
may be a 'mistaken' subjective construction of a complex reality that can be
interpreted in a totally different way. From a clinical-therapeutic point of
view, it is essential that one should proceed on the basis of the phenomenological constructions, however bizarre and unreal they may seem. The
ultimate aim is that, thanks to therapeutic action in a safe climate, each
group member should discover alternatives and more realistic interpretations about themselves and about their significant others.

This phenomenological-dialectic personality model can be a workable
frame of reference for the psychodramatist (Verhofstadt-Denève 1988,
1995, 2000, 2001, 2003; Verhofstadt-Denève et al. 2004).

Dialectics

In this framework, the dialectic concept acquires a decisive significance as
the motive force behind the process of development. An important aspect
of this view is the positive interpretation of the individual meeting with
oppositions and experiencing crises. These are read as motivational forces,
or at the very least as signs of dynamic events, psychic activity and potential
personality development. This view is underpinned by my own follow-up

research and by theoretical interpretation of dialectic developmental psychology (Buss 1979; Basseches 1984; Verhofstadt-Denève 1997; Verhofstadt-Denève and Schittekatte 1996; Conville 1998).

The assumption is that the six personality dimensions (Self-Image, Ideal-Self, Alter-Image, Ideal-Alter, Meta-Self, Ideal-Meta-Self) relate to each other in dialectic constructive oppositions. An important corollary is that effective *I–Me* reflection should soften and integrate too rigid, habitual constructions about oneself and significant others. Thus there might be exclusive *inter*dimensional oppositions between the Self-Image and the Ideal-Self: 'With my poor potential I will never be able to find a good job'; between the Self-Image and the Alter-Image: 'She is so much stronger than me'; between the Self-Image and the Meta-Self: 'He thinks I do not love him, but I do desperately!' Likewise, the possibility can be taken into account that there are *intra*dimensional oppositions, for example, between external and internal contents, between phenomenological constructions and 'reality,' and between contents in different times: 'As a child I was loved by my parents, but now they are disappointed in me.'

In other words, with self-reflection and empathy people can become conscious of their extreme oppositions and rigid interpretations. When they have acquired this awareness (a process sometimes combined with the experience of a crisis), they can move on to taking a more qualified view and to constructing alternative, more flexible images of themselves and important others. How to work with this dialectical process will be explained later in this chapter, but now we will try to explain what we mean in this context by 'dialectics.'

The *Historisches Wörterbuch der Philosophie* (Ritter 1972) needs more than 60 pages to deal with the entry on dialectic. Over the millennia, different cultures (Hindi, Chinese, Ancient Greek, Western) have given the term the most diverse meanings. We confine ourselves here to highlighting a number of crucial elements (for further reading, see Verhofstadt-Denève 2000: 19–40).

Making due allowance for Rychlak's warning against trying to apply a single, fixed definition to the concept of dialectic (Rychlak 1976), we do believe that it is necessary to try and define this key concept by considering its chief characteristics. The following is an attempt to illustrate the general course of human development by means of a much simplified example originally outlined by Hegel (1770–1831), the father of modern dialectics (Hegel 1952).

The *child* grows into an adult, thus becoming fundamentally different, and in this process negating itself. The *adult* appears to lose many of his former childlike characteristics (his carefree and spontaneous behaviour, his playfulness, his wondering at 'everyday' and 'unimportant' things, etc.), but he also gains a number of positive characteristics (rationality, conscious self-reflection, sense of responsibility, perseverance, etc.), which did not seem to be explicitly present in the child. But the adult, when reaching *old age*, negates himself as he appears to lose much of what he had gained (physical and mental involution), though he acquires fundamentally new characteristics as well, doing so by means of the integration of characteristics from the two previous stages. After all, we often see in older people a typical interplay of carefree repose (in spite of physical pain and approaching death), playfulness and interest in small things for which many adults have no patience, combined with wisdom, reason and integrity. In brief, the child has returned to itself, to the 'simplicity' of its early years, but that simplicity has now been *mediated, resolved* by the experiences from adulthood. Hegel uses in this context the term 'aufgehoben', defined later in this chapter.

This process reminds us of Fichte's trilogy of *thesis-antithesis-synthesis*, in which a higher synthesis is achieved thanks to a double negation (Basseches 1984). However, Fichte's schema is only useful as an ordering principle and a guideline. In fact it would not be possible to force all dialectical processes into this construction, since the process as a whole cannot be clearly split up into separate parts. Moreover, this process can happen very swiftly, for example in self-dialogue, or it can be spread over several generations and historical ages.

Furthermore, Rychlak points out that one particular thesis can be opposed to more than one antithesis. Should there be only one antithesis, this would imply a high degree of predictability, which cannot be reconciled with the concept of dialectical developments: If the outcome is known in advance, then a truly dialectical encounter cannot take place (Rychlak 1976).

Finally, Rychlak emphasises that antithesis and synthesis are potentially present in the thesis. The process is one of self-actualisation. The person that the child will become in adulthood and in old age is present from the very beginning as a possible outcome. Concepts such as 'opposition' and 'alternating periods of crises and relative equilibrium' crop up in the theories of many psychologists and psychotherapists. The following are examples of such 'contrastive thinking': Jung (1931); Piaget (1949); Busemann (1953); Kelly (1955); Festinger (1957); Erikson (1968); Kohlberg (1976); Vygotsky (1979); Minuchin and Fishman (1981); Yalom (1995). See also Barton (1994) in relation to dynamic systems and chaos theory.

Though the interaction of oppositions may be a prerequisite for dialectic processes, it does not follow that all oppositions will of necessity result in dialectical developments. Referring, amongst others, to Altman *et al.* (1981) and Adler (1927), we believe the major characteristic of dialectic contradictions to be that their components must simultaneously have opposition as well as complementarity. *Complementarity* means that the opposing poles should: (a) depend on each other; (b) belong to the same system of a higher order; (c) be of comparable strength, so that they cannot exclude one another. *Opposition*, on the other hand, contains: (d) the motive force for effecting change at every stage. These four characteristics will now be explained.

1   The two poles of the opposition are *mutually dependent*. This means that the two poles must be able to flow into each other. It is in this way that the child can become the adult and that the adult can be reborn as the child in old age.
2   Mutual dependence implies that the opposing poles are closely related and belong to *the same system of a higher order*. Being a child and being an adult, for example, are two intrinsic stages of ontogenesis – the development of every individual.
3   It is an essential requirement that *the two poles should be of comparable strength*, for if they are not, one will wipe out the other and a fully fledged dialectical process will become impossible. When a child grows into an adult, some of its earlier features may continue to dominate, so that the individual develops a strong resistance to becoming an adult. For reasons of anxiety, uncertainty, lack of confidence, etc., someone can refuse to assume the responsibilities of adulthood and seek refuge in childlike, egocentric dreams. Dialectically speaking, the adult pole in the child is suppressed. If one pole prevails over the other, the dialectical nature of development is at risk. Likewise, there can be no dialectically founded relation between partners if one of the partners feels that he or she is completely dominated by the other.
4   What is the nature and function of the opposing poles in the various stages of the dialectical process? We have already pointed out that Rychlak (1976) believes that antithesis and synthesis are potentially included in the thesis stage. Within our view, the opposing poles are present in every stage of the dialectical process, but the relation to each other is different at each stage (i.e. implicit, explicit and partially integrated). Moreover, at each stage the tension between the poles provides the indispensable driving force which makes the transition to the next phase possible (see Figure 8.2).

   In stage one (thesis stage) there is only one pole (A, the thesis pole: childhood) which is explicitly present. The antithesis pole (B: adulthood) is surely present, but only in the background as a potentiality. Only one of the two poles is actualised (A), and the other (B) is implicit, connected in an undifferentiated way with the actualised pole (A). However, the implicit pole (B) operates in a hidden fashion, since it is part of the opposition which will inevitably force the thesis pole to negate itself.

   The first negation is realised in stage two, the stage of the antithesis. The thesis pole remains in the background and the antithesis pole is now actualised. This second stage often goes hand in hand with crisis and conflict ('I miss the rich creative spontaneity of childhood'). The implicit

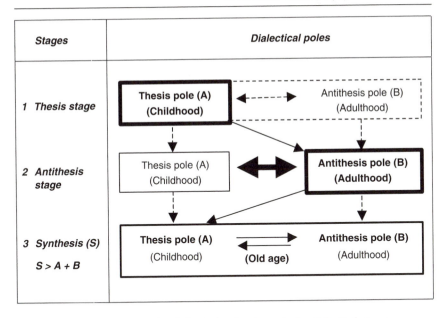

Stages	Dialectical poles

Figure 8.2 Relation between the dialectical poles through the dialectical stages (schematic representation)

opposition of stage one is now actualised. Stage two is that of the explicit unfolding of the contradiction. We have already emphasised the fundamentally positive character of the antithesis stage. The explicit contradiction arising from the actualisation of B becomes the prerequisite for the all-important second negation in stage three.

In stage three – the stage of the synthesis – the antithesis pole (B) is in its turn negated, so that it can now be partially integrated in the thesis pole (A), resulting in a 'higher' synthesis which is richer than the sum of A and B. The outcomes of dialectical processes are always in some part unpredictable. What takes place in the synthesis or the transcendence of oppositions? Hegel says that the oppositions using a threefold ambiguity in the German verb 'aufheben'(see Jonkers 1978: 122):

- The first meaning of the verb 'Aufheben' is to remove, to destroy, *to repeal* (as in 'to repeal a law') (see Kruithof 1959: 177). This means that the opposites of thesis and antithesis no longer exist in their original form. The older individual is not a child but has also become different from what he was in adulthood.
- Secondly, the term has a sense of to keep, *to preserve*: 'In the synthesis, the contradiction is preserved, and in the reconciliation the opposing poles never merge completely. Should they merge completely, everything would stop moving' (Kruithof 1959: 178). Some of the characteristics

of being a child and of being an adult are found once again in the older person.

- Finally, 'Aufheben' also has a meaning of to raise, *to lift*; in a figurative sense to grow, to change, to develop. 'The speculative reconciliation is not the sum of the elements but rather a lively structure in which the two sides become what they are in essence' (Kruithof 1959: 178). Thanks to his active participation in the earlier stages, the older person is more than the mere sum of child + adult; he goes beyond the characteristics from the earlier stages and brings them to a (qualitatively) higher synthesis. What the qualitatively higher synthesis will consist of will partly depend on the content given to the dialectical process.

The notion of a growth towards some form of ideal synthesis underlies many religious, philosophical and psychological theories. The fact is that the optimum integration, i.e. synthesis, of opposites is never completed. Altman *et al.* (1981) and Adler (1927) make this point when they observe that the synthesis of opposites can never be complete since the result would be no opposition, which would eliminate a dialectic system. In every synthesis there is the potential of a new thesis, which may start a new dialectical cycle. It needs to be emphasised that dialectic processes originate out of an *inherent necessity*, which is typical of the principle of self-regulation in every living organism.

Before looking at the meaning of dialectics for a better understanding of psychodrama practice, we will mention the existential axis as an important aspect of the human personality.

Existential questions

While dialectic forces can be considered to underlie the developmental *process*, it is existential issues which constitute the major *content* (though not the only content) of the *I–Me* reflection in the various stages of life (Verhofstadt-Denève 2000). Research shows that it is at a much earlier stage than one would expect that children, and later on adolescents as well, are very much concerned with fundamental existential issues closely bound up with the specific human condition (Anthony 1971).

When a therapeutic group has reached a high degree of familiarity and security, the members will inevitably raise thoroughly human existential issues about origin, destiny, and finiteness of oneself and important others; about personal freedom, choice, responsibility, separation, loss and aging (Verhofstadt-Denève 2000: 41–66). All this is frequently imbued with feelings of depression, anxiety, guilt and loneliness (Mijuskovic 1977; Yalom 1980). It is important that individuals should recognise these issues, and that they should interpret and accept feelings of anxiety and guilt as normal and ontological, so that they may be able to enjoy to the full every moment of life, vividly and consciously (May 1983; Mullan 1992).

Psychodrama and an existential-dialectic theory

In this part we outline the connection between the starting points of an existential-dialectic developmental psychology as highlighted above, and existential-dialectic psychodrama.

Why is psychodrama such a powerful tool in the stimulation of group and individual development? We will try to explain that the power of psychodrama can to a great extent be explained by the intrinsic dialectical nature of the three-stage course of a psychodrama session and the fundamental psychodrama techniques used. Moreover, deeply grounded existential themes and issues will inevitably be triggered in the course of intensive psychodrama group sessions. What are the basic aims of (existential-dialectic) psychodrama interventions?

Elsewhere, the author has explained the activation of dialectic processes in the developmental process of the subtle relationship between group and protagonist during the typical psychodrama three-stage session (Verhofstadt-Denève 2000: 181–186). Within this chapter, we restrict ourselves to the elaboration of the following examples:

1   Activation of *dialectic processes* in each group member through the stimulation of *I–Me* reflection using self-reflective action techniques such as role taking, role reversal, doubling, mirroring and other techniques;
2   Optimisation of *existential perception*: consciousness and acceptance of the 'human condition,' i.e. ontological anxiety, loneliness and guilt, in relation to personal development.

Stimulation of I–Me reflection and dialectical processes in individual group members

In existential-psychological terms, it can be said that psychodrama aims to kindle critical reflection on one's own essence (the content of one's existence): 'Who am I, who is thinking, feeling, acting in these existential conditions?' 'Who is this *I* who plays *these* roles and has *these* social ties?'

Some of the most striking effects of psychodrama are a raised self-awareness and a better knowledge and understanding of the other person. Self-reflective potential and empathy can be stimulated very effectively through the classical dialectical psychodrama techniques.

Nearly all psychodrama techniques aim at activating the *I–Me* dynamic in the form of reflection on oneself, and other people in relation to oneself.

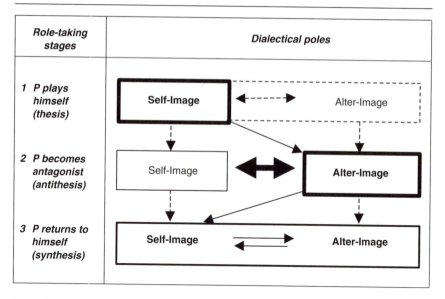

Figure 8.3 The dialectical relationship between Self-Image and Alter-Image through the three stages of role taking (schematically, see also Figure 8.2)

This is a clear aim during, for example, role taking (protagonist plays the role of another person) and role reversal (where the protagonist and 'antagonist' exchange places). In these two techniques, the *dual dialectical negation process* along the three dialectical *stages* is clearly recognisable, as illustrated in the following example. Let us look at John, the protagonist, an adolescent enacting the relational problems with his father, the antagonist (see Figure 8.3).

In the first stage, John starts out by *being himself*. He situates his *person* in his space. He acts as John in his (social) environment. He reflects on his actions in relation to his thoughts and feelings. He exteriorises his *Self-Image*. This stage could be called the thesis or the 'homogeneous' stage.

The picture changes completely when John takes over the role of his father (via role taking or role reversal). He is now obliged to speak from the point of view of his father and, to a certain degree, psychologically negates himself. He has to distance himself from his personal (egoistic) feelings as much as possible in order to be able to 'become' his father. He *becomes someone else*, his opposite. He becomes a part of his *Alter-Image*. In dialectical terms, this is obviously the negation, antithesis or 'differentiation' stage.

When the protagonist *becomes himself* again in the synthesis stage, this involves a second negation: he negates the father image (*Alter-Image*) in himself and returns to the *Self-Image*. However, the direct confrontation with the activated father image in the negation stage has changed the protagonist's *Self-Image*; his father-image has changed as well. The two original images have been partly cancelled out or destroyed (note the first meaning of 'Aufheben,' outlined earlier). At the same time, a degree of opposition persists: the protagonist has come round to some of his father's conceptions and feelings, but not to all of them. Both the *Self-Image* and the father image display a certain continuity (note the second meaning of 'Aufheben'). Most importantly, however, the protagonist has grown as a person during the synthesis stage of role reversal. He has been raised to a higher level (the third meaning of 'Aufheben'). By first becoming the other and then returning to himself, enriched with his conscious *Alter-Image*, the protagonist is better capable of understanding his feelings towards his father (his *Self-Image* has been enriched). In the meantime, he has learned to empathically understand his father's feelings and thoughts (his *Ideal-Alter* has developed) and he is more understanding towards the way his father should act (his *Alter-Image* has been corrected). He can also better imagine what image his father has conceived of him and what his father expects of him (broadened perception of his *Meta-Self*). Rigid conceptions in the *Self-Image* have been softened by this stimulating dialectical process and have been partially integrated during the 'integration stage.' This does not automatically and necessarily imply improved contacts with the real father, but the new insights may pave the way. Role taking and role reversal are extremely powerful instruments for activating these personality dynamics.

The other characteristics proper to dialectical processes also apply in role taking and even more explicitly in role reversal: both poles of the contradiction are *partially opposed and partially complementary*. They are interdependent: from the beginning of the process, the protagonist's *Self-Image* stands in relation to the image he has conceived of his father (*Alter-Image*). Both images give one another sense and meaning.

This cohesion results from the fact that both images represent related elements of a higher whole, the network of the protagonist's subjective images of the so-called 'significant others' (Mead 1934) in relation to the *Self-Image*. Moreno (1934) uses the term 'social atom' in this context, and Kelly (1955) refers to the 'role constructs' which the subject uses to construe his significant others into a hierarchic structure, mutually and in relation to himself. It would lead too far to illustrate the dialectical background for all the techniques, but such a background can also apply to the soliloquy, mirroring and to the key technique of doubling.

Summarising, we can say that psychodrama starts from the conscious phenomenological constructions the protagonist has construed of himself in relation to his material and social world. The psychodrama method and techniques imply an integration of cognitive, emotional and action techniques which will activate the *I–Me* dynamic and dialectical processes. In this way the contradictions (and similarities) within and among the subjective phenomenological self-constructions are better defined. In addition, some pre-conscious and unconscious contents can be expressed as well. The whole system of constructions is set in motion, requiring a redefinition and opening perspectives for integration into a renewed synthesis.

Stimulating the acceptance of the 'human condition'

It is generally agreed that psychodrama intensifies awareness of self, other people and the world. However, opinions diverge when it comes to the contents of this awareness process. What should the protagonist and the other group members become aware of in order to acquire the best chance of personal development? In the existential-dialectic view, we consider the central existential themes to be fundamental (not the only ones, but very important ones).

Since the existential 'human condition' is a highly valuable but also precarious one – constantly marked by the impending, inescapable separation of beloved persons (and animals and objects), and with the clear realisation of one's own finiteness – *existential anxiety* and *loneliness* are largely inevitable. The absence of anxiety and feelings of loneliness should be viewed as negative signals. This absence may be caused by the avoidance of responsibility, freedom and realistic self-reflection. In this context we can refer to the concept of Blaise Pascal (1670/1912): the danger of escaping into *divertissements*, when sham values – for example, seeking power or hoarding possessions – are used in order to avoid facing the harsh, cruel existential condition.

Guilt is also a normal feeling: guilt towards oneself because one has not succeeded in developing all potentialities; guilt towards significant other people because one does not do or has not done enough, or because the relationship is felt to be unfair or superficial. Similarly to the absence of anxiety, the absence of guilt is usually a negative signal.

In psychodrama, the intensive activation of the *I–Me* reflection inevitably emphasises this existential anxiety, loneliness and guilt. One becomes intensely aware of how much significant other people mean to us, and how painful a (permanent) separation may be. This insight may lead to the significant intention to spend one's time as meaningfully as possible with the loved one, experiencing every moment intensely and consciously. The classic psychodrama techniques (role taking, doubling, role reversal, etc.) and the exchanges during sharing may stimulate the awareness during psychodrama that anxiety is inherent to human existence and should be accepted as such. Anxiety should of course not be heightened, but it would be wrong to dismiss it completely. In such a case, the danger exists that after the sudden and rude awakening, this existential anxiety erupts with great intensity. This should be avoided. On the contrary, a conscious experience and acceptance of existential anxiety should broaden and deepen our interactions with people (especially significant and beloved people), and also with our natural environment.

The same applies to *existential guilt*. It is no use constantly blaming oneself for insufficiently developing one's skills or potentialities or not seizing all the opportunities offered. One should become aware that full self-realisation is more a forward-moving direction rather than a single goal. According to the psychoanalyst Blos, the de-idealisation process of self and object (others) is one of the most painful experiences during adolescence:

> The adolescent patient needs to be exposed – gradually and repeatedly – to a disillusionment in self and object. Over time, this leads to a *tolerance of imperfection*, first in the object and finally extending to the self. How difficult and painful the process of de-idealisation of object and self is for the adolescent never ceases to impress me.
>
> (Blos 1979: 16, author's italics)

The opposition to the 'tolerance of imperfection' may also come into play in adulthood and old age. However, we should learn to realistically accept weaknesses and mistakes in ourselves and in others. This in no way hampers the striving for self-realisation and harmonious cohabitation. On the contrary: not all oppositions and contradictions should be resolved. It is sometimes necessary to learn to live with compromises. Personal development is possible only if one accepts a healthy share of anxiety, loneliness and guilt in oneself (and others). There is no point in wasting energy on condemning or even 'revolting' against an existence which can be deemed – in Camus' not exclusively negative meaning – 'absurd' (Camus 1965). Freedom, imposed choices, personal responsibility, the need to accept and experience the positive aspects of existential anxiety, loneliness and guilt are themes which can be dealt with very effectively in a secure psychodrama group. Intense experience and a growing awareness of oneself in relation to the significant others automatically leads to a confrontation with those existential themes. A supportive, understanding group can provide very effective help in the process.

Illustrative in this regard are the studies referred to by Yalom (1995) concerning the so-called 'healing factors' in group therapy. In one of these studies, 20 patients were asked to rate 60 items (in relation to their effect on their recovery) corresponding to various categories: altruism, group cohesion, universality, learning from one another (giving and receiving information), guidance, catharsis, identification, reliving of existential factors. In his discussion of the results, Yalom reaches the following conclusion:

> It is clear that the existential items strike responsive chords in patients . . . [One of the items], 'Learning that I must take ultimate responsibility for

the way I lead my life no matter how much guidance and support I get from others,' was highly ranked by the patients.

(Yalom 1995: 89)

According to Yalom, these patients realised that, although they were able to feel closely tied to others, there was a borderline beyond which no one could accompany them: there is an existential being alone in existence which everyone has to face and which cannot be escaped. Indeed, there are two types of loneliness: *existential* and *social loneliness*. The first type refers to the original loneliness proper to 'being' human; the second relates to the incapacity of 'being with.' The resolution of social loneliness may make existential loneliness more bearable and favour its acceptance, but it can in no way solve or replace it (Yalom 1980: 376–377). However, the mistake is sometimes made that group members convert existential problems into interpersonal problems, which are easier for the group to address. This is an escape via a 'higher' form of 'divertissement,' an attempt at evading existential reality. If this process is not identified and named, existential loneliness may be mistaken for social loneliness (Yalom 1995).

Of course, these themes do not emerge only in psychodrama groups. However, through the intensification of the *I–Me* dialectic, these themes are bound to crop up. A secure group is therefore an excellent medium for tackling this fundamental problem constructively and can contribute to the optimisation and the adjustment of existential perception and personal development.

References

Adler, M. J. (1927) *Dialectic*, New York: Harcourt.

Altman, I., Vinsel, A. and Brown, B. (1981) 'Dialectic conceptions in social psychology: an application to social penetration and privacy regulation', in L. Berkowitz (ed.) *Advances in Experimental Social Psychology*, New York: Academic Press.

Anthony, S. (1971) *The Discovery of Death in Childhood and After*, Harmondsworth: Penguin.

Barton, S. (1994) 'Chaos, self-organization, and psychology', *American Psychologist*, 49, 1: 5–14.

Basseches, M. (1984) *Dialectical Thinking and Adult Development*, Norwood, NJ: Ablex.

Blos, P. (1979) 'Modifications in the classical psychoanalytical model of adolescence', in S. C. Feinstein and P. L. Giovacchini (eds) *Adolescent Psychiatry: Developmental and Clinical Studies*, Vol. 8, Chicago: Chicago University Press.

Busemann, A. (1953) *Krisenjahre im Ablauf der menschlichen Jugend* [*The Crisis Years in the Course of Human Youth*], Ratingen: Aloys Henn Verlag.

Buss, A. R. (1979) *A Dialectical Psychology*, New York: Wiley.

Camus, A. (1965). 'Le mythe de Sisyphe', in A. Camus, *Essais*, Bruges: Editions Gallimard, Bibliothèque de la Pléiade.

Conville, R. (1998) 'Telling stories: dialectics of relational transition', in B. M. Montgomery and L. A. Baxter (eds) *Dialectical Approaches to Studying Personal Relationships*, Hove, UK: Lawrence Erlbaum Associates Ltd.

Erikson, E. H. (1968) *Identity, Youth and Crisis*, New York: Norton.

Festinger, L. (1957) *A Theory of Cognitive Dissonance*, Stanford: Stanford University Press

Hegel, G. W. F. (1952) *Phänomenologie des Geistes* [*Phenomenology of the Mind*], Hamburg: Meiner (originally published 1807).

Hermans, H. J. M. (2003) 'The construction and reconstruction of a dialogical self', *Journal of Constructivist Psychology*, 16, 2: 89–130.

James, W. (1950) *The Principles of Psychology*, New York: Dover (originally published 1890).

Jonkers, P. (1978) 'Verklarende noten' [Clarifying notes], in G. W. F Hegel, *Het wetenschappelijk denken* [*Scientific Thinking*], Amsterdam/Meppel: Boom.

Jung, C. G. (1931) *Seelenprobleme der Gegenwart* [*Soul Problems for the Present*], Zurich: Rascher.

Kelly, G. A. (1955) *The Psychology of Personal Constructs*, New York: Norton.

Kohlberg, L. (1976) 'Moral stages and moralization: the cognitive-developmental approach', in T. Lickona (ed.) *Moral Development and Behavior: Theory, Research and Social Issues*, New York: Holt, Rinehart & Winston.

Kruithof, J. (1959) *Het uitgangspunt van Hegel's ontologie* [*The Starting Point of Hegel's Ontology*], Brugge: De Tempel.

May, R. (1983) *The Discovery of Being: Writings in Existential Psychology*, London: Norton.

Mead, G. H. (1934). *Mind, Self and Society*, Chicago: University of Chicago Press.

Mijuskovic, B. L. (1977) 'Loneliness: an interdisciplinary approach', *Psychiatry*, 40, 2: 113–132.

Minuchin, S. and Fishman, H. C. (1981) *Family Therapy Techniques*, Cambridge: Harvard University Press.

Moreno, J. L. (1934) *Who Shall Survive? A New Approach to the Problem of Human Interrelations*, Washington, DC: Nervous and Mental Disease Publishing. Revised 1953, Beacon, NY: Beacon House.

Mullan, H. (1992) 'Existential therapists and their group therapy practices', *International Journal of Group Psychotherapy*, 42: 453–468.

Pascal, B. (1670/1912) *Pensées et Opuscules* [*Thoughts and Opuscules*], Paris: Librairie Hachette, Imprimerie Tessier (first edition 1670).

Piaget, J. (1949) *La psychologie de l'intelligence*, Paris: Colin.

Ritter, J. (1972) *Historisches Wörterbuch der Philosophie* [*Historical Dictionary of Philosophy*], Darmstadt: Wissenschaftliche Buchgesellschaft.

Rychlak, J. F. (1976) 'The multiple meanings of "Dialectic"', in J. F. Rychlak (ed.) *Dialectic, Humanistic Rationale for Behavior and Development: Contributions to Human Development*, Basel: Karger.

Sartre, J.-P. (1949) *L'être et le néant: Essai d'ontologie phénoménologique* [*Being and Nothingness*], Paris: Gallimard.

Verhofstadt-Denève, L. (1988) 'The phenomenal-dialectic personality model: a frame of reference for the psychodramatist', *Journal of Group Psychotherapy, Psychodrama & Sociometry*, 41, 1: 3–20.

—— (1995) 'How to work with dreams in psychodrama: developmental therapy from an existential-dialectical viewpoint', *International Journal of Group Psychotherapy*, 45, 3: 405–435.

—— (1997) 'Using conflict in a developmental therapeutic model', *International Journal of Adolescent Medicine and Health*, 9, 2: 151–164.

—— (2000) *Theory and Practice of Action and Drama Techniques: Developmental Psychotherapy from an Existential-Dialectical Viewpoint*, London: Jessica Kingsley Publishers.

—— (2001) 'The "magic shop" technique in psychodrama: an existential-dialectical view', *International Journal of Action Methods*, 53: 3–15.

—— (2003) 'The psychodramatic "social atom method": dialogical self in dialectical action', *Journal of Constructivist Psychology*, 16: 183–212.

Verhofstadt-Denève, L. and Schittekatte, M. (1996) 'Adolescents have become adults: a 15-year follow-up', in L. Verhofstadt-Denève, I. Kienhorst and C. Braet (eds) *Conflict and Development in Adolescence*, Leiden: DSWO Press.

Verhofstadt-Denève, L., Dillen, L., Helskens, D. and Siongers, M. (2004) 'The psychodramatical "social atom method" with children: dialogical self in dialectical action', in H. Hermans and G. Dimaggio *The Dialogical Self in Psychotherapy*, Hove and New York: Brunner-Routledge.

Vygotsky, L. S. (1979) *Mind in Society: The Development of Higher Psychological Processes*, Cambridge, MA: Harvard University Press.

Yalom, I. D. (1980) *Existential Psychotherapy*, New York: Basic Books.

—— (1995) *The Theory and Practice of Group Psychotherapy* (4th edn), New York: Basic Books.

Chapter 9

How does psychodrama work?

How theory is embedded in the psychodramatic method

José Luís Pio-Abreu and Cristina Villares-Oliveira

Introduction

Three decades after J. L. Moreno's death, psychodrama has expanded around the world. During this time, it has often been observed that psychodrama does not appear to have its own underlying theory, and a range of psychological theories has been used to augment the theoretical basis of psychodrama. Moreno himself may be partly responsible for this, as he proposed action instead of theoretical 'cultural conserves'. It is also true that external theories may be purposefully and beneficially adapted to psychodrama practice. In this chapter we explore these and related issues and describe how theory is embedded in the psychodramatic method.

There is a complex relationship between psychotherapeutic methods, psychological theories and scientific research. Sometimes, experimental research gives rise to psychotherapeutic methods (e.g. behaviourism), with theory developing afterwards. In other instances, theory is born of psychotherapy (e.g. psychoanalysis). In some cases, a non-psychological concept defines a new psychotherapy (e.g. systemic family therapy). Philosophical attitudes also influence psychotherapeutic models and theories.

Specific research is often done within each psychotherapeutic discipline, and often reveals limited results with patients who have complex disorders or across groups of patients with different disorders (Guthrie 2000). Research does, however, indicate that some types of psychotherapy work better with certain 'pure' disorders, and therefore shows that there is not a general theory about pathology and healing. New research paradigms are being developed, and it is acknowledged that this field is a long way from reaching a general consensus on this matter.

Irrespective of theory, the key elements of psychodrama remain consistent. There is a wide consensus about separation of the *group* and *dramatic* contexts, and about the psychodrama instruments: the *director* (the therapist), the *protagonist* (the client of therapy), the *auxiliary egos* (co-therapists, who can be chosen from among the audience), the *audience* (the members of the group), and the *stage* (Rojas-Bermudez 1980; Kellermann

1992; Karp 1998; Pio-Abreu 2002).

The evolution of a psychodrama session is also consistent. First, the director promotes an *unspecific warming up*, in order to see who emerges as protagonist. Then, the protagonist and director occupy the stage and cooperate to define the dramatization: the auxiliary egos are put in place, certain techniques are used, the meeting begins and the *specific warming up* starts the *dramatization*. The director progressively fades out, allowing the protagonist to act spontaneously. Once the dramatization ends, there is an opportunity for verbal *feedback* or *sharing*. The critical points of this process are the proposal of the dramatization and application of specific techniques, which are the director's decisions, made according to the therapeutic purpose. Thus, the director must know the ways of recovering health, and hence be familiar with some theory.

To develop a theory, Moreno provided the concepts of *role, spontaneity, tele* and *acting out*. Furthermore, he presented a model of psychological suffering (i.e. something that blocks spontaneity) and recovering (i.e. *catharsis of integration*, or jumping to a new psychological universe), which fits life crises and personality dysfunctions and provides a powerful framework for personal transformation. A wide range of psychodramatists agree that, after psychodrama therapy, the personality of the protagonist changes for the better (Kellermann 1992: 25). Thus, the question is: How does psychodrama work?

Matrix of identity

To answer this question, we must first recall that Moreno also provided a model of personality development. This model – called the *matrix of identity* – is frequently quoted in Moreno's writings, but only a few times is it described in detail. In *Psychodrama, Volume One* (Moreno 1978: 112–132), he describes three stages of child development – a *total non-differentiated matrix*, a *total differentiated matrix* and the *breakdown between fantasy and reality (the second universe)*. In *Psychodrama and Group Psychotherapy* (Moreno 1959: 115–118), he relates these stages to psychodrama techniques, calling them the *doubling stage, mirror stage* and *role reversal stage*. This is to say that children spontaneously use the techniques of psychodrama to develop their personality and cognitive apparatus. These specific techniques allow them to overcome each stage. In the first they use mainly the *doubling*, in the second they resort to the *mirror*, and the third is characterized by *role reversal*.

Moreno's observations about child development are similar to those of subsequent researchers that directly studied children's behaviour. One of them was Piaget, who demonstrated that children's activities, which are generally seen as children's games, have a certain sequence and are essential for cognitive development. Interestingly, these descriptions correspond to the usual techniques of psychodrama. Thus, it is worth reviewing these techniques and matching them with the age children perform them and their role in cognitive or emotional development (Pio-Abreu and Villares 1996).

Doubling

The double is an auxiliary ego who assumes the identity of the protagonist and develops activities the latter is unable to do. The comparison with parents and child caregivers is immediate. The feeling of confidence depends on the early and attentive presence of these 'auxiliary egos'. Sometimes, the auxiliary ego makes clear hidden parts of the protagonist's behaviour: for instance, expressing his feelings, or beginning a subjective speech.

This technique recalls the early interaction between the mother and child. Such 'conversational dances' (Brazelton and Tronick 1980) have been studied by Stern, who calls the resulting process 'attunement'. Speaking to Daniel Goleman, Stern observes that attunement differs from simple imitation:

> If you just imitate a baby, that only shows you know what he did, not how he felt. To let him know you sense how he feels, you have to play back his inner feelings in another way (for instance, the baby shakes his rattle, and the mother gives him a quick shimmy in response). Then, the baby knows he is understood.
>
> (Goleman 1996: 114)

These are the roots of healthy attachment.

Interpolation of resistances

This technique is referred to by Moreno (1959: 271; 1978: 283) while describing the cases of 'Robert' and 'Mary'. It consists of asking auxiliary egos to play in a different way from the protagonist's expectation. For Moreno (1959: 123), interpolation of resistances is a function of reality. In fact, Piaget (1978: 50) describes how offering resistance to the expectation of his daughter, Jacqueline, led her to spontaneously represent with her own body the expected but missed response. Thus, a symbolic cognitive activity takes place.

This process is not exclusively a child's resource. Without it, life would be an eternal repetition. Fortunately, reality itself offers continuous resistance to human expectation and so it makes knowledge grow. However, in psychodrama we can amplify this pedagogic resource, allowing the protagonist to be more flexible and spontaneous.

Role playing and sculptures

We have seen that children, when they cannot have an expected object, represent it with their own body. They can then move their representing body in order to discover how the object works (for instance, opening one's mouth while trying to open a small box). Piaget (1978: 48–94) makes a number of observations, explaining how these representations are the base of cognitive activities. By the age of two, children spend most of their time representing not only objects but also people they know or meet. Frequently, they act out professional activities. Of course this game is not merely playful; it is the background for cognitive and emotional development. Thus, before the first year of life, children are able to remember and recognize objects and people, but only after the age of two do they recognize that other people have different desires and beliefs from themselves (Welman and Lagattuta 2000).

These activities are similar to psychodrama sculpture and role playing. Through a sculpture, the protagonist can represent on the stage something that is problematic for him. Frequently, the director asks him to place himself inside the sculpture. This placement can begin a dramatization. Role playing, in its turn, is the best known psychodrama technique. It can be played by the protagonist, for instance, training for a difficult future interview, or by the auxiliary egos when playing the complementary roles of the protagonist.

Mirror

Everyone who interacts with children under the age of three knows the complex interaction they have with mirrors. As Moreno points out, babies are not initially aware that their mirror image is related to them. This awareness is acquired by the third year, when the child speaks in the first person. The 'mirror stage' is well known by Lacanian psychoanalysts (Lacan 1949). The mirror is seen as a tool of self-knowledge, and its role during this critical stage of development is quite plausible.

In a psychodrama session, the mirror technique can be used in several ways. In every case, the protagonist is an onlooker, observing their own appearance and behaviour, which is played by the auxiliary ego. The protagonist is frequently surprised, if not distressed, with this presentation (like the first reaction of children). However, if he accepts the mirror image, a new step in his self-knowledge begins.

Symbolic realization

This technique was described by Moreno (1978: 256) and defined by other psychodramatists (Rojas-Bermudez 1980: 41). Some authors (Langley 1998) call it 'metaphor' and observe that it is more commonly used in dramatherapy. However, it is also used in psychodrama, either changing the emerging situation for therapeutic purposes, or when a real scene cannot be represented on the stage (for example, sex or violence). To a certain extent, every psychodrama dramatization is a symbolic realization, since real activities cannot be completely represented.

Between the ages of three and four, children's spontaneous playing gets more and more complex and symbolic. Piaget (1978: 165) calls it 'symbolic combinations'. The analysis of these games of 'pretend' reveals a number of features. First, they develop a structure of thinking with interchangeable contents (for example, ants, cats or people alternately sharing the same events in the same place and with the same supposed furniture). Second, the child alternately represents himself and these imagined personages. Finally, the child gives his feelings and desires to other people and characters, apparently to accept some rules and prohibitions after seeing his forbidden desires projected onto others (Piaget 1978: 170).

Symbolic realization is a powerful resource for the development of imagination, freedom of thinking and autonomy. Children's games of pretence also seem to be important in helping them to understand other people's minds and to develop empathy. Children play these games extensively, until the cognitive development following the fourth year imposes a progressive preoccupation with more realistic games (Piaget 1978: 176). In psychodrama, there is an opportunity to revert to this enriched form of imaginative learning.

Soliloquy

In psychodrama, the protagonist is sometimes asked to think aloud. Depending on the timing of and opportunity for the request (sometimes at the end of a dramatization), such a soliloquy can be very clarifying. It is a way of assuming attitudes, feelings and qualities that were previously ignored. Thus, the technique of soliloquy is also an instrument of self-knowledge and self-definition, complementary to the mirror. Sometimes, a soliloquy can become an opportunity to make a commitment to changing one's way of life.

Soliloquy is abundant in children's spontaneous play. It is, however, mainly displayed at around the third year, after the development of language and self-recognition. Self-definition then develops, sometimes leading to an oppositional attitude at around the fourth year of life. Eric Berne (1983: 295) underlines some early decisions of older children that can subsequently affect their later lives. These decisions can be expressed by a simple soliloquy (for instance, 'I will never trust men'). Since it concerns interpersonal relationships, it promotes a sort of repetitive and standard-ized interpersonal 'game' with an anticipated end, in order to maintain a self-fulfilling prophecy (for instance: 'all men are bad').

Role reversal

The central technique of psychodrama is role reversal. After age four, children use this technique spontaneously, depending on the co-players they have (Piaget 1978: 179). The function of spontaneous role reversal in the play of children seems to be socialization and adaptation to complementary roles. From the fourth year on, children are more concerned with reality and collective rules (Piaget 1978: 180) and begin to develop moral judge-ment. Moreno and Moreno (1983: 159) describe how their son, Jonathan, corrected his upsetting behaviour after playing in role reversal with his mother. The Morenos emphasize the utility of role reversal for accepting rules and promoting socialization, in addition to a number of other functions (Moreno and Moreno 1983: 171–174).

In fact, role reversal is a complex exercise. While playing the inter-locutor's role, the protagonist also sees himself as in a mirror. Returning to his role, he can appropriately correct his performance and adapt it to the other's expectation. This exercise is frequently performed in one's imagina-tion during adult life, in order to understand the intention of others and adapt to it. Psychodrama provides the opportunity to actively engage in role reversal.

At this point, we can understand how psychodrama works. It is a new opportunity for the protagonist to develop exercises that construct his or her personality. This window of opportunity is open during childhood, but it is progressively closed during adolescence and adult life. Some people can take this opportunity at the appropriate time, others cannot. But everyone can recover these missed activities during life, and psychodrama aims to do this.

The philosophy of encounter

The term 'matrix of identity' can seem strange. However, it is coherent with Moreno's general theory about life and its underlying energy. In fact, Moreno (1959: 74) recurrently resorts to a trinity:

1   The *matrix*, which is the source of life, like a seed, an ovule, a child or a sensitive part of his body (the *zone*);
2   The *locus*, which is the appropriate environment of the matrix;

3   The *status nascendi*, which is the dynamic development of the *matrix* when it meets its *locus*.

Thus, Moreno is concerned with these beginnings of life – the *status nascendi* and the *warming up* – when everything is undecided but dynamic energy is growing. This energy, which is acquired by meeting the appropriate conditions, is called *spontaneity*. Moreno's *spontaneity* substitutes Freud's *libido* as the motor of behaviour. However, this new concept is more comprehensive, visible and compatible with known sciences than the postulated but hidden libido. In the present state of research, emotions and affective life have begun to be studied in psychology and neurosciences (Ekman and Davidson 1994), and they are candidates to substitute the general concept of libido as the energy of behaviour (and pathology). Moreno's theory is compatible with this.

In a psychodrama session, the *matrix* is the protagonist, the *locus* is the psychodrama stage and the *status nascendi* is the warming up. The function of the director is to help the protagonist in organizing the stage to create an appropriate locus. Then, the meeting proceeds, and the warming up develops. This basic scheme is very simple, but it is open to all the complexities of interpersonal relationships. Moreno was aware of this, and tried hard to develop the concept of *human encounter*, based on the growing ideas of phenomenology. He particularly felt that the ego was made up of the incorporation of other significant people, and could be enriched by new meetings.

Therefore, his model was directed outwards rather than inwards to the psychic life, and concerned with health rather than pathology. The ideal concept of *tele* (opposed to the concept of transference) was added to it (Blatner 1994). The theory of roles is also outward looking, although the division between *psychosomatic*, *psychodramatic* and *social* roles recalls Freudian instances (id, ego and super-ego). Moreno did not deny the psychoanalytic influence, but he was critical of it, and avoided going into its 'worn out concepts' (Moreno 1959: 56). Marcia Karp (1998) regrets this position, and argues that post-Freudian development of object relations theory is applicable to psychodrama and widely incorporated in its language.

In fact, the subtleties of the interpersonal relationship are precisely the focus of psychodrama. This is a complex issue, which has been making new advances since the study of autistic children, who have interpersonal difficulties. The present state of research (Baron-Cohen *et al.* 2000) observes that autistic children cannot understand the mind of other people (i.e. they don't have a 'theory of mind'). In non-autistic children, this ability begins early in childhood and can develop during life. Incorporating the mind of others by imitation and games of pretence has been recognized as important for this, since specific imitating neurons ('mirror neurons') have been discovered (Williams *et al.* 2001).

Empathizing by incorporating the mind of other people is an early and pervasive idea of Moreno's. It is what he describes in his well-known poem:

> A meeting of two: eye to eye, face to face.
> And when you are near I will tear your eyes out
> and place them instead of mine,
> and you will tear my eyes out
> and will place them instead of yours,
> then I will look at you with your eyes
> and you will look at me with mine.
>
> (Moreno 1978: Preface)

This view is surely influenced by phenomenology (the 'intersubjective community'), but it is also now a good metaphor for the recent discoveries of 'mirror neurons' and their relation to 'theory of mind'.

Body language

In spite of the importance of spoken language in the human being, meetings that promote life and, surely, the human encounter, go further than verbal conversation. Emotional communication, posture and proximity are the basic framework of human communication, and these are made visible in psychodrama. Words are superimposed on this basic framework, but they can be organized to falsify the true communication and, more than this, our feelings and emotions. Since the majority of psychotherapies are mediated by verbal language, they must have a way of discovering the hidden contents and tendencies. Psychoanalysis resorts to dreams. Psychodrama resorts directly to body language.

Members of a psychodrama group are encouraged to comment on the dramatization, including distances, postures and body movements (what they have seen and felt), rather than the open discourse and self-narrative (what they have heard). Body language and verbal discourse are frequently contradictory. As for the protagonist, he has the bodily experience of the dramatization. Thus, he takes home the bodily memory, and he has, at the very least, to reframe his narratives and self-definition.

People generally communicate by language. Through words, they try to modify and adjust reciprocal behaviour. This attempt is frequently ineffective, since the implicit memory prevails over the semantic one in organizing behaviour and personality. This is why pathological behaviour is not rational and behaviour therapists have resorted to conditioning. In psychodrama, there is direct access to implicit memory and body conditioning. The same occurs in children, who construct their personalities and cognitive apparatus not only by speaking or listening to adult talk, but mainly by playing and experiencing.

The group factor

Psychodrama is generally conducted in a group, although this is not an absolute requirement. Individual psychodrama is also possible as long as one or two (sometimes more) co-therapists perform the function of auxiliary egos. Some psychodramatists admit the possibility of the director alternately performing his own function and the function of the auxiliary egos. At the other extreme, an anonymous audience in public psychodrama replaces the group. In each instance, however, the presence of other people is indeed required to represent the complementary roles the protagonist has in mind.

In fact, wherever a healthy subject lives, he lives in small communities, which shape his behaviour and personality. Family therapy reveals how these communities, beginning with the family, have their own tacit rules, which are frequently more prevalent than the action and the intention of each member in it. Furthermore, people have the possibility of belonging to several groups – family, friends, playmates, school and professional teams – on an alternate or successive basis. The psychodrama group is, at first glance, one more of these possibilities.

However, psychodrama is not a therapy of the group, but an individual psychotherapy carried out within a group. This ideal purpose does not allow the director to neglect the dynamics of the group and the tacit rules emerging in it. He must be concerned with and work alternately or simultaneously with the protagonist (including the group 'in the mind' of the protagonist) and the actual group, in a well-balanced way. Although this seems difficult, it is what spontaneously occurs in natural groups, where people interact and also talk about themselves and their relationships. Thus, nothing is new, but a more conscious process and a therapeutic context closer to the reality of life.

Furthermore, the group is an interested audience that witnesses the protagonist's dramatization. Little is known about the influence of audiences on human behaviour. However, evaluating it from public personalities, their impact is decisive. People also assume professional or social roles in rituals (weddings, celebrations), which are witnessed by an audience (the guests) and remain in the collective memory. In the same way, assuming a role in a psychodrama dramatization can have the same impact as social rituals, where protagonist and audience come to a consensus about the legitimacy of performing the role. Thus, the group, as an audience, maximizes the strength of the protagonist's decisions.

The various audiences of our life do not need to be present. In an implicit or explicit way, people have in mind the result of their behaviour upon selected spectators. Sometimes it seems that the unhealthy life of a person is a spectacle to cause impact on a selected audience, which can be constituted by a social group or by only one person (father, mother, husband, wife or son). In the psychodrama context, Alfredo Soeiro (1990) developed this theme, speaking about the human 'instinct for audience'. If you modify the audience or make it respond in a different way, the spectacle will change.

In a psychodrama group, there are some people who avoid talking about or dramatizing their conflicts and problems, but they also improve while watching and commenting on others' performances. Life changes can even occur after leaving the group rather than during the therapy. In spite of explanations about psychotherapeutic strategies, the intimate process of sustained human change remains to be clarified. It can include new learning, reframing cognitions, modifying beliefs and non-specific factors. However, to be sustained, personal decisions must be free and not necessarily requested by therapists. Therapy within a group allows this freedom, all the more since the final comments are multiple and may differ. The ultimate decision belongs to the protagonist, after a process of psychic 'digestion' of the dramatization experience and feedback from the audience, auxiliary egos and director.

Conclusion

Some models of psychotherapy recommend a 'healthy' way of life and offer explanations – sometimes without scientific support – for the patient's suffering. Moreover, they are mediated by language and promote emotional dependence on the therapist. Thus, we can ask if they are not using the most primitive and directive form of psychotherapy: *suggestion*. Psychodrama may not be free of this sin, particularly if it adopts closed models of illness. However, if Moreno's view is adopted, it must be the least directive of psychotherapies. We note that the client of psychodrama is not called the patient or the subject, but the *protagonist*. Clients are the protagonist of their own healing. If you give them the initiative to the protagonist, they have the opportunity to develop all the resources of their unique personality. Thus psychodrama may not need a definitive, once-and-for-all theory. Its processes work in accordance with recent discoveries about the human brain, and it is open to new scientific contributions. However, to work with each specific protagonist, the director of psychodrama must be aware of these contributions. Psychodrama is a strong tool for personal development and change, but, as with all psychotherapies, it is not a universal panacea.

References

Baron-Cohen, S., Tager-Flushberg, H. and Cohen, D. J. (2000) *Understanding Other Minds: Perspectives from Developmental Cognitive Neuroscience.* Oxford: Oxford University Press.

Berne, E. (1983) *Introducción al Terapia de Grupo* [*Principles of Group Therapy*], Barcelona: Grijalbo.

Blatner, A. (1994) 'Tele: the dynamics of interpersonal preference', in P. Holmes, M. Karp and M. Watson (eds) *Psychodrama Since Moreno*, London: Routledge.

Brazelton, T. B. and Tronick, E. (1980) 'Preverbal communication between mothers and infants', in D. R. Olson (ed.) *The Social Foundations of Language and Thought*, New York: Norton.

Ekman, P. and Davidson, R. J. (1994) *The Nature of Emotion: Fundamental Questions*, Oxford: Oxford University Press.

Goleman, D. (1996) *Emotional Intelligence: Why It Can Matter More than IQ*, New York: Bantam.

Guthrie, E. (2000) 'Psychotherapy for patients with complex disorders and chronic symptoms: the need for a new research paradigm', *British Journal of Psychiatry*, 177: 131–137.

Karp, M. (1998) 'An introduction to psychodrama', in M. Karp, P. Holmes and K. B. Tauvon (eds) *The Handbook of Psychodrama*, London: Routledge.

Kellermann, P. F. (1992) *Focus on Psychodrama*, London: Jessica Kingsley Publishers.

Lacan, J. (1949) 'Le stade du miroir comme formateur de la fonction du Je' [The mirror stage in promoting the 'I' function], in J. Lacan, *Écrits I*, Paris: Éditions du Seuil.

Langley, D. (1998) 'The relationship between psychodrama and dramatherapy', in M. Karp, P. Holmes and K. B. Tauvon (eds) *The Handbook of Psychodrama*, London: Routledge.

Moreno, J. L. (1959) *Psicoterapia de Grupo e Psicodrama* [*Psychodrama and Group Psychotherapy*], São Paulo: Mestre Jou.

—— (1978) *Psicodrama*, São Paulo: Cultrix. (Originally published in English as *Psychodrama, Volume One*, Beacon, NY: Beacon House.)

Moreno, J. L. and Moreno, Z. T. (1983) *Fundamentos do Psicodrama*. São Paulo: Sumus. (Originally published in English as *Psychodrama, Volume Two: Foundations of Psychotherapy*, Beacon, NY: Beacon House.)

Piaget, J. (1978) *A Formação do Símbolo na Criança* [*The Origin of the Symbol in the Child*], Rio de Janeiro: Zahar.

Pio-Abreu, J. L. (2002) *O Modelo do Psicodrama Moreniano* [*The Model of the Morenian Psychodrama*], Coimbra: Quarteto.

Pio-Abreu, J. L. and Villares, C. (1996) 'Como lidar com mudos e quedos' [How to deal with uncooperative subjects], *Psicodrama, Revista da Sociedade Portuguesa de Psicodrama*, 4: 17–25.

Rojas-Bermudez, J. G. (1980) *Introdução ao Psicodrama* [*An Introduction to Psychodrama*], São Paulo: Mestre Jou.

Soeiro, A. C. (1990) *O Instinto de Plateia* [*The Instinct of the Audience*], Porto: Afrontamento.

Welman, H. M. and Lagattuta, K. H. (2000) 'Developing understanding of minds', in S. Baron-Cohen, H. Tager-Flushberg and D. J. Cohen (eds) *Understanding Other Minds* (2nd edn), Oxford: Oxford University Press.

Williams, J. H., Whiten, A., Suddendorf, T. and Perrett, D. I. (2001) 'Imitation, mirror neurons and autism', *Neuroscience Biobehaviour Revue*, 25, 4: 287–295.

Chapter 10

A postmodern approach to psychodrama theory

Renée Oudijk

> My Stegreiftheater book had three aims: To define spontaneity, especially in its relation to creativity; to explore the possibilities of interpersonal measurement; to experiment with the spontaneous interaction of small groups. As I had no precedent in this I had to introduce many new terms which made the book difficult reading.
>
> (Moreno 1955: 27)

Psychodrama theory

A legitimacy problem

While psychodrama is utilized in many countries around the world, its practitioners often look to other therapies to support its theoretical underpinnings because of a perceived lack of theoretical depth to psychodrama. Many psychodramatists work from other theoretical frameworks and often neglect J. L. Moreno's wide-ranging writing on theory and practice. Psychodramatists working from his legacy call their work *classical psychodrama*. Some other practitioners refer to psychodrama as only a psychotherapeutic method (as in *technique*). Such practitioners may be limited in their understanding of Moreno's wider vision, which is reflected, for example, in his statement that he founded psychodrama to spread his philosophy about man as creator and co-creator in the here and now of the human encounter.

As a psychodrama trainer and educator for more than 30 years, I have often asked myself: 'How can I help students to use psychodrama theory to reflect on their practice?' This chapter mirrors my search for an epistemological framework that helps readers living in postmodern times better to understand Moreno's theoretical position in the scientific field.

Structure and process of meaning-giving

I define the aim of psychodrama theory and practice as *understanding human meaning-giving*. According to Wikipedia, the free web encyclopedia, 'meaning' is an important aspect of philosophy but also a difficult concept to pin down, especially for scientific approaches that build their epistemology on the gap between thinking and being, object and subject, knowledge and values. While in meaning-giving both aspects are involved, Moreno argues that knowledge is not in the first place a reflective but an active, spontaneous-creative and unique process, that neither can be reached exclusively by observation nor by 'Verstehen' (a term from sociology and anthropology meaning, approximately, empathic understanding). As early as 1909 he developed *action research* as a participative, observing research method (Moreno 1955). He studied spontaneity–creativity, using *theatre* as a laboratory, and the *stage* as test tube (Moreno 1993). His subject was the human capacity to *take and give roles* and by doing so to create the own role, the World, and the Self.

Even before he went to university, Moreno started to develop psychodrama using the *as-if situation* of children's symbolic play and experiment (Moreno 1989). Using action methods, he researched meaning-giving as an experiential and social learning process of construction, deconstruction and reconstruction. Based on this early work, he designed a structure and process in which group members learn to research – as co-researchers – their main themes, under the pacing and guidance of a director/researcher.

Psychodrama: an epistemological problem in historic perspective

While J. L. Moreno was in a constant dialogue with the social and scientific thinking of his day, this dialogue is perhaps not as vigorous as it could be among modern practitioners of his methods. Psychodrama practitioners often say that their work cannot be explained by theory, without being aware of the epistemological background of their opinion. In fact, during the 65 years that J. L. Moreno developed psychodrama, many epistemological developments took shape that influenced his thinking. From a historic perspective, important influences can be detected in psychodrama theory. For example, Moreno developed his theoretical framework in encounter – sometimes antagonistic encounter – with the work of such thinkers as Freud, Marx and Darwin.

Looking at the essence of Moreno's writings helps us to approach his deepest motivation: the wish to turn human tragedy into *co-creativity*. As he often mentioned, Moreno found inspiration in the theatre of ancient Greece, reflecting the life force of Dionysus (Oudijk 1990). His wish to help and to heal was fed by his Jewish roots and wider religious inspiration. One of the resulting characteristics of his approach is a social-psycho-biological mental health approach, using *group psychotherapy* and *catharsis*. Sometimes he called his method *Shakespearean psychiatry*.

Furthermore, Dr. Moreno and his wife, Zerka Toeman Moreno, positioned themselves from the start – in practice and in theory – with their basic assumption that 'knowledge' has its origin in *encounter*. They called their method *action research* and organized clients, students and assistants as *co-researchers*. They researched all angles in practice and writing, in experiment and in discussion, in an attempt to integrate all knowledge in one integrated theory based on their shared notion of *humans as creators of meaning* (Moreno and Moreno 1969, 1975).

Moreno combined in his work an existential humanistic philosophical belief system related to Spinoza, with an expressive research approach. The results of encounter and role reversal he worked out in his *Theatre of Spontaneity*, using the qualitative approach of *Interpretivism* (Moreno 1983; Taylor 1991). A strong link to Positivism, as worked out by the Wiener Kreis (explained below) – mirroring the quantitative scientific methods of the natural sciences of prediction based on measurements and tests – is recognizable in his standard work on sociometry (Moreno 1993), and is also present in *Theatre of Spontaneity* (Moreno 1983).

Pragmatic constructivism and postmodern epistemology

During J. L. Moreno's lifetime, the epistemology of social science was developing, and Vienna in the first quarter of the twentieth century was an important cultural and scientific centre. The name of Weber (1864–1920) is strongly connected with *Interpretivism*, the qualitative method of 'Verstehen,' while the so-called 'Wiener Kreis' (1922–1936) – a group of philosophers and scientists organized by Schlick and Carnap – tried to bring the quantitative method into social science. They call their method *Logical Positivism*.

In this milieu, Moreno – even before his twentieth birthday – positioned himself as a man of encounter. He encouraged children to enlarge their imaginations and (co-)creative potential. He believed that people could improve their situation together, as they share central concerns. Putting this into practice, he organized the first self-help group of prostitutes (Marineau 1989). Spontaneity–creativity and co-creativity were concepts he investigated.

By 1925, aware of growing Austrian nationalism, Moreno was ready to leave Vienna. He considered moving to both Russia and the USA, and chose the latter. Later, he told his wife Zerka that he decided on 'the land of Dewey.' However interested he was in scientific developments, Moreno was a man of spontaneous action. This attracted him to the USA and to Dewey (1859–1952), known as one of the main founders of *Pragmatism* – also called *Constructive Pragmatism* or *Constructivism* – an epistemological direction that distinguishes itself as '*knowing by doing*.' Moreno's work often breathes with a constructive scientific spirit, so it is no surprise that many of his main concepts show remarkable agreement with Dewey's (Oudijk 2005).

A fourth form of epistemology that influenced Moreno's work is *Postmodernism*. This form of epistemology was born out of the arts. Living in Vienna, even before World War I Moreno was practising expressive arts in writing and the theatre. His involvement in expressionism, surrealism, Dadaism and absurdism laid the foundation for the postmodern character of his scientific work. Whereas some directions of epistemology tried to dominate the field, Moreno synthesized his ideas in a co-creative epistemological framework. Psychodrama philosophy practices a fluent process embedded within a clear structure. Construction, deconstruction and reconstruction of meaning are served by a multi-theoretical practice. One of his former students – a co-founder of *surrealistic psychodrama* – told me that Moreno used to say 'Das auch' (that too) when students came up with theories to explain psychodrama (Shearon, personal communication 2005).

Encouraged by Ella Mae Shearon and others, I studied the complexity of Moreno's theory in the light of a postmodern perspective. Unexpectedly and surprisingly, deconstructive philosophers such as Lyotard (1984), Derrida (1982, 1985) and Saussure (1974), constructive philosophers such as Dewey (1896, 1980, 1997, 2002), Piaget (1976) and Rorty (1979), and hermeneutic philosophers such as Gadamer (1977) and Taylor (1989, 1991) helped me to realize the overall congruency of Moreno's thinking. Reading these other authors, Moreno's texts became more and more clear.

The cornerstones of psychodrama theory

The first cornerstone: the canon of creativity

Before going further in the epistemology, I searched for the fundamental elements of psychodrama theory and found three cornerstones. The first one, the *canon of creativity* (Figure 10.1), is Moreno's model of the human interactional meaning-giving capability, and his axiom of psychodrama theory. The heart of this model is *man as creator of his universe*. While all six billion of us have the same gift, in order to let all this creativity not become co-destructive it is our duty to learn how to practise this potential as *co-creativity*.

In the canon of creativity, Moreno shows how creative and constructive meaning-giving forms the self (self-organization). All movement starts with *spontaneity*. Moreno's most quoted definition of spontaneity can be found in *Who Shall Survive?*: 'Spontaneity propels the individual toward an adequate response to a new situation or a new response to an old situation' (Moreno 1993: 42). According to Moreno, spontaneity – with us since conception – awakes *the creator* in us. By using our spontaneity–creativity, we give meaning to the here and now. In the experiential and social

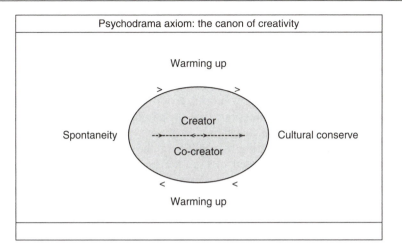

Figure 10.1 Moreno's concept of man as creator and co-creator

framework of meaning-giving, we create our unique, social, cultural and collective selves and our reality.

What is created in this model is called the *cultural conserve*, the result/effect of meaning-giving in the form of pre-formed *warm-ups, roles, role clusters and institutions*. For example, 'role' is a personal, interactional, social, cultural and collective concept. It is also an interactive phenomenon: by giving someone a role we create our meaning of 'the other' and at the same time, as a kind of counterpart, a role for our self. According to Moreno, *the self emerges from the roles* (Moreno 1985). Living in the here and now of spontaneous *encounter* ('Begegnung'), our cultural conserve contains our constructed meaning. This 'reservoir' functions for us as reassurance and as warm-up. Through encounter, meaning-giving structures are contents to deconstruct and reconstruct by spontaneity–creativity.

The second cornerstone: action research

Psychodrama as a method demonstrates the *canon of creativity*. Group members, caught to one degree or another in fixed cultural conserves, are invited to research their situation in a spontaneous, creative way, in the midst of the group (as an enlargement of their social, cultural and collective self). Before going further into the theory, I would like to show how this research works in action. The following is presented with the kind permission of Bep Lovink:

In the third session of a partly intramural assertiveness group, participants recount their experiences of the past week. One of them,

Lindsey, says she does not feel comfortable in her work. She feels left out by her colleagues. When questioned by the director, she explains that this feeling is new to her. She used to be quite communicative. The director proposes to play the situation. The group and Lindsey agree and Lindsey is invited to stand alongside the director, who asks Lindsey how she is feeling right now, in this group. Lindsey hesitantly admits to feeling left out, but points out that she is relatively new in this group.

Lindsey is asked to place eight cushions on the playing floor, with each cushion representing a member of the group consisting of eight women. Next, she is asked to take her place on one of the cushions. When she does, she spontaneously says that she is beginning to feel left out.

When asked to tell this directly to the other 'cushions,' she hesitates. She feels clumsy because her dialect is apparent. Once she has expressed this, she tells that this is why she often does not dare speaking her mind at work. She used to have more colleagues speaking the same dialect, but now two of them are gone, the dialect is out.

The director asks Lindsey to leave the play now and to retake her place in the group. The other participants are asked whether they recognize something in the play. Almost every group member can now tap into the own experience to tell about feeling left out, feeling inferior, being insecure, not daring to talk because of insecurity, blaming one's self for this, etc. Lindsey is visibly touched by the appreciation and recognition. Following the exchange of experiences, a lively discussion on experiences and the background of the participants takes place, and it is noted that Lindsey's problem, at least within this group, is gone for the time being.

(Lovink 2005, 2006)

The scene described here seems quite simple and easy to understand. Starting with Lindsey's first remark, the situation develops, guided by the director, in a natural and casual way. Playful Lindsey starts to develop her blocked meaning in a spontaneous–creative process of experiential and social learning. However, this simplicity is deceptive. Actually, a thorough four to seven years of theoretical and practical training, including self-experience and supervised practice, is needed to learn how to get and hold adults safely, in the context of a group, in such a spontaneous, open and vulnerable way, so that they are able to research their problems with naturalness and effectiveness in the midst of others.

The third cornerstone: the triadic structure

To understand psychodrama theory, it is important to notice its triadic structure. Figure 10.2 shows an image of the *grand theory of psychodrama*,

Figure 10.2 The Moreno building – psychodrama as a triadic system

pictured as a building with three wings, centred on an 'encounter plaza,' built on theory piles, with floors marked for research, methods and strategies/techniques, and as a roof garden, the actual practice of psychodrama. The three wings of this 'Moreno building' give space to the concepts that are united in psychodrama: 'Theatre of Spontaneity,' 'Sociometry' and 'Group Psychotherapy.' On the roof, around the 'Encounter Plaza,' so to say in the here and now, Lindsey's drama takes place. It is worth noting that I am using the term 'triadic system' in this instance to focus in particular on psychodrama. This is somewhat different from Moreno's use of the term 'triadic system,' which he used to describe his work as a whole (Moreno 1970; Lipman 2003).

From my perspective as a psychodrama trainer and educator, trained psychodramatists should know their way around this building. Based on strong foundations of theory, psychodramatists start the action research by trusting the method in which group members are considered as co-researchers. They know the techniques that can lead the group to spontaneity–creativity. When all develop well, the group witnesses the birth of 'insight' when the protagonists, with the help of auxiliaries and director, deliver at the encounter plaza. The connection between the words theatre–theory, abridged as: 'making a wonder visible,' in my view captures a key aim of psychodrama.

The postmodern approach as a fitting framework

To find a fitting framework for the richness and diversity of psychodrama, a postmodern epistemological approach is proposed. Following Crook et al. (1992), the value of postmodern theory is that it searches deep into the historic and structural roots of complex cultural meaning systems, and at the same time looks at aspects on the periphery. Under the surface and away from the centre, 'grand theories' show not their fulfilling stability but their fragility, their over-fragmentation and monocentric isolation. Postmodern theorists want to destabilize those underlying patterns. They see evolution in deconstruction, expecting that across the old boundaries new combinations will arise from fragments of the old (Bradley 1996). Psychodrama theory about *humans as meaning-giving creators* – developed by J. L. Moreno in often sharp contrast to other social and psychotherapeutic thought – seems to fit well in the framework and method of postmodern thinking, as it crosses the borders of scientific approaches and disciplines.

Analyzing Lindsey's play

Crook et al. (1992) analyze the basic dynamic process of postmodernization in culture, society and science on two axes: *differentiation and organization*: 'Putting these two together, cultural dynamics not only reverse conventional hierarchies of material and ideal determination, but play a crucial role in disrupting the autonomous and predictable developmental logics of human behaviour' (Crook et al. 1992: 229).

With the help of Table 10.1, it is possible to analyze Lindsey's play in more depth. Looking at the nine boxes, the most simple and at the same time diffuse way of describing her drama is as equivalent to children's symbolic play (1). Indeed, Moreno began to create his theory of psychodrama when he experienced and experimented with children's play in the gardens of Vienna (Moreno 1955, 1989).

In a more differentiated way, Lindsey's drama can be seen as a symbolic construction (2). Facilitated by the director, Lindsey – warmed up by the stories of the group members – tells her story and experiences strong emotions. Reading her sensory-motor signals, the director helps Lindsey to explore what is beneath her feelings.

In psychodrama terms, Lindsey's drama is called an *enactment* (3). This is the second phase of the psychodrama structure/process, consisting of warm-up, enactment, sharing and processing.

By looking at the next level of organization, more systematic observation shows that Lindsey's meaning-giving action of construction, deconstruction and reconstruction (4) is guided by the director in subtle but nevertheless firm ways. It is the director's friendly, open and trustworthy invitation to encounter which brings Lindsey from a state of experiencing difficult

Table 10.1 Psychodrama theory: a postmodern view

Psychodrama theory: developmental processes in state of	Differentiation		
Organization	*Simple*	*Complex*	*Hyper differentiation or fragmentation*
Diffuse	1 Children's play	2 Symbolic construction by sensomotoric and affective play	3 Enactment
Systematic	4 Mental construction, deconstruction and reconstruction	5 Psychodrama research	6 Healing by dynamic emotional and ritual social involvement
Monocentric 'grand theory'	7 Action insight by experiential and social learning	8 Didactic and psychotherapeutic method	9 Psychodrama as triadic system – 'the Moreno Building'

emotions and restricted spontaneity to spontaneous experiential learning. In accordance with the observations of Gadamer, we notice: 'The truth of experience always contains an orientation towards new experience. That is why a person who is called "experienced" has become such not only through experiences, but is also open to new experiences' (Delacour 2002). In fact this is one of the main objectives of psychodrama: to enlarge in participants their trust and capacity to be open for the experience of experiential and social learning (7).

To see how this postmodern framework helps a psychodrama trainee to analyze their directing, I invite you to look at the action analyses the director wrote (as supervisor I encourage my supervisees to write in the present tense):

1. As director, I invite Lindsey to explore in the group in a symbolic way her work situation and wait for assent from Lindsey and the group members. Lindsey will explore her situation not only in front of the group, but also as a kind of stand-in for the group. In psychodrama terms she is called protagonist = representative of individual interpersonal-social-universal human condition.
2. By doubling, I note that Lindsey, standing in front of the group, apparently is in an emotional state that is more or less comparable to 'feeling left out' in the setting of her work.
3. I wait for a sign of confirmation, and then ask Lindsey to stage the group situation in the as-if situation of a scene, which refers to child

play. I ask her to use the cushions to validate her 'constructed meaning' in a sensory-motor, affective and symbolic way.

4. For Lindsey, this clearly works as a warming up. Once she takes her place in the scene, the spontaneity of the creative process of meaning- and role-giving resurfaces and she recognizes the nature of the distortion. That I have done a good job in choosing this scene, is also apparent from the spontaneous transfer (Edelstien 1984) and recognition that this is the same problem she faced at work.

5. At this point, I make the didactic/therapeutic choice to have the group and Lindsey take advantage of the sharing of recognized feelings, in order to deepen and widen the theme, lessen the feelings of shame and strengthen group cohesion.

6. In the subsequent discussion, the group members help each other to mirror themselves and each other in an exchange of the increased self-insight.

7. It is typical of psychodrama that the vulnerability Lindsey tried to hide at first in order to prevent social loss of face, once staged, strengthens the group solidarity. The ritual of the symbolic play in the as-if situation is what facilitates this transformation.

(Lovink 2005, 2006 – presented with the kind permission of the author)

The analysis above demonstrates how a co-creative process of group, protagonist and director is structured by various concepts, mentioned in Table 10.1. It also shows that the director is not only skilled in the philosophy of the *canon of creativity* and the method of action research, but is thoroughly trained in the aspects of the triadic system.

Proposals for further discussion

Gadamer, in his book *Die Aktualität des Schönen* (1977), says that art is a topical issue, raising more questions than ever, since art is about truth. According to Gadamer, the uniqueness of art (and especially drama) is that it exposes the core of the human condition. Positivistic science and its objective, quantitative method ascribe great value to predictability and 'generalizability,' but the value of art is the truth of authenticity and uniqueness.

John Dewey warned a hundred years ago about the danger of splitting the world into thinking and valuing. One hundred years later, the supremacy of rationalism has in no way decreased. This is partly because of the far-reaching effects of successful technological developments on our daily lives. In psychotherapy, we see the results of the 'power struggle' in which the positivistic epistemology – in the Netherlands strongly connected to psychology – results in a strong belief in cognitive behavioral psychotherapy. Sometimes it seems as if humans can only imagine a choice between an objective, rationally oriented attitude and a subjective, irrationally orientated one. Constructivism and postmodern thinking offer ways to relink the far-reaching fragmentation of our world, which we create ourselves. That is one of the main reasons that the importance of Dewey's work is recognized by postmodern philosophers like Rorty and Derrida.

In this chapter, I have explored psychodrama theory from a constructionist and postmodern point of view. My purpose has been to encourage a full and wide-ranging discussion within the field of psychodrama regarding the richness of its underlying theory. I consider this to be an urgently needed discussion. Therefore I encourage my colleagues to contribute to the epistemological debate (see also Verhofstadt-Denève 2000 and in this volume), especially because the newest post-constructionist developments contain much of what Moreno described already 80 years ago.

References

Bradley, H. (1996) *Fractured Identities: Changing Patterns of Inequality*, Bristol: Polity Press.

Crook, S., Pakulski, J. and Waters, M. (1992) *Post-Modernization: Change in Advanced Society*, London: Sage.

Delacour, J. (2002) *The Heart of Things – Saturday 16th March 2002 – Obituary of Gadamer*, <http://weblog.delacour.net/archives/2002/03/the_truth_of_experience.php> (accessed May 2006).

Derrida, J. (1982) *Margins of Philosophy*, Brighton: Harvester Press.

—— (1985) 'Racism's last word', *Critical Inquiry*, Autumn: 290–292.

Dewey, J. (1896) 'The reflex arc concept in psychology', *Psychological Review*, 3: 357–370. Also <http://psychclassics.yorku.ca/Dewey/reflex.htm> (accessed April 2005).

—— (1980) *Art as Experience*, New York: Penguin Putnam.

—— (1997) *Experience and Education*, New York: Simon & Schuster.

—— (2002) *Human Nature and Conduct*, Mineola, NY: Dover Publications.

Gadamer, H.-G. (1977) *Die Aktualität des Schönen: Kunst als Spiel, Symbol unde Fest* [*The Relevance of the Beautiful, and Other Essays*], Stuttgart: Philipp Reclam jun. English translation published 1986, Cambridge: Cambridge University Press.

Lipman, L. (2003) 'The triadic system: sociometry, psychodrama and group psychotherapy', in J. Gershoni (ed.) *Psychodrama in the 21st Century: Clinical and Educational Applications*, New York: Springer.

Lovink, B. (2005) Unpublished notes. Some of the quoted material has also been presented in the course program for the School of Psychodrama in the Netherlands.

—— (2006) 'Psychodrama: toepassingen in Assertiviteitstraining van het AMW' ['Psychodrama in an assertiveness training program of a welfare institution'], *Maatwerk* [*Social Work*], 3: 4–6.

Lyotard, J.-F. (1984) *The Postmodern Condition: A Report on Knowledge*, Manchester: Manchester University Press.

Marineau, R. F. (1989) *Jacob Levy Moreno 1889–1974: Father of Psychodrama, Sociometry, and Group Psychotherapy*, London: Tavistock/Routledge.

Moreno, J. L. (1955) *Preludes to my Autobiography: Introduction to Who Shall Survive*, Beacon, NY: Beacon House.

—— (1970) 'The triadic system: psychodrama – sociometry – group psychotherapy', *Group Psychotherapy and Psychodrama*, 23: 16.

—— (1983) *Theatre of Spontaneity*, Ambler, PA: Beacon House.

—— (1985) *Psychodrama, Volume One*, Beacon, NY: Beacon House. (Originally published 1946.)

—— (ed.) (1989) 'The autobiography of J. L. Moreno, M.D. (abridged)', *Journal of Group Psychotherapy, Psychodrama & Sociometry*, 42: 1.

—— (1993) *Who Shall Survive?: Foundations of Sociometry, Group Psychotherapy and Sociodrama* (2nd edn), Beacon, NY: Beacon House.

Moreno, J. L. and Moreno, Z. T. (1969) *Psychodrama, Volume Three: Action and Principles of Practice*, Beacon, NY: Beacon House.

—— (1975) *Psychodrama, Volume Two: Foundations of Psychotherapy*, Beacon, NY: Beacon House. (Originally published 1959.)

Oudijk, R. (1990) 'Het koor' ['The chorus'], *Psychodrama Bulletin*.

—— (1998) 'The concept of the chorus in psychodrama training', in P. Fontaine (ed.) *Psychodrama Training: A European View*, Louvain-B: Fepto Publications.

—— (2005) 'Moreno en het pragmatisch constructivisme van John Dewey' ['Moreno and the pragmatic constructivism of John Dewey'], (workshop handout), Sittard-NL: School of Psychodrama.

Piaget, J. (1976) 'Genetische epistemologie: een studie van de ontwikkeling van denken en kennen' [Genetic epistemology: a study of the development of thinking and knowing], Meppel: Boom. Translated from the original (1970) *Epistémologie génétique*, Paris: Presses Universitaires de France.

Rorty, R. (1979) *Philosophy and the Mirror of Nature*, Princeton: Princeton University Press.

Saussure, F. de (1974) *Course in General Linguistics*, London: Fontana.

Taylor, C. (1989) *Sources of the Self: The Making of the Modern Identity*, Cambridge, MA: Harvard University Press.

—— (1991) *The Malaise of Modernity*, Ontario: Stoddart.

Verhofstadt-Denève, L. (2000) *Theory and Practice of Action and Drama Techniques: Developmental Psychotherapy from an Existential-Dialectical Viewpoint*, London: Jessica Kingsley Publishers.

Developments in psychodrama practice and research

The chapters in Part II include a range of interdisciplinary views that explain new developments in psychodrama practice and research. The authors describe work with different clinical groups and consider the full spectrum of psychological disorders. A consistent theme that emerges from their work is the central importance of psychodrama's positive, strength-focused, holistic approach, which emphasizes each person's capacity to heal themselves and improve their psychological integration when they are helped to gain confidence in their personal potential and increase their spontaneity.

Chapter 11 starts us off with a fascinating encounter with the transgenerational application of psychodrama. In 'Transgenerational Analysis and Psychodrama: Applying and Extending Moreno's Concepts of the Co-unconscious and the Social Atom to Transgenerational Links', Anne Ancelin Schützenberger discusses how awareness of life events in previous family generations is of great help to the living generations and their mental and physical well-being. The author presents research and theory demonstrating evidence for this. She also addresses Moreno's original concepts of co-conscious and family co-unconscious and develops these from Moreno's original formulation. Concepts such as unfinished business, the anniversary syndrome and hidden loyalties are used in the analysis of transgenerational links. Some clinical cases and methods of psychogenealogy and transgenerational therapy are described, including the genosociogram – a concept created from the standard genogram and social atom.

In Chapter 12, M. Katherine Hudgins describes her adaptation of the psychodramatic method for working with trauma. In 'Clinical Foundations of the Therapeutic Spiral Model: Theoretical Orientations and Principles of Change', Hudgins explains that the Therapeutic Spiral Model™ (TSM) provides a safe and effective model of experiential psychotherapy for people who show symptoms of post-traumatic stress, and mood and dissociative disorders following the experience of extremes of violence and/or natural catastrophes. The model develops from a well-defined and integrated theoretical base drawing on neurobiology, cognitive behavioral theory, attachment theory, object relations theory, classical psychodrama and experiential psychotherapy research. Hudgins also describes a clear and realistic definition of psychological health following the experience of traumatic stress.

The important themes raised by Schützenberger and Hudgins are nicely complemented by Connie Miller in Chapter 13, 'Psychodrama, Spirituality and Souldrama', where she describes her method of Souldrama®, which integrates psychology and spirituality through action. Souldrama is intended to help people see and understand their psycho-spiritual evolution. Miller discusses the importance of taking into account the patient's or client's spirituality as a part of their mental health. Many clinicians tend to think of spirituality and therapy as being mutually at odds – a kind of 'church-and-state mentality' – yet Miller reminds us that spirituality is not a synonym for religion. She also discusses how taking into account a client's spiritual life is likely to help them develop a higher sense of psycho-spiritual coherence which, in a health-focused model, prepares them for a more positive and meaningful life.

Chapter 14 offers the reader a captivating insight into the work of John Casson and other clinicians who use distancing and projected play methods in their work with clients. In 'Psychodrama in Miniature' Casson explores methods of psychotherapy which employ miniature objects to empower clients, and offers examples of working tools that can assist in the process of working in miniature. Casson also presents a historic overview over psychotherapeutic techniques based on symbols and play activities. He explains how the regulation of distance afforded by the use of miniature objects is a key element in their effectiveness, for example, in sculpting: placing objects into a symbolic arrangement with the aim of clarifying intrapsychic or interpersonal themes, in the service of the therapeutic process. The playfulness of working in miniature also attracts, energizes and frees the person to explore difficulties, solve problems and find new solutions.

In Chapter 15, 'Sociometric Scenarios and Psychotherapy', Anna Maria Knobel offers her innovative views of sociometry. For her, sociometry represents the 'understanding of relationship scenarios', which gives access to the way we see the world and can promote growth, making life more worth living. Knobel's approach to sociometry offers a model for understanding how groups function and how group relationships develop in phases – a useful framework for group practitioners. Knobel's model demonstrates how Moreno's tools for social analysis and intervention are also useful in helping us to understand and attend to the demands that our patients and participants present us with daily. This application of sociometry can help us to create responsive spaces that counter the oppressive realities of contemporary life while also helping us to rediscover what is most valuable to us in our lives and relationships.

Psychotherapists are increasingly taking into account crucial research into neurobiology and how psychopathology may link with the functions and development of the brain. In Chapter 16, 'A Neuroscience Perspective on Psychodrama', Edward Hug provides an overview of the key findings of neuroscience that are most relevant to psychodrama. He also demonstrates the neuroscientific basis of several psychodrama techniques. The author acknowledges important work by previous authors who have written on neuroscience in relation to psychodrama. He goes on to explore subjects such as: how hemispheric brain functions may inform the concept of spontaneity; how 'mirror neurons' may be seen as representing the neuronal basis for empathy and tele; and how the psychodrama director may deliberately choose techniques to assist integration of both right brain (e.g. emotional and body-oriented) and left brain (e.g. language, logic) systems. This chapter is full of insights about psychodrama and its foundations, and offers what may become new core elements of psychodrama training.

Anne Bannister also acknowledges the importance of developmental neurobiology, and its links with attachment theory in Chapter 17, 'Psychodrama and Child Development: Working with Children'. After an overview of Moreno's theory of child development and how it relates to later developments in attachment theory and neurobiological research, Bannister also conveys how Moreno's psychodramatic techniques are based on early childhood developmental stages and how psychodrama provides a way of correcting our present behaviour so that we will continue to evolve and develop through our lifespan. Bannister describes how psychodrama is particularly helpful for people who have suffered early endangering attachments or trauma. She shows how rehearsing the possibility of new ways of behaving can offer clients a gentle introduction to a new way of being and relating to other people.

Many psychotherapists, especially those working within hospital or mental health service contexts, understand how important it is to link mainstream psychiatric diagnoses with specific psychotherapeutic treatments in order to provide an effective treatment that all clinicians can understand and endorse. In Chapter 18, 'Psychodrama and Psychopathology: Purposefully Adapting the Method to Address Different Pathologies', Fernando Vieira and Marta Risques attempt to reconcile the values of growth, maturation and encounter in psychodrama with those of psychopathological diagnosis and treatment. The authors also consider how the psychodrama director may need to emphasize his or her differing roles according to the task and context. The authors show how an understanding of different psychopathologies can help the psychodramatist to strategically and safely direct psychodrama sessions that are sensitive to the needs and capacities of different clients or patients. They remind us that psychodrama offers a wide range of techniques that may be purposefully and effectively chosen and applied to address many different psychological conditions.

Continuing the theme of adaptations to psychodrama, in Chapter 19, 'Jungian Psychodrama: From Theoretical to Creative Roots', Maurizio Gasseau and Wilma Scategni present their approach to psychodrama as an articulation of the analytical theory of Carl Jung. The authors describe how the Jungian approach to psychodrama combines the important innovations and techniques of the psychodrama model from J. L. Moreno (for example, role reversal, doubling and the mirror technique) with Jung's approach to depth psychology on dreams, collective unconsciousness, archetypal medicine, the tendency towards individuation and the concepts of net and matrix.

While it is increasingly the case that psychodrama and related experiential therapies are recommended as the treatment of choice for people suffering from trauma and abuse, we must acknowledge the importance of ongoing research to further establish psychodrama's benefits. Part II concludes with an important meta-analysis of research on psychodrama's effectiveness. In Chapter 20, 'Studies on Treatment Effects of Psychodrama Psychotherapy', Michael Wieser explores the statistical evidence that we have for the effectiveness of psychodrama psychotherapy. He provides a survey and description of existing studies into the effectiveness of psychodrama psychotherapy, shaped as a narrative literature review. Wieser helpfully arranges the research papers according to the systematic categories of ICD-10 (*International Classification of Diseases, Version 10*), produced by the World Health Organization. He makes observations about the strengths and weaknesses in the research into psychodrama, and offers a number of indications of where further research is needed.

Chapter 11

Transgenerational analysis and psychodrama

Applying and extending Moreno's concepts of the co-unconscious and the social atom to transgenerational links

Anne Ancelin Schützenberger

Introduction

> The fathers have eaten sour grapes, and the children's teeth are set on edge.
>
> (Ezekiel ch. 18, v. 2)

Fair or unfair, it is an ancient adage that the sins and mistakes of the ancestors are passed down, to be paid for by succeeding generations. The Bible's metaphor of the unripe grapes is a metaphor for sins, faults, mistakes and errors, resulting in the more commonly known proverb: 'The sins of the fathers shall be visited upon the children.' It is only recently that we have tried to come back to another important saying, this time from Jeremiah, which holds that a person should have to pay only for what they have done themselves:

> In those days they shall no longer say, 'The fathers ate unripe grapes, and the children's teeth are set on edge.' . . . But through his own fault only shall anyone die: the teeth of him who eats the unripe grapes shall be set on edge.
>
> (Jeremiah 31: 29–30)

If we stay with the first quote for a moment, and consider its meaning for psychotherapists, we encounter a concept that can be understood as the *intergenerational* and *transgenerational* transmission of unfinished business. We distinguish what is known and consciously understood about the legacies from prior generations (intergenerational) from what is forgotten, not worked through or elaborated into words (transgenerational). I would add that it is not just sin, faults, mistakes and errors that may be passed down unaddressed from generation to generation, but also unresolved traumas, unmourned losses, family or personal secrets and any other unfinished business pertaining to animal, vegetable or mineral. These unfinished dramas and traumas from previous generations may be passed down and affect succeeding generations in myriad and profound ways.

Overview of transgenerational analysis and its implications

Can family patterns and problems, even traumas, be transmitted through generations as part of an invisible, unconscious but very present family inheritance? This is part of the unresolved larger debate over what is innate and what is acquired, which has been brought to a head by the recent development of transgenerational therapy.

Recent clinical observations and research (Hildgard 1989; Cyrulnik 1999; Ancelin Schützenberger 1993, 1998a, 2000) have demonstrated that images of past traumas and past family traumas can be passed down from generation to generation, for example, via nightmares and also by the occurrence of accidents on specific and significant dates. This can include unexpected deaths taking place on anniversary dates of specific family events, including the anniversary dates of past war traumas. Sometimes these accidents or deaths occur on the very day of the anniversary. These traumas are repeated by the transmission of visual images, smells, sounds, tastes in the mouth, fluctuations in body temperature (e.g. freezing cold, boiling hot), and sometimes physical sensations such as running, choking, sweating, feeling good, relaxed, happy, fatigued or terrified. These images and sensations are not experienced as hallucinations but as profoundly real events – an event relived – and they can continue down the generations, often until they end up some 14 generations later or even longer.

This perspective into family events profoundly changes our understanding of the make-up of the human mind and feelings, of personal and family history, and of psychotherapy and psychoanalysis. This perspective sheds light on family repetitions and has helped to overcome many dramas, difficulties, sicknesses and illnesses.

Hildgard's (1989) respected but not widely known research has shown that intergenerational or transgenerational transmission of trauma and unfinished business is a statistically significant factor in the development of some cases of adult psychosis, and our research has shown the repetition of car, mountain or hunting accidents, early deaths and traumatic events on the anniversary of the first one (when the first could be discovered). In some cases, these repetitions of the same event go back one or two centuries before – in France, up to the French Revolution (1789) and the terror of the guillotine (1793), in America as far back as the Civil War (1860–1864) and the War of Independence (1774–1783), in Ireland back to the time of the great uprising against England (1798) and the potato famine (1846–1847) and in England as far back as the Civil War (1625–1649). This kind of research and therapy, based on an awareness of prior generations, is a great help to the living generations and their mental and physical well-being.

How does transgenerational transmission occur?

We make the distinction between what is clear in a transmission, called intergenerational, and what is secret, hidden, unspoken or not worked through – but even more active – called transgenerational. Underlying the importance of recognizing transgenerational links is our observation that trauma and unfinished business that is not put into meaningful words expresses itself in illness, tragic death or accidents.

The hidden elements are like a hot potato, burning people's hands, which is quickly gotten rid of and passed down over and over, from generation to generation. This is a kind of backlash trauma, an open wound that needs to be revealed, attended to and contained by a therapeutic *holding* (Winnicott 1965; Ancelin Schützenberger and Devroede 2005).

This is how the French-Hungarian psychoanalyst Nicolas Abraham sought to explain the cases of certain clients who did not correspond to a Freudian theoretical model (Abraham and Török 1978; personal notes and discussions 1967–1970). It was as though someone else was speaking through the mouth of the client, as a ventriloquist. The client seemed to be 'possessed' by this 'ghost' carrying a dark, hidden family secret and 'emerging from a crypt' inside a descendant to manifest either physically or psychically in order to be heard. (This is reminiscent of the Russian-Jewish folktale of the *Dybbuk*.) It is only through beginning to see, understand and disinter the secret through listening and 'holding' its manifestation that a cure can take place (more on treatment later).

Relation to the co-conscious and co-unconscious

Freud (1953) gave us the theory of *individual unconscious*, Jung (1964) the *collective unconscious* and Moreno the *co-conscious* and the *co-unconscious* of families and groups. Hildgard (1989) and myself have separately identified the *anniversary syndrome*, and I use the concept of *extended family unconscious* as one way of understanding transgenerational links. I have also extended Boszormenyi-Nagy's concept of *invisible loyalties* to include *hidden family loyalties* and *invisible small group loyalties* in the analysis of transgenerational links (Boszormenyi-Nagy and Spark 1973).

Years ago, in the 1950s and afterward, I heard J. L. Moreno develop, in his front garden at Beacon, New York and all over the world, the idea of the co-conscious and co-unconscious as encompassing everything that happens between people in families and groups of close friends, teams of workers, and war buddies or pals (as in a surgical team or a platoon of soldiers at war). This theory was developed by J. L. Moreno primarily through his spoken lectures and demonstrations, and through discussions. He wrote relatively little on the topic. I rely on my memory of various long discussions with J. L. Moreno, here and there, during many years of professional association with him and his wife Zerka, and many informal discussions during more than 25 years. On the subject of the co-unconscious, J. L. Moreno writes:

> People who live in close symbiosis, like mother and child or like the famous old couple of Greek folklore Philemon and Beaucis, develop in the course of time a common content, or what might be called a 'co-unconscious.' I have frequently been confronted with emotional difficulties arising between individuals living in close proximity. I was then not treating one person or the other, but an interpersonal relationship or what one may call an interpersonal neurosis.
>
> (J. L. Moreno 1975: 50)

Moreno is describing here a process by which two or more individuals are interlocked in a co-unconscious system (see also Moreno 1980: vii).

The 'interpsyche' of a group or team can be made explicit by various psychodramatic techniques, thus making apparent the *tele*, the co-conscious and the co-unconscious states. These states are jointly experienced by partners, family members and closely connected group members, and can be enacted and shared. Moreno explains this a little more, writing:

> A co-conscious or co-unconscious state can not be the property of one individual only. It is always a *common* property.
>
> (Moreno's emphasis; J. L. Moreno 1980: vii)

Moreno's concept of the co-unconscious is not the same as Jung's concept of the collective unconscious: it is about team and family links and not generalized to the whole society. It is important not to confuse these differing terminologies. (Our own family's story is not the same as our culture's folklore, even if sometimes there is a contagion, or an overlap, between an individual family and the wider society and culture.)

During the 1950s I felt – and continue to feel now – that the concepts of the co-conscious and the co-unconscious are very important ideas – a 'key' for the world, for therapy and psychodrama. It is my considered opinion, after more than 50 years of practicing and teaching psychodrama over five continents, that the conceptualization of the co-unconscious and the family co-conscious and co-unconscious are among Moreno's most fertile ideas, as important as *role reversal, future projection, sociometry* and the *social atom* (Schützenberger 1948; Ancelin Schützenberger 1966; Moreno 1980, 1993).

J. L. Moreno had so many creative, seminal ideas that he did not, unfortunately, have the time to develop them all and to properly prove many of them. Some of us took up this new concept and worked on family co-conscious and family and small team co-unconscious to research and develop it from Moreno's original formulation. I have developed the concept of co-unconscious over more than 20 years in my work on family transgenerational links, family loyalty and the anniversary syndrome, psychogenealogy and transgenerational therapy. In this work I use the *genosociogram* – a concept I created from the standard genogram and social atom (more later) – as well as *psychodrama vignettes* and *surplus reality* enlarged.

The anniversary syndrome

The anniversary syndrome is like an imprint, repetitive and unconscious, of bad, terrible, unspeakable or even unthinkable traumas, and also happy events – in fact all the important *life events* in the family memory. It can include repetitions of marriage dates, and also birth dates (e.g. a baby born on the anniversary date of a grandfather's death, or a great-grandmother's birthday).

As further examples, the anniversary syndrome may occur when similar symptoms manifest in a descendant at about the same age as their ancestor was when an event with similar symptoms (trauma, illness, internment, bereavement) occurred. The syndrome could also manifest itself through a link in dates or periods, so that particular symptoms such as nightmares or panic attacks will occur or begin in the same month or even the same day as the original trauma sustained by the ancestor.

The American psychoanalyst and medical doctor Josephine Hildgard (1989) has demonstrated that, in the case of adult psychosis among women, there is frequently a repetition of the same symptoms through generations. For example, symptoms would be repeated when a daughter reached the age her mother was when she 'disappeared' (either through death or psychiatric hospitalization). When her own daughter (the third generation) reaches the same age, this daughter herself has the same symptoms as her grandmother and also her mother at the time of her traumatic disappearance.

The study, carried out on the patients in Californian Veterans Administration hospitals over a four-year period, found this correlation to be statistically significant in cases involving mother and daughter, and frequent but not statistically significant in any other family relationship. This is an example of the working of the anniversary syndrome in psychiatry.

I have found the same mechanism in operation among cancer patients, in the case of accidents (going back three or five generations) and also in certain illnesses linked to the upper respiratory tract, such as bronchitis, asthma or tuberculosis. For example, patients will be 'coughing and spitting,' reproducing the symptoms of a grandfather gassed in World War I at Ypres 22–25 April 1915) or at Verdun (1916) about a century ago. Such symptoms may be a sign of unconscious family loyalty and a symptom of the negative anniversary syndrome, which can occur in several siblings and cousins in the same family.

The anniversary syndrome can also manifest itself positively. For example, dates of births and marriages are often repeated through many generations. An example of this is the marriage of 'Renée' in French Canada (Québec) to a Frenchman on 28 August 1971, ten generations after her ancestor Françoise married a man called René on 28 August 1728. We had the chance to discover this because in French Canada there are registers of family history going back to the seventeenth century. For many families, such research about ancestors is possible.

Historical imprints: the case of the Kosovo

Invisible loyalties and the transgenerational transmission of trauma are often linked with special historical events as well as individual life events and family traumas. These historical events can include disasters, plagues, wars, religious conflicts, uprootings, killings or the displacement of various ethnic populations, for example, throughout central Europe – e.g., Greeks, Armenians, Slavs, Slovenians and the victims of battles in former Yugoslavia, including Kosovo.

The case of the repetitive traumas in Kosovo also points to the repetitive complexity of unfinished business among peoples, with loss, death and trauma being repeated there since 1389. This case illustrates the repetition of historical events on anniversary dates. The 'Great War' of 1914–18 was sparked by the political assassination of the Archduke Franz Ferdinand, heir to the throne of the Austro-Hungarian Empire, by a Serb activist, Gavrilo Prinzip, on 28 June 1914 in Sarajevo. The Prince's visit to Serbia was perceived as an intrusion on the territory and as 'another humiliation for Serbia.' His murder led to millions of deaths in World War I.

The date of 28 June is highly significant. It is the anniversary of the famous Kosovo battle of 28 June 1389, in which the Serbs were defeated by the Ottomans, and both leaders were killed/assassinated (including the Serbian leader, Prince Lazar). The memory of this defeat has been rekindled many times since. Most recently it was reopened – and the killing repeated – by the Serbian leader, Slobodan Milosevic. On 28 June 1989 – the six hundredth anniversary of the famous battle – he opened a new memorial monument in Kosovo, and made a declaration to an enormous crowd reminding the Serbs of the assassination of (Saint) Prince Lazar on the very place he was standing, and of his motto: 'Ottomans shall be stopped.' Never again, Milosevic told the crowd, would Serbia be enslaved.

The symbolism could not have been more potent, as Milosovic made his declaration in front of the monument erected to store the returned remains of the canonized Prince Lazar. Soon after, the killing of Muslims and the central European Kosovo war started, with fighting and massacres spread throughout the former Yugoslavia. This is a clear example of unfinished business and unfinished trauma, and it has returned for more than 600 years to the same place – Kosovo Polje – a place of ancient bloodshed (Volkan 1997).

The Zeigarnik effect (unfinished tasks)

Before working on group dynamics in the USA, the psychologist Kurt Lewin worked at the Berlin Institute of Psychology, mainly concentrating on Gestalt theory. In 1928, the Russian student Bluma Zeigarnik (still living in Moscow in 1980) was asked to research the topic of finished and unfinished tasks, supervised by Kurt Lewin. She demonstrated that unfinished and/or interrupted tasks continue to creep into our minds. These tasks stay in the mind and in our memories, often for a long time, as we ruminate about the unfinished task or what we could have done differently. By contrast, completed tasks are stored in the memory and can be forgotten in our day-to-day lives, allowing us to 'turn the page' and move on.

Myself and colleagues use the concept of the Zeigarnik effect to work with people who have cancer and other illnesses, including *frozen life situations* where a person's life comes to a frozen stop after a loss or trauma (Lewin 1948, 1952). We use the Zeigarnik effect concept to address the current and past stresses affecting the person's life, including personal and professional trauma. This work is aimed at helping these people to heal open wounds and past traumas that cause constant rumination – thoughts about what was left unsaid, 'unshouted,' 'uncried' and 'unfelt.' The hurt of injustice is felt, the pain of trauma acknowledged and contained. This unfinished business can include instances of sexual abuse, war and mass ethnic killing and unfinished mourning (Ancelin Schützenberger and Jeufroy 2005).

These sorrows and worries, and the hunger for revenge or repair, can prevent these patients from being in peace and able to relax and concentrate on healing and getting well again. Instead, they are full of stress, aggression and anxiety. Making the connection to the unfinished tasks helps them to start working on their health problems. Patients offered this help often get better and also frequently recover completely (Ancelin Schützenberger 1985, 1991; Simonton *et al.* 1978).

The Zeigarnik effect may be applied to all unfinished business, including that going back generations, such as family secrets, tragic deaths or unspeakable war traumas, for which mourning was impossible. Because they are often related to such past traumas, we look at the transgenerational patterns in cases of trauma, psychosomatic and somato-psychical illnesses. The 'unfinished business' can leave its imprint with events and physical and mental illnesses that repeat themselves through generations, following the rule that unfinished tasks need to have a 'closure.' The Zeigarnik effect of the interruption (called *unfinished gestalten* by the Gestalt schools of philosophy and psychotherapy) describes feelings and traumas that tend to be 'ruminated' (as in, 'chewed over') from one stomach to another, and repeated until they are fully 'digested,' because their meaning needs to be clarified (Zeigarnik 1927; Ancelin Schützenberger and Devroede 2005).

Biological and neurobiological research about transgenerational transmission of trauma

As mentioned earlier, Nicolas Abraham and Marie Török (1978) have suggested the 'ventriloquist' or ghost theory – observing that transgenerational transmission is like a ghost that is held inside a burial tomb inside a descendant. This 'ghost' is a formation of the unconscious which has never been conscious, and which passes from the unconscious of a parent to the unconscious of his or her child or grandchildren, or possibly also to other people in the extended family.

How might this process work? Many hypotheses have been put forward. These range from notions about the co-unconscious of the mother–child relationship, to the concept of *morphogenic waves* (Sheldrake 1995) and ideas about family and small group co-unconscious (J. L. Moreno).

How are family secrets transmitted? From the outside, things may look straightforward. The 'forbidden topic' may be conveyed through a frown or breaking of eye contact between parent and child about some topics, dates, names or periods of history or regions. Or it may be conveyed with a special silence or tension related to certain photos in family albums, or parts of movies, television programmes or 'home movies.' These behaviours cause the child to learn that certain topics, places, people, thoughts, emotions or actions are 'no go' areas – dangerous and to be avoided, and never to be questioned.

However, this process may not be as straightforward as it first appears, because these behaviours between parent and child, conveying and responding to the 'forbidden topics,' may not be consciously controlled by the parent or consciously perceived by the child. Nevertheless, they may still be conveyed by the parent and unconsciously remembered by the child. Professor Jean-Pol Tassin, neurobiologist and specialist in the processes of memory at Inserm, College de France (Paris), has proposed that certain types of interpersonal transmission of information occur in milliseconds, beyond a person's conscious awareness. Tassin has observed that certain types of data – e.g. memory of a traumatic event – may be stored in the memory not by the slow, conscious, 'cognitive' mode, but instead through an 'analogical' mode that occurs within milliseconds, beyond conscious awareness (personal communication 2005–2006; Vincent 2003). Thus we begin to see the neurobiological basis for the notion of 'unconscious transmission,' where information is conveyed without either person even being conscious of the facts or aware that traumas or 'forbidden topics' may be embedded in the communication.

Even though these memories may be beyond conscious awareness, they may still act on us, without our knowledge. To the extent that we are constrained by these unconscious memories, we may, alas, be no more than marionettes – puppets controlled by strings that are out of view of the 'public,' beyond and above our heads and our awareness.

However, it need not be a fate cast upon us that we must be haunted and controlled by these ghosts of previous generations. When *invisible loyalty* is constraining our freedom and chaining us, it is important to make it *visible* and stop unwanted, unhappy, unhealthy – even deadly – repetitions of the trauma, death or sickness.

There may be further biological (or bio-electric) factors involved in transgenerational transmission. As medical science and research progresses to discover more about the electrical and biological composition of the cell, we will learn more about the widely various mechanisms by which transgenerational and intergenerational patterns and memory may be passed down (Sheldrake 1995; Suomi and Levine 1998; Tassin 1998a, 1998b, 1999, 2001, and personal communication 2005–2006; Yehuda *et al.* 1998; Panksepp *et al.* 2002; Vincent 2003). For example, we may learn more about how some parts of the cell may store emotion, or how trauma may affect reproductive cells and even our DNA. The emerging field of *epigenetics* is helping us to better understand how social and environmental factors can influence the expression of genes (Petronis 2004). We are learning more about how *epigenetic signals* at the gene and cellular level may be inherited and transmitted across generations (Panksepp 2004). From an evolutionary perspective, one may hypothesise – and further research may bear out – that natural selection may favour not just the retention of the fittest genes but also the retention of transgenerational information about threat and danger, necessary to survival.

But we academics must be scientific, and thus cautious. Research in these domains is far from complete, and any 'biological decoding' is premature and will probably not be achieved for several decades or more. We mention the biological aspect of transgenerational transmission to note the important work being done in this area and also to bring this important question further into the realm of scientific focus and attention. But we must advise the reader to 'wait and see' as the research progresses and further evidence accumulates.

Treatment of transgenerational transmission

'We judge a tree according to his fruits' goes the saying, and we can also judge an action by its long-distance consequences for ourselves, our descendants and the wider world. To find the key to many family accidents and unexpected deaths, losses of home or money, or losses of mind (suicides or psychiatric cases), we often need to go up a minimum of three to seven generations (two centuries) to see the origins of the problem. The anniversary syndrome and its effects can sometimes be clinically halted, as we and some others have experienced and shown. We must look at and understand the repetitions of past events from many generations before, sometimes up to the grandparents of the grandparents (Dolto 1971; personal communications between the author and Dolto during tutorials from Dolto, then professional collaborations with her from 1955–1980; Ancelin Schützenberger 1993, 2004).

The recent developments in *chaos theory* and the understanding of *fractals* (Mandelbrot 1975, 1982, 1997; see also Chapter 7 by Remer *et al.*) might point to research into endless repetitions of the same family events. Chaos theory has already been applied to the management of financial crises and the building of highly resistant, irregular barriers against brutal sea waves. Chaos theory helps us to understand the beautiful creations of nature, such as a snowflake, a cauliflower or the coast of Brittany in western France. It can also help us to understand fatal repetitions, as in the replication of cancer cells. This same line of thinking may have the potential to be applied to repetitions of human events through the generations.

The repetition of traumas seldom stops naturally. It usually needs a strong, supportive holding container, a neutral place for the trauma, loss or unfinished business to be addressed, enacted, unburdened, whispered, cried or shouted at – a safe place for the story to be told, shared and held. It is like a decompression chamber in deep-sea diving. The clinician must offer unconditional support for whatever the client or patient says (Stuart and Lieberman 2002). Likewise, the clinician must let the client feel free to take any comment made by the therapist as a hypothesis waiting to be proved (not a 'truth' to be passively accepted). The client must also be allowed to end the encounter at any time, with no strings attached. This is what is meant by therapeutic holding (Winnicott 1986): a safe, neutral and nevertheless completely supportive space.

When we consider the treatment of transgenerational traumas, we should also be aware that words (talk therapy) may have limited use if the trauma is stored mainly in the body and in the limbic brain. Bessel van der Kolk and colleagues (1996) have provided evidence about how the prolonged stress of trauma permanently alters the way in which a person (or any organism) deals with future stresses and organizes to protect themselves. His and related neurobiological research has shown how trauma can be 'locked' in the body when we are unable to put into action our most basic, animal instincts for survival. Looked at in this way, the concept of 'unfinished business' is a very real concept. It refers to the body's unfinished, instinctive actions of *fight* (fighting off the attack), *flight* (escape), *pairing* (clinging to allies for protection and also to form a coalition) or *freeze* (to avoid being seen and attacked). Where such defensive actions are left unfinished, they may remain as undischarged energy in the body's nervous system for many years. This undischarged energy may present itself through the symptoms of *post-traumatic stress disorder* (PTSD) and may also be passed down to future generations in the ways described in the previous section. Psychodrama and related therapies such as dramatherapy, art therapy, somatic experiencing therapy and body psychotherapy, being forms of therapy that involve the body and emotions as much as the neocortical (front) brain, may bring great relief to the protagonist when the protagonist is allowed, during the session, to finally flee, fight back, be protected, avoid, mourn or otherwise respond spontaneously to (or bring to a close) a traumatic event or attack (Sykes Wylie 2004). This applies even when the trauma or event took place in previous generations and was not directly experienced by the protagonist, as the two clinical case studies later in this chapter demonstrate.

The instruments of psychogenealogy: the genosociogram and the social atom

We can address the issues of the Zeigarnik effect, unfinished business and transgenerational patterns with the help of genealogy, psychogenealogy (i.e., combining an extended genogram and genosociogram) and psychodrama vignettes that emphasize *surplus reality*, *closure* and *sharing*.

To offer a contrast, in classical or modern psychoanalysis, only the individual person is under disclosure or 'investigation' (Freud 1938). The treatment examines the individual's experiences, failings, sufferings and traumas, through their subjective point of view. However, in the intergenerational and transgenerational approach, we are concerned not only with the 'client,' but also with their whole cultural and family milieu going back many generations, which forms the framework within which the individual story unfolds and the individual brain and habits of thinking and acting (or not acting) are created and 'imprinted.'

The genosociogram

The genosociogram is an in-depth investigation into family and transgenerational problems. It can usually be done in one or two hours, especially when there is a focus in mind, for example, a terminal illness, the threat of early death, examining blocks to emotional health or considering patterns of financial breakdown or insecurity, bankruptcy, or the occurance of tragic deaths. If you are focusing on a single query or theme, the genosociogram can be done more quickly. It is better to have an identified quest or issue, to maintain the focus of the work or investigation.

The genosociogram is begun using the classic 'family tree.' To this is added all that the client remembers about the important *life events* and details of the parents, grandparents and further ancestors. This may include family sagas and family secrets – things that were at the time unspeakable or unthinkable, an avoidance of too painful reality. The genosociogram can be supplemented with further research via government and church archives, tombstones, churchyards, notaries, wills, old documents, war archives and war monuments.

The genosociogram also focuses on the bonds of affection and repulsion among and between family members in the family tree. It provides a quick and very useful, deep and encompassing look into unsolved family problems and unresolved mourning. It allows the client and the therapist to trace, like a red thread running through – and using a real red pen – the similarities in events across different generations, making visible the links between traumas, sicknesses, illnesses, and accidents occurring through generations. This can include occurrences of the anniversary syndrome and hidden family loyalties. Unspoken sorrows, griefs and grievances, various occurrences left hanging or stuck in the throat (*en travers de la gorge*) may be finally dislodged, or the 'bison's bump' (an abnormal hump between the shoulder blades, not related to spinal deformity) may be suddenly relieved when the weight of burden of unresolved issues is lifted.

This work is also the elaboration of a family story – a kind of legend or novel – encompassing three to eight generations, tracing and analysing the paths, through the events marking them. To look back at their specific family history – to put together and glance at 200 years in one look, with a clear red line running through and connecting significant events – allows each client to see how their own individual past is influenced – sometimes as plainly as a blueprint copy – by the events of other significant persons in their family history. The genosociogram shows to what extent the individual is the product of a family history, out of which he or she seeks to become an autonomous and free person (Rogers and Stevens 1967). There can be a profoundly freeing and relaxing effect when one sees at once the repetitions of traumas going back several generations or more. One can understand and let go of the burden of once again repeating the history. This relief helps to generate a rebalancing and a reinhabiting of one's own body, without tensions due to passed down burdens and pain. One can move normally and effectively, like a horseman firmly remounted in the saddle, finding his centre and balance again (or, at last and for the first time), free to create, explore and enjoy his own road.

The social atom

The social atom (Moreno 1993; Ancelin Schützenberger 1993, 1998b) is a drawing or other representation of the nucleus – the 'atom' – of what is deeply important for a person: their family and friends (living or dead), colleagues, pets, heroes and foes, their favourite books or music, their home or garden, or their fancy for guitar, piano, horses and cars. It also includes their beliefs (for example, some people want to die, and do die, at age 33, through their deep identification with Jesus Christ), and their 'inner objects' (what makes their essence – the thread of this person's life).

Working with psychogenealogy through surplus reality: two clinical cases

An example of war trauma being lived by a descendant may be seen in the case of 'Barbara.'

Barbara

Barbara had always wondered why she had such a 'barbaric' sounding name which had not appeared previously in her family. It so happened that on 4 August 1994, several months after the fiftieth anniversary commemorations of the D-Day landings of the Allied forces in Normandy (6 June 1944) – the beginning of the end of World War II – and several weeks before the commemorations of the Allied forces' liberation of Paris (25 August 1944), Barbara began to suffer from repeated nightmares, panic attacks and periods of insomnia. Her distress had occurred during the height of the anniversary commemorations of the war, when war imagery and recollections were omnipresent in the media and the public attention. She called for help during August.

We began working first on the images in her nightmares and on the timing – why they had started on 4 August specifically. When I started to ask questions, she replied, 'No, no, no! It's not what you think! It's not the fourth of August 1789.' (This is the date of the abolition of privileges for the aristocracy during the French Revolution, a cornerstone date in French history, as well known to French people as the 4th July is to Americans. My first thought on hearing that her nightmares had begun on the fourth of August had been to make this too obvious connection, which proved incorrect, as we shall see as the story unfolds.)

Barbara's nightmares were very detailed, with almost a cinematic quality. In them, she could clearly see men in grey, wearing a kind of 'round pot' (she described it as a chamber pot with something protuberant on the top or the side) and galloping down the hills on horseback. 'The Prussians?' I suggested. She suddenly exclaimed, 'Oh, the Uhlans!' as she realized that she was seeing the round, pointed helmets of the nineteenth-century Prussian cavalry, called the Uhlans.

We then worked on Barbara's family history and she drew her geno-sociogram, going back five generations. Our research brought us to a family in the Ardennes to which she was related. Having made contact, she visited them and found herself reliving vivid memories with her distant relative of the war of 1870 and the Sedan massacre of 1–2 September 1870. This massacre took place during the Franco-Prussian war, with Bismark sending his Prussian troops against the French Emperor Napoleon III.

The trip brought Barbara to the ossuary at Flouing (near Sedan) and to the memory of the barbarous carnage which had taken place there: 25,000 dead, 83,000 taken prisoners, thousands of horses disembowelled, and that is without taking the civilian population into account.

In our sessions, Barbara revived these memories in a psychodrama vignette. She spoke about and mourned the past. After this, she was able to sleep normally again. Her nightmares were gone, although a certain remnant of pain remained. So she went on looking, and she found out why her nightmares and panic attacks had begun on 4 August. In the Franco-Prussian War, the battle of Wissembourg occurred on 4 August 1870, a battle in which several of her family members had taken part and where one great uncle was wounded.

Barbara's discoveries highlight the importance of doing what we call a *frame analysis*, encompassing the *ecological niche* – a *psycho-historic* view of long-distance family life events taking into account all the information around an event, both 'inside' the frame of events and also that information which may be tangentially related. A frame analysis involves a free-floating series of connections within the psychotherapist's mind and memory. As Sherlock Homes stated, referring to his detective work: 'Breadth of view is one of the essentials of our profession. The interplay of ideas and the *oblique uses of knowledge* [emphasis mine] are often of extraordinary interest' (Doyle 1981: Part One, Chapter 7). It can be a great benefit for the psychotherapist to have a Holmesian respect for seemingly oblique cultural connections, so we do not make assumptions – for example, assumptions about generalized dates. In Barbara's case, her connections took her to the year 1870, not 1789, as I first thought. When using frame analysis, be cautious of the obvious. It is easy to think you are right, but only the client really knows.

Even after her discovery, Barbara continued exploring her transgenerational links with her family's past. For instance, when I asked her why she had bought a house in Normandy, close to the sea, she replied, 'If the Prussians come, I shall take a boat and row to England.'

'But the 1870 war has been over for more than a century!' I answered. 'And the Prussians from 1870 aren't about to give chase to you, and you do not need to escape by sea.'

It soon emerged that Barbara needed to relive and work through the nightmarish horror of Jules, her great-grandfather. At the age of six, Jules had witnessed the Sedan massacre (1870) while hidden underneath a tree, clutching the hand of his own grandfather and not daring to make a sound for fear of being heard and killed. We enacted in a psychodramatic vignette the battle of Sedan with Barbara (in a role reversal) playing the role of Jules as a six-year-old child. We hoped this would give her a lasting catharsis of this traumatic aspect of her family's past. I should stress here the importance of adequate de-roling. Just as we warm up to a role, we must also warm down. This applies even to secondary auxiliaries or those taking smaller roles in the psychodrama. De-roling is especially important when the person is taking the role of someone who is sick, traumatized, dying or dead, because without proper de-roling the person may be left feeling sick or unwell for a long time without knowing why. They would still be *out of their real body*. De-roling allows one to get back to oneself and avoid these negative effects.

Barbara seemed to have inherited a deep-seated fear of the 'barbarians,' holding inside herself a 'crypt' in which the unexpressed anguish of this suffering and death had been hidden and buried more than a hundred years ago, for four generations.

In general, to better understand how these transgenerational war traumas function, we look through family and general history, going through dates and places, especially (given the country where I work) those linked to Franco-German and Allied-German wars from 1870 until the end of the twentieth century. I have found that a number of these transgenerational trauma links are connected with August and September and also to the remembrance of Sedan, a place that figures not only in the Franco-Prussian War but also in both world wars (Sedan was near one end of the French Maginot Line at the time of World War I, and also the area through which the Nazis invaded France in World War II).

The cold reach of the guillotine (French Revolution 1793)

A psychotherapist – let us call her Marie-Paule – consulted me after having undergone many years of psychoanalysis and also treatment for problems with her throat. Her concern for the future focused on her responsibility for her disabled young brother François, who had been dependent on her since the death of their parents. She explained that her brother was disabled after an attack of croup at the age of six months. So: two throat problems. From clinical experience, I suggested that there may be a connection with the gas attack at Verdun in 1915, during World War I. Indeed this was correct: her mother's father had been gassed, 'coughing and spitting,' at Verdun. Having made this connection, she felt better and her breathing improved.

But something in Marie-Paule's non-verbal communication – hand held to her throat, her short red necklace, her birth in January, her attacks of freezing coldness, similar to Raynaud's syndrome – I associated with the French Revolution and the guillotine. She denied any knowledge of such a connection, but on a hunch I insisted that she investigate this possibility further.

Returning home, she did a computerized search for her grandmother's birth certificate at her birthplace in Vendée. By chance or serendipity (a term coined in 1754 by Horace Walpole, based of the ancient fable *The Three Princes of Serendip*, who were always discovering by lucky chance what they were not looking for but needed), the computer also produced a long family history and, to her shock, a picture of the guillotine with the names of five ancestors who were guillotined in 1793, and one named François, guillotined on 9 January 1793. Her disabled brother François was born on 9 January 1963.

With the shock also came a sensation of release in her throat. At her next appointment with her consultant, Marie-Paule insisted on a full examination, which revealed a striking change. Her throat, which had been constricted 'permanently' since birth (and considered innate), was now open and normal. The consultant could offer no medical explanation for this transformation of a condition that had been considered innate.

Three months later she reported being well, except for some terrible attacks of cold. We looked up the battles which had taken place in and around Vendée during the French Revolution, and found that one had taken place on 6 June. This was the date on which her brother François, aged six months, had the attack of croup which left him disabled. We discussed the horrors of the war, and the deaths. We looked up the June dates in a historical chronology and found a massacre on 6 June. At this, the temperature of her body came back to normal. Later on, the health of her brother improved somewhat, when he understood that there is an element of repetition to his long-term illness (i.e., he became ill on an anniversary date of a massacre at a place near where his family was from). He found this knowledge was helpful to him and eased his symptoms.

I have seen about 20 similar cases of people presenting with throat problems, and some dozen people diagnosed with Raynaud's syndrome. These clients have all improved using similar explorations of the unfinished business of bereavement in their past family life (transgenerational links of their illness).

Reflections and connections

Wittingly or unwittingly, fair or unfair, we can grow up appropriating – or ignoring or even suffering from – our family's past. But eventually we must differentiate ourselves from our parents and grandparents, and from their problems, secrets, traumas and beliefs. *Becoming a person* is a difficult task, needing separation of self from others, and cutting the umbilical cord. We must do this not only to be able to live our own lives, but also to survive in a fast-changing world, where strict past rules may prevent us from survival or adaptation. *To really live means to take life as a chance, a mystery to enjoy – and not as a problem to be solved.*

Life is movement, life is change – and thus it is unstable. As Kurt Lewin (1948, 1952) observed, the world around us is in a *quasi-stable equilibrium* – a small push can change it completely and forever. One could, of course, choose illusion, and refuse to open eyes or ears to the presence of life's demands and to the changing world. This refusal can lead to great tension between those with 'closed minds' and those who seek a deeper understanding of the world around them. Think of poor Galileo: having been forced – in order to save his life – to abjure his discovery that the earth is rotating and constantly moving in orbit, he still whispered 'and nevertheless she turns.'

It is no longer possible to rely on just our reptilian brain, which long ago helped us to understand either/or – for example, safe/danger, night/day, friend/enemy or mate/rival. Living in our past brain, we see a world of opposites and little in between: heaven or hell, right or wrong, black or white, master or slave, 'with me or against me.' Living with such an outlook, it is as if one hopes to somehow survive and, even more, hopes that one's children might survive, with the mindset of dinosaurs (Lewis *et al.* 2001). It is a craving for the sweet garden of paradise, or prehistoric times, or pre-industrial times, or, as Peter Pan calls it, Never-Neverland (Barrie 1940; Kelley-Lainé 2005).

Yet facts are facts, and time has moved on. The demands of our modern age – perhaps the most important being the growing recognition of the effects we are having on the earth's climate – require the greatest possible use of our modern brains and our awareness of our interdependence, our co-conscious and co-unconscious. Facts are stubborn, and one can never hide them completely, not from one's own body and unconscious, and not from the curiosity of great-grandchildren (or their imaginations, which can turn difficult unspoken reality into something far worse). Recovering family history through talking with relatives and doing research to find the open and the hidden story can help a person to mature, to become free, to *be*, to think, to evaluate or re-evaluate, to choose and become their own person – remembering the past, but free to choose their personal future.

We all have, somewhere in the past, a ghost in the closet, hinted at or hidden. As the Greek legend of King Midas reminds us, when one tries to bury a secret in the sand, in the soil or in a grave, the earth whispers, 'Midas, King Midas, has ass's ears.' I close with the words of the traditional song:

Make new friends,
But keep the old.
The ones are silver,
But the others are gold.

And my working motto:

Acknowledge the past, be faithful to yourself,
open your future, with no strings attached.

Acknowledgements

Some elements in this chapter were first published in *Caduceus*, 35, 1997. Reproduced with the kind permission of the journal. This chapter, written in English by the French author, was revised by Clark Baim in collaboration with the author, with thanks.

References

Abraham, N. and Török, M. (1978) *L'Ecorce et le Noyau*, Paris: Aubier Flammarion. (Translated 1994, *The Shell and the Kernel*, Chicago: University of Chicago Press.)

Ancelin Schützenberger, A. (1966) *Précis de Psychodrame*, Paris: Editions Universitaires.

—— (1985) *Vouloir guérir, l'aide aux malades atteints d'un cancer* [*Getting Well Again: Helping Patients with Cancer*], Paris: La Méridienne et DDB.

—— (1991) 'The drama of seriously ill patients: fifteen years of experience with psychodrama and cancer', in P. Holmes and M. Karp (eds) *Psychodrama: Inspiration and Technique*, London and New York: Routledge.

—— (1993) *Aïe mes Aïeux* [*Ouch – My Ancestors*], Paris: Desclée De Brouwer. (English trans. A. Trager 1998, *The Ancestor Syndrome: Transgenerational Psychotherapy and the Hidden Links in the Family Tree*, London: Routledge.)

—— (1998a) Discussant: 'Kosovo and unfinished business with war traumas', at opening presentation by Vladimir Volkan at 13th International Conference of the International Association of Group Psychotherapy – 'Annihilation, Survival and Re-creation', London.

—— (1998b) 'Epilogue', in M. Karp, P. Holmes and K. Bradshaw Tauvon (eds) *The Handbook of Psychodrama*, London: Routledge.

—— (2000) 'Le génosociogramme: introduction à la psychogénéalogie trangénérationelle' ['The genosociogram: introduction to transgenerational psychogenealogy'], *Cahiers critiques de thérapie familiale et de pratique des réseaux* [*Critical Leaflets of Family Therapy*], 25: 61–83.

—— (2004) 'Françoise Dolto (1908–1988): A glimpse at her life, ideas and work with small children', *British Journal of Psychodrama and Sociodrama*, 19, 1: 21–30.

Ancelin Schützenberger, A. and Devroede, G. (2005) *Suffering in Silence: The*

Legacy of Unsolved Family Traumas, New Orleans: Gestalt Institute Press. First published 2005 in a longer version as *Ces enfants malades de leurs parents* [*The Children Made Ill Through their Parents*], Paris: Payot.

Ancelin Schützenberger, A. and Jeufroy, E. B. (2005) *Sortir du deuil, surmonter son chagrin et réapprendre à vivre* [*Get Out of Bereavement, Get Over Sadness and Learn to Live Again*], Paris: Payot.

Barrie, J. M. (1940) *Peter Pan and Wendy*, New York: Charles Scribner's Sons.

Boszormenyi-Nagy, I. and Spark, G. M. (1973) *Invisible Loyalties*, New York: Harper & Row.

Cyrulnik, B. (1999) *Un Merveilleux Malheur* [*A Marvellous Misfortune*], Paris: Odile Jacob.

Dolto, F. (1971) *Le Cas Dominique* [*The Case of Dominique*], Paris: Le Seuil. (Summarised in English in Ancelin Schützenberger 2004.)

Doyle, A. C. (1981) *The Valley of Fear*, London: Penguin.

Freud, S. (1938) *The Basic Writings of Sigmund Freud*, New York: Modern Library.

—— (1953) *Family Romance*, in *The Complete Psychological works of Sigmund Freud, Vol. 5*, London: Hogarth Press.

Hildgard, J. (1989) 'The anniversary syndrome as related to late appearing mental illnesses in hospitalized patients', in A. L. S. Silver (ed.) *Psychoanalysis and Psychosis*, Madison, CN: International University Press.

Jung, C. (1964) *Man and His Symbols*, Garden City, NY: Doubleday.

Kelley-Lainé, K. (2005) *Peter Pan ou l'enfant triste* [*Peter Pan or the Sad Child*], Paris: Calmann Levy.

Lewin, K. (1948) *Resolving Social Conflicts*, New York: Harper.

—— (1952) *Field Theory and Social Sciences*, New York: Harper.

Lewis, T., Amini, F. and Lannon, R. (2001) *A General Theory of Love*, New York: Vantage Books.

Mandelbrot, B. (1975) *Les Objectifs fractals* [*Fractals and Fractal Objects*], Paris: Flammarion.

—— (1982) *The Fractal Geometry of Nature*, New York: Freeman.

—— (1997) *Fractals, hasards et finances* [*Fractals, Chance and Finances*], Paris: Flammarion.

Moreno, J. L. (1980) *Psychodrama, Volume One*, Beacon, NY: Beacon House. (Originally published 1946.)

—— (1993) *Who Shall Survive? Foundations of Sociometry, Group Psychotherapy and Sociodrama*, (2nd edn), Mclean, VA: American Society of Group Psychotherapy and Psychodrama. (Originally published 1934 and enlarged 1953.)

Moreno, J. L. and Moreno, Z. T. (1975) *Psychodrama, Volume Two: Foundations of Psychotherapy*, Beacon, NY: Beacon House. (Originally published 1959.)

Panksepp, J. (ed.) (2004) *Textbook of Biological Psychiatry*, Hoboken, NJ: Wiley-Liss.

Panksepp, J., Moskal, J. R., Panksepp, J. B. and Kroes, R. (2002) 'Comparative approaches in evolutionary psychology: molecular neuroscience meets the mind', *Human Ethology and Evolutionary Psychology*, 23, 4: 105–115.

Petronis, A. (2004) 'Schizophrenia, neurodevelopment, and epigenetics', in M. Keshavan, J. Kennedy and R. Murray (eds) *Neurodevelopment and Schizophrenia*, Cambridge: Cambridge University Press.

Rogers, C. and Stevens, B. (1967) *Person to Person: The Problem of Being Human*, Lafayette, CA: Real People Press.

Schützenberger, A. [see Ancelin Schützenberger]

Schützenberger, M.-P. (1948) 'Étude statistique d'un problème de sociométrie' ['Statistical studies of a sociometric problem'], *Gallica Biologica Acta*, 1, 1: 96–104.

Sheldrake, R. (1995) *The Presence of the Past: Morphic Resonance and the Habits of Nature*, Rochester, VT: Inner Traditions.

Simonton, C. O., Simonton, M. S. and Creighton, J. (1978) *Getting Well Again*, Los Angeles: Tolcher.

Stuart, M. and Lieberman, J. (2002) *The Fifteen Minute Hour: Applied Psychotherapy for the Primary Care Physician*, New York: Praeger.

Suomi, S. J., and Levine, S. (1998) 'Psychobiology of intergenerational effects of trauma: evidence from animal studies', in Y. Danieli (ed.) *International Handbook of Multigenerational Legacies of Trauma*, New York: Springer.

Sykes Wylie, M. (2004) 'The limits of talk: Bessel van der Kolk wants to transform the treatment of trauma', *Psychotherapy Networker*, 28, 1: 30–41.

Tassin, J. P. (1998a) 'Ontogénèse du fonctionnement psychique: de l'analogique au cognitif' ['Ontogenesis of psychic functioning from analogic to cognitive'], in R. Frydman and M. Szejer (eds) *Le bébé dans tous ses états* [*The Baby in all its States*], Paris: Odile Jacob.

—— (1998b) 'Qu'est-ce que l'intelligence?' ['What is intelligence?'], *Pour La Science*, December: 30–33.

—— (1999) 'Le rêve naît du réveil' ['Dreams start when waking up'], *Le journal des Psychologues*, December 1999/January 2000: 54–61.

—— (2001) 'A quel moment survient le rêve au cours d'une nuit de sommeil?', ['When does a dream appear in a night's sleep?'], *Journal de la Psychanalyse de l'Enfant*, 28: 83–94.

van der Kolk, B., McFarlane, A. C. and Weisaeth, L. (eds) (1996) *Traumatic Stress: The Effects of Overwhelming Experience on Mind, Body, and Society*, New York: Guilford Press.

Vincent, C. (2003) 'Quand les ancêtres deviennent fantômes' ['When ancestors become ghosts'], *Le Monde*, 8 October.

Volkan, V. (1997) *Bloodlines: From Ethnic Pride to Ethnic Terrorism*, New York: Farhar, Straus and Giroud.

Winnicott, D. W. (1965) *The Maturational Process and the Facilitating Environment*, New York: International Universities Press.

—— (1986) *Home is Where We Start From: Essays by a Psychoanalyst*, London: Penguin.

Yehuda, R., Schmeidler, J., Elkin, A., Housmand, E., Siever, L., Binder-Brynes, K. *et al.* (1998) 'Phenomenology and psychobiology of the intergenerational response to trauma', in Y. Danieli (ed.) *International Handbook of Multigenerational Legacies of Trauma*, New York: Plenum Press.

Zeigarnik, B. (1927) 'Das Behalten erledigter und unerledigter Handlungen', *Psychologische Forschung*, 9: 1–85. English version (1967) 'On finished and unfinished tasks', in W. D. Ellis (ed.) *A Sourcebook of Gestalt Psychology*, New York: Humanities Press.

Chapter 12

Clinical foundations of the Therapeutic Spiral Model™

Theoretical orientations and principles of change

M. Katherine Hudgins

Introduction

This chapter presents the theoretical foundations of the Therapeutic Spiral Model™, a clinically modified system of psychodrama that makes practice safer for people working on trauma-related issues (Hudgins 1998, 2000, 2002a, in press). The Therapeutic Spiral Model, or TSM as it is colloquially called, has clinically modified psychodrama interventions that are anchored into well-accepted theoretical orientations and principles of change for treating the effects of trauma. TSM provides a safe and effective model of experiential psychotherapy for people who show symptoms of post-traumatic stress, mood, and dissociative disorders following the experience of extremes of violence and/or natural catastrophes.

This chapter presents the expanded theoretical foundation behind TSM and the principles of change that make it effective with people across cultures, space and time. Most importantly, it offers an operational definition of spontaneity that is simply a number of roles that can be replicated and measured for training and research.

Goldfried (1980) wrote a seminal article stating that all psychological models of therapy must include three levels of definition to be reliable and testable. His categorization is still followed today by most psychologists and is the basis of the theory, practice and research of TSM (Hudgins 2000, 2002a, in press). Goldfried's three levels include: theoretical orientations, principles of change, operationalized (manualized) interventions.

Theoretical orientations

An effective model of psychotherapy must have one or more guiding theories of child development, personality development and interpersonal relationships that explain why humans act like they do. As you will see, TSM advances an integrated clinical theory base to define psychological health following the experience of traumatic stress, drawing on neuro-biology, cognitive behavioral theory, attachment theory, object relations theory, classical psychodrama and experiential psychotherapy research. Together, they define the eight 'prescriptive roles' needed to access spontaneity as the curative agent of change.

Principles of change

A good model of psychotherapy must have one or more explanations of what makes people change. Research has shown that there are some principles of change that cause change in any good psychotherapy session, for example, empathy and unconditional positive regard (Rogers 1957). In fact, a number of the change agents in experiential therapy, such as active experiencing, have been found to create change regardless of theoretical orientation (Elliott *et al.* 2002). In the case of the TSM, there are six principles of change that safely guide experiential methods with people who have post-traumatic stress disorder (PTSD) and other stress-related problems:

* active experiencing of self-organization
* empathic bonding with others
* accessing spontaneity and creativity for new self-organization
* safe adaptive use of affect for emotional release and repair
* controlled regression in the service of the ego
* accurate labeling for new personal narratives to guide the future.

These six theoretical principles of change are discussed in more detail on p. 181.

Operationalized (manualized) interventions

In Goldfried's system, each intervention must have written step-by-step directions about how to teach, implement and research it, so effectiveness can be trained and tested. Manualized interventions also make it clinically possible to reliably predict what will happen when your intervention is used, thus making psychodrama safer for all. The TSM has 14 intrapsychic 'advanced action intervention modules,' with two of them, the 'body double' and the 'containing double,' currently in research studies.

Therapeutic Spiral Model™

The TSM is such a clearly defined clinical model of intrapsychic psychological change. TSM is a system of modified psychodrama for people who have suffered traumatic stress and/or violence in their lives. TSM has been used to treat survivors of war, political and religious persecution, cult and clergy abuse, torture, kidnapping, forced resettlement, poverty, racism, sexual and physical abuse, addiction, earthquakes, floods, fires, illness and accidents.

A crucial aspect of TSM is that it is conducted by a team of clinicians – the action trauma team. Each team consists of trained clinicians including a team leader, an assistant leader and number of trained auxiliary egos. All of the team members are trained to use the modified psychodrama methods of TSM with trauma survivors. It is my belief that deep experiential work with trauma survivors should not be done alone, if at all possible. It is too draining on the providers and may not be containing enough for clients. The primitive defenses and vulnerable self-organization of most trauma survivors must be treated with respect in order to prevent the risk of retraumatization, uncontrolled regression or unconscious abreaction with experiential methods (Hudgins 2002a).

TSM uses Terr's definition of trauma as 'an external blow or series of blows rendering the person temporarily helpless and breaking past ordinary coping and defensive operations' (Terr 1991: 12). This definition is inclusive and based on how a person actually experiences a traumatic event, not on what caused the stress. It shows the effects of trauma are caused by a real event.

In terms of theoretical advances in psychodrama, TSM focuses on intrapsychic change and has operationally defined the state of spontaneity. From the perspective of the TSM model, spontaneity results from the enactment of eight 'prescriptive roles' that can produce stable self-organization in the face of trauma. TSM also contributes an advanced clinical map to guide the safe use of all experiential interventions: the 'trauma survivor's intrapsychic role atom' (TSIRA; more on this in the following sections).

Theoretical orientations in TSM

The Therapeutic Spiral Model™ provides a comprehensive theoretical foundation for treating the effects of trauma in the global community. Drawing on the original theories of human development that influenced TSM, this chapter includes a broader theoretical perspective to understand how overwhelming stress affects body, mind, emotion and spirit. Together these theories describe healthy self-organization as the operationalized state of spontaneity – the goal of all psychodrama interventions (Moreno 1973). These include the following medical, psychological and behavioral theories of human functioning.

The neurobiology of trauma: body

Using brain imagery, researchers have shown that unprocessed trauma experiences are stored in the nonverbal, emotional centers of the limbic system, where they are inaccessible to words. This clearly suggests experiential therapy, such as TSM, is a treatment of choice for people who have experienced violence and overwhelming stress (van der Kolk 2003). (See Chapter 16 by Hug; Hug in press, describing the neurobiological correlates of several TSM operationalized interventions.)

Cognitive behavioral therapy: mind

The theories of mind in cognitive behavioural therapy (CBT) explain the role of cognitive schemas, negative introjects and maladaptive coping strategies that are internalized by traumatic experiences. Many of the CBT and classical psychodrama interventions are remarkably alike (Treadwell *et al.* 2003). Drawing on CBT, TSM places an equal emphasis on cognitive and expressive interventions, aiming at all times to maintain a state of conscious spontaneity where new roles can be created for psychological change.

Attachment theory: mind/emotion

Research into family therapy and social systems shows that the psychological and neurophysiological attachment bond to self and others is damaged when someone experiences traumatic stress, especially when it is human-caused violence (Siegel 1999). TSM builds intrapsychic strengths and interpersonal connections through its 'prescriptive roles' to form healthy attachment bonds to self, others and the world as part of clinical treatment.

Object relations theory: mind/emotion

The psychodynamic view of self-development shows the importance of early childhood experiences on stable self-organization (Stern 1985, 1990). Object relations theory describes the intrapsychic internalization of representative templates of 'self and object/other' and how they are affected by overwhelming stress and the experience of helplessness (Holmes 1992). Following trauma, a person may internalize what the TSM model describes as the trauma-based roles of victim, perpetrator and abandoning authority. To counteract those internalized roles, TSM prescribes roles of observation, restoration and containment for healthy personality development.

Spontaneity and creativity theory: spirit

Drawing on the essence of classical psychodrama, TSM views psychological health as the development of spontaneity and creativity (Moreno 1953; Moreno *et al.* 2000). For people who have experienced the true helplessness of PTSD, the view of self as spontaneous and creative is an antidote to years of despair. TSM operationally defines spontaneity in the following way (Hudgins 2002a, 2000b):

> Spontaneity develops when the protagonist actively experiences the eight TSM 'prescriptive roles' to demonstrate stable self-organization and connection to others.

Increasing creativity is the goal of all experiential interventions in the Therapeutic Spiral Model™.

Role theory: integrating body, mind, emotion and spirit

Role theory, another core theory of psychodrama (Moreno and Moreno 1969; Blatner 1991) helps 'normalize' the pathology people can experience as a result of the right-brained, nonverbal, emotional, limbic system symptoms of PTSD: body memories, flashbacks, ego state shifts, and dissociation. Instead of psychiatric labels, TSM uses the 'trauma survivor's intrapsychic role atom' (TSIRA; Hudgins 2002a), to assess personality functioning and pinpoint where there are decreases in spontaneity. Just as a social atom depicts the minimum number of roles needed for interpersonal equilibrium, the TSIRA details the minimum number of internal roles needed for stable personality functioning following traumatic stress. The TSIRA is a clinical map of 'prescriptive,' 'trauma-based,' and 'transformative' roles that guide clinical action interventions at all times in TSM.

Summary of theoretical orientation

In summary of its theoretical orientations, TSM views human functioning from an experiential perspective on personality. As Moreno wrote:

> The spontaneity state . . . does not arise automatically; it is not pre-existent. It is brought forth by an act of will.
>
> (Moreno 1973: 44)

> The self is like a river, it springs from spontaneity but it has many [tributaries] which carry supply to it.
>
> (Moreno 1973: 8)

More specifically, TSM defines the state of spontaneity that promotes stable self-organization following the experience of stress. The eight prescriptive roles are:

1   'Observing ego.'
2   The 'client role.'

3 'Intrapsychic strength.'
4 'Interpersonal strength.'
5 'Transpersonal strength.'
6 'Body double.'
7 'Containing double.'
8 'Manager of defenses.'

The model is more fully explained in Hudgins (2002a). For many survivors of trauma, the image of a spontaneous and creative self brings hope amidst despair for the first time.

Experiential psychotherapy research: the evidence

Research now shows that experiential methods *are equal to* psychodynamic and cognitive behavioral methods of treatment for general psychiatric difficulties, and *better* for stress-related diagnoses such as PTSD and anxiety disorders (Elliott *et al.* 1998, 2002; Greenberg *et al.* 1998). In fact, the *Handbook of Psychotherapy and Behavior Change* (Greenberg *et al.* 1994; Lambert *et al.* 2003), the psychologist's bible in the USA, details success over two decades of quantitative research on experiential psychotherapy.

In the past ten years, classical psychodrama has shown success with populations from addictions (Dayton 2000) to dissociative identity disorder (Altman 2000; Leutz 2000) to sexual offenders (Baim 2000; Robson 2000). It has been used with adolescents (Cossa 2002) and families (Chimera 2002).

Johnson (2000) calls for a clinical system of experiential therapy to test its effectiveness on PTSD. TSM is the answer to this call, with its definition of spontaneity, operationalized experiential interventions, and the clinical map of the TSIRA.

Research on TSM has shown treatment effectiveness across populations and applications. Client and therapist self-report measures show an average 92 per cent improvement in trauma symptoms after a three-day TSM workshop. A single-case design with a client diagnosed with PTSD demonstrated a decrease in dissociation and general trauma symptoms across three individual therapy sessions using the containing double (Hudgins *et al.* 2000). Another study showed effectiveness with addictions (Forst 2001). An eight-day program of education, training and self-care for community leaders affected by the terrorist attack in Washington, DC, funded by the University of Virginia, found significant decreases in post-traumatic anxiety and depression (Hudgins in press). A change-process study identifying moments of change shows a number of therapeutic factors contribute to the success of TSM (McVea and Gow 2006).

A pilot study on the effectiveness of TSM across cultures has collected pre-and-post test data on all training and personal growth workshops using

TSM. The data from Canada, mainland China, England, South Africa, Taiwan and the USA show similar decreases in anxiety, depression and dissociation across cultures.

TSM clinical principles of change

We now turn to the six theoretical principles of change that guide all of the TSM clinically modified psychodrama interventions shown in the following clinical case examples:

- active experiencing of self-organization
- empathic bonding with others
- accessing spontaneity and creativity for new self-organization
- safe adaptive use of affect for emotional release and repair
- controlled regression in the service of the ego
- accurate labeling for new personal narratives to guide the future.

Each principle is briefly described. A few are illustrated by composite clinical examples using the TSIRA to guide TSM practice with protagonists working on stories of trauma or violence. The client examples have been significantly changed in order to protect the confidentiality of the many protagonists who have used TSM in the past 15 years.

Active experiencing of self-organization

Defined by Gendlin (1996), active experiencing is the ability to be consciously aware of the flow of bodily felt experience from sensation and perception to integrated self-organization in the here and now. Active experiencing is the ability to both experience the self in the present moment, while simultaneously being able to self-reflect and make meaning of that experiencing.

All experiential psychotherapies directly target changes in active experiencing of self in ways that talk therapy does not. Moving one's body, noticing breathing, taking a walk with your client – all of these are standard interventions in experiential therapies. Zerka Moreno et al. (2000) describes it as 'surplus reality,' a rich source of experiential information about one's internal reality that is accessible in the here and now. TSM sees people as having a core state of spontaneity and creativity that must be actively experienced for trauma repair. In the following example, I direct a protagonist from a state of depletion and terror to the state of spontaneity and stable self-organization provided by the TSM 'prescriptive roles'.

Mei Feng is a middle-aged woman in a TSM group in Nantou County, Taiwan. She asks to develop the strength to leave her husband who is domestically violent. The group chooses her to be the protagonist.

Mei Feng begins her drama by collapsing into tears the moment we begin a walk and talk to establish a clinical contract for this session. She says, 'I am afraid to even work on this question. I am afraid he will know I am doing it.' Clearly, her limbic system is taking over her cognitive functions and she is losing her ability to stay present in the here and now. Rather than following her to the past, I clinically intervene to help increase her active experiencing of the TSM prescriptive roles to stabilize self-organization and increase spontaneity.

As a clinical director, I immediately interrupt the seductive pull down into the trauma spiral of unprocessed, right-brained images, sensations, body memories, intense affect, and survival coping skills that is trying to take over her active experience of needed strengths and connections. I step in as her 'body double' (Hudgins 2002b; Burden and Ciotola 2003; Ciotola 2004) in order to increase her active experience of healthy body awareness, to focus her attention in the present. I tell her. 'We need to stop right here and get you some strengths and support, so you can, in fact, face some of your fears about being hurt by your husband. Take a few deep breaths to steady yourself. I am going to stand next to you and become your body double and help you ground in the present. I will speak in the first person, as a helpful part of you. A part that can help you stay safe in the moment. OK?' [Protagonist gives nonverbal nod OK.]

I step in as body double, standing beside the protagonist, and speak: 'I can take a few deep breaths . . . and . . . as I . . . [audible breathing by BD] do this, my mind slows down . . . and I feel a bit calmer. I can look around this room. I am at the social services TSM group. I am safe. Silence . . . breath . . . Maybe, I can draw on the image of a strong, sturdy tree. [More audible breathing by BD.] I can feel my roots go into the ground . . . ah, yes . . . that is . . . better. I am a big strong tree that has faced a lot of storms and is still standing.'

Protagonist: [Audible breathing in response.] 'I can slow down. Yes, I can look around the room and see the other people in the group. I can feel . . . myself . . . as a tree . . . a Chinese tree . . . that has been around for . . . 3000 years. I have given solace to many and I am well rooted in the earth.'

Kate as Director: 'Great, so pick someone to be that tree and we can concretize it as a transpersonal strength. Something you will no doubt need if you are going to face your fears today. I'd also like to ask you to pick someone to be your body double, so it can walk beside you throughout the drama.'

The scene continues until the prescriptive roles stabilize her self-organization and increase her spontaneity.

Empathic bonding with others

The second TSM principle of change – empathic bonding with others – is a long-established standard of adequate psychotherapy treatment. In the example above, you can see how important it was for me to establish an immediate, nonverbal, empathic bond with my protagonist in order to help stabilize her self-organization as we began her drama. The 'body double' increases empathic bonding and helps the protagonist move toward spontaneity and creativity.

Accessing spontaneity and creativity for new self-organization

In many ways, this third TSM principle of change, accessing spontaneity and creativity, is the most essential for healing PTSD (Moreno 2006). In Moreno's book, *Who Shall Survive?* (1953) he states that only people who are spontaneous will survive. In classical psychodrama, he and Zerka, his wife and co-creator, gave us the tools to become spontaneous (Moreno and Moreno 1969).

In TSM, spontaneity and creativity are present on the stage when the protagonist has enough of the eight 'prescriptive roles' for healthy psychological functioning in the moment. The prescriptive roles provide the psychological functions of observation, restoration, and containment to assist the protagonist to be in a balance between left and right brain, between thinking and feeling, so that new creative solutions can be found. The development of the state of spontaneity through the prescriptive roles is always scene one in a TSM drama or session.

Below are the prescriptive roles enacted by a protagonist in South Africa. She is Nonhlanhla, a community leader who guides youth at risk in the local township of Ivory Park. She wants to work on trauma repair from a gang rape when she was eight years old.

First, we mark a place for her 'observing ego' (prescriptive role 1). It is a quickly drawn picture of a lookout point in a tree where she goes to watch what happens in her community sometimes. Today, she says it is to protect her, to watch out for her, to keep her safe. She tapes it on the wall near the window where you can see a big pod tree outside.

Next, Nonhlanhla chooses group members to play the following 'restorative roles' for her: (prescriptive role 2) a fierce lioness protecting her cubs; (3) a large waterbird that has sharp eyes and a sharp beak; (4) her wise great-grandmother, who carried the teachings of indigenous medicine; (5) her older sister, who always wished she was able to stop the rape.

At times, the protagonist goes into trance and chants in her native language. As Director, I assess the need for containment and prescribe the 'containing double' (prescriptive role 6) for her. I want to help her stay connected to words as well as sensorimotor information, to the group as well as the self.

Now Nonhlanhla is in a state of spontaneity as shown by stable self-organization through the six prescriptive roles she has enacted. She is ready to confront the men who gang raped her at eight years old in her local township. She does this from her adult ego state, supported by the prescriptive roles as above.

Safe adaptive use of affect for emotional release and repair

There are the two risks when using experiential methods with people who have experienced violence: unchosen catharsis and uncontrolled regression. As a clinical model of change, TSM uses the TSIRA to guide decisions about how to use affect and regression 'in the service of the ego' (Slavson 1951). What that means is that TSM does not, once again, overwhelm the brain by intense, uncontrolled expressions of affect when someone is triggered by a nonverbal, limbic system association in a drama. Instead, TSM increases the active experience of the protagonist's 'prescriptive roles' so that expression of feelings is done by conscious choice.

TSM also addresses when to role reverse someone into the trauma-based roles of victim, perpetrator or abandoning authority roles. The TSM answer is: not very often and *only* with the full support of the prescriptive roles, so the protagonist is not overwhelmed by ego state changes or uncontrolled, dissociated intense affect.

Controlled regression in the service of the ego

Controlled regression in the service of the ego means that you only support regression to child states for people working on trauma when they can be done with full conscious left-brain connection to right-brain awareness.

In this way, you keep the trauma-based scene safe for even the more dissociative clients.

When there is a clinical reason for the protagonist to be role reversed into the role we call 'the wounded child,' a body double or containing double is always there, so the child state experiences repair not retraumatization in the face of the perpetrators (Hudgins 2002a, 2002b).

> At the end of scene two, Nonhlanhla puts her 'wounded child' next to her great-grandmother. She has rescued her child self from the internal flashback of being raped and abandoned. Now, she goes over to her child self. She asks for forgiveness: 'I know I have shamed you over and over for being a bad child. Today, I know you are a beautiful child of God. I ask for your forgiveness. I want you to stand by great-grandmother and witness what I want to say to those boys that hurt you years ago.'
>
> She walks over to several members of the TSM team who are playing the role of the boys, who are now standing in a judges' box. She says: 'You were wrong to hurt me when I was just a little girl. I know you were hurting too, but this is not the way for us to act. You must do as I have and stop the violence. Do not repeat it another generation. Take up your responsibility as men. Only then are you forgiven.'

Accurate labeling for new personal narratives to guide the future

In TSM, there is a clinical emphasis on maintaining cognitive and emotional balance for the protagonist at all times through the prescriptive roles. TSM delineates a type of drama, called initial discovery and accurate labeling of trauma. It concretizes those experiences that are consciously remembered and allows the protagonist to observe those experiences and give them an accurate label. For example, an abusive experience will be labeled as abusive. A situation of powerless confusion will be labeled as such; likewise a wrenching loss or a terrifying ordeal.

The accurate label helps the protagonist to make sense of the experience and begin to form new perceptions based on accurate information. The previous errors, omissions, distortions or deceptions regarding the experience are revealed in the scenes of discovery and accurate labeling. For example, in the scene described above, we can see how Nonhlanhla begins to form a new perception of herself as a young child. She sees her younger self not as a 'bad child' who should be shamed, but instead as a beautiful 'child of God.' The accurate labeling of the experience helps her to give the responsibility for the abuse back to the boys who had raped her.

Summary

This chapter has described the theoretical orientations and clinical principles of change that underlie the use of the Therapeutic Spiral Model™ to treat post-traumatic stress and other disorders in today's world of increasing violence. TSM has operationalized spontaneity as the enactment of the eight 'prescriptive roles' to establish stable self-organization and conscious awareness in the here and now. The TSIRA provides a clinical map to direct people how to develop their spontaneity and creativity. This has profound implications for the practice and research of psychodrama and its core principle of change – spontaneity.

Author's note

More information on TSM can be found at www.therapeuticspiral.org.

References

Altman, K. P. (2000) 'Psychodramatic treatment of dissociative identity disorder', in P. F. Kellermann and M. K. Hudgins (eds) *Psychodrama with Trauma Survivors: Acting Out Your Pain*, London: Jessica Kingsley Publishers.

Baim, C. (2000) 'Time's distorted mirror: trauma work with adult male sex offenders', in P. F. Kellermann and M. K. Hudgins (eds) *Psychodrama with Trauma Survivors: Acting Out Your Pain*, London: Jessica Kingsley Publishers.

Blatner, A. (1991) 'Role dynamics', *Journal of Group Psychotherapy, Psychodrama and Sociometry*, 44, 1: 33–40.

Burden, K. and Ciotola, L. (2003) *Report from a Body Double: An Advanced Clinical Action Intervention Module in the Therapeutic Spiral Model* (workshop handout), Charlottesville, VA: Therapeutic Spiral International.

Chimera, C. (2002) 'The yellow brick road: helping children and adolescents to recover a coherent story following abusive family experiences', in A. Bannister and A. Huntington (eds) *Communicating with Children and Adolescents: Action for Change*, London: Jessica Kingsley Publishers.

Ciotola, L. (2004) *The Body Dialogue* (workshop handout), Charlottesville, VA: Therapeutic Spiral International.

Cossa, M. (2002) 'Drago-drama: archetypal sociodrama with adolescents', in A. Bannister and A. Huntington (eds) *Communicating with Children and Adolescents: Action for Change*, London: Jessica Kingsley Publishers.

Dayton, T. (2000) *Trauma and Addiction*, Deerfield Beach, FL: Health Communications.

Elliott, R., Davis, K. L. and Slatick, E. (1998) 'Process-experiential therapy for posttraumatic stress difficulties', in L. S. Greenberg, J. C. Watson and G. Lietaer (eds) *Handbook of Experiential Psychotherapy*, New York: Guilford Press.

Elliott, R., Greenberg, L. S. and Lietaer, G. (2002) 'Research on experiential therapies', in M. Lambert, A. Bergin and S. Garfield (eds) *Handbook of Psychotherapy and Behavior Change* (5th edn), New York: Wiley.

Forst, M. (2001) 'The therapeutic spiral model: a qualitative enquiry of its effectiveness in the treatment of trauma and addiction', unpublished master's thesis, University of Ottawa.

Gendlin, E. T. (1996) *Focusing-oriented Psychotherapy: A Manual of the Experiential Method*, New York: Guilford Press.

Goldfried, M. R. (1980) 'Toward a delineation of therapeutic change principles', *American Psychologist*, 35: 991–999.

Greenberg, L. S., Elliott, R. K. and Lietaer, G. (1994) 'Research on experiential psychotherapies', in A. E. Bergin and S. L. Garfield (eds) *Handbook of Psychotherapy and Behavior Change*, New York: Wiley.

Greenberg, L. S., Watson, J. C. and Lietaer, G. (eds) (1998) *Handbook of Experiential Psychotherapy*, New York: Guilford Press.

Holmes, P. (1992) *The Inner World Outside: Object Relations Theory and Psychodrama*, New York: Routledge.

Hudgins, M. K. (1998) 'Experiential psychodrama with sexual trauma', in L. S. Greenberg, J. C. Watson and G. Lietaer (eds) *Handbook of Experiential Psychotherapy*, New York: Guilford Press.

—— (2000) 'The therapeutic spiral model: treating PTSD in action', in P. F. Kellermann and M. K. Hudgins (eds) *Psychodrama with Trauma Survivors: Acting Out Your Pain*, London: Jessica Kingsley Publishers.

—— (2002a) *Experiential Treatment for PTSD: The Therapeutic Spiral Model*, New York: Springer.

—— (2002b) *The Body Double: A Prescriptive Role for Containment in the Therapeutic Spiral Model*, Charlottesville, VA: Therapeutic Spiral International.

—— (in press) *A Trainer's Manual for Community Workers using the Therapeutic Spiral Model*, Charlottesville, VA: Virginia Foundation for the Humanities, University of Virginia.

Hudgins, M. K., Drucker, K. and Metcalf, K. (2000) 'The containing double: a clinically effective psychodrama intervention for PTSD', *British Journal of Psychodrama and Sociodrama*, 15, 1: 58–77.

Hug, E. (in press) 'The neurobiology of trauma', in M. K. Hudgins (ed.) *Action Against Trauma: A Trainer's Manual for Using Experiential Methods In Post-Violence Communities*, Charlottesville, VA: Virginia Foundation for the Humanities, University of Virginia.

Johnson, D. R. (2000) 'Creative therapies', in E. B. Foa, T. M. Keane and M. J. Friedman (eds) *Effective Treatments for PTSD*, New York: Guilford Press.

Lambert, M., Bergin, A. and Garfield, S. (eds) (2003) *Handbook of Psychotherapy and Behavior Change* (5th edn), New York: Wiley.

Leutz, G. A. (2000) 'Appearance and treatment of dissociative states of consciousness in psychodrama', in P. F. Kellermann and M. K. Hudgins (eds) *Psychodrama with Trauma Survivors: Acting Out Your Pain*, London: Jessica Kingsley Publishers.

McVea, C. and Gow, K. (2006) 'Healing a mother's emotional pain: protagonist and director of a TSM session', *Journal of Group Psychotherapy, Psychodrama and Sociometry*, 59: 1: 3-22.

Moreno, J. L. (1953) *Who shall survive? Foundations of Sociometry, Group Psychotherapy and Sociodrama* (2nd edn), Beacon, NY: Beacon House. (Originally published 1934.)

Moreno, J. L. (1973) *Theatre of Spontaneity*, Mclean, VA: American Society of Group Psychotherapy and Psychodrama.

Moreno, J. L. and Moreno, Z. T. (1969) *Psychodrama, Volume Three: Action Therapy and Principles of Practice*, Beacon, NY: Beacon House.

Moreno, Z. T. (2006) *The Quintessential Zerka*, London: Routledge.

Moreno, Z. T., Blomkvist, L. D. and Rützel, T. (2000) *Psychodrama, Surplus Reality and the Art of Healing*, London: Routledge.

Robson, M. (2000) 'Psychodrama with adolescent sex offenders', in P. F. Kellermann and M. K. Hudgins (eds) *Psychodrama with Trauma Survivors: Acting Out Your Pain*, London: Jessica Kingsley.

Rogers, C. R. (1957) 'The necessary and sufficient conditions of therapeutic personality change', *Journal of Consulting Psychology*, 21: 95–103.

Siegel, D. J. (1999) *The Developing Mind: How Relationships and the Brain Interact to Shape Who We Are*, New York: Guilford Press.

Slavson, S. R. (1951) 'Catharsis in group psychotherapy', *Psychoanalytic Review*, 38: 39–52.

Stern, D. N. (1985) *The Interpersonal World of the Infant: A View from Psychoanalysis and Developmental Psychology*, New York: Basic Books.

Stern, D. N. (1990) *Diary of a Baby*, New York: Basic Books.

Terr, L. C. (1991) 'Childhood trauma: an outline and overview', *American Journal of Psychiatry*, 148, 1: 10–20.

Treadwell, T., Kumar, V. K. and Wright, J. (2003) 'Enriching psychodrama through the use of cognitive behavioral therapy techniques', *Journal of Group Psychotherapy, Psychodrama & Sociometry*, 55, 3: 55–65.

van der Kolk, B. (2003) 'In terror's grip', *Connections*, Feb/March.

Chapter 13

Psychodrama, spirituality and Souldrama®

Connie Miller

Intuition

> The intuitive mind is a sacred gift and the rational mind is a faithful servant. We have created a society that honors the servant and has forgotten the gift.
>
> (Albert Einstein)

Spirituality is universal, as is the desire to manifest our life's intentions. The goal of psychodrama is to access, concretize and experience a state of learning and creativity to heal past traumatic experiences. Psychodrama builds community, self-awareness and problem solving abilities. Psycho-spiritual psychodrama is aimed at integrating psychology and spirituality through action. It is intended to help people see and understand their psychospiritual evolution and addresses ways to enhance the psychospiritual roles we play in life. Souldrama® (Miller 2000, 2004) is a developmental process that leads a person through stages of spiritual development, aligning the ego and soul. This helps the person to recognize and move on to their higher purpose, creating that which is desired. By doing this, the soul becomes a co-creator in a person's life. This is the soul's mission: co-creation. Souldrama incorporates the new concept of spiritual intelligence and further supports Moreno's work through a new spiritual model.

There is a spiritual movement in the field of psychology today that cannot be ignored. As various holistic healing practices become more accepted, the trend is to integrate psychology with other methods of healing. Brief, time-limited approaches to therapy are aimed at treating specific symptoms, rather than dealing with issues of a more existential and spiritual nature. When people seek therapy, they are often feeling personally diminished and disconnected from others. They may feel spiritually impoverished as well as anxious and depressed. Addressing these deeper, more spiritual issues can effect lasting change. Yet many treatment programs minimize or discourage the importance of spirituality, especially when the treatment in question is aimed primarily at symptom relief.

The experience of feeling 'stuck' with clients is a common problem in our profession and leaves therapists searching for 'creative' solutions to clinical problems. Clinical creativity is always an interactive process, inseparable from the imagination and creativity of the client. One of the most effective ways to tap into that creativity is to broaden the client's frame of reference from the literal to the metaphorical. People's inner logic is often best expressed through metaphors, symbols, fantasies, rituals and stories. These co-creative approaches can be powerful channels for changing people's perceptions and experiences. As mental health professionals, we address psychological aspects of a client's problems but largely overlook the significance of their spirituality. This is because spirituality wasn't part of our training and we tend to think of spirituality and therapy as mutually exclusive – a kind of 'separation of church and state' mentality. But spirituality isn't a synonym for religion. It is universal. It defines the way we view our world. When we access this perspective, it empowers us with a higher sense of coherence and courage to resolve problems and move ahead.

For Antonovsky (1979), the 'sense of coherence' is a good predictor for health. Antonovsky coined the phrase 'salutogenesis' in the context of survivors of the Holocaust. He was fascinated by the phenomenon of survival when he considered how some people came through the horrors of the Holocaust seemingly unscathed as human beings. For him, salutogenesis is an interior phenomenon, linked to what others call resilience. Macdonald (2006) extends the term beyond the psychological to the environmental, to encompass an interest in what is salutogenic, health enhancing in the contexts of people's lives: their physical, emotional, economic and cultural environments. There is need for a mindset which counters the medical concern with the pathological with a salutogenic vision of populations, be it adolescents, older people, or in this instance, our clients.

The pathogenic view is dominant in mental health work. The focus is on dealing with what is dysfunctional, pathological, on repairing the damage of past experiences and controlling the pathologies. All this is a necessary part of any mental health system, but it is biased in the sense that there is much less emphasis on understanding what is salutogenic, healthy and wholesome.

Some humanistic psychologists claim that Abraham Maslow, and Carl Rogers, came up with the concept of 'salutogenic' factors 40 years ago. However, Seligman (Gillham and Seligman 1999; Seligman and Csikszentmihalyi 2000) observes that there is a significant difference between humanistic psychology and positive psychology. One of the goals of the positive psychology movement includes the development of two complementary branches of science and practice: one that alleviates and prevents negative traits and feelings, and another that promotes well-being as well as changing the nature of psychotherapy by developing ways to identify and nurture patients' strengths.

After World War II psychology became a science largely devoted to healing. It concentrated on repairing damage, using a disease model of human functioning. This almost exclusive attention to pathology neglected the idea of a fulfilled individual and a thriving community, and it neglected the possibility that building strength is the most potent weapon in the arsenal of therapy. The aim of positive psychology is to catalyze a change in psychology from a preoccupation only with repairing the worst things in life to also building the best qualities in life. To redress the previous imbalance, we must bring the building of strength to the forefront in the treatment and prevention of mental illness.

At the subjective level, positive psychology is about positive subjective experience: well-being and satisfaction (past), and flow, joy, the sensual pleasures, and happiness (present), and constructive cognitions about the future: optimism, hope and faith. At the individual level, positive psychology is about positive individual traits: the capacity for love and vocation, courage, interpersonal skill, aesthetic sensibility, perseverance, forgiveness, originality, future-mindedness, high talent and wisdom. At the group level, positive psychology is about the civic virtues and the institutions that move people toward better citizenship: responsibility, nurturance, altruism, civility, moderation, tolerance and a work ethic (Gillham and Seligman 1999; Seligman and Csikszentmihalyi 2000).

What is spiritual intelligence?

In the early part of the twentieth century, IQ, or rational intelligence, was the big issue. More recently, emotional intelligence (EQ) has been identified as a requirement for the effective use of IQ. Now there exists much scientific data that points to the presence of a spiritual intelligence (SQ), the ultimate intelligence that serves as a necessary foundation for the effective functioning of both IQ and EQ. This category of skills is crucial for wholeness, happiness, and effective living.

The word 'religion' comes from roots that mean to 'tie together,' recognizing that spiritual matters involve not only faith, prayer and values, but also obligations to and support from others. Spiritual Intelligence® (Kravitz 2002) refers to the skills, abilities and behaviors we need to help us balance the expansive love that flows through our hearts and all of creation with the need for discipline and responsibility. When we successfully balance these polarities in our own feelings and in how we treat others and the world, we are able to create forgiveness, healing and connection (Khavari 1995). Spiritual Intelligence® also refers to the skills, abilities and behaviors required to develop and maintain a relationship to the 'ultimate source of all being.' When we access this intelligence, we can better succeed in the search for meaning in life, find a moral and ethical path to help guide us through life, and act out our sense of meaning and values in our personal life and in our interpersonal relationships (Kravitz 2002). Another definition of SQ is:

> the intelligence with which we address and solve problems of meaning and value, the intelligence with which we can place our actions and our lives in a wider, richer, meaning-giving context, the intelligence with which we can assess that one course of action or one life-path is more meaningful than another.
>
> (Zohar and Marshall 2000: 2–3)

Spiritual Intelligence offers an expansion of psychology as a science, and posits the need for a new psychological model of the human self and of human personality. In doing so, it combines mystical and mythological structures found within human spiritual thought, both ancient and modern, carefully pointing out that SQ is not necessarily about being religious, but rather it is an internal and innate ability of the human brain and psyche (Ramachandran and Blakeslee 1998; Zohar and Marshall 2000, 2001).

Spiritual intelligence in psychodrama

J. L. Moreno's philosophical and theological views greatly influenced the theory and practice of psychodrama. Theoretically speaking, psychodrama is a holistic form of therapy addressing, among other aspects of life, our implicit, subconscious concepts of God, or spiritual intelligence. For Moreno (1972), part of living consciously is addressing individual views about God and spirituality. Moreover, Moreno saw spirituality as essential to clinical activities.

New methods are needed now to connect to our spiritual intelligence and wisdom and discover how to use energy in a group setting. Moreno's suggestion that God is immanent, creative and the supreme co-creator, promotes respect and honor between group members. To see the light of God in each group member and to gain an understanding of the universal struggles of all human beings discourages what Moreno called the 'cultural conserve' while encouraging conscious living in each and every moment. This includes examining fundamental existential concerns universal to the human experience, such as choice, freedom, self-determination and the responsibility to shape one's life. Moreno developed methods to tap into our spiritual intelligence.

Psychodrama is one way to access this concept of spiritual intelligence. Moreno (1920) called spontaneity and creativity the 'godhead' in classical psychodrama. He stated that each person has a god-within that can be drawn on as a guide for a creative life and healing force. Toward the end of *Who Shall Survive?* (1953) Moreno describes his hope for humanity: the transformation of human consciousness through the integration of creative play, spontaneity and psychological theory. Moreno's methodology is a growth model, emphasizing individual responsibility and the creating of one's destiny (Moreno 1946). Unique to psychodrama is the use of primarily role play in therapy to promote joy, enthusiasm, excitement, playfulness, vitality, deep feelings, sharing, and the integration of these emotions with the greater spiritual self (Blatner 2000).

Moreno's theory has metaphysical and theological underpinnings. In the mid 1930s, when Moreno published some of his first books in English, psychology and spirituality were seen as different and separate. Yet Moreno (1972) boldly suggested that individuals are co-creators with God, indicating self-responsibility in what one creates in life and in the world in general. God is not seen as separate, but rather as the indwelling of the Supreme Being. By this definition, all existence and each being is an expression of God.

Additionally, Moreno (1972) suggested that God acts within the creativity of each individual person. Such creativity and spontaneity is believed to be a connection with God as an expression of transpersonal identification. Rather than being a moralistic God, Moreno (1972) proposed that God encourages aesthetic values which highlight pleasure in creativity, discovery and celebration of life. Therefore God does not act in the role of a judge, but is instead one who invites caring, compassion and the achievement of our full potential.

Souldrama®: a psychospiritual technique to access spiritual intelligence

A great deal of study in psychology has been done so that a client might understand the scars and abuses of childhood and to help them heal. Not enough attention has been paid to vision: vision for moving forward and living lives of joy and purpose. After a certain point in therapy, vision seems to be more powerful in the recovery process than clearing away the 'baggage' of the past. Without vision, many clients lose enthusiasm for life – the will to live it joyfully and creatively, and the passion for interests and projects. Many clients have lost the ability to appreciate the positives in life and, more importantly, have lost a commitment to action. Complete recovery needs to be of the body, mind and spirit. It involves controlling addictions, removing abuses, learning new behaviors and putting vision into life.

Many clients have developed distorted internalized object relationships with the spiritual beings in their lives. Childhood emotions have often been transferred on to present-day relationships. Many of these relationships have become contaminated with residuals of childhood traumas and misunderstandings. When a person learns to look outside of themselves for love and validation, they create a distance from their spiritual nature, creating a gap or emptiness within the self. Often, as a client grows into adulthood, childish attitudes toward their 'higher power' remain and their relationship to God is one that remains outside of them, being one that is superficial and inconsistent. The client feels they must 'do' something in order to get God's love, which they see as being inconsistently outside of themselves as opposed to within. Instead of moving forward, they engage in self-sabotaging behavior, further compounding their problems. Their energy comes from problems and not from the joy in life. Spirituality is a state of 'being,' not 'getting.' Spiritual work has to do with reconnecting with spirit, to the divine within, to their spiritual intelligence.

Blatner (1998) defines spirituality as the activity of deepening our connectedness with the 'Greater Wholeness of Being.' He urges the need for creativity and imagery within the therapeutic process so humans can see themselves as co-creators and not victims of omnipotent strength. When God is seen as being inside and not outside of oneself, a greater sense of co-creative responsibility exists.

Blatner (1998) states that one of the most important functions of process thought is that it offers core conceptual tools to aid in the 'conscious transformation of consciousness itself,' promoting a mature state of mind and a sense of co-creative responsibility toward one's higher power. The process view of God as caring organism can lure but not force healthy relationships, reframing the relationship of the individual to the 'greater wholeness' as one of responsibility and actively aligning, participating with, taking inspiration, but not passive reliance.

Furthermore Blatner (1999) urges us to rediscover the storylines in our lives, and to elaborate that storytelling in order to enrich and develop the soul–ego connection, which is an important element in spiritual development and psychological healing and resiliency. Helping people to retell their stories in order to reconstruct them in a more positive fashion can lead one to thinking more hopefully about oneself and one's life. Storytelling is one of the ways to develop a relationship with the soul. It also is socially bonding and cathartic, and acts in the group process in that dynamic Yalom called 'universalization' (Yalom 1975). 'Soul does not think in terms of prose and facts but rather in images and stories' (Blatner 1999). Soul is not a thing but a quality or dimension of experiencing life within ourselves. The challenge of healing, therefore, is to align these two roles of ego and soul. If we learn how to serve the soul, we will rebuild our relationship with spontaneity. To support clients in identifying their vision and moving forward in achieving their life's purpose, we need new, creative therapeutic tools.

Moreno observed that the major challenge for humanity is that of living creatively. Spontaneity refers to the spirit of opening to the creative possibilities in a situation. Much of Moreno's work may be understood as being methods and ideas for promoting spontaneity in the service of creativity (Blatner 2000). Now we need ways to access our spiritual intelligence. A lack of spirituality reflects itself when one feels separate from others. The ego developed in early childhood can obstruct or distort one's relationship with the divine. It can manifest a far richer consciousness in everyday life if brought into alignment with the soul.

Souldrama® helps a person to define their relationship to a higher power and thus to themselves as one that is all loving and not based on the internalized image of their parents or outside authoritarian figures. The process of Souldrama fits into the fourth role category (the first three being psychosomatic, sociocultural and psychodramatic roles; see Moreno 1946: 77 and Winters 2000) of psychodrama – that of the psychospiritual – and as an action-oriented multidisciplinary training system it adds a psychospiritual element to psychodrama. This new model of Souldrama utilizes the process of the veils as the ultimate symbol of the spiritually intelligent self. It is a way to combine the great eastern and western traditions of the self with the latest insights from science to move past resistance.

Souldrama (Miller 2000, 2004) is an action-oriented method that takes groups and individuals through a six-stage process of spiritual growth and discovery. Each stage allows one to enter into a higher state of consciousness, aligning the ego and soul. This unique psychospiritual approach uses psychodrama, spontaneous affirmation, prayer, art, guided meditation, props and the metaphor of angels as a messenger between the heavenly world and the human world so the soul can truly hear what the divine is saying.

Souldrama enables people to discover their life's purpose by releasing emotional and mental blocks that inhibit psychospiritual growth. It guides group members to experience the divine within so that they can act as co-creators with God and define their own personal gifts and soul's mission. This process blends group psychotherapy, psychodrama and Souldrama to stimulate creativity and enhance spiritual intelligence.

During a Souldrama, through the help of the auxiliaries (the presence of a loving soul and an angel), one is able to feel the vibration of the power and presence of one's real self. As one goes into higher stages of consciousness, one is in a higher level of vibration (Zimberoff and Hartman 1999). The group energy becomes more cohesive as the protagonist passes through the veils and more ego is left behind. Various psychodramatic techniques are employed such as role reversal and doubling, and each veil leaves much to the creative process of the director. What makes Souldrama unique is that it is not linear but progressive in its healing stages. Each veil progresses into the next level of healing, and one must repeatedly go through the veils in the same sequence. Thus, each time, each positive level of healing is reinforced and repeated. Each veil defines a stage of spiritual growth and development and opens up the participants to greater self-awareness to truly hear what the soul is saying or to tune into that spiritual intelligence.

The veils present a challenge for the group. There is a group conscious-ness and a group lesson and a unified karma. The director must surrender to the higher will of the group as they have their own spiritual rhythm. The group will not be able to move through the sequence of the veils unless they are ready as a group to progress on to the next veil. The energy of love has to be present and increased over the life of the group, the ego decreased and the group cohesion increased over that time period.

Accessing this spiritual intelligence helps a client to reframe their gifts from childhood. Curiously, the things we lacked in childhood can become the gifts we are able to give others, skills that prepare us for our life's work. Gifts that we can compassionately give to others often come from what we lacked as children, from our wounds. Often we are unable to integrate these gifts into our own hearts because we resist the donor or how the gifts were given. We gladly give away our gifts to others as fast as we can, without ever accepting them first into our own hearts. One way to accept them is to move past the negativity and resistance. We may spend years refusing to forgive and, therefore, do not use the gifts bestowed by our parents, gifts that could lead us to our higher purpose. Interestingly enough, what we choose as our higher purpose is often connected to the time when we felt the most loved. One of the qualities of spiritual intelligence is wisdom. This includes knowing the limits of our knowledge. Other ingredients are values such as courage, integrity, intuition and compassion. With SQ, more is less, so as you learn the process may involve unlearning what other people have taught us.

Conclusion

After years of therapy, many clients remain blocked, afraid to take further risks, 'waiting' for something to happen. When a client learns to connect to the divine and to use 'soul' as a verb, to retrieve the soul they lost as a child, they regain a connection to life. One learns to live life in the moment, giving attention to living in the present with total joy.

When you have faith, you have joy and you move forward. We learn to heed the voice of spirit that is quiet and non-demanding as opposed to the voice of fear that is loud and threatening. We learn that it is not the material world that causes things to happen but our awareness of our divine inner reality. When we are in tune with the voice of spirit, with intuition and creativity, we realize that we are always the creators of our own lives because we come from a center of higher awareness. Our work needs to become our higher purpose, our ministry performed from love, joy and spontaneity. We need to learn that the receiving comes from our 'being' which later becomes manifest in our 'doing,' which is our work or our higher purpose. We need to understand that we do not need to 'do' any-thing in order to be.

Our creativity holds the key to our life dream, purpose or calling. However, we place many obstacles between our creative gifts and ourselves. Creativity is the ability to manifest what has real meaning and purpose for us, our soul's mission. When creativity is shut down in childhood in order to stay safe, we remain in jobs and relationships that we have outgrown, that no longer serve us. When we learn to listen to the inner voice of our own spirit as opposed to the internalized critical voice of our parents (or other powerful or significant figures in our lives), we are able to follow the voice that leads us toward fulfilled, creative lives. All the signals from that spiritual or soul voice are for the purpose of giving us back our lives as creators. That spiritual voice is difficult to hear if you are struggling with learned beliefs, trying to control the outcome of situations and enmeshed in expectations of the way things 'should' turn out. When we are on our soul's purpose, we stop defending and begin to truly live.

One of our most important relationships is with the soul. When you lose yourself, you lose the attributes of spontaneity, creativity and openness, the attributes of the spiritual self. Instead of damaging the soul with negative, fearful thinking, we must learn to use all of our experiences to nourish the soul and to live our dreams. When you spend your life doing what you love, you are nourishing the soul. When you listen to your inner callings, you practice the art of self-love. Spirituality is missing when love of life is absent.

We need more methods to nourish our souls, rather than more analytical thinking. Our soul is ever present and the connection to inner peace is only a moment away. Spiritual intelligence typically becomes a focus later, as we begin to search for meaning and ask 'Is this all there is?' People are living longer today, and they often begin to seek therapy in the latter part of their lives. It becomes a time to discover the soul's purpose and to live a life full of joy, transformation and fulfillment.

Today we look for the purpose of our individual and collective experience as we have created it and search again for the meaning of life. We must look for ways to recreate ourselves. 'Generativity' takes center stage in the seventh stage of Erik Erikson's (1963) eight-stage model of the human life course. In each stage, the developing person confronts a central psychological issue. The seventh stage is 'middle adulthood', the stage Erikson calls 'generativity versus stagnation,' where one asks 'How can I fashion a legacy of the self?' The eighth and final stage is 'old age,' the stage Erikson calls 'ego-integrity versus despair,' where one asks 'How can I accept the gift of my life?'

Erik Erikson believed that in order to be 'generative' as opposed to 'stagnant,' people must have 'a belief in the species.' They must have faith that despite suffering and setback, despite evil, human beings are potentially good and human life can be good for generations to come. The more generative a person becomes, the more they can constantly imagine such futures and they envision a better world for themselves and society. Generativity takes us beyond the short-term gains we often seek in daily life and orients us to the long run: 'I am what survives me.'

Recent approaches, for example, Kate Hudgins' Therapeutic Spiral Model™ (see Chapter 12), Natalie Winters' psychospiritual model (Winters 2000), Dan Tomasulo's cultural double (Tomasulo 2001) as well as the technique of Souldrama® (Miller 2000) are only some of the newer action techniques to be employed in the therapeutic group process, born from Moreno's philosophy and designed to move one through stagnation and despair. Only then can a person tend to see their own lives in redemptive terms as they move forward onto their higher purpose. Holding out hope for our ultimate redemption gives us faith and hope that our legacies will be good and that our life has had a higher purpose. What we can do as therapists is to help others to re-create themselves anew. This is the time for teaching, healing and generating new action techniques, for we are all one and must become co-creators with each other to become spiritual activists and healers.

Much education is based on the model of cognitive intelligence. In our society we have developed the intellect while neglecting our emotions and our spiritual life. If our education were more holistic, as students we would learn to balance our intellect with our emotional and spiritual growth. As therapists we would take responsibility for our personal as well as our professional growth. If cognitive intelligence is about thinking and emotional intelligence is about feeling, then spiritual intelligence is about being (Dayton 1995). In a holistic view of life, we are creatures with a mind, a body and a spirit, all interconnected and arranged in a pattern that means that the whole is greater than the sum of the parts (Bateson 1979; Tomasulo 2004). In the same way we can look at our intelligences.

'Health,' 'whole' and 'healing' all come from the same root. In the course of a therapeutic career, we need knowledge and skills for our modern roles as therapists. We heal because of who we are and not because of what we do.

References

Antonovsky, A. (1979) *Health, Stress and Coping*, San Francisco: Jossey-Bass.

Bateson, G. (1979) *Mind and Nature: A Necessary Unity*, New York: Bantam.

Blatner, A. (1998) 'Why process thought is relevant: a psychiatrist's perspective', presentation at the Silver Anniversary Whitehead Conference, Center for Process Studies, Claremont, CA. See also <www.blatner.com>

—— (1999) 'Re-story-ing the soul', keynote presentation to the 1999 meeting of the American Society for Group Psychotherapy and Psychodrama, Philadelphia. See also <www.blatner.com>

—— (2000) *Foundations of Psychodrama: History, Theory and Practice*, New York: Springer.

Dayton, T. (1995) *The Quiet Voice of The Soul*, Deerfield Beach, FL: Health Communications.

Erikson, E. (1963) *Childhood and Society*, Harmondsworth: Penguin.

Gillham, J. E. and Seligman, M. E. P. (1999) 'Footsteps on the road to positive psychology', *Behaviour Research and Therapy*, 37: S163–S173.

Khavari, K. (1995) *Spiritual Intelligence*, Ontario: White Mountain Publications.

Kravitz, Y. (2002) <www.spiritualintelligence.com> Spiritual Intelligence® is registered as a Service Mark in the US Patent and Trademark Office, since March 2000. © Yaacov J. Kravitz, 2002. All rights reserved.

Macdonald, J. (2006) *Environments for Health*, London: Earthscan.

Miller, C. (2000) 'The technique of Souldrama and its applications', *The International Journal of Action Methods*, 52, 4: 173–186.

Miller, C. (2004) *Souldrama: A Journey into the Heart of God*, NJ: Self-published.

Moreno, J. L. (1920) *Das Testament des Vaters*, Berlin: Gustav Kiepenheuer Verlag. (English translation 1941 published as *The Words of the Father*, Beacon, NY: Beacon House.)

—— (1946) *Psychodrama, Volume One*, Beacon, NY: Beacon House.

—— (1953) *Who Shall Survive? Foundations of Sociometry, Group Psychotherapy and Sociodrama* (2nd edn), Beacon, NY: Beacon House.

—— (1972) 'The religion of God-Father', in P. E. Johnson (ed.) *Healer of the Mind: A Psychiatrist's Search for Faith*, Nashville, TN: Abington.

Ramachandran, V. and Blakeslee, S. (1998) *Phantoms in the Brain: Probing the Mysteries of the Human Mind*, New York: William Morrow.

Seligman, M. and Csikszentmihalyi, M. (2000) 'Positive psychology: an introduction', *American Psychologist*, 55: 5–14.

Tomasulo, D. (2001) 'Culture in action: diversity training with a cultural double', *The International Journal of Action Methods: Psychodrama, Skill Training, and Role Playing*, 53, 2: 51–65.

—— (2004) <www.thehealingcrowd.com>

Winters. N. (2000) 'The psychospiritual in psychodrama: a fourth role category', *International Journal of Action Methods*, 52, 4: 163–171.

Yalom, I. (1975) *The Theory and Practice of Group Psychotherapy*, New York: Basic Books.

Zimberoff, D. and Hartman, D. (1999) 'Heart-centered energetic psychodrama', *Journal of Heart-Centered Therapies*, 2, 1: 77–98.

Zohar, D. and Marshall I. (2000) *SQ: Connecting with our Spiritual Intelligence*, London: Bloomsbury.

—— (2001) *SQ – Spiritual Intelligence: The Ultimate Intelligence*, London: Bloomsbury.

Chapter 14

Psychodrama in miniature

John Casson

This chapter explores methods of psychotherapy which employ miniature objects to empower clients. I explore theory that has emerged from practice and practice that has developed from theory – there being nothing as practical as a good theory. When clients find a method useful we must ask why and research our own practice. From such research develops further theory and practice, as illustrated by two examples of working in miniature: the Rosenthal Process – a miniature psychodrama theatre – and the Communicube (Casson 2002) – a new method invented during research.

A miniature history

Throughout human history, powerful symbolic objects have been used in rituals to facilitate healing and manage change processes. The miniature has fascinated human kind. The earliest artefacts were painted pebbles, small statues, carved bones. In many cultures there are festivals in which miniature figures play an important role in representing significant deities and powers. Jewels, miniature paintings, coins, Japanese netsuke, doll's houses, have fascinated adults. From childhood, the small world of toys has been a source of delight and wonder, empowering children to achieve a sense of mastery. Peter Slade (1980, 1995), the founder of dramatherapy in Britain, named these activities 'projected play' and suggested they were an important stage of child development. Many therapists have used various projective methods from the Rorschach test to button sculpting.

Historical background

In 1911, H. G. Wells published *Floor Games*, about playing with children on the floor with toys. In 1917, Caldwell Cook in *The Play Way* recommended drama in schools as a rehearsal for living. His methods included the creation of miniature worlds with toys. Margaret Lowenfeld (1935), a child psychotherapist and the creator of Jungian sandplay, was inspired by Wells and from 1929 developed her therapeutic play method. In 1937,

Rosenzweig and Shakow used toy furniture and bricks, in a controlled experiment, using play techniques with patients diagnosed with schizophrenia and other psychoses. They concluded:

> Patients may be able to act out in pantomime what they are not ready to put into words, or they may be able to convey more quickly in a material medium of representation what words would disclose only after a considerably longer time [. . .] play is a better adapted means than conversation to elicit personal content from patients.
>
> (Rosenzweig and Shakow 1937: 33, 34, 42)

Methods of working in miniature

Matrioshka dolls

Matrioshka dolls are sets of wooden dolls of decreasing size that are nested one inside the other. The word 'matrioshka' means grandmother and the dolls are of eastern European origin. McLuskie described the use of these dolls:

> They can be set up by the group and given identities, especially as families. By putting a finger on a doll, anyone in the group can speak for that character. Sometimes people find it a lot easier to show their feelings and problems sideways.
>
> (McLuskie 1983: 25)

Karp described her use of matrioshka dolls to focus on developmental blocks that prohibit spontaneous expression (Holmes *et al.* 1994). I have also used these dolls in work with people who hear voices (Casson 2004a).

Katerina

Katerina had received a diagnosis of schizoaffective disorder. I met her in a secure hospital unit where she was living many years after the death of her baby. She had been convicted of killing the child and was detained under the Mental Health Act. She had attempted to kill herself at the time she killed the child, in response to difficult family circumstances which included domestic violence, isolation from her family and being depressed. I was asked to assess her for individual therapy. Katerina had a great need to speak: she had a torrent of words, hardly pausing for breath and giving me very little space for any creative intervention. She wanted me to listen but was speaking at me rather than to/with me. I had a feeling she might not let me in, but would instead present a barrage of feeling, complaint and talk.

Each year, as the anniversary of the child's death approached, Katerina would become ill and this disturbed period could extend for months. I knew if therapy was to be useful we must address the grief for this lost child. I was aware that if I approached this too directly Katerina would ricochet away from therapy – the death was just too painful. I wondered what method I could use. I needed to find an intervention that was sufficiently distanced yet appropriate.

During one of her sessions, I discovered that Katerina's parents were from eastern Europe, and that family members had died in a terrible famine. I was familiar with the intergenerational transmission of trauma in the aetiology of schizophrenia (Casson 2004a; see also Chapter 11 by Ancelin Schützenberger). I wondered if the matrioshka doll would be useful for her. I took my collection into the next session. Katerina looked through the collection and immediately chose two dolls: a large, beautiful doll, which was painted with a young eastern European couple of lovers, and a smaller mother doll holding a baby. She was delighted by the colours and remembered the dolls from her family's culture.

As the work proceeded, Katerina cradled the larger doll and wept for her child. She told the child that she had loved her. I asked what the child would say in reply. She said the child loved her.

I was sure that what made the doll effective was the fact that Katerina could hold the matrioshka and look into its eyes, and because it was appropriate to her ancestral culture. I was also aware that by using the dolls I had enabled her to play – to choose to get closer to the material through the distance of the doll. Katerina later told me that this one session had prevented her from becoming ill during the anniversary period. It was perhaps the single most useful session of her therapy.

COMMENT

This example signals that it is the distance afforded by the use of miniature objects that is a key element in their effectiveness. They promote the ability to play and enable clients to see things from different perspectives. The potency of symbolic objects is also seen here. Arranging such objects into patterns (sculpting) further develops the method.

Sculpting

Jennings (1986) used miniature objects in sculpting – placing objects (or people) into a symbolic arrangement with the aim of clarifying intrapsychic or interpersonal elements or issues and also for creative purposes (see also Jennings 1990). Jennings invented the micro-sculpt (in the palm of the hand, perhaps with Guatemalan 'worry dolls') and the mini-sculpt (with toys such as plastic animals, which she called a 'spectogram'). I have used Guatemalan worry dolls in assessment and therapy sessions (Casson

2004a). These tiny figures may be used to represent either real or imaginary people – family members, significant others or parts of the self. Sculpts may be thematic ('Make a pattern of buttons or stones representing members of your family') or be without any specific theme. Indeed, it may be best to start the work without stipulating any theme and trust the unconscious process of pattern making to promote the emergence of significant material. Thus the method may be: first make a pattern without speaking; then decide whether to change or add anything; then speak of what the arrangement shows you (to the therapist or a partner in a group).

Why is sculpting effective?

Sculpting combines pattern making, spatial awareness, symbolism, non-verbal expression and embodiment, in the service of the therapeutic process. Sculpting evokes the subdominant right brain, with its emotional knowledge, and then processes this into verbal expression and understanding, thus bringing the left brain (with its analytic abilities) into relationship and play (Casson 1998). Through this method, the dynamics of the group and the psychological needs of the members, or any individual, are revealed more effectively than by talk alone.

The following processes are common to all sculpting:

1 To start nonverbally and create/explore a pattern in space.
2 To offer the option to change the pattern.
3 Only then, verbalise.

The sculpt gives the person sculpting the opportunity to:

- create a pattern
- step back and observe
- change the arrangement
- speak to and interact with the sculpt
- consider what is missing
- have power and be in control.

After a sculpt has been made a useful question is: 'What would you like to change, add or take away?' The sculpt can then become a source of drama, can be dramatised by the client giving voice to different parts of the sculpt, or by other members of the group taking the roles. A useful question to ask different elements in a sculpt is: 'What do you want?'

Sculpting therefore provides a flexible structure for storytelling, exploration, expression and working through issues. It can be used in individual work and groups. It can be miniature (whereby the client experiences themselves as being in total control) or on a human or even epic scale. Sculpting enables engagement and provides safe distance: the person can review the sculpt, stepping back, and engage their observer ego (see also Chapter 12 by Hudgins). Sculpting can be revealing, empowering and fun (Casson 2004b).

Toys and puppets

Miniature toys and objects seem to empower people by putting them in control. Doll's house furniture can be used even without figures – the empty chair is a useful tool whatever the size of the chair. Indeed, for some clients a full size adult chair might be too large. For example, if a client is working on their experience of abuse and is regressed to a child state and is then asked to locate their abuser in an empty chair, they may experience the 'abuser' in the chair as much larger than them. This could be retraumatising. If the abuser is represented by a miniature chair, or if he is represented by a toy animal, the client is much larger and in control. To give some examples: 'Gloria' used a toy gorilla to represent the man who raped her. This gave her the confidence to confront him. 'Diane' used animal puppets to tell the story of her sexual abuse (Casson 2004a: 105).

Bannister (2000) stated that puppets provide safe distance and such miniaturisation makes action more manageable. Furthermore, when adults may find confronting an abuser potentially overwhelming, miniaturisation distances and empowers. As another option, flat card figures can be used – just five to ten inches tall, and used as standing in for the abuser, instead of an adult auxiliary. These card figures may be created by the client or provided as a template tool by the therapist. Features might be drawn on the card by the client and the figure can also be bent, crumpled, distorted or even attacked. Such miniaturisation may permit the safe expression of violent and revengeful feelings. These may be especially useful where the room available for psychodrama is too small for sufficient safe physical distance between the protagonist and an abusive figure. I have written elsewhere of the value of safe distance in ensuring clients are not overwhelmed during the work (see Casson 2004a: chapter 7). Flat card figures may also be used and contained in a toy theatre.

Toy theatres

Miniature theatres were popular during the nineteenth century. I have developed their use in dramatherapy (Casson 2004a). They provide a fascinating, focused container for material that can be played with at a safe distance – the metaphors of the theatre being a vehicle for the drama of the client's psyche.

Dillon

Dillon, who heard persecutory voices, used the toy theatre I had made from a cardboard box to create an epic political play, designing sets and scenarios, writing speeches and improvising music over several sessions. He said the play was to enable people to transcend death, find healing and achieve a transcendental view. He continued to think about this play between sessions and felt better. The creativity gave him a sense of purpose. He wanted the audience to feel the power of the actors and so feel empowered themselves. The play was about power, violence and spirituality. He was able to project his delusional ideas into the drama and get satisfaction from this creativity. His desire for power led him to identify with power figures.

Many of Dillon's dramas were about political and spiritual power and control – whether someone could survive through violence. His relatives had died in the Nazi concentration camps. He believed he was controlled by a deity, an extremely hard, violent taskmaster. Theatre offered him the opportunity to explore being powerful without being actually destructive. Through creative action, he could experience having some control when in life he was powerless, isolated and felt controlled by extra terrestrial deities (Casson 2004a: 111).

The Rosenthal Process

Annie Rosenthal (2004) has recently developed a miniature psychodrama theatre. This is a portable wooden box which opens to reveal a scale model of Moreno's original theatre. The client uses toy figures and objects to represent the significant figures in their drama (Figure 14.1).

Rosenthal has found that simple geometric shapes such as balls and blocks can, by their very neutrality, be useful symbols for clients who might not at first be prepared to use toy figures. She values the nonverbal stage of the work when the client is selecting figures and setting the scene on stage (Rosenthal 2004). She might begin by inviting the client to choose a figure to represent himself or herself and then proceed to work with whatever other figures might emerge, whether real or imaginary. Dialogues and action can then develop between figures, with the client being both director and narrator, simultaneously in the action and in the audience.

Rosenthal uses the theatre with individuals and couples. It is a powerful and effective method. I have used it and found that even a single empty toy chair on the stage can be remarkably evocative. I have used it with clients to explore their dreams and fantasies: it is especially useful with survivors of abuse, for whom work on a larger scale might be overwhelming. It also engages the client in play, putting them in control and enabling them to look at scenes from a safe distance. (For further information on the Rosenthal Process see www.rosenthalstage.com.au.)

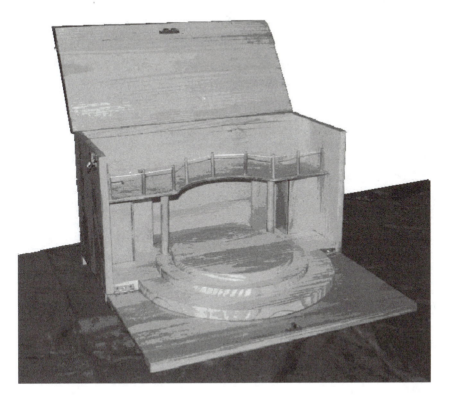

Figure 14.1 The Rosenthal Stage

The Communicube

The Communicube is a development of button sculpting which was invented during research with people who hear voices and struggle with psychotic experiences (Casson 2002, 2004a, 2005). It was originally called the Five Story Self Structure (Figure 14.2).

The Communicube is a transparent, open, five-level container. Light reflects off the shelves, which are each printed with a grid of 25 squares. These grids float within the structure like a series of transparent chessboards, one above the other. Clients are invited to choose buttons, stones or other small objects and place them on the structure, creating patterns and symbolising parts of the self and significant issues in their lives or relationships.

Viewed from above, the whole is instantly visible – a mandala containing disparate elements yet integrated in one world. The Communicube is a twenty-first-century communication tool for use in individual, group, couple

Figure 14.2 The Communicube

and family therapy, supervision, team building, life coaching, education and play. It is flexible, empowering and containing, and provides sufficient distance from material that might otherwise overwhelm.

A circular version, the Communiwell, is also available. Instead of a grid of squares, it has three concentric circles on each level (Figure 14.3).

Using the Communicube in individual therapy

In this chapter there is not sufficient space to describe all of the uses for the Communicube and the Communiwell, so I will focus on their use in individual therapy:

1   I show the person the structure and ask them what they see, notice and imagine it is. Often the structure has reminded people of the three-dimensional chess set in *Star Trek* or, alternatively, a multistorey car park, office block, department store or house. We might explore this image and develop a story. The structure clearly intrigues people, and if they are willing to continue to use it we move on to stage 2.

2   I offer the client the opportunity to choose buttons and place them wherever they wish. This might lead to developing a pattern and to storymaking. This step may be useful in enabling the person to use the structure. It is more distanced than the next step and in not stipulating what the pattern might be, this step gives the person maximum freedom

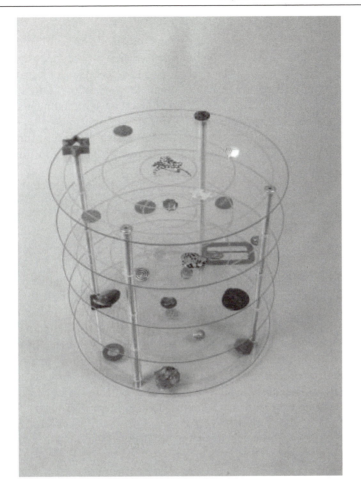

Figure 14.3 The Communiwell

to project whatever they will on to the structure. Alternatively we might pass straight to stage 3.

3 I invite the person to choose one button to represent themselves: 'to be you: place it wherever you feel you are or wish to be'. (This might lead to two buttons being chosen – a real self and an ideal self.)

4 'Choose more buttons to represent other aspects of yourself or people or things in your life and place them.' As clients talk of various elements in their experience, I encourage them to symbolise each element. For example, when someone says 'I feel stuck' I would invite them to find a button that represents their 'stuckness' and place it where they feel it is in the structure.

5 Once the elements and people are symbolised in the structure, dialogues may be developed between them and buttons can be moved as they dialogue. The miniature psychodrama emerges spontaneously.

6 'Step back and look at the pattern you have created: look at the scene from different sides and angles. What do you notice?' Often shadows and reflections of buttons on different levels or new alignments between elements become apparent during this observing stage.

7 'Look down from above so you can see the whole pattern through the different layers (of the transparent shelves). What do you notice? Are there any changes you want to make?'

8 'Reflect, express how you feel and discuss what you notice.'

How and why is the Communicube effective?

The Communicube has proved to be an extraordinarily flexible and useful method. The structure enables play and concentration – it fascinates and focuses, thus enabling people to concentrate. It enables people to explore creatively through stories and patterns (right brain activities) their mental and spiritual 'geography' – 'the hidden strata of the self' (Porter 2002: 187). People using it can, in effect, create a three-dimensional model of their whole psyche, their relationships with others and the world. In doing so, they see structure emerge from chaos. With such structure emerges meaning. It has sometimes been breathtaking to watch this process as people have realised insights through placing the buttons in relation to one another. The process leads to dramatised encounters with parts of self and other people symbolically held in the structure – in other words, miniature psychodrama. The effective elements in the process of using the Communicube include:

- the value of a containing structure;
- the buttons and objects hold roles and enable the client to see the relationships between these different aspects of self and other;
- the integrative holding of diverse elements and polarities so that the whole is visible;
- the focusing effect of the structure: its ability to encourage concentration;
- the distance afforded by the use of miniature objects to symbolise aspects of people's experience that might otherwise be overwhelming;
- the different perspectives available and the development of the observer ego;
- the generative power of the structure, which evokes archetypal imagery and energy;
- its open flexibility and neutrality: meaning emerges but the meaning is decided by the client;

- the value of the structure as an intermediary/transitional object between client and therapist, evoking Winnicott's 'playground' (1991: 47) and Bannister's 'the space between' (2003: 27);
- the creative fun of pattern making.

Pattern recognition is a right brain activity. When we are born, the right brain hemisphere is more developed than the left brain. This ensures that within hours and days of being born, babies can recognise their mother's face (facial recognition being an instantaneous appreciation of a complex pattern). This helps to promote attachment and forms the bedrock of human psychological development. Faces communicate feelings, and so there is a close relationship in the right brain between patterns, faces, feelings and communication. The way the mother/caregiver looks at the baby promotes brain development and affect regulation (Schore 1994). Through the subtle modulation of facial patterns, the parent communicates, nonverbally, potentially integrative and developmental signals (or their reverse: destructive, negative messages). The infant absorbs these messages and patterns into the very fabric of their nascent self-structure.

Often, when we struggle in life, the patterns we have difficulty with are those that are fundamental to our struggle: the patterns of our emotional life, our relationships, the different parts of ourselves. The Communicube facilitates communication about these complex patterns. Psychotherapy has not only to do with examining old, dysfunctional patterns but also with creating and exploring new patterns. Using the Communicube we can build a more complex picture of ourselves, create new patterns and gain an overview of the whole, thus achieving greater insight and integration. Anne Makin, a gestalt psychotherapist, has found the Communicube useful with clients who dissociate. Reflecting on it, she writes:

> The German word 'gestalt,' when put into English, translates into 'the whole is greater than the sum of the parts.' The Communicube contains the parts and also allows the whole, which is greater than the sum of these, to gradually emerge for both client and therapist. The 'whole' is a dynamic experienced in the moment and will, by definition therefore, be experienced differently over time; it is this phenomenon that allows the client to experience, chew over, assimilate, integrate and move on at the pace that is in line with their changing capacities. Providing the therapist accompanies the client at his/her pace, I believe that the Communicube can be a very user-friendly means of developing inter-personal and intra-personal communication.
>
> (Anne Makin, personal communication, 5 April 2005)

We all need structure in our lives. When people are struggling with the chaos of trauma, complex feelings or conflicted interpersonal relations, the Communicube and the Communiwell can provide a containing structure to achieve some order and discover meaning. This innovative therapeutic method promotes communication in a way that can be both powerful and fun. (For further information on the Communicube see www. communicube.co.uk.)

Conclusion

Working in miniature empowers the client, as they are in control and much larger than these containing structures and their contents. Indeed the client has total power while using the Rosenthal Process and the Communicube, where they are the director, casting agent, stage manager, scriptwriter and audience (see also Chapter 4 by Blatner on the meta-role). Both methods promote the development of the observer ego, enabling clients to gain insight and liberating distance from material that might otherwise overwhelm. The playfulness of the methods also attracts, energises and frees the person to explore difficulties, solve problems and find new solutions. They discover resources and points of view of which they were unaware. Symbolisation through miniatures promotes disclosure and thinking. The Rosenthal Process and the Communicube are containing structures which facilitate the emergence of meaning and creative, therapeutic work in safe and playful ways.

References

Bannister, A. (2000) 'Prisoners of the family: psychodrama with abused children', in P. F Kellermann and M. K. Hudgins (2000) *Psychodrama with Trauma Survivors: Acting Out Your Pain*, London: Jessica Kingsley Publishers.
—— (2003) *Creative Therapies with Traumatised Children*, London: Jessica Kingsley Publishers.
Casson, J. (1998) 'Right/left brain and dramatherapy', *Journal of the British Association for Dramatherapists*, 20, 1: 12–15.
—— (2002) 'Dramatherapy and psychodrama as psychotherapeutic interventions with people who hear voices (auditory hallucinations)', unpublished PhD thesis, Manchester Metropolitan University.
—— (2004a) *Drama, Psychotherapy and Psychosis: Dramatherapy and Psychodrama with People who Hear Voices*, Hove: Brunner-Routledge.
—— (2004b) 'Sculpting', *Prompt: Newsletter of the British Association of Dramatherapists*, Summer.
—— (2005) *The Communicube: An Instruction Manual for the Therapeutic Method of The Five Storey Self Structure: Concerning Theory and Practice*. Manchester: Communicube (www.communicube.co.uk).
Cook, C. (1917) *The Play Way*, London: Heineman.
Holmes, P., Karp, M. and Watson, M. (1994) *Psychodrama since Moreno*, London: Routledge.

Jennings, S. (1986) *Creative Drama in Groupwork*, Bicester: Winslow Press.

—— (1990) *Dramatherapy with Families, Groups and Individuals: Waiting in the Wings*, London: Jessica Kingsley Publishers.

Lowenfeld, M. (1935) *Play in Childhood*, London: Gollancz.

McLuskie, M. (1983) 'Dramatherapy in a psychiatric hospital', *Journal of the British Association of Dramatherapists*, 6, 2: 20–25.

Porter, R. (2002) *Madness: A Brief History*, Oxford: Oxford University Press.

Rosenthal, A. (2004) *The Rosenthal Process, Manual No 1*, private publication (see www.learninginaction.info).

Rosenzweig, S. and Shakow, D. (1937) 'Play technique in schizophrenia and other psychoses', *American Journal of Orthopsychiatry*, 7: 32–47.

Schore, A. N. (1994) *Affect Regulation and the Origin of the Self: The Neurobiology of Emotional Development*, Mahwah, NJ: Lawrence Erlbaum Associates, Inc.

Slade, P. (1980) *Child Drama*, London: Hodder and Stoughton.

—— (1995) *Child Play: Its Importance for Human Development*, London: Jessica Kingsley Publishers.

Wells, H. G. (1911) *Floor Games*, London: Frank Palmer (republished 1931, London: Dent).

Winnicott, D. W. (1991) *Playing and Reality*, London: Tavistock/Routledge.

Chapter 15

Sociometric scenarios and psychotherapy

Anna Maria Knobel

Introduction

While J. L. Moreno considered that the human baby is born with the gift of spontaneity, he also observed that, in order for the child to develop, favourable relationships are necessary. The simple passage of time does not guarantee that a person matures well.

Psychodramatic theory has a specific field that covers the understanding of relationship scenarios – sociometry – and this chapter will explore sociometry from a clinical perspective. I will leave aside the aspects related to measuring relationships, already widely discussed (Bustos 1979; Hale 1981). I will focus instead on an exploration of how our subjective relationships construct the way we see the world from a personal perspective and promote growth, making life worth living.

Moreno's sociometric focus

While studying Moreno's writing about his experiences with groups, I observed that there is a clear and definite mark in his sociometric practices. They always begin from situations where there is discomfort, suffering or rejection, and aim at reaching group inclusion. This movement occurs by way of:

- the development of telic-spontaneous states between people who relate with each other
- by the management of a shared action
- by the acceptance of multiplicity, differences and the unexpected.

Another characteristic of Moreno's sociometric focus is that it is linked to the description of relational phenomena that occur *between* people and not to theoretical conceptions of life events. Thus the sociometric procedures tend to be closely related to natural processes that encourage the human being to grow, understand the world and to know himself or herself. These sociometric processes, while paralleling natural processes, stimulate each person involved to be an active agent, capable of empathic social behaviour and capable also of expanding their view of their own life and the lives of people around them.

Sociometry also looks for feeling and understanding coming from within the group, as the sociometric researcher uses the information originating from the participants themselves. Moreno says: 'The cornerstone of socio-metry is its *doctrine of spontaneity and creativity* . . . it gives its subjects research status by changing them from subjects into participating and evaluating actors' (Moreno 1953: 18). In this way 'the organism in the field becomes the actor in situ' (Moreno 1953: 61).

Action research

Lewin called this type of method 'action-research': 'an action at realistic level, always followed by an objective self-critical reflection of the results. [. . .] We do not want action without research, nor research without action' (Barbier 2002: 29). Moreno complements this idea when he observes: 'especially in the human sphere one cannot understand the social present unless he tries to change it' (Moreno 1972: 9). Thus we have flow and interplay between action, reflection and change.

Barbier (2002) points to different perspectives on action research. Among his perspectives, one that best describes Moreno's different sociometric interventions is the 'axiological perspective' that aims 'to render human suffering less difficult, working with social dysfunctions and to privilege the forms of democratic management' (Barbier 2002: 31). Other perspectives are:

- 'praxiology' which optimizes action and facilitates decision
- 'methodological,' combining clinical work and experimentation
- 'epistemologic,' as Kurt Lewin proposes – a theory of the field.

A category system for sociometry

Moreno's sociometric theory and experiments enabled the construction of a fascinating and useful micro socio-psychology that allows us to understand and to work with the relationships of groups. However, in spite of the fact that he created refined and complex instruments for sociometric research (Moreno 1953), his writing can at times appear unclear and this may prompt methodological lapses. Trying to organize and apprehend Moreno's sociometric ideas in a whole and integral way, I suggest a new organization based on their functional categories:

- category one: spatial features of sociometry
- category two: dramatic concepts within sociometry

- category three: sociometry and human motivation
- category four: sociometry and co-conscious and co-unconscious states.

Category one: spatial features of sociometry

The first category is organized around the spatial nature of some sociometric terms. This includes concepts such as: social atom; sociometric network; locus; central, peripheral and isolated sociometric positions; sociogram; relational structures with their configurations (pairs, chains, triangles, circles); and also the techniques of the double and the mirror.

To what does this way of thinking relate? To a vision of man as a *being-among-others*, that is *structured being with*. In this universe, personal life is constituted and gains its unique characteristics from relational proximity and distance.

In order to adequately develop, a child must be seen and valued by its caretakers, having its needs met in an empathetic manner. In many ways, the child's needs must come first, and capable and attuned parents understand this when they prioritize the child's needs. Castello de Almeida (personal communication, ca. 1990) observes that sociometry may embrace the 'narcissistic core' in the individual because it enables the understanding of the fluctuating set of relationships that influence the definition of each one's value – that is, the constellation of positions and sociometric status present in the social atom where it is inserted. In the social atom we are at the centre of the world.

Sociometry is still highly contemporary, even though it was created more than 70 years ago with a vocabulary and conceptual apparatus that appears distant. Sociometry theory may benefit from some of the more recent dynamic theories such as cybernetics and the notion of a cybernetic network. This may enrich our notion of the sociometric network. The concept of the cybernetic network includes within it the idea that what is *between* is movable and what is movable is in a chain without beginning or end – more a continuous flow than a structure. This idea is more fully explored in the following sections.

Category two: dramatic concepts within sociometry

The second set of concepts is linked to the theatre, with the notions of warming up, protagonist, stage, scenario, audience, role, spontaneous theatre, role playing, role reversal, actor (in the sense of agent of his own action), auxiliary ego, and spontaneity and role tests. These are all notions deeply interconnected to Moreno's sociometric practices, even though they do not immediately present themselves as being among the techniques of measuring relational structures. We recall that in his work in Hudson, New York, after mapping groups based on girls' sociometric choices, Moreno worked with role playing, as he thought that 'they must hang together by spontaneous affinities in order that one becomes a therapeutic agent of the other' (Moreno 1953: 712).

To what does the theatre point when we think about being in a group and in relationships? It points to the idea of action, but a type of action that occurs in distinct contexts, configured in space – temporal scenes and sequences. The theatre allows an amalgam between present time and memory that moves in the flexible and complex field of *here and now* as a scene lived and evoked. Theatre allows for the generation of images, thoughts, affections and impulses that belong to the past, present and future, all of this lived and experienced in a shared and collective way, in the 'inter-intra' of relationships. The theatre enables the experimentation with characters, and the exercise of being many others. This can help to challenge repetitions and stereotypes, opening many perspectives and different ways of seeing past experiences.

Theatre also leads us, by way of role performance, to action and cultural and personal guidelines. These are described by Moreno when he says that every role is a fusion of individual and collective elements, being composed of two parts, its 'collective denominators' and its 'individual differentials' (Moreno 1953: 75). Contro understands the 'collective denominators' as most closely relating to sociocultural analysis, and he relates the 'individual differentials' to the field of experiences of each person with their closest partners: 'I understand them as confluent angles of the same phenomenon [. . .] they are in constant and mutual interaction, not existing distinctly' (Contro 2004: 62).

Category three: sociometry and human motivation

A third set of concepts is organized around motivations, that is to say, what mobilizes each person in their interactions with other people, both in a positive way (as expectation or experience of satisfaction) and a negative way (as repulse or displeasure in living together). Included in this category are the movements of coming closer, growing apart and indifference between people, and various concepts such as criteria, social and emotional expansiveness, saturation point, sociodynamic law, identification, opinion, social and psychological currents and sociometric status.

According to Moreno, if the sociometric choices show the position of each member of the group in the relational structures, 'the motivations given, however inarticulated, disclose how individualistic the reactions are' (Moreno 1953: 329). The choices map the emotional needs, the projects and expectations that each person believes are important for him or her.

Motivations reveal a kind of entrance door to each person's sense of self-identity, configured over their lifetime. Put another way, the emotional expression that each person brings to their social roles reflects what that person experienced in their 'matrix of identity' (Moreno 1972) and in other previous relationships and experiences.

This perspective enables us to follow Moreno in his search for the 'locus', the 'matrix' and the 'status nascendi' (Moreno 1972) of people's values, practices and myths, as well as their symptoms, stereotype behaviours and inhibitions, whether they are individual or collective. The histories and enactments resulting from this search reveal conceptual forms that each individual or group takes up when speaking about himself or herself (or the group). Mascarenhas (1995) calls this mosaic of versions of reality the 'founding myth'.

Starting from any element in a session that presents an obstacle to fluidity in the relationships, spontaneity or individual or group protagonist atmosphere, Perazzo (1994) defines a sequence of phases for addressing such hindrances using psychodramatic processes. He suggests a strategy of using psychodrama processes to follow the 'enchaining of transferential links' in order to reach the origins of the symptoms. During this journey, 'an imaginary role that is rigid becomes a spontaneous and creative psychodramatic role, opening a path for the catharsis of integration that will only become visible in the evolution of the process' (Perazzo 1994: 74).

Category four: sociometry and co-conscious and co-unconscious states

The fourth category concerns co-conscious and co-unconscious states. These states are difficult to define because, as Moreno observed, they 'are by definition, such states which the partners have experienced and produced jointly and which can, therefore be only jointly reproduced or re-enacted [. . .] a co-conscious or a co-unconscious state can not be property of one individual only' (Moreno 1972: vii).

From this perspective, the unconscious contents are part of these relationships, configuring an interpersonal and transpersonal field of events that happens between and beyond people. The co-unconscious can be described as the shared states, the matrix of what is good or destructive, the group fantasies, atmosphere, climate, coincidences of thought and action, feelings of synchronicity and emotional consonances that may occur among people. Another way to say this is that the co-unconscious is what is everywhere but it is not seen, yet it is sometimes felt. It evokes what was experienced far from there and becomes a complex of experiences, emotions, thoughts and multipersonal sensations. It is kept beyond the time and space of real relationships, involving and also depending on the facilitator who, by his or her way of being, influences the style of the group.

I believe that from this perspective we may interpret that the 'tele' function implies a certain quality of emotions that enables the consonances and emotional intersections to evoke simultaneously unique subjective states in two or more people. In being enlightened by a relational focus, the subjective states organize and transform themselves into representations that may be shared. This process produces in people a sensation of familiarity, intimacy and even momentary fusion, in which each one understands the other existentially. In this transformation, there is no loss of the unique richness of the events. This transformation of particular experiences in shared mental states remains anchored in the specificity of experiences they result from.

Volpe (1990) has made a systematic study of Moreno's concept of the co-unconscious, describing it as a set of phantasm-like mental formations originating from the ancestors (therefore transgenerational). These mental representations are embodied by descendants who, without knowing, fulfil the mandates of prior generations. Volpe notes a correlation between the notion of *tele* and that of *destiny* in the universe of tragic heroes. Thus, 'psycho-sociodrama presents man constituted by the dimension of mystery, de-centered from him/herself [. . .] To know him/herself, a human being must recognize that we are all preceded by a definitive script going back many generations, a script that is beyond our control and may even overtake us' (Volpe 1990: 94).

In this complex and moveable universe created by socio-psychodrama, auxiliary (surplus reality) worlds enable us to have in the *here and now* of shared scenes experiences that modify the senses and disassemble the codes of these crystallized pre-scripted roles, opening channels for spontaneous forces.

Another question to be considered from co-unconscious phenomena refers to the transit between the public and the private, between sociodrama and psychodrama. It is up to the director of the group to evaluate when and if this passage is validated by the contract and by the group project, so that no member of the group is exposed and transformed into a scapegoat of defensive group dynamics. In the same way, one must be careful not to understand social situations by means of reducing them to psychological dynamics.

Where these concepts take us

What may we conclude from our journey through these four conceptual categories? First, we can observe that here is a collection of ideas – proximity and distance; action structured in scenes, plots and characters; human motivation; and co-conscious and co-unconscious effects – that mutually interweave and interdetermine each other, forming an articulate theoretical construction, as vivid as the phenomena they describe. In addition, the sociometric practices configure an empirical field where specific themes (social and emotional expansiveness; sociometric status, position and criteria; sociogram; sociometric networks; psychological currents; social atom; and relational structures) can be articulated. Within the context of this empirical field, the basic notions of psychodrama (spontaneity, tele, warming up, roles, role playing) can be better understood. As Moreno writes: 'No concept has a meaning by itself. Terms and concepts are interdependent within the entire system. No one factor is an independent variable. The more significant the factor, the more dependent it is upon others' (Moreno 1953: 719).

A second branch of this conceptual journey makes it clear that quantitative research is just the first sociometric strategy. It delineates the contours of the group that will be exposed to different methods. In this way, sociometry organically integrates itself with the conceptual body of psychodrama. If a person has a problem created as a result of inadequate relationships, in order to be transformed the person needs boundaried and congruent relationships.

Such a theoretical position depends on practices that can generate an empathetic co-existence in the group, creating a kind of social womb, to be offered to people who suffer psychologically or socially. The constitution of this welcoming relational matrix is systematically repeated in all practices by Moreno. Thus, it is a constant within the psychodramatic method. Other constants include the acceptance of the client and his or her way of being in the world and the acting out of the protagonist in the 'as if' (Knobel 2004).

A third result of our journey makes it evident that the group facilitator who uses a sociometric approach is in the position of 'holder of other people's truth'. The facilitator recognizes that they are immersed in the group co-conscious/co-unconscious system, acting as the decipherer of the group's sense and of the forces in struggle. The facilitator recognizes that, in these conditions, they have a central role in the warm-up of the group and potential protagonists. The role of facilitator demands a capacity for empathy, the ability to engage in telic-spontaneous states and, perhaps most of all, consistent theoretical knowledge on which to base the work.

Developing relationships in the group

In discussing contemporary ways of understanding sociometry and with the intention of exploring its clinical applications, I next present a device for the understanding and direction of groups that seems to me to be useful to orient the action of the group facilitator. This is centred on the understanding of the *development of relationships* in groups, how relationships are organized and how they evolve.

Moreno observes: 'The three directions or tendencies of structure we have described for baby groups, *organic isolation, horizontal differentiation* and *vertical differentiation* [my italics], are fundamental features in the development of groups. We find them appearing again and again, however extensive and complex the groups become' (Moreno 1953: 202). With this observation of Moreno's in mind, I have assembled a set of strategies for direction that enable the facilitator to understand and intervene in the functioning of groups (Knobel 1996). I use the terminology proposed by Moreno, characterizing these three phases.

It is important to say that these are not phases that, once lived, do not repeat themselves. Instead they are phases that occur alternately and constantly in the life of groups. They refer to processes of evolution that have their focus in the collective, not being mere transpositions of individual phenomena to group situations.

Phase 1: isolation

In a recently formed group, where people hardly know each other, the first moment is that of isolation. There are few contacts, practically no possibility of discrimination of individual characteristics or repertoire of roles present in the group. The possibility of an organized action together is at a minimum and the group project is a virtual concept, yet to be attained.

Each person knows about himself or herself, but little or nothing about the other people. In general, the atmosphere in the group is that of tension and curiosity. The most anxious people may act in an impulsive or defensive manner. For the participants, the basic rule in this phase is to be with oneself, to exercise the capacity of introspection, to respect one's own rhythm, to support the isolation and to observe the movements of the group.

In this phase, it is up to the facilitator to centralize communication and be the focus of attention; to promote warming up; to describe and reaffirm the objectives of this activity; to work with the group to define the contract of the group; to provide participants with minimum conditions of calm and boundaries so that they can deal with their fears and anxieties; to understand the need of a first self-centred movement that allows the participants to take up the role of a member in the group; and to propose different types of introspective exercises (physical, mental or emotional) with which one can establish brief contacts between people. These tasks, as they are consonant with the early phase of the group, facilitate the experience of the group process and the passage to the next phase.

Phase 2: horizontal differentiation

The moment of horizontal differentiation has as a characteristic the need from each participant to distinguish the other people from each other. It works with the different identities that exist in the group. In this phase, each person gets closer, sees, examines, meets the other people and also shows themselves to the group. Each person can signal the attention of the others, and may do this with different degrees of appropriateness and success. The action tends to be individual, but turned to the others.

Many movements of approach and separation come up between people. Contacts tend to be quick, forming pairs or trios that soon fall apart. In this phase, some people may get together in a defensive manner and, indeed, sometimes coupling occurs. The atmosphere is that of tumult, agitation, many people talking at the same time, without a centralizing action, in spite of the fact that there is already some possibility of organization.

The most common feelings are those of pleasure in the experimentation, showing off, seeing the other people and discovering the unknown. There may be some frustration for lack of success in showing oneself off, for not finding complementary people or experiencing the desired admiration. Discouragement, anger, feelings of emptiness and the desire to run away from the group may also appear.

The action of the facilitator is still directive. The facilitator's functions in this phase are: to value diversity and the unique aspects of each person; to propose activities that increase the power and safety of participants; to enable many contacts between participants; to facilitate exchanges in different kinds of actions and roles. The offer of different roles is very important, because the different roles promote the manifestation of unique ways of social interaction and provide specific structures for spontaneity and psychic functioning. In addition, different kinds of experiences, and warming up for spontaneous states, favour the inclusion of all the group members. These strategies help each individual to live this moment, as well as the transit to the next phase.

Phase 3: vertical differentiation

In the moment of vertical differentiation, one of the group members focuses the attention of the others. Group leaders emerge, and people who are interested follow them. The group generates various proposals that are attractive to some people, and there is the possibility of identification, whether with ideas or people.

Because the group members have begun to discriminate those to whom they are more or less attracted, cooperation becomes possible. This cooperation is assisted by the fact that common objectives are emerging. Subgroups are organized, resulting from the need to belong and look for equals with the aim of collective work. In this phase, the group can attain complex collective objectives. The atmosphere oscillates between collaboration and dispute. The feelings may become radical and part of the group may dominate others. Tension may grow and action in the group may become intense. There may be curiosity, admiration and pleasure in being with the other people, as well as space disputes, anger and envy.

In this phase, it is important that the facilitator promotes leadership. The facilitator will focus on reciprocity and common objectives, make evident and guide digressions, favour actions based on the objectives of the group, note proposals that oppose the contract or the objectives of the group, and close activities when needed.

Benefits for the group

This set of facilitator strategies tends to guarantee the turn and voice of everyone and subgroups, enabling successive levels of representation for collective actions. In addition, in favouring the inclusion of minority voices within the group, the facilitator promotes the functioning of the group, as people who are isolated tend to have difficulties integrating by themselves and need the attention and intervention of the facilitator (or some leader) to participate. Even more importantly, people who are isolated in the group serve to indicate that changes are needed in the group and how it is working. When the force of those not integrated overcomes group cohesion, this results in difficulties in the functioning of the group, which can lose sight of its objectives and often collapses.

However, even if after many movements and efforts a person does not find a place in the group, it is up to the facilitator to help them leave in a dignified manner.

Conclusion

Closing this journey through the world of sociometry and relationships, which Moreno advocated and valued so much, I believe that we may recognize sociometry as a privileged field. It is an extraordinary approach for understanding the forces involved in interpersonal relationships and for instilling a certain empathetic proximity, crucial to the vitality of human encounters.

Moreno's sociometric tools for social analysis and intervention are also useful in helping us to understand and attend to the demands that our patients and participants daily present us with. They enable us to create responsive spaces that can help to counter some of the oppressive realities of contemporary life, such as loneliness, exacerbated competition and deep distortions regarding what is of most value in human beings and their relationships.

References

Barbier, R. (2002) *A pesquisa Ação* [*Action Research*], Brasília: Plano Editora.
Bustos, D. (1979) *O teste sociométrico* [*The Sociometric Test*], São Paulo: Brasiliense.

Contro, L. (2004) *Nos jardins do Psicodrama* [*In the Gardens of Psychodrama*], Campinas: Editora Alínea.

Hale, A. (1981) *Conducting Clinical Sociometric Explorations: A Manual for Psychodramatists and Sociometrists*, Roanoke, VA: Royal Publishing Company.

Knobel, A. (1996) 'Estratégias de direção grupal' [Strategies of group direction], *Revista Brasileira de Psicodrama* 4, 1: 49–62.

——— (2000) 'Átomo social, o pulsar das relações' [Social atom, the pulsating of relationships], in R. Pamplona da Costa (ed.) *Um homem a frente do seu tempo, o psicodrama no século XXI* [*A Man Ahead of his Time: Psychodrama in the 21st Century*], São Paulo: Agora.

——— (2004) *Moreno em ato, a construção do psicodrama a partir das práticas* [*Moreno in Action: The Construction of Psychodrama from Practice*], São Paulo: Agora.

Mascarenhas, P. (1995) 'Multiplicação dramática: uma poética do psicodrama' [Dramatic multiplication: the poetics of psychodrama], unpublished monograph, São Paulo.

Moreno, J. L. (1953) *Who shall survive? Foundations of Sociometry, Group Psychotherapy and Sociodrama* (2nd edn), Beacon, NY: Beacon House. (Originally published 1934.)

——— (1972) *Psychodrama, Volume One*, Mclean, VA: American Society for Group Psychotherapy and Psychodrama. (Originally published 1946.)

Perazzo, S. (1994) *Ainda e sempre psicodrama* [*Still and Always Psychodrama*], São Paulo: Agora.

Volpe, J. A. (1990) *Édipo, psicodrama do destino* [*Oedipus, Psychodrama of Destiny*], São Paulo: Agora.

Chapter 16

A neuroscience perspective on psychodrama

Edward Hug

Introduction

In this chapter I will introduce the reader to some recent neuroscience research as it seems relevant to the practice of psychodrama. The 1990s were the 'Decade of the Brain' and neuroscience has been expanding quickly in terms of hard, peer-reviewed science dedicated to understanding the brain and its relationship to cognition, affect, addictions, behaviors and therapies. We are living at a time in which psychology is becoming more open to incorporating neurological understanding.

The brain is an action-oriented organ, so it should not be surprising that its integrative potential is realized through action. Where words are inadequate or blocked from access to primary material, the brain is open to other avenues of expression. The psychological dynamics explored by psychodrama reflect fundamental operations within the brain/body in which emotional dynamics favor more subcortical layers and rational modes favor more neocortical layers of the brain.

The protagonist in the action phase of a psychodrama enters a state of mild regression which involves two things: a partial return to an earlier stage of development, and a re-use of a more primary mode of functioning. This regression involves a partial diminishing of the prefrontal cortex's inhibiting system so that information in the corticolimbic system may emerge and be integrated. This information is more accessible to the image-oriented right cerebral hemisphere than to the linguistic left hemisphere. Healing may be framed in terms of integration between hemispheres or integration between prefrontal and corticolimbic systems (Cozolino 2002).

The dominant cerebral hemisphere (usually the left) tends to form narratives more related to social adaptations than to inner images. It is, in many ways, a 'confabulation machine' – confabulation being the fabrication of stories not actually recalled (a concept often used in connection with 'false memories'). The dominant hemisphere rationalizes and distorts inner realities to fit what appears to be the 'reality' of the social group and the social context, i.e. the cultural conserve.

This presents a limitation to purely cognitive therapies. The recessive cerebral hemisphere (usually the right) is the image-forming side of the brain, and is better connected to the body's somatosensory systems, to childhood attachment experiences and traumatic experiences, and to affect regulation processes. It is the primary resource for the 'truth of the body.' Experiential approaches to psychotherapy, such as psychodrama, bridge these two modes, promoting psychological integration.

Our two 'brains' – that is, the left and right hemispheres of our brain – are connected primarily through (a) the Corpus Callosum, a large bundle of nerves connecting the two hemispheres of our brain; and (b) their shared body, i.e. the rest of our body. Research is consistently pointing to a striking neurobiological and developmental reality: what we have not integrated through the Corpus Callosum (internal to the brain) will get integrated through the body, possibly in the form of psychosomatic symptoms, compulsions or unregulated behaviors.

Psychodrama and the potential space

There is a world where play and reality are not antithetical, nor clearly separate either. It is into this world that the action phase of psychodrama places its protagonist. Play arises from the same subcortical layers of our brain which we share with our fellow mammals (Panksepp 1998), and it also profoundly influences cortical functioning. It is this urge to play that arises in the 'potential space of the child,' a term which D. W. Winnicott (1989) used to describe that intermediate space between inner and outer realities. The 'potential space' is especially active in children at times of increasing language ability, and when they are learning, through play, the normative values of their culture.

In neurological terms, the 'potential space' corresponds to a stage of brain development in which the left brain is increasingly active in establishing a narrative of the self and finding appropriate connections to the right brain. Prior to this stage, the right brain has been particularly active in regulating attachment processes and establishing a 'core' self (Schore 1999).

Case example: Annie

This case takes place during a psychodrama session which I am directing in a 'partial hospital program' at a hospital in Connecticut, USA. Annie has emerged from the group as the protagonist. Her issue is that she has just gone through a divorce and is very poor, almost not able to live on her own. Her father has offered to take her in, but she wants to be independent and not go back to living with her father, with whom she cannot communicate effectively. We play a psychodramatic 'current scene' between her and her father and discover her huge anxiety to even speak with her father about needing help. I ask her when she has experienced this specific kind of anxiety in the past, and she remembers a scene at the beach when she was five years old.

The second scene of the psychodrama is at the beach. Annie is playing near the water, with her parents a short distance away. Suddenly, a large wave comes and overwhelms her, knocking her over. She goes screaming to her father and sits in his lap. Her father comforts her just a little, and then sends her off to play again. But for little Annie, her father has sent her away too soon! 'I needed him to hold me longer, until I was ready to go back and play!' She goes back to playing but with a heightened feeling of anxiety (and therefore with less spontaneity).

So for the third scene, we replay the second scene (on the beach) 'the way it could have been.' Annie goes screaming to her father and sits in his lap. But this time her father *holds* her, and keeps holding her until she is 'finished needing to be held,' until she has really calmed down. *Then* she goes back to playing, but this time with less anxiety (and therefore more spontaneity).

The fourth scene takes place back in the 'current time,' and in this scene she is able to *negotiate* with her father about needing help, and to accept limited help while preserving her own sense of autonomy.

Discussion

This (much simplified) case example illustrates how psychodrama can be seen as a return to the play space of the child, and addresses the question of how affective memory can be changed through psychodrama in service of current coping skills. To provide a quick review of affective memory, this is the memory system that involves: (a) the amygdala, which is the part of the brain responsible for conditioned responses and affective appraisal; (b) the orbital-frontal cortex, which is responsible for attributing the salience of information and sensory inputs. The affective memory system is contrasted with the explicit memory system, which is centered in the hippocampus.

Let us consider the neurological aspects of this life event and its consequences for Annie, and the effect of the psychodrama on her neurobiology. In the early scene (five-year-old Annie on the beach), the wave feels life threatening to Annie, and her father feels like he is (or should be) her harbor of safety. When the wave overwhelms her, this event registers in her amygdala-based fear memory system as 'dangerous' (the amygdala, mentioned earlier, is the principle organ in the limbic brain which registers fearful memories and the emotional qualities of other memories). This produces, among other responses, an increase in stress hormones (principally cortisol). This set of responses prepares Annie to flee the danger.

However, such a high level of stress hormones interferes with Annie's natural spontaneity, in part by compromising her hippocampus, which serves an integrative function for new experiences coming into the brain. Annie's natural need is to reduce anxiety and she does this (quite appropriately) by allowing herself to be held by her father. But her father's holding is inadequate, and so she is left with unresolved anxiety, which remains as a memory residue in the amygdala-based fear-memory system of her right brain, only to resurface later in a stressful situation with regard to her father. Her adult inability to regulate her stress is a direct result of not having learned it at an earlier age. The role of the right brain in such 'affect regulation' is very well explored by Allan Schore (1999, 2003).

A word about 'holding': Annie's traumatic event activates her hypothalamic-pituitary-adrenal (HPA) axis, producing an ongoing release of high levels of stress hormones such as cortisol which, if not diminished, may disrupt the neural maturation of her developing brain. Such disturbances may lead to a vulnerability to psychiatric disorders developing later in life, such as depression, chronic anxiety and attention deficit hyperactivity disorder (ADHD). Secure, empathic holding is needed by the affect regulating system in her right orbital prefrontal cortex, and is extremely important for the neural development of this child.

By using psychodrama to re-enter the old scene (on the beach), we are also reactivating Annie's 'fear system' which is centered on the amygdala. Once we are inside the fear system, we can help Annie learn something new and give her a better experience of being held. This gives her a new affective memory in support of her capacity to 'self-soothe' and receive appropriate holding and support from other people.

Lateralization in the brain: core vs narrative consciousness

The right brain is the seat of body awareness, spatial orientation, image formation and 'core consciousness,' while the left brain (especially Broca's Area) is the seat of serialization (i.e. sequencing) of coordinated action, language and 'narrative consciousness.' Psychodrama has to do with connecting body and language through enactment and action.

The left brain memory system is much less accurate at registering experiences than the right brain (Gazzaniga 2002). Evidence for this comes from tests with split-brain patients – patients whose Corpus Callosum has been cut, usually to stop epilepsies. When such patients are presented with new information and later tested, their left brains generate many false reports while the right brain provides a much more accurate account. At Dartmouth, Margaret Funnel has shown that the right brain simply pays attention to raw perceptions, whereas the left brain actively places its experiences in a larger context (Gazzaniga 2002).

Joseph LeDoux, a neuroscientist at New York University, has traced this malleability of memory to a 'reconsolidation' process centered in the hippocampus, a limbic structure which integrates conscious memories (LeDoux 2002). Gazzaniga's experiments suggest that this malleability is a process peculiar to the 'left hemisphere interpreter,' whose perceptions are based on context and surrounding events, and is central to self-narrative and social coping skills (Gazzaniga 2002). As in the case example of Annie, this malleability of memory can be employed to implant modified memories in service of the person's coping skills.

It is interesting to note that the concept of the malleability of memory was put forth long ago by Freud. In a letter to Fleiss, dated 6 December 1896, Freud used the word 'nachträglichkeit' (afterwardsness) to describe a process in which memory is not isomorphic with experience, but laid down many times during successive developmental periods, for each of which a new transcription takes place.

As most body/action oriented psychotherapists know, the body remembers what the conscious mind may confabulate or may not remember at all. Central to the responsible conduct of psychodrama is the process of helping the protagonist to recognize and integrate what the right brain is trying to communicate without upsetting the social coping skills of the left brain. 'Act hunger' is one way of describing this core right brain motive.

Caveat

My emphasis on the 'cerebral lateralization' (right–left) paradigm would be questioned by some people in the neuroscience community whose perspective is more 'front–back' (frontal lobe–corticolimbic system). I believe the truth to be mixed. Since lateralization of function came late in the evolution of our brains (nonhuman mammals and preverbal children have very little functional lateralization), our own earlier subcortical structures are probably not as lateralized as our later ones. Notwithstanding this, the left–right paradigm is a most useful lens for describing human behavior and the underlying brain mechanisms of psychotherapy.

The attentional system

Alan Kingstone of the University of Alberta (Kingstone *et al.* 2000) suggests that the brain's left hemisphere, dominant for self-narrative, can 'hijack' the operations of the right hemisphere in the act of recalling body and earlier emotional states, thus subverting the process of integration. This suggests why psychodrama may be useful, because the action phase engages the body and emotional memories, with the left hemisphere narrative processes momentarily set aside.

During a psychodrama, the left brain attentional system may be re-engaged in forms of narrative. More importantly, attentional resources are so limited that the more one hemisphere works, the harder it is for the other hemisphere to carry out its own tasks. When the protagonist in a psychodrama is engaged in the action of a scene, language and body resources are calling upon one another. At the same time, narrative (reflective) consciousness may not be receiving many attentional resources, so that the director may call for an 'aside' to bring the attentional resources of the protagonist to bear in providing a narrative of the action (mainly a left brain activity). The director of a psychodrama has an impressive power to influence the attentional resources of the protagonist's brain, directing it to affective or reflective resources, to imagery or sensory foci.

Warm-up: anxiety, act hunger and the window of tolerance

Though our left brain narrative consciousness largely defines our ordinary 'self,' it may become progressively estranged from the core consciousness of our right brain. This may give rise to 'act hunger' or other symptoms. But the left brain's 'interest' in preserving the coherence of its narrative will tend to generate defenses (e.g. rationalization) against access by right brain ego-alien consciousness. This produces stress and anxiety.

Anxiety produces adrenal stress hormones which, if excessive, reduce the capacity of our hippocampus to integrate new data. This impairs our spontaneity. Warming up is essential to reducing anxiety and defenses. On the other hand, it is under stress (but not too much stress) that the brain changes its focus to new learning. And new learning, according to Goldberg (2001: 49) involves a shift of emphasis to right brain processes.

How much stress is 'just right?' The hippocampus responds to 'emotional charge' signals from the amygdala according to an 'inverted U' (van der Kolk et al. 1996: 295). This means that too little stimulation from the amygdala produces little integration. Too much stimulation from the amygdala also produces little integration. There is an optimum level of stimulation which produces maximum integration in the hippocampus, which defines a 'window of tolerance.'

The encounter of the narrative consciousness with core consciousness may be experienced as ego alien. Nevertheless, out of this encounter may emerge a deeper level of ego integration, as it incorporates aspects of core consciousness heretofore excluded from narrative consciousness. The group's support for the protagonist during this process is vital for the stabilization of the new learning. This is especially true during the sharing phase, in which the new learning finds resonance with the group.

Doubling, empathy and tele

In the mid-1990s, Vittorio Gallese, Giacomo Rizzolatti and colleagues at the University of Parma identified a new class of neurons. These neurons were active not only when a person performed a certain task, but also when the person observed someone else performing that same task. The team dubbed this new class of neurons 'mirror neurons' and, together with Vilayanur Ramachandran (2004) of the University of California at San Diego, introduced a new paradigm into neuroscience. Mirror neurons are becoming recognized as playing a pivotal role in the way we understand the intentions of others, an 'important part of the mosaic that explains our social abilities' (Gallese 2004). They are also the basis of our brain's ability to represent the intentions of another brain, which goes to the core of psychodramatic doubling.

Using mirror neurons, the observer's brain forms an 'action representation' of the behavior of the other person. Observing the behavior of another person activates two regions of the left brain, the 'superior temporal sulcus' and part of Broca's area – an area associated with speech production. So mirror neurons provide a 'bridge' between 'doing' and 'communicating.' The core of language itself is in pre-motor action representations, and action representations are the core of empathy and doubling.

The meaning of an object, action or social situation may be common to several individuals because they energize distributed patterns of neural activation in their corresponding brains. Decety and Sommerville (2003) at the University of Washington are actively studying the neuroscience of shared representations and their role in interpersonal awareness. It is a direction of current research that may elucidate a neural basis of 'tele.'

Moreno defined tele (or 'valency') as a process 'that attracts individuals to each other or which repels them, that flow of feeling of which the social atom and the networks are apparently composed' (Moreno 1937: 213, quoted in Blatner 1994: 283). In a group, there is for each individual a valency with respect to each other group member. So why are we attracted to certain individuals and repelled by others, even without knowing them?

According to Gazzaniga (1998), split-brain patients respond behaviorally to emotion-provoking stimuli (which reach the right brain) even though they cannot say (with their left brain) what they saw. We recognize faces by virtue of certain regions in our right temporal lobe. But the appraisal/ affective aspect of recognition takes place in areas of the amygdala and orbital frontal cortex. So it is possible to be predisposed toward or away from another person based on amygdala/OFC appraisal with no actual recognition. Certain brain areas serve the purpose of creating emotional valency even without literal recognition.

Spontaneity and the cultural conserve

In order to define spontaneity in terms that can be related to neuro-biological processes, let us draw from Moreno's (1953: 42) definition:

'Spontaneity operates in the present, now and here; it propels the individual towards an adequate response to a new situation or a new response to an old situation.' Based on this definition, can we find a neurological basis of spontaneity? Spontaneity seems to especially involve the right medial temporal lobe. A glimpse into the brain basis of spontaneity derives from an experiment by Alex Martin and his colleagues at the National Institute of Mental Health (Martin *et al.* 1997). In the experiment, levels of neural activation were measured when subjects were performing novel tasks and again when the tasks were no longer novel. When the task was novel, the medial temporal structures of the right brain were especially active, but this activation decreased in subsequent ('routine') exposure to the same task. In contrast, the level of activation was constant in the medial temporal structures of the left brain between novel and routine exposures. Response to novel tasks seems to require cooperation of right brain with left brain medial temporal structures, while routine tasks can be handled by left brain alone. This result was pervasive across differing modalities: verbal, visual and kinesthetic.

Interestingly, the right medial temporal lobe, amygdala and associated limbic lobe structures seem to be involved in out-of-body and religious experiences, as evidenced by investigations of temporal lobe lesions, direct electrical stimulation, and the experience of temporal lobe epileptics. So it may not be surprising that 'spontaneity' is associated with 'beyond the ordinary' experiences.

Elkhonon Goldberg offers an explanation regarding why psychodrama promotes spontaneity (2001: chapter 5): 'The difference between the two cerebral hemispheres revolves around the difference between cognitive routines (left brain dominant) and cognitive novelty (right brain more participatory).' Moreno considered the psychodramatic encounter to be essential for evoking spontaneity. If the brain's approach to confronting novel tasks is to awaken right brain/left brain balance, whatever facilitates this balance should improve 'spontaneity.' The action phase of psychodrama may be framed in neurological terms as the activation of right brain emotional structures through scene setting, imagery and motion within the space of the stage, and connecting this activation with left brain structures through verbalization.

Goldberg's notion of novel response arising from a balance of right and left brain resources suggests an encounter between an interior self (right brain 'core self') and an exterior self (left brain 'consensual self'). It is such an encounter between self and other which was envisaged by Moreno as engaging our spontaneity.

Lesions in the right prefrontal areas of the brain tend to produce 'extreme context dependence' in the patient (Goldberg 2001). Following Goldberg's theory (left brain for routine), the brain's connectivity to the 'cultural conserve' would be primarily through the left brain. The person in whom the left brain is dominant but unbalanced by the right brain is a person running on habitual response – a captive of the cultural conserve.

Involved in all of this is a profound encounter: Somewhere between embracing the culture and embracing interior reality lies an intermediate realm of 'play' – the realm of Winnicott's 'potential space.' This is the locus of development of the culturally adapted, yet individually expressive, ego. The current neuro-psychoanalytic viewpoint, represented by Schore (1999, 2003), is to frame this encounter as arising between right brain ('core' based) and left brain ('narrative' based). Accepting Moreno's perspective that the encounter (between persons) is the progenitor of spontaneity, I propose that this encounter has an internal biological basis, expressed at the highest levels of human neural organization, as an encounter between our own left and right cerebral hemispheres.

Conclusions

In this short chapter I have highlighted several findings of neuroscience which appear relevant to psychodramatists. Not included is any discussion of neurotransmitters, hormones or glial cells. I have also not developed aspects of the social brain pertinent to sociometry and the social atom, or to the neurobiology of roles. Much else can, and doubtless will, be explored in this fertile terrain between neuroscience and psychodrama. Here is a brief summary of what I have touched upon:

1   The brain is an action-oriented organ, and natural psychodramas regularly take place in the 'theater of the body.' Cognition is derivative of motor behavior. Movement is core to growth.
2   The two distinct hemispheres of our brain have different orientations, the left brain to language and narrative and consensual reality, the right to body and imagery and 'core' reality. The relationship between them is a primary one within us and underlies interpersonal relationships.
3   'Mental health' requires an adequate relationship between these hemispheres, and one in which the linguistic hemisphere is dominant, since we are social animals and consensual reality is vital to 'coping skills.'
4   A similar statement can be made about the relationship between the prefrontal cortex (the 'executive brain' and the seat of what Ramachandran (2004) calls the 'meta-representational brain') and the underlying corticolimbic system. (See also Chapter 4 by Blatner on the meta-role.)
5   Psychodrama is a form of play that creates a world in which imagination and reality are not antithetical, nor clearly separate. This world is a conjunction of two worlds, a dynamic encounter between representations internal and external to the organism.

6 Memory is malleable. Ordinary memory (left brain, narrative based) is very open to modification, as it is the end product of a series of reconsolidations in which new information may be imposed. This is particularly useful in psychodramatic 'how it might have been' (surplus reality) scenes.

7 For neuro-psychological change to occur, the correct level of stress is required – not too much and not too little. If the emotional level is too great, the hippocampus (which coordinates the short-term integration of experience) is overwhelmed, and this produces little integration. Too little and there is no change. This defines a 'window of tolerance' for the work.

8 Spontaneity involves a dynamic, balanced use of left and right brain resources. The left brain is mainly oriented to establishing routines (cultural conservation) while successful engagement with novel problems involves right brain structures. It may well be for this reason that the power of psychodrama to balance left brain with right brain processes promotes spontaneity.

9 There is a neurobiological basis of interconnectedness. Language, imitative learning and empathy are linked, and rooted in 'mirror neurons' whose function is 'action representation,' within the brain, of behavior observed in other people.

10 Distributed patterns of neural activation occur when individuals exchange (through encounter) their action representations. This produces shared meanings of objects, actions and social situations, as part of our shared evolution as social mammals. These shared representations as well as amygdala/OFC-based appraisal (which is largely unconscious) have a functional role in interpersonal awareness, including tele.

11 The brain's 'attentional system' is shared between our two hemispheres, but involves two separate searching systems, one for the left and one for the right hemisphere. The searching system of the linguistic left hemisphere is dominant, and can hijack an integrated attentional system, thus interfering with the operations of the right hemisphere in the act of recalling emotional states, and thus subverting the process of integration. The power of the psychodrama action phase is to engage body/emotional memory. The psychodrama director may re-engage the narrative attentional system by means of aside, soliloquy, etc. Part of the power and responsibility of the director is to manage the attentional system of the protagonist.

At a psychodrama conference in Miami, in 2005, Esly Carvalho introduced what may be the first fusion of psychodrama with a direct neurological intervention, Eye Motion Desensitization and Retraining (EMDR). As we further understand the neurological basis of psychotherapeutic interventions, we are likely to see more neuro-psychological interventions.

Acknowledgements

I want to acknowledge Dr. Jaime Rojas-Bermudez, who set me on the path of interest in the neurobiological underpinnings of psychodrama, an approach he has refined into what he calls 'scientific psychodrama,' an extension of the Argentine School of Psychodrama (Hug 1997; Rojas-Bermudez 1997).

References

Blatner, A. (1994) 'Tele: the dynamics of interpersonal preference', in P. Holmes, M. Karp and M. Watson (eds) *Psychodrama since Moreno: Innovations in Theory and Practice*, London: Routledge.

Cozolino, L. (2002) *The Neuroscience of Psychotherapy*, New York: Norton.

Decety, J. and Sommerville, J. A. (2003) 'Shared representations between self and others: a social cognitive neuroscience view', *Trends in Cognitive Science*, 7: 527–533.

Gallese, V. (2004) 'Intentional attunement: from mirror neurons to empathy', paper presented at the Fourth International Conference on Neuroesthetics: Empathy in the Brain and in Art, Berkeley: Minerva Foundation.

Gazzaniga, M. S. (1998) *Mind Matters*, Boston: Houghton Mifflin.

—— (2002) 'The split-brain revisited,' *Scientific American*, special issue on the 'Hidden Mind', 27–31.

Goldberg, E. (2001) The *Executive Brain: Frontal Lobes and the Civilized Mind*, New York: Oxford University Press.

Hug E. (1997) 'Current trends in psychodrama: eclectic and analytic dimensions', *Arts in Psychotherapy*, 24, 1.

Kingstone, A., Friesen, C. K. and Gazzaniga, M. S. (2000) 'Reflexive joint attention depends on lateral and cortical connections', *Psychological Science*, 11: 159–166.

LeDoux, J. (2002) 'Cellular and systems reconsolidation in the hippocampus', *Neuron*, 36, 3: 527–538.

Martin, A., Wiggs, C. and Weisberg, J. (1997) 'Modulation of human medial temporal lobe activity by form, meaning and experience', *Hippocampus*, 7, 6: 587–593.

Moreno, J. L. (1937) 'Sociometry in relation to other social sciences', *Sociometry* 1, 1–2: 206–219.

—— (1953) *Who Shall Survive? Foundations of Sociometry, Group Psychotherapy and Sociodrama* (2nd edn), Beacon, NY: Beacon House. (Originally published 1934.)

Panksepp, J. (1998) *Affective Neuroscience*, New York: Oxford University Press.

Ramachandran, V. S. (2004) *A Brief Tour of Human Consciousness*, New York: Pearson.

Rojas-Bermudez, J. G. (1997) *Teoria y Tecnica Psicodramaticas* [*Theory and Technique of Psychodrama*], Barcelona: Paidòs and Buenos Aires: Editorial Celsius.

Schore, A. (1999) *Affect Regulation and the Origin of the Self: The Neurobiology of Emotional Development*, Hillsdale NJ: Lawrence Erlbaum Associates, Inc.

—— (2003) *Affect Regulation and the Repair of the Self*, New York: Norton.

van der Kolk, B., McFarlane, A. C. and Weisaeth, L. (eds) (1996) *Traumatic Stress: The Effects of Overwhelming Experience on Mind, Body, and Society*, New York: Guilford Press.

Winnicott, D. W. (1989) *Playing and Reality*, New York: Routledge.

Chapter 17

Psychodrama and child development
Working with children

Anne Bannister

Introduction

As a therapist working with severely traumatized children, I have always remembered that J. L. Moreno's early ideas about psychodrama came from watching children play. He drew inspiration from memories of his own early childhood play and his later observations in Vienna, during the first decade of the twentieth century, where he formed groups of children for impromptu play. This developed into the Theatre of Spontaneity and, eventually, into psychodrama (Moreno 1977).

In this chapter I provide an overview of Moreno's theory of child development and how this theory relates to later developments in attachment theory and neurobiological research. I explain how Moreno's thinking has informed my psychodramatic practice with traumatized children, and I also provide the reader with some guidance on working with children, based on my experiences.

The need to work directly with children

I first used psychodrama with groups of women who were having difficulty in mothering their children. Within a short time it became clear that each of these women had, to a greater or lesser extent, suffered a traumatic childhood. In some cases, the memories of abuse had been deeply repressed. One woman was living with a physically abusive husband when she began to hit her own small child. In psychodrama, she re-enacted scenes of sadistic physical abuse by her own father, but she felt she could not own these memories. After making contact with her older sister, from whom she had been estranged, she was able to accept the memories. Several psychodrama sessions later, she was able to understand her place in the cycle of abuse and to rebuild her relationships with her husband and child.

Psychodrama helped many women in this situation, but I realized that the cycle of abuse may have been prevented if these abused children had received therapy before growing up and raising children of their own. Later, when I was working therapeutically with children who had been sexually abused, it became obvious to me that children who had suffered any kind of abuse could be helped by therapy, and that psychodrama was particularly effective with children. Young people, in solo or group play with me, often spontaneously re-enacted scenes from their lives, or they enacted metaphors of actual events. It was clear to me that psychodrama could help them to work through trauma.

Attachment

To understand how this process works, we must return to theories of attachment. Through the work of Bowlby (1953, 1969), we can understand the importance of children's early relationships with their parent(s) or caregiver(s). Bowlby's work was extended by Ainsworth and her colleagues (1978) who described various types of attachments, some of them less functional than others. It soon became clear that in cases where parental figures were inconsistent or rejecting, children had to accommodate their own needs to those of their caregivers. The dysfunctional attachments which they formed had a major effect on their later ability to attach to their own offspring.

To understand the attachment process more fully, we need to look at more recent work, for instance that of Schore (1997). His studies of the brain show that non-verbal and largely unconscious information passes between the mother–infant dyad and that in adulthood this can continue between the private self of one person and the private self of another (see also Chapter 11 by Anne Ancelin Schützenberger). Schore observes that this communication represents transactions directly between the right brain hemispheres of those concerned. He confirms that infants are sensorially based, not cognitively, and so it is clear that bodily based experiences are an essential part of the attachment process.

This is a major argument in favor of using psychodrama, which is a sensorial, whole-person therapy. Psychodrama uses the whole body and the body's position in relation to other people. This can arouse powerful feelings which may be difficult to articulate (even for adults).

Moreno's theory of child development

The way that psychodrama works is intrinsically bound up with J. L. Moreno's theory of child development. He suggested that the development of an infant is accomplished in three stages: the first stage of finding identity, the second stage of recognizing the self and the third stage of recognizing the other. Each of these stages can only take place in conjunction with one or more attachment figures. Such figures (who may include older siblings or companions) often reflect the child's feelings and assist in their expression. Usually, children who have been surrounded by other people who are willing to interact with them in an attuned way proceed more quickly through the various stages.

Finding identity – the crucial role of the double

Babies realize their 'separateness' from their mother, and others, when there is acknowledgement of the baby's feelings and when the response by the caretaker is appropriate. This interaction is very similar to the psychodramatic technique of 'doubling' where the director (or members of the group) assume the bodily stance and facial expression of the protagonist in order to help the protagonist to recognize his or her unexpressed feelings. We can observe this in attuned caregivers who spontaneously double for the baby when they give words to the baby's non-verbal expressions, for example, 'That toy is boring,' 'Oops! All gone!' or 'Oh, that's exciting!' Existentially, the baby is learning, in effect, that 'I exist and I have these feelings and thoughts.' However, at this stage there is not yet a full separation between self and other. Babies who receive plenty of attuned acknowledgement from their attachment figure(s), both in speech and touch, naturally respond better to other people and move more quickly to the second stage of development, which is 'mirroring' (see the next section).

Another point about the use of the double with children is that they have spent less time than adults in trying to hide their true feelings and so their body positions and facial expressions more accurately reflect their inner consciousness. Psychodrama therapists can empathize by taking up the child's position (doubling) and stating what they feel. As they reflect this back, the child often expresses feelings of relief. This method of doubling also avoids the tendency of some adults to make assumptions about children's feelings. For instance, we may assume that, after being parted from a parent, the child's primary feeling is sadness, when it may well be anger, terror, or relief.

Recognizing the self – the 'mirror' stage

Through experiencing their own feelings mirrored back by their caring parental figures, infants begin to form their own identity. This identity is reflected back to them from those who are closest, and so their personality begins to form in large part based on this feedback. Through this process of interaction, the infant begins to understand how they are separate from the other person. Sometimes, siblings or other children also assist in this stage of development by copying the baby's actions.

Anyone who has been in a room full of babies can see the distinction between the first and second stages of development. In the first stage of development, when one baby starts to cry, the others follow. As the infants grow, however, and identity becomes firmer in the second stage of development, older babies will look concernedly at a crying infant and then look to adults to satisfy the crying child. They can mentally separate themselves from the other baby. Existentially, the infant has learned that 'there is me and then there are other people and things that are not me.' This can be very frightening and frustrating for the infant, especially when the other people and things do not do exactly as the infant wishes. If the infant/young child is helped to negotiate this dilemma through caring and attuned guidance, he or she can move on to the next developmental stage.

Recognizing the other person – the stage of role reversal

The third stage of child development, according to Moreno, is role reversal. Children practice this from around the age of three to four, as they play at 'dressing up' or other improvised games. Boys and girls will role reverse and become inanimate objects such as trains, or animals (real or imaginary), as well as people such as friends, parents or other authority figures (doctors and teachers). It is important that young children are able to interact with adults or other children so that their own role reversals have substance. Illustrated books and films are also helpful to feed their imagination and give them a wide opportunity of experiencing different behaviors and roles.

Role reversal is intrinsic to psychodrama and is one of its most powerful techniques. Moreno used a harsh metaphor when in 'Invitation to an Encounter' he wrote:

> A meeting of two: eye to eye, face to face.
> And when you are near I will tear your eyes out
> and place them instead of mine,
> and you will tear my eyes out
> and will place them instead of yours,
> then I will look at you with your eyes
> and you will look at me with mine.
> (Moreno 1977: Preface)

This description of role reversal describes very well the strong feelings which are aroused when it is used in psychodrama, and the powerful effects of such feelings. Role reversal is, perhaps, a sophisticated form of play. Around the age of four or five, most children are adept at taking the roles of adults or fantasy figures. Holmes (1992) suggests that psychodrama, which uses playing and illusion, serves the same purpose as play. The psychodrama space is filled with creativity, fantasy and imagination and, in addition, it contains elements of the 'here and now.'

Working therapeutically with abused or neglected children

We can only work therapeutically with children (and the same applies to adults) by totally accepting their feelings and assisting in some expression of those feelings. When this is accomplished well, the next part of psychotherapy is facilitating the rehearsal of a scenario where these feelings can be expressed with those members of the family or the friends who will be affected. The child's expectations of the results of this can be seen and addressed and different behavior can be rehearsed. The change may be fully integrated into the child's life or it may be rejected. The result is usually a better understanding by the child that some things can be changed and others may be better endured by being understood.

However, many children may be unable to work therapeutically in such a direct way. After all, the child may still be living with the parent who originally facilitated the dysfunctional attachment. There may be no other choice. It is often desirable for these parents to also receive therapy, but this is not always possible.

In my experience, most children show me their family situation through metaphor. Younger children may show graphic scenes of disasters in their drawings or play. Others devise stories in which the children are rescued or in which they are the rescuer. It is important to accept this play at its face value and not to try to alter it. After the therapist and child have built their own functional attachment, then it may be possible for children to show a different kind of play and to be able to practice different behavior in their home situation.

Some children who have been abused or neglected during their early years appear to be stilted in their emotional development. They may be unable to understand or appreciate the feelings of other people and they may find it difficult to accept the reality of their own behavior and will try to deny this. (It is easy to see how this can escalate into criminal behavior.) Their own vision of themselves is distorted, as is their vision of others, so they are also unable to put themselves 'in the shoes of' another person. They have to be helped to play. I have given many examples of such children (Bannister 1990, 1992, 1997) who were helped to work through the metaphors of stories, using painting or role play (according to their preference and age).

Most children are able to invent their own stories, but some need the help of a therapist to suggest storylines from legend or fairy tales. In what I have termed 'the space between' (Bannister 2003), the children are able to complete development which has been blocked or delayed. The therapist must respect 'the space between' (which is an actively creative space between two people) and allow the child to express their needs, only making suggestions which arise from the child's behaviour or demeanor. I will illustrate this with the case of Frank:

> Frank was a little seven-year-old boy who had been brought up in a loving but rather repressive household. Sexual matters were never mentioned and he was very aware, because his father had impressed it upon him, of his masculine role in protecting his mother from unpleasant happenings. Consequently, when he was caught up in a child sex ring along with other boys, he was unable to tell either parent. He thought that his mother could not listen because she would be shocked and hurt and his father could not listen because he would be angry. In fact his assessment was entirely correct. When the sex ring was discovered, through another child, Frank became depressed and withdrawn and failed to show any interest in school or friends, and his mother complained that she could not reach him.
>
> Frank moved slowly with me at first, trying to discover whether I would react to his story angrily or with shock and horror. There was a long period of reassurance where we talked about familiar things and played dramatic games with puppets. He tested me out by picking up a boy doll. 'This boy is naughty, he takes his clothes off.' We explored the statement. When was it OK to take your clothes off and when was it not OK? 'What if a man tells him to take his clothes off?' he asked. We agreed that the boy doll couldn't help it if the man was big. He played the role of the man for a few moments, relishing the power and control that gave him. Without any direction, he moved into the 'mirror technique' and picked up a puppet that he said was the monster man. He asked me to make the monster frighten the little boy doll. He watched intently while I demonstrated. I did not, of course, show specific sexual abuse, because he had not revealed this to me at this stage, but I showed the usual sort of scary monster that appears in children's stories. 'He likes being scared,' he said calmly, giving me a clue that part of Frank's problem may be about coping with the pleasure as well as the pain of abuse.
>
> Later on in therapy, he was able to use the 'mirror' technique again, this time using anatomically correct dolls which he controlled himself to show me exactly what happened. 'I liked it a little bit and I was scared as well,' he said. He was able to express all his feelings, not just those he thought I wanted to hear. After three sessions, Frank's mother reported a great improvement and his teacher was delighted that Frank was again showing interest in schoolwork. Of course, his mother received parallel work from another worker to help her cope in the future.
>
> (Bannister 1990: 161–162)

Plasticity and emotional development

Allan Schore (1994) suggests that the brain is capable of 'plasticity,' especially during childhood, so it seems reasonable that a therapy which engages all the senses can have a permanent effect. For many children, this means that they can complete their delayed emotional development. Children can become more sensitive to the feelings of others, can understand their own behavior and its effect upon others, and, if they are old enough to have reached the third stage of development, they can even understand the feelings and behaviour of other people.

Historically, the phrase 'emotional development' would not have been understood. The emotions were seen as separate from reason and later as irrational and not a fit subject for study. More recently, emotions have been studied in those with neurological disease and the relevance of emotions to certain stimuli in parts of the brain is much clearer (Damasio 2000). In addition, neurological studies are now easier to accomplish with the invention of photon emission tomography and other types of brain scans. It is now possible to confirm how the brain is reacting and to confirm or deny the information which we already knew through very careful observation of behavior.

Schore (1997) also refers to the work of Melanie Klein, and in particular her well-known work on projective identification. This she defined as an early developmental interactive process between two individuals, wherein largely unconscious information is projected from the sender to the recipient. Schore observes that this process arises in the mother–infant dyad and that for the rest of the lifespan it represents a process of non-verbal emotional communication between two people. This may also be essential in the transmission of attachment patterns between adults. The communication is necessarily sensory, illustrating how basic this is in all our relationships. I believe that Moreno's description of 'tele' between two people is something similar. Tele may be positive or negative and may represent different kinds of attachment behaviour.

We can also see how important our early attachments are in respect of our future relationships. Sometimes a dysfunctional relationship, where one partner has much more power than the other, can feel so familiar that we may seek to replicate it, often with unhappy or fatal results.

Conclusion

Psychodrama therapy is particularly helpful for people who have suffered early dysfunctional attachments. As one example is played out in a psychodramatic representation, other scenes come to mind and the protagonist soon begins to understand his or her life experiences and their relationship to the present situation. Rehearsing the possibility of new ways of behavior is a gentle introduction to a new life for many people. In addition, people who are chosen to play auxiliary roles in such a psychodrama may recognize their own dysfunctional attachments and resolve to make some changes.

The human race has always devised 'cures' for our various ailments, whether physical or emotional. Sometimes these cures can be confirmed by science and sometimes there are no rational reasons why they work. The placebo effect is cited for many things that we do not understand. It has been shown to have a positive effect in many cases, thus 'proving' the power of mind over matter. However, through science, we now understand very much more about both child development and attachment. Moreno's observations of children have borne fruit. Psychodramatic techniques are based on early childhood developmental stages. Our emotional development continues throughout life, so psychodrama provides a way of honing and correcting our present behavior so that we will continue to develop. This, I believe, was Moreno's greatest legacy.

References

Ainsworth, M. D. S., Blehar, M., Aters, E. and Wall, S. (1978) *Patterns of Attachment: A Psychological Study of the Strange Situation*, Hillsdale, NJ: Lawrence Erlbaum Associates, Inc.

Bannister, A. (1990) 'Listening and learning: psychodramatic techniques with children', in A. Bannister, K. Barrett and E. Shearer (eds) *Listening to Children: The Professional Response to Hearing the Abused Child*, Harlow: Longman.

—— (ed.) (1992) *From Hearing to Healing: Working with the Aftermath of Child Sexual Abuse*, Harlow: Longman.

—— (1997) *The Healing Drama: Psychodrama and Dramatherapy with Abused Children*, London: Free Association Books.

—— (2003) *Creative Therapies with Traumatized Children*, London: Jessica Kingsley Publishers.

Bowlby, J. (1953) *Child Care and the Growth of Love*, Harmondsworth: Pelican.

—— (1969) *Attachment and Loss, Vol. 1: Attachment*, London: Tavistock.

Damasio, A. (2000) *The Feeling of What Happens: Body, Emotion and the Making of Consciousness*, London: Vintage.

Holmes, P. (1992) *The Inner World Outside: Object Relations Theory and Psychodrama*, London: Routledge.

Moreno, J. L. (1977) *Psychodrama, Volume One*, Beacon, NY: Beacon House. (Originally published 1946.)

Schore, A. N. (1994) *Affect Regulation and the Origin of the Self*, Hillsdale, NJ: Lawrence Erlbaum Associates Inc.

—— (1997) 'The neurodevelopmental aspects of projective identification', paper presented at Psychoanalysis in Clinical Social Work National Conference, Seattle.

Chapter 18

Psychodrama and psychopathology
Purposefully adapting the method to address different pathologies

Fernando Vieira and Marta Risques

Introduction

A psychopathological diagnosis is a process used to identify an illness and to categorize it based on its signs and symptoms. Knowing that diagnoses are not always consensual, the more existentialist therapists tend to deny the philosophy of diagnosis. They believe it is fundamental to participate in the therapeutic relationship with the client or patient, more as a person and less as a psychologist or psychiatrist (Kellermann 1998). In this chapter, we address the question of whether it is possible to reconcile the values of growth, maturation and encounter with those of psychopathological diagnosis and treatment. We will also consider how the psychodrama director may need to emphasize his or her differing roles according to the task and context.

The Morenian psychodramatic model is mainly existentialist and, probably due to that, it resists integrating more rigid therapeutic aspects into its approach. Therefore, psychodrama therapists do not usually differentiate groups, nor do they commonly direct sessions based on nosological criteria. In psychodrama, anything is possible, but the 'psychopathological label' may impoverish the dramatization, eventually taking away from the labeled individual the chance to be spontaneous. More than working with 'people with psychopathologies,' psychodrama therapists focus on 'psychopathological relationships' among people. In other words, the diagnosed illness or psychopathology may in fact be considered one of the roles one has developed in a rigid and out-of-context manner. It is the patient's role, and from it we can reach the most frequent relationship pattern which prevents other roles and relationships or bonds from emerging. From a psychodramatic point of view, in an 'ill' person the psychopathological, rigid roles disguise or dominate a number of healthy or adaptive roles. The therapy group can be the catalyst that helps the 'ill' patient's role to be less rigid, creating spontaneous functioning alternatives.

The mental illness appears as the inadequate manifestation or pathology of spontaneity and creativity (Moreno and Moreno 1984). The psychopathological diagnosis, despite the label's inconvenience, allows us to understand how a person limits his spontaneity. For instance, a patient with an obsessive-compulsive disorder or obsessive personality disorder will tend to think 'too much' and act 'too little.' He will show a tendency to rationalize in the sharing part of the psychodrama session, minimizing his personal experiences. He will do little action in the second, action phase of the psychodrama session, and he will warm up slowly and only verbally (for instance, he will tend to avoid warm-up games in the first phase of the session). If the director has knowledge of this psychopathological diagnosis, they may facilitate a warm-up without words and with games. They will drive the dramatization towards the search for experiences instead of 'cold' descriptions, not allowing rationalizations or non-affective comments in the sharing.

On the other hand, in patients with hysterical personality disorders, dissociation disorders or somatoform disorders, the psychodrama director will try a verbal warm-up and avoid excessive 'drama' in the dramatization, preferring the cognitive elaboration rather than excessive emotional sharing in the closure. In the case of alcohol and drug addiction, the dramatizations show the addiction as a way of inhibiting spontaneity which, being possible when the diagnosis is known, allows focused work on autonomy. In patients with psychosomatic disorders or psychological symptoms associated with a physical illness, knowing that diagnosis may lead the director to suggest a dramatization without words, developing the abilities of the right hemisphere, working metaphorically, and using symbolic acts as much as possible. In patients with borderline and antisocial personalities, previously knowing the diagnosis enables the director to expect incidents due to impulsiveness and aggressiveness. The director can anticipate the occurrence of acting out, and may facilitate soliloquies which will be useful to elaborate strongly felt emotions. This may be complemented by the use of cooling down techniques when needed.

To sum up, diagnoses help the psychodrama therapist to more purposefully and strategically direct and better lead the psychodrama sessions, avoiding risks that may arise from the uninformed use of powerful processes (Langley and Langley 1983).

Furthermore, within the psychodrama family it is becoming evident that resistance to the notions of diagnosis and assessment of psychopathology may result in the loss of credibility and therefore isolation in the mental illness field. This isolation will be exacerbated if psychodrama neglects the importance of research and does not establish a formulation of therapeutic indications (Kellermann 1998). Therefore, it will be helpful to analyze which psychodrama technique applies to a certain diagnosis and which technique or dramatization applies to certain psychopathological symptoms. This can be better understood with reference to Figure 18.1.

Protagonist-centered approach to psychodrama (top arrow): directing the scenes of the psychodrama towards the protagonist's stated needs and 'act hunger'. Note that the role of 'The Patient' will often hide other healthier roles.

PSYCHODRAMA   **NOSOLOGY**

Psychodrama techniques informed by nosology (bottom arrow): used in a purposeful and adaptable way to address clusters of psychopathological symptoms and underlying problems.

Therapeutic indications: used to inform an appropriate balance between the two arrows, i.e., the priorities of protagonist-centered psychodrama and the nosologically defined symptoms and underlying problems.

Figure 18.1 The balance between psychodrama and nosology

Purposeful applications of the psychodramatic method with differing psychopathologies

What would Moreno think of this? We are sure that the author of 'Psychodramatic Treatment of Psychoses' (Moreno 1987) and other articles referencing diagnoses would consider this a path to be explored, while other more recent psychodrama therapists have also mentioned this subject. We will explain these aspects and give examples of the psychodrama techniques and adaptations that may be particularly effective with people diagnosed with different psychiatric disorders. We start with drug addiction, an area in which we have the greatest professional experience. We follow with the topics of depression and anxiety disorders, because of their frequency and clinical importance. After exploring a number of further diagnoses, we conclude with personality disorders, due to the complexity of this diagnosis and the privileged way in which psychodrama – with its holistic and interactional approach – can help people with such disorders.

Drug abuse and addiction

The use of psychodrama with people who have misused drugs is nowadays mainly associated with therapeutic communities, which is understandable, as both settings (psychodrama and the therapeutic community) provide a space where life is practiced in a safer way, where people can experience new ways of feeling, thinking or acting.

The psychodrama session creates the therapeutic milieu. It introduces, more than verbalizations, the physical body of the protagonist. This is important, because in many drug addicts the body is mainly experienced as an 'exchange frontier' with the consumed product. In this clinical picture, psychodrama, instead of blocking the way to the act, tries to stimulate it in a specific context – dramatization – giving room for different satisfaction of impulses, teaching the protagonist at the same time how to deal with frustration. The main role is given to the protagonist drug addict, who watches his or her narcissistic potentialities in order to later listen to the comments and to the group sharing. While acting as a drug addict character, the player, who is also a drug addict, can criticize the character without feeling harm to his self-esteem. On the other hand, during dramatization, due to the exchange of roles, the drug addict experiences the other side, perceiving how it feels to deal with an addict in real life, which is therapeutic. In the stage's 'time machine,' one can go backwards, to the first consumption of the drug, to the existential causes of drug abuse; or alternatively into the future, whether being substance free, being in prison for dealing drugs, or death by overdose. It will be the drug addict by himself or herself who is going to choose their path in life.

The social atom is a useful technique for working with drug addicts, and the therapist must be aware of the importance of the family matrix to these patients. For instance, as far as alcoholics are concerned, we try to help them pass from an exhausted and immature relationship matrix to a new, more mature and creative matrix, encouraging growth, autonomy and more adaptive defense mechanisms. By adding value to the individual's total gestalt, psychodrama surpasses the focus on feelings emphasized by psychodynamic currents, the focus on thoughts emphasized by the cognitivists, the focus on behaviors emphasized by the behaviorists or the focus on the environment emphasized by the systemics. It also takes into account an existential, hermeneutical and affective side, working on isolation, despair, guilt, aggressiveness, social aspects, coping and, if necessary, we may resort to catharsis with subsequent group support (Olsson 1972; Moreno 1973; Wood 1979; Olsson and Barth 1983; Ruscombe King 1984; Zarcone 1984; Monroe 1986; Duffy 1990; Moffett and Bruto 1990).

Depression

In the presence of depressed patients, psychodrama therapists pay more attention to the person and less to the depression. In the psychodramatic perspective, the depressed patient interconnects, in a rigid and stereotyped way, false roles in all his matrices and relationships (social, family and professional). In order to break with rigid behavioral responses, it is necessary that the depressed person sets free his spontaneity and creativity, exercising, in the psychodramatic session, new roles, or better, stimulating atrophied and less developed roles, breaking with depressive stereotypes.

In psychodrama, the group is a key factor in the treatment, because the cohesion and sharing increase self-esteem, providing the learning models and/or development of roles, support and empathy, which counteract the feeling of isolation of the depressed person. The depressed person also presents a decrease in the rhythm and speed of their behavior, as if the depression was a slow and passive adaptation when facing a problem, thus impeding free interactions with situations. On the other hand, depressed people often deal badly with their own aggression, sometimes turning it against themselves through attempts at suicide. The slow and expectant behavior, and the aggression channeled into the interior, can be worked with in a psychodramatic context by stimulating and exploring behaviors that are feared by the patient, which should be reinforced and supported by the group through sharing. The protagonist has to re-learn the aggressive response, first redirecting it to the exterior and not to oneself and then transforming it into assertiveness.

There are different ways of doing a psychodramatic session with the purpose of reformulating the depressed person's existential suffering: addressing the instinct for non-participation by understanding the defensive process; putting out one's hand and empathically inviting the patient to the stage; using soliloquy to reveal the patient's thoughts; using role exchange with the empty chair; and, on occasion, using the mirror technique (this should only be used in specific contexts).

The psychodramatic model can assist in the mourning process, helping the need to express painful emotions, like an adaptive process to a loss. Similar to the burial rituals, the psychodramatic session allows integrating all the stages of the mourning process, dramatizing the associated psycho-pathological symptoms (avoidance, idealization of the deceased, denial and non-adaptive identification). Frequently, the interpersonal relation-ships of the person who mourns become disrupted. These relationships can also be the focus of particular attention in the psychodramatic approach (Kaminsky 1981). The same happens to the phobic places that can emerge (e.g. cemetery, hospital). For this reason, the dramatization of 'saying goodbye' to the person who died, the promotion of new relationships and the reinforcement of the net of connections to life should be the techniques used, so long as trust and group cohesion are assured.

Panic disorder and general anxiety

Lantican and Mayorga (1993) report the efficacy of psychodrama when applied to 26 female patients institutionalized in a psychiatric hospital and suffering from panic attacks, depression, eating disorders and marital dysfunction. With patients suffering from panic disorder, we frequently facilitate the dramatization of specific situations in which the panic occurs. We have seen that it is possible, through the use of techniques such as soliloquy and role exchange with an empty chair, for patients to learn to manage their internal dialogue when the anxiety attack occurs. Simultaneously, the handling of dysfunctional thoughts is trained, be it through dramatization or through the audience's commentaries. It is also important to demystify the severity of the crisis, for example, through the explanation of the physiological mechanisms associated with the panic crisis (Kipper and Giladi 1978). The use of humor or of relaxing and breathing exercises has also proven to be useful, helping to demystify the 'fear of having fear' (Stevenson 1990, 1992).

Phobias and post-traumatic stress

A treatment generally described as effective with phobias and post-traumatic stress is the phobogenic stimulus exposure, done in an imagined or real situation. This draws on behaviorist theory. In the psychodramatic approach, something similar can be done by using a 'covered and revealed' psychodrama (usually where the protagonist can control the 'covering' and 'revealing'), in which the protagonist is encouraged to keep internally calm while he or she experiences events that lead to his or her avoidance reactions. This leads to the deconditioning of the anxious response. More than imagining the phobic situation, the psychodrama promotes an 'exposition in experienced imagination,' since the protagonist works within a total gestalt (in space and time). This symbolic and metaphoric work has shown good results in our clinical experience (Newburger 1987; Winn 1994).

Obsessive-compulsive disorder

The obsessive patients tend to speak in great detail and with a high power of argumentation, demanding a significant warm-up at the start of the session in order that some emotional variation can be expressed. The promotion of affective and emotional language, blocking the propensity to excessive cognitive elaborations, is achieved through bodily expression and the use of symbolic objects, by insisting in the spontaneous improvisation method (inviting the patient to an invented and imagined role, rather than putting his life in focus) and by inviting the patient to participate in projective activities.

Social anxiety/social phobia

The therapeutic emphasis with these patients should be placed on bodily expression and non-verbal communication. For psychodramatists, as for dramatherapists, the achievement of the following social skills (among others) is a therapeutic goal (Langley and Langley 1983):

- ability to keep eye contact in a socially acceptable way
- notion of own status and the status of other people with whom one relates
- knowledge of what one wants to offer to the members of a group, and an understanding of what they are ready to accept
- differentiation of assertiveness and body proximity limits, including socially accepted touch and 'personal space' issues
- perception of body language, always aiming at the capacity to deal effectively with daily problems and issues.

Technically, the psychodrama director may use the mirror technique to provide feedback to the protagonist. The director may also model the skill (or have more able group members model the skill) and may invite the protagonist to practice the skill at increasing levels of difficulty. The director may also ask the protagonist to train their internal dialogue (self-talk) through soliloquy and/or role exchange with an empty chair (Figge 1982).

Psychosomatic disorders

In psychodramatic language, the psychosomatic illness is understood to be the 'physical expression of an existential hindrance,' or rather, a dysfunction of the life course, in which the psychosomatic symptom has resulted from an interaction with the environment or a disturbance of interpersonal relationships. One of the aims of psychodrama in this clinical context will be to increase the patient's insight about the relation between the interpersonal situation/emotional reactions and the physical symptoms.

Thus, psychodrama is the therapeutic acting out, which opposes the acting in of the action over internal organs, promoting the impulses' passage to the exterior, to the stage, rather than being discharged to the interior. On the other hand, psychosomatic patients have an operating thought that drives the illness, and they find it difficult to elaborate the conflict, to fantasize and to dream, being extremely fluent in defensive verbalizations and intellectualizations. Psychodrama invites the use of metaphor, inspires creativity and promotes healing spontaneity, while also objectifying (making external and 'concrete') the patient's internal dialogue. So it is important to focus on the alexithymic (distancing feelings) functioning styles and on the dysfunctional family characteristics common to these patients. Likewise, it is important to decipher possible secondary benefits of the physical illness. This can be done using symbolic and metaphoric language, resorting to sculpts and dramatizations without words (expression with body movement only).

Hysteria and hypochondria

The person with hysteria lives in constant symbolism. This person may give priority to bodily sensations, emotions and feelings (they 'feel too much'). To a hysterical person, feelings are more important than thinking. Feelings are maximized, and other people may be seen as cold, rational and insensitive. Therefore, in dramatizations, they frequently adopt seductive behavior, exaggerating appearance and shape, looking for admiration, and being always ready to go on stage, rapidly changing their state of mind (Soeiro 1976).

In the psychodramatic approach, the important thing is to help the hysterical person to unlearn their patient role, which provides them with primary gains (anxiety and avoidance reduction) and secondary gains (calls for attention and pity). It is important to deepen other roles, always being alert to the seduction, to kindliness, and even to the suggestion of dramatizing scenes, full of symptoms to overcome. Technically, the drama helps to 'externalize' the internal dialogue. The role exchange with significant people helps the training of adult assertive roles. The mirror technique provokes and helps the observation of immature, inadequate and childish behaviors. It is equally essential to dramatize scenes that examine future consequences or expectations of change, questioning the hysterical person about the need for immaturity or the reason for the systematic demand of the exaggerated feelings.

As far as hypochondria is concerned, if on the one hand it is similar to hysteria, on the other hand it has aspects that resemble anxious disorders. In fact, the state of anxiety in hypochondria may result from the creation of danger or menace cognitions, as in phobias. The maintenance also results from unrealistic interpretations of physical and irrelevant sensations like panic. The intrusiveness has a parallel with obsessive-compulsive disorder.

These different prevailing aspects demand different handling by the psychodramatist. It is important to expose, in the live experience of the imagination, scenes from the hypothetical consequences of the illness and from the experienced fear. It is also important to externalize the internal dialogue, training the patient to better respond to dysfunctional cognitions or to confront himself or herself before anguish. The patient can similarly be helped to detect catastrophic automatic thoughts through the soliloquy technique. It may also be useful to model adequate responses, asking the audience for representation of and commentary on the expressed dysfunctionality. The psychodramatist may also direct the construction of sculpts of the feared illnesses or affected organs, dramatizing along with them the dialogues in which the hysterical person exchanges role with his or her own complaint (Clayton 1973; Lisk 1982).

Eating disorders

As in psychosomatic disorders, the psychodramatic approach to eating disorders dares to bring the body to the therapy, with the embodiment of emotions. For that, it is necessary to develop a symbolic and metaphoric language, which provides access to rigidified feelings, integrating it creatively in the patient's personality. The focus is on encouraging the patient to search for and develop their autonomy in a new constellation of interpersonal relationships. The patient is helped to work directly with relational stress focused on the body and is also helped to explore new social and individual roles, like the woman's role and her expectations about femininity. In these cases, one resorts frequently to conceptual representation with the body, through sculpting; to the act of touching/being touched; to corporal/bodily metaphors, rather than psychological metaphors, in order that the corporal image of oneself will no longer be distorted. The distortion itself can be enacted and shaped, in the present, past or future. The desired or feared fantasies may be enacted on stage. The body deterioration in a hospital can be dramatized by the extension of an additional reality. The focus can also be on the behavior-learning process or on role training, modeling the adequate eating pattern, maximizing the anxiety reduction strategies and the behavioral rehearsals/social skills (Levens 1994; Dokter 1996).

Schizomorph syndromes

In psychodramatic theory, psychoses are conceptualized as emerging from disorders that occur at an early developmental stage. Some disorders emerge in the passage from the non-differentiated identity matrix (in which the child can't distinguish himself from the exterior) to the differentiated identity matrix, in which the difference between the self and the mother/primary caregiver is established. Disturbances arising during this stage may result in confusion between what is real and what is imagined. Moreno used to provide psychotics with the means and context for the expression of their delusion, since the more disturbed the mental organization, the more help through auxiliary egos would have to be provided. Sometimes a whole 'auxiliary world' was required, where the therapists acted as 'theatrical points,' providing an anchor to reality and gradually bringing the patient to the healthy side. The representation of delusion and hallucinations therefore converts them into external objects, accessible to psychotherapeutic intervention and, above all, accessible to the protagonist's control.

Bermudez (Soeiro 1976) develops the concept of the intermediary object, using marionettes with psychotic patients to ease the communication, and to allow the overcoming of the psychological barrier, without causing alarm reactions typical of these patients. Music and dance are also valuable auxiliaries in the therapeutical approach. The play consists in the protagonist acting like somebody they are not, and knowing that they are not that person. This form of drama is especially useful in working with schizophrenia, as the therapist can help the patient to keep and differentiate the frontiers between real and not real. Grainger (1990, 1992), Johnson (1984), Landy (1986) and Casson (2004) have been interested in psychotic pathology, and have made significant contributions to the use of dramatherapy and psychodrama with these patients.

More recently, in psychotic patients, psychodrama has focused more on rehabilitation, and is being recognized as a treatment of choice in day hospitals. In this context, psychodrama can work as a corrective therapy, developing roles and increasing tolerance and boundaries, and stimulating interpersonal interaction. The object is the socialization and improvement of communication with other people (including at an affective level), suiting likewise the corporal movement and expression/image (Moreno 1978). Using psychodrama, it is possible to maximize the training outcomes of social skills, exceeding the mere warm-up and the training standardization, reaching the level of internal and affective experiences. With schizophrenic patients, when we speak of affect and emotion, we note that sometimes these patients have to be trained in anger control, or helped to overcome the anxiety inherent in interpersonal relationships. In these cases psychodrama can be quite useful in helping patients develop communication and self-management skills while also developing a truer perception of the world. Psychodrama can help them develop skills of emotional expression, setting future goals and decision making. It helps encourage motivation and the development of many skills relating to interpersonal relationships (Bielanska *et al.* 1991; Altman 1992; Honig 1993).

Personality disorders

We can speak of personality disorders when there is a set of inflexible and poorly adaptive patterns that emerge in an interpersonal context. Translating into a Morenean conceptualization, we could say that the interactions with others would be rigid and inflexible. We would be in the presence of false roles, rather than true roles, mere models or cultural conserves.

In personality disorders, the expression of the true 'self' is restrained, due to the dysfunction of the spontaneity factor, and the individual does not respond in a free, new or adequate way. Thus, what will be at stake is the lost ability for self-updating based on new potentials. There is also an incongruity between the interior drama and exterior presentation. The psychodramatic setting makes personality disorders evident, since when the exterior drama of the protagonist is reproduced, the incongruence of the interior drama and the ego-dystonic and alloplastic outward symptoms, in harmony only with the usual rigidity, becomes visible. Therefore, what psychodrama tries to do with these patients is to ease the growing, the maturation, and the fight against rigidness; to develop spontaneity and, through the group, to provide an adequate atmosphere of congruence, comprehension and empathic sharing.

It is also possible to purposefully adapt psychodrama techniques to incorporate general notions from other psychotherapeutic currents that are recognized as effective in working with personality disordered individuals. Such an adaptation of psychodrama would focus more on the person's behavior (that is, their interactions), rather than on explanations. There is more confrontation than interpretation, but very importantly it is the protagonist who confronts himself or herself. The limits are defined and the structure is provided, depending on the sessions and the difference imposed by the distinction between social, group and dramatic context. Through the group, the emotional discharges are contained; the cognitive (and spoken) elaboration of acting-out behaviours is encouraged, for example, through the technique of soliloquy. Dysfunctional beliefs and automatic thoughts are discussed, and are made conscious and manifest through enactment. The unproductive behavior and the stereotyped and repetitive complaints are taken into the dramatic context, sometimes emerging as insight arising from caricature (using the mirror technique). Finally, the use of modeling and social reinforcement by the various group members can be very effective.

One tries to structure the acting-out behaviors to stay within the specific context of the dramatization, trying to contain them away from the daily routine. When a disruptive behavior is underway, the technique of role exchange will allow the experience, in the patient's own flesh, of the disruptive behavior, and the look through the other's eyes at his or her own behavior. When proposing dramatizations, we also strive to help individuals to explore their own (maladaptive) defense mechanisms, developing them at a more adaptive level, in order to use more adequate coping strategies.

The processes of splitting, projection or projective identification can be rapidly visualized through the use of the double and role exchange techniques. For example, the auxiliary ego can help to reshape the split ego, building a dialogue. The members of the group may be asked to double for the protagonist, encouraging insight. Or, using role exchange, the protagonist assumes the role of the projected characteristics she or he has placed on to other people, identifying himself or herself again with these characteristics. The protagonist finds that it is no longer useful to project the perverse characteristics on to others, because the director puts the protagonist inside the projected person: the statement '*He made himself angry*' is converted into '*I was angry at him.*'

Denial is another defense that becomes unsustainable with dramatization, in front of an attentive group. The self-idealization that contributes to denial can be worked out through a dialogue between an auxiliary ego and a protagonist, representing both the real and the ideal ego. Alternatively, a similar effect can be gained through an intense dialogue between the self and a 'Jiminy Cricket' character – a sort of verbalized conscience figure borrowed from the Disney version of Pinocchio. Such techniques may help to reveal not just aspects of denial but also aspects of narcissistic omnipotence. On stage, these can be exaggerated and extreme, which can produce humor and insight. We should also remember that beyond the disruptive behavior of a patient with a personality disorder can also be a deficit of social skills, which can be trained, or depression or low self-esteem. These other factors may become the focus of treatment where they are primary sources of suffering (Sidorskl 1984).

Conclusion

We have intended to demonstrate the possibility of reconciling the approach of psychopathology diagnosis with the existential approach of psychodrama. We recognize that the notion of diagnosis is, and perhaps always will be, controversial among psychodramatists. In conclusion, we may say that in the present state of the art, it is too soon to establish strict diagnostic implications for psychodrama. We must also emphasize that no therapy, including psychodrama, can be considered a universal panacea. Nevertheless, psychodrama does offer a large range of techniques that may be purposefully and effectively chosen and applied by psychodramatists to address many different psychological conditions.

References

Altman, K. P. (1992) 'Psychodramatic treatment of multiple personality disorder and dissociative disorders', *Dissociation Progress in the Dissociative Disorders*, 5, 2: 104–108.

Bielanska, A., Cechnicki, A. and Budzyna-Dawidowski, P. (1991) 'Drama therapy as a means of rehabilitation for schizophrenic patients', *American Journal of Psychotherapy*, 45, 4: 566–575.

Casson, J. (2004) *Drama, Psychotherapy and Psychosis: Dramatherapy and Psychodrama with People who Hear Voices*, London: Brunner-Routledge.

Clayton, M. (1973) 'Psychodrama with the hysteric', *Group Psychotherapy and Psychodrama*, 26, 3–4: 31–36.

Dokter, D. (1996) 'Dramatherapy and clients with eating disorders: fragile board', in S. Mitchell (ed.) *Dramatherapy Clinical Studies*, London: Jessica Kingsley Publishers.

Duffy, T. K. (1990) 'Psychodrama in beginning recovery: an illustration of goals and methods', *Alcoholism Treatment Quarterly*, 7, 2: 79–109.

Figge, P. A. W. (1982) 'Dramatherapy and social anxiety: results of the use of drama in behaviour therapy', *Dramatherapy*, 6, 1: 3–19.

Grainger, R. (1990) *Drama and Healing: The Roots of Drama Therapy*, London: Jessica Kingsley Publishers.

—— (1992) 'Dramatherapy and thought disorder', in S. Jennings (ed.) *Dramatherapy: Theory and Practice 2*, London: Routledge.

Honig, A. M. (1993) 'Psychotherapy with command hallucinations in chronic schizophrenia: the use of action techniques within a surrogate family setting', *Journal of the British Psychodrama Association*, 7, 2: 19–38.

Johnson, D. R. (1984) 'Representation of the internal world in catatonic schizophrenia', *Psychiatry*, 47, 4: 299–314.

Kaminsky, R. C. (1981) 'Saying good-bye: an example of using a "good-bye technique" and concomitant psychodrama in the resolving of family grief', *Journal of Group Psychotherapy, Psychodrama and Sociometry*, 34: 100–111.

Kellermann, P. F. (1998) 'Diagnosis in psychodrama', *Revista da S. P. P.*, 5: 25–32.

Kipper, D. A. and Giladi, D. (1978) 'Effectiveness of structured psychodrama and systematic desensitization in reducing test anxiety', *Journal of Counseling Psychology*, 25, 6: 499–505.

Landy, R. (1986) *Dramatherapy: Concepts and Practices*, Springfield, IL: Charles Thomas.

Langley, D. M. and Langley, G. E. (1983) *Dramatherapy and Psychiatry*, London: Croom Helm.

Lantican, L. S. and Mayorga, J. (1993) 'Effectiveness of a women's mental health treatment program: a pilot study', *Issues in Mental Health Nursing*, 14, 1: 31–39.

Levens, M. (1994) 'Art therapy and psychodrama with eating disordered patients: the use of concrete metaphors for the body', in D. Dokter (ed.) *Arts Therapies and Clients with Eating Disorders: Fragile Board*, London: Jessica Kingsley Publishers.

Lisk, G. L. (1982) 'Psychophysiological hysterical reaction', *Journal of Group Psychotherapy Psychodrama and Sociometry*, 35: 18–23.

Moffett, L. and Bruto, L. (1990) 'Therapeutic theatre with personality-disordered substance abusers: characters in search of different characters', *Arts in Psychotherapy*, 17, 4: 339–348.

Monroe, C. (1986) Psychodrama – an effective treatment for the alcoholic', *Journal of the British Psychodrama Association*, 1, 2: 30–36.

Moreno, J. L. (1973) 'Note on indications and contra-indications for acting-out in psychodrama', *Group Psychotherapy and Psychodrama*, 26, 1–2: 23–24.

—— (1987) 'Psychodramatic treatment of psychoses', in J. Fox (ed.) *The Essential Moreno: Writings on Psychodrama, Group Method and Spontaneity*, New York: Springer.

Moreno, Z. T. (1978) 'The function of the auxiliary ego in psychodrama with special reference to psychotic patients', *Journal of Group Psychotherapy, Psychodrama and Sociometry*, 31: 163–166.

Moreno, Z. T. and Moreno, J. D. (1984) 'The psychodramatic model of madness', *Journal of the British Psychodrama Association*, 1, 1: 24–34.

Newburger, H. M. (1987) 'The covert psychodrama of phobias', *Journal of Group Psychotherapy, Psychodrama and Sociometry*, 40, 1: 33–36.

Olsson, P. (1972) 'Psychodrama and group therapy with young heroin addicts returning from duty in Vietnam', *Group Psychotherapy and Psychodrama*, 25, 4: 141–147.

Olsson, P. and Barth, P. A. (1983) 'New uses of psychodrama', *Journal of Operational Psychiatry*, 14, 2: 95–101.

Ruscombe King, G. (1984) 'Psychodrama: a treatment approach to alcoholism', *Dramatherapy*, 8, 1.

Sidorskl, S. (1984) 'The psychodramatic treatment of the borderline personality', *Journal of Group Psychotherapy Psychodrama and Sociometry*, 37, 3: 117–125.

Soeiro, A. C. (1976) *Psicodrama e Psicoterapia [Psychodrama and Psychotherapy]*, São Paulo: Ed. Natura.

Stevenson, M. (1990) 'Psychodrama and cognitive therapy: some similarities and differences', *Journal of the British Psychodrama Association*, 5, 1: 25–38.

—— (1992) 'Maria: dealing with panic attacks with the help of psychodrama and cognitive therapy', *British Journal of Psychodrama and Sociodrama*, 7, 1: 11–21.

Winn, L. (1994) *Post Traumatic Stress Disorder and Dramatherapy: Treatment and Risk Reduction*, London: Jessica Kingsley Publishers.

Wood, D. (1979) 'Psychodrama with an alcohol abuse population', *Group Psychotherapy, Psychodrama and Sociometry*, 32: 75–88.

Zarcone, V. (1984) 'Gestalt techniques in a therapeutic community for the treatment of addicts', *Journal of Psychoactive Drugs*, 16, 1: 43–46.

Chapter 19

Jungian psychodrama
From theoretical to creative roots

Maurizio Gasseau and Wilma Scategni

Introduction

Jungian psychodrama is an approach to psychodrama that is articulated in reference to the analytical theory of Carl Jung (Gasseau 1992; Scategni 1994). The notion of a Jungian approach to psychodrama combines the important innovations of J. L. Moreno (for example, role reversal, doubling and the mirror technique) with Jung's approach to depth psychology on dreams, collective unconsciousness, archetypal medicine, the tendency towards individuation and the concept of net and matrix (Foulkes 1964; Jung 1964). In this chapter we explain and explore some of our central ideas about the application of Jungian psychodrama.

Originally, Jung had fears about the investigation of dreams in a group setting. This fear was connected with the fear of suggestion by the masses, the loss of critical competencies, the development of regressive tendencies in the belly of the group and the fear of losing one's self and one's personal perceptions and maturity. In 1955, Jung elaborated an archetype in which the opposites are individuality and collectivity. In recognition of this archetype, he came to believe that personal analysis and group psychotherapy are complementary and equally useful approaches. Individual analysis elaborates the archetypal polarity of the individual, whereas group therapy explores collective themes of being with others.

Jungian psychodrama is intended to be a versatile and widely applicable approach, rather than dogmatic and narrow. It can be used as a therapeutic approach in the public and private spheres, in health care, mental health and prevention work, and as a supervision tool for therapists.

Basic elements

We will now describe how some of the basic elements of Jungian psychodrama have their roots in Morenean thought.

Setting

Jungian psychodrama sessions typically last two hours, during which there will usually be more than one protagonist. The group participants (7–12 members) will be seated in a circle in order to protect and contain the process of transformation occurring in the protagonist's drama.

Enactment

In Jungian terminology, the psychodramatic enactment of scenes from life focuses on the 'emotional complexes.' These emotional complexes – present in all people – consist of interconnected thoughts, feelings and images. The emotional complexes, according to Jung, may become 'autonomous' wherever they are disconnected from the person's awareness.

By definition, when the emotional complexes manifest themselves, they bring with them emotions, memories, physical feelings, images and thoughts. Psychodramatic enactment can reveal these emotional complexes. A scene may reveal a significant emotional difficulty or blockage in the protagonist (and also potentially in the auxiliary egos and observers). In any instant, the emotional complexes can change their visibility and their intensity. Psychodramatic enactment may enhance the protagonist's self-awareness about these emotional complexes and how they might be addressed and managed.

'Autonomous complexes' – those aspects of the emotional complexes that remain out of awareness – can be made visible on the psychodrama stage in the form of, for example, characters from a dream. They may also take the form of characters from narrative literature. Characters from narrative literature, like characters in a dream, belong to the psyche of the 'author.' We see a good example of this in the Magic Theatre of Herman Hesse's *Steppenwolf* (Hesse 2002) and in Luigi Pirandello's *Six Characters in Search of an Author* (Pirandello 1998). In the cinema, Woody Allen's 1997 film *Deconstructing Harry* is a good example of the way in which the characters created by a writer can develop a life of their own (thus echoing the 'autonomous complexes').

Role reversal

In Jungian terms, when we reverse roles with different characters in a psychodrama (especially with the 'antagonists') we have the opportunity to encounter the other person's 'shadow.' This shadow is the part of one's self that contains the feelings, images and thoughts that are undesired or denied – aspects of self that a person does not want to recognize and which are unconsciously projected on to other people.

For Jung, the shadow is the opposite of what he calls the 'persona.' Persona is the way in which the 'ego' likes to present itself in public life and in the eyes of the world. Because such a high priority is given to this outward presentation, other feelings, thoughts and images that are in contrast with this person may be rejected, banished to the unconscious.

Role reversal can reveal aspects of the shadow in surprising ways. For example, when we reverse roles and encounter the shadow part of someone with whom we are in conflict, we may discover unanticipated connections between their shadow and parts of our own. Similarly, when taking the role of ourselves in a dream, we may discover surprising aspects of our shadow self (for example, a dream where the protagonist feels ashamed because she is walking naked through the streets).

Role reversal offers the opportunity to contact these shadow parts of one's self and other people in order to create new connections, dialogue and relationships inside the different parts of the ego, awareness and unconscious. Many examples of the shadow can be seen in literature, for example in Edgar Allan Poe's *William Wilson* (Poe 1966) and Robert Louis Stevenson's *The Strange Case of Doctor Jekyll and Mister Hyde* (1991).

The double

Doubling facilitates the development of the 'inner voice' of the protagonist. In Jungian psychodrama, this function is normally one of the functions of the director. If we can go back to the examples from literature, we can find in the story of *Pinocchio* (Collodi 1996) the character of the wise, speaking grasshopper (Jiminy Cricket in the Disney version). This grasshopper functions as a vivid double, only with a more pedagogical intent. During the whole story, he leads Pinocchio with a voice of good self-awareness, as the wooden puppet metamorphoses into a real human being.

Pinocchio's transformation is also an apt metaphor for Jung's concept of 'individuating processes' – the metamorphosis of the protagonist from being manipulated by other people or by their own 'autonomous complexes,' to becoming self-determined and taking personal responsibility based on a deep understanding of one's true self.

Returning to Jungian psychodrama, the double has the function of expressing the protagonist's inner thoughts – sometimes already known, sometimes only partially recognized, and sometimes quite unconscious. The function of the double is to suggest these kinds of thoughts, feelings and emotions to the protagonist. In this way, it is possible to encourage an inner dialogue between the conscious and unconscious of the protagonist. In Jungian terms, the conscious self of the protagonist is moving towards the manifestation of the individuating process, helped along by the continuous dialogue between the conscious and unconscious. In Morenean terminology, the manifestation of 'spontaneity' can only be realized when somebody is working with their individuating process.

In the version of Jungian psychodrama developed by Helmut and Ellynor Barz of the Institute for Psychodrama and Jungian Psychology in Switzerland, the double is the function of the co-therapist or co-director. This person accompanies the protagonist during the entire session. At the end, during the sharing, this person shares the feelings and emotions that have arisen for them during the doubling.

Surplus reality – dreams

Jungian psychodrama gives great prominence to dreams and to what is called, in Morenean terms, 'surplus reality.' Dreams are considered a never-ending and faithful mirror of the individuating process occurring in the unconscious. The psychodrama stage is the place where dreams can be concretely represented. In this context, autonomous complexes (the emotional complexes that are free floating and out of awareness) can be made manifest in flesh and blood, where they may contribute to the creation of the atmosphere and emotional color of the dream.

Jungian psychodrama pays particular attention to the aspects of the dream that connect with the present, everyday life of the protagonist/dreamer. Great importance is also given to how the dream connects with the people in the group and the present state of the group. The concept of 'sharing dreams' was explored many years ago by the Jungian analyst Peter Tatham, connected with Gordon Lawrence, who used the concept of the 'social dreaming matrix.' We have used the concept of the social dreaming matrix and combined it with the use of Jungian psychodrama, where we take the dreams back to the group where they arose to explore connections between the protagonist, the group and individuals in the group.

Theory

We now explore important aspects of Jungian psychodramatic theory, in a short exposition of seven basic elements of psychodrama.

The stage

On the psychodrama stage, images and fantasies from the lives of the group members find their space next to images that emerge from their unconscious, such as images from dreams. All of these images are incarnated in the concrete reality of scenic representation. Thus, in psychodrama, the stage functions as the meeting place of two realities:

- the concrete reality represented by the group and its members, who mark off the stage's borders;
- the reality of the inner world of the protagonist – that is, the subjective reality of the images of the unconscious through their scenic representation.

It is this continuous dialogue between conscious and unconscious – between external and internal reality – that takes form on the stage (Scategni 1994).

The protagonist

The attention paid to the protagonist in Jungian psychodrama is equally balanced by the attention paid to the group as a whole. This is perhaps a different balance than that given to the group in classical, 'protagonist-centered' psychodrama. (This is an area of some variation among differing practitioners of Morenian psychodrama.)

The director

In addition to the various functions that Kellermann (1992) describes well, the director guides the group in its explorations inside the labyrinth of relationships, fantasies, encounters, feelings, emotions, images and memories, and searches out some sense in all of these, giving them a direction.

Analytical psychology recognizes four fundamental functions in the individual: intuition, thought, sensation and feeling. It may be said that a psychodrama director, seeking the harmonious interaction of all four of these functions, should engage all of these functions in order to lead a group.

The dramatic scene

Psychodrama based on Jungian psychology stresses that the content of the scenes played out can involve different time dimensions: it can be a recent memory, an impression, or a fantasy that involves the 'here and now,' a memory that goes back many months or years, or the sequence of a dream that belongs to a space without time – the dream world.

The group and the auxiliary ego

In Jungian psychodrama, we generally do not use 'auxiliary egos' who have a stable function, except in some particular contexts, such as psychodrama with psychotic patients, or other situations that require figures who, for example, function as containers for the emotions. In our groups the term auxiliary ego is commonly extended to all the members of the group whom the protagonist chooses to play the roles of the characters. This is also how Moreno used the group members when not working with psychotic persons.

Observations

We add 'observations' to the basic elements of Jungian psychodrama. The observations follow the 'sharing' and conclude the sessions. The observations give back to the group connections, images and links that are open to several readings and reflect back each group member's different ways of seeing and feeling. They act as a sort of frame that borders the work that has been done and gives it back to the group members.

The observer speaks at the end of the session, using a narrative style to convey their sense of the dreams and stories that have been told. The observer enriches the narrative with mythical-poetic amplifications as they reconstruct the stories of the personal events and the group dynamic.

The three phases of psychodrama

Warming up

Typically, ongoing Jungian psychodrama groups rarely use warm-ups. When they are used, this would normally be to 'unblock' situations. They may also be used in single-session workshops. Warming up can at times be used for entire sessions and become the key technique for continuous groups. This approach might be used in some groups with chronically ill psychotic patients who have deteriorated to a point where they may not be able to work on more personal material.

Dramatization – enactment

There is only a small difference between the use of enactment in Jungian psychodrama and classical psychodrama. One possible difference is that, in Jungian psychodrama, we will place great emphasis on finding the 'concatenation among different successive scenes' – in other words, the linking factors between scenes. This approach is intended to shed light on the otherwise hidden links between different scenes in a dream or an event.

Sharing

Sharing is done in the same way in both classical and Jungian psychodrama.

Connections with other Jungian topics

Play, myth, ritual and tragedy

There are deep relationships between the dramatic play, the myth and the ritual in Jungian psychodrama. Dramatic plays contain rules (or 'messages') that place order on the confused experience of suffering and the chaotic experience of the unconsciousness. Similarly, Jungian psychodrama has strong elements of ritual process which are intended to protect against the unboundaried inflation of the unconscious. The protagonist in a Jungian psychodrama feels themselves to be part of a mythical reality which places them in a universal environment. This helps them to move beyond a hindering experience of alienation into an experience felt to be in common with all humanity. As Cassirer (1946) has observed, 'the myth aspires to totality.'

There is also an interesting relationship between Jungian psychodrama and Greek tragedy. In both forms, the audience/observers do not give advice to the characters, but instead the characters must go through their process on the stage. As with Greek tragedy, in the aftermath of a Jungian psychodrama there may be energy present like that following the end of a storm (we recall Aristotle's notion of the audience catharsis). This changes the group. There are also interesting connections between the lament of the chorus in Greek tragedy and the function of the 'observer' in Jungian psychodrama (described earlier in this chapter). At the end of the sessions, the protagonist and all participants are given back to the group reality of here and now. They leave the ritual background and return to their everyday life, as with any audience member leaving the ancient theatre.

Dream work

When we think about dream work, we start with Jung's concept that the structure of dreams is not different from the structure of drama. The dream is a theatre where the dreamer is scene, actor, promoter, player, author, public and critic together (Scategni 2001a). In Jungian psychodrama, dreams of all categories are enacted: symbolic dreams, visionary dreams, nightmares, oracle dreams, recurrent dreams and social dreams (Scategni 1994, 2001a, 2001b, 2002). The technique of 'incubation' of dreams is also investigated by Gasseau according to the ancient ideas of Asclepion (Gasseau 1992).

Relationship between Jungian psychodrama and shamanic rituals

As in the shamanic practices, there are times when Jungian psychodrama explores the relationship between the protagonist and the spirit/memory of people who have died. These are psychodramatic scenes that take place in virtual places, beyond time and space. From the role of this spirit person, the protagonist, after a sufficient preparation, will be able to give themselves deep and meaningful messages. The director will work to ensure adequate doubling is offered where necessary during the protagonist's encounter with this psychic afterlife of thoughts, images and feelings.

The message taken from this encounter is then brought back to the here and now of the protagonist and the group itself. The group members will, over time, each have an opportunity for such an encounter, because these other dimensions are different for each person.

Imaginative work

Jungian psychodrama is a work of imaginative psychology in which the director's task is to gather together and bring into focus the images present in the stories of the participants which can be useful for the protagonist (this will include images, memories, dreams and actively imagined scenes). Role representation is important in Jungian psychodrama, and so is the representation of the imaginative realm. Particular attention is paid to how some of the images presented by individuals constitute a 'group emergence,' that is, they contain meanings which are prospectively useful for the whole group.

Collective unconsciousness and co-unconsciousness

In Jungian psychodrama, there is a deep relationship between the Jungian concept of individual and collective unconsciousness and Foulkes' concept of the basic and intergenerational matrix (Foulkes 1964). The concept of the collective unconscious can be well integrated with Moreno's inspired concept of tele and co-unconsciousness.

Therapeutic effectivness

We have used Jungian psychodrama for many years with great effectiveness and benefits for our clients. If the reader is drawn to using this approach, we suggest that the therapeutic effectiveness of Jungian psychodrama may be evaluated by focussing on the following points of benefit for the participants:

- increased self-awareness, attained while also finding the similarities and differences between one's self and the different roles played
- sharing concrete experiences with the group, and developing the ability to work collaboratively

- ability to observe one's own relational dynamics, e.g. through participating in a psychodrama and observing through the 'mirror' technique
- ability to empathize with the other (e.g. through double and role reversal)
- spontaneous manifestation of creativity, developing the possibility of finding 'new answers to old questions'
- ability to reflect on, compare and contrast thoughts in images and dreams with thoughts resulting from having enacted those images and dreams in psychodrama
- rediscovery of the relation between images and emotions, through directly experiencing the connections on the stage
- recognition that one's own individual path may also be influenced by and open to the needs and desires of other people.

References

Cassirer, E. (1946) *Language and Myth*, New York: Dover Publications.

Collodi, C. (1996) *Pinocchio*, London: Puffin.

Foulkes, S. (1964) *Therapeutic Group Analysis*, London: Allen and Unwin.

Gasseau, M. (1992) *Lo Psicodramma Junghiano* [*Jungian Psychodrama*], Torino: Boringhieri.

Hesse, H. (2002) *Steppenwolf*, New York: Picador.

Jung, C. (1964) *Man and his Symbols*, Garden City, NY: Doubleday.

Kellermann, P. F. (1992) *Focus on Psychodrama*, London: Jessica Kingsley Publishers.

Pirandello, L. (1998) *Six Characters in Search of an Author*, New York: Signet.

Poe, E. A. (1966) *Complete Poems and Stories of Edgar Allen Poe*, New York: Doubleday.

Scategni, W. (1994) *Das Psychodrama zwischen alltaglicher und archetypischer Erfahrungswelt* [*Psychodrama Between the Archetypal World and Everyday Life*], Solothurn and Dusseldorf: Walter Verlag.

—— (1999) 'Some reflections on Jungian psychodrama training', in P. Fontaine (ed.) *Psychodrama Training: A European View*, Leuven: Federation of European Psychodrama Training Organisations (FEPTO).

—— (2001a) 'La materia dei sogni: dall'immagine onirica all'immagine psicodrammatica' [The stuff of dreams: from dream image to psychodramatic image], in W. Scategni (ed.) *International Review of Psychodrama and Analytical Psychology*, Turin: Ananke.

—— (2001b) 'The social dream in psychodrama', in W. Scategni (ed.) *International Review of Psychodrama and Analytical Psychology*, Turin: Ananke.

—— (2002) *Psychodrama, Group Processes and Dreams: Archetypal Images of Individuation*, London: Routledge.

Stevenson, R. L. (1991) *The Strange Case of Dr. Jekyll and Mr. Hyde*, New York: Tor.

Chapter 20

Studies on treatment effects of psychodrama psychotherapy

Michael Wieser

Introduction

Psychodrama as psychotherapy is based on theories of spontaneity, creativity and action. It is probably due to this association that the study of psychodrama's effectiveness, in a controlled and more rigid academic way, has been neglected. Consequently, psychodrama psychotherapy, despite being one of the first recognized psychotherapies, still has a relatively tentative status in the scientific fields of psychology, psychiatry and psychotherapy. Systematic research will provide us with answers with regard to which treatment effect can be associated with which research method and type of measurement.

In this area of investigation, there is documentation in Germany (Burmeister *et al.* n.d.), but there are problems in matching the mainstream standards in evidence-based psychotherapy. The same is true in Switzerland, in the meta-analysis developed by Grawe *et al.* (1994). (Meta-analysis is where existing studies in treatment effectiveness are systematically compared; Wieser 2006a.) Similar studies, conducted outside German-speaking countries (Kipper 1978; Schramski and Harvey 1983; Kellermann 1987; Greenberg *et al.* 1994; Kipper and Ritchie 2003; Elliott *et al.* 2004) also point to problems with research design.

Psychodrama psychotherapy has been accredited by the government and social insurance systems in Austria (Ottomeyer and Wieser 1996), in Hungary (Pintér 2001), and by the European Association of Psychotherapy (Wieser *et al.* 2005). However, the scientific status of psychodrama psychotherapy has not yet been recognised by the scientific community at large, since studies done in this field seem to have failed to attain mainstream standards. Nevertheless, a closer analysis of studies on the treatment effects of psychodrama therapy should be carried out on the background of *ICD-10* to identify the constraints of research encountered in this field and to suggest possible avenues for future research. *ICD-10* stands for the *International Classification of Diseases, Version 10*, produced by the World Health Organization (1992). Chapter F00–99 covers mental and behavioural disorders. This classification is negotiated and agreed world-wide, is culturally sensitive, and insurance systems often ask for diagnoses that reference it.

The aim of this chapter is to explore the kinds of statistical evidence that we have for the effectiveness of psychodrama psychotherapy. This involves a survey and description of existing studies into the effectiveness of psychodrama psychotherapy, shaped as a narrative literature review. A collection of research papers has been grouped according to the systematic categories of *ICD-10*. The analysis is based on statistically significant results regarding the treatment effects of psychodrama therapy.

Sample characteristics

The sample consists of a wide variety of papers retrieved from PsycINFO (American Psychological Association) and PsyNDEX (University of Trier, Germany), and other databases in English and German, going back several decades. These studies are concerned with different aspects of investigation into treatment effectiveness within the field of psychodrama psychotherapy.

The selection process of the sample was not based on a particular topic of investigation, such as age (children, youths, adults, elderly patients), type of disorder (acute to chronic), treatment program (inpatients, outpatients, prisoners), setting (individual, couple, family, group) or length of treatment (one session, weekend, marathon, long term).

The sample also includes comparative studies. These compare psycho-drama psychotherapy with other psychotherapeutic methods and pharma-ceutical therapy as well as outcome studies (where the main interest lies in the difference between the beginning and end of psychotherapy) and process research (where every single session is of interest). Investigations of cost efficiency analyses are not known in this field at the moment.

Some studies included in this sample do not use measuring instruments that would satisfy high standards. At the very least, studies included here must include a systematic self-report or measurement of interpersonal relations by means of sociometry. Drop-out rate in psychotherapy and research should be noticed and reflected, but was not part of the selection criteria for studies reported here. In addition, most of the subjects/patients must have a diagnosis included in *ICD-10* (as opposed to self-referral where there is no diagnosis). Psychodramatists do not typically use a manualized approach as some cognitive behaviour therapists do, so there is no requirement for manualized treatment for studies to be included here. The studies included here are both published and unpublished, e.g., as a manuscript. All together, there are 52 studies included. Eight studies are randomized clinical trials, 14 are controlled studies, and 30 are naturalistic studies.

Method of description

In order to broaden the scope of research, the description involves classification of the studies according to the research method. Three main categories were used. The first consists of those studies which follow the 'gold standard' of the randomized clinical trial. In studies in this category, two groups of patients are chosen at random. Typically, one group is given psychotherapeutic treatment while the other, for example, has to wait.

The second category comprises studies using controlled methods. For example, a psychotherapy group may be compared with a non-treated group.

A third group is made up of naturalistic studies, which investigate patients in normal psychotherapeutic practice. Single case studies are a subgroup of naturalistic studies. They must be systematic in some way and controlled by a qualitative or quantitative method. One of the disadvantages in analyzing single case studies is that they do not lend themselves to statistical testing, since the study is only done on one particular subject.

Comparative studies may be thought of as a subgroup of randomized clinical trials, or controlled or naturalistic studies, depending on their area of focus.

All of the above groups include 'pre- and post' measures (at the beginning and end of treatment) and some include a follow-up (for example, one year after treatment).

In analyzing the effectiveness of psychodrama psychotherapy in each study, the approach in this chapter is to look for positive statistical significance and not for effect sizes. A standard procedure to obtain statistical evidence on effectiveness is through the counting of effect sizes (ES). The parameter is normally set as ES>0.5. However, this procedure poses a problem with this parameter, because not all studies provide necessary information on areas such as change, the scale used, population (n), mean (m) and standard deviation (s_d). This data would be measured before treatment (pre), post-treatment, possibly in a follow-up, and at the same time in a non-treated control group. (Effect size is expressed as: $ES = m_t - m_c/s_{dc}$, where t = treatment and c = control.) Qualitative studies have mostly been excluded because they do not allow for rigorous statistical testing. This does not mean that qualitative studies (Kipper and Hundal 2003) are not scientific. Nevertheless, if psychodrama psychotherapy is to be accredited by states, social and health insurance agencies, and professional and scientific associations, it must use mainstream standards of measurement.

Results

Where studies have found statistically significant effects, these are marked with asterisks (one, two or three according the significance level). In order to have a criterion for what is evidence of treatment effectiveness, there should be at least one study according to each main category of research methods and classification of disorders.

Organic, including symptomatic, mental disorders (ICD-10 F00–F09)

To date, no studies have been reviewed.

Mental and behavioral disorders due to psychoactive substance abuse (ICD-10 F10–F19)

Four studies report positive results for adults and two of them also for youths (Waniczek *et al.* 2005; Wood *et al.* 1979). The research design is mostly naturalistic (see Table 20.1).

Comment

Mental and behavioral disorders due to psychoactive substance abuse can be treated successfully with psychodrama therapy, as reported by eight statistically significant results. Randomized and controlled clinical studies should be added.

Schizophrenia, schizotypal and delusional disorders (ICD-10 F20–F29)

Four of five studies have good results, even with chronic schizophrenics and people with delusions who are in short-term psychodrama psychotherapy (see Table 20.2).

Comment

Peters and Jones (1951) is one of the pioneer studies. Normally, 1952 is known as the beginning of controlled psychotherapy research. Schizophrenia, schizotypal and delusional disorders are well evaluated by five statistically significant results for psychodrama therapy, and overall support the use of psychodrama with these disorders. A better randomized clinical trial could follow. Under mixed groups of disorders, research has been done by Bender *et al.* (1979, 1981), where schizophrenia and delusion are among the main disorders.

Mood (affective) disorders (ICD-10 F30–F39)

Three studies with good results have been reported in this field (see Table 20.3).

Table 20.1 ICD-10 F10–F19 mental and behavioral disorders due to psychoactive substance abuse

Study	Research method	Measure	Findings
Mann and Janis (1968)	Controlled trial, follow-up (2 weeks, 18 months)	Questionnaire, interview	Less cigarette consumption after emotional role playing* (p<0.05, probability of error in percent)
Wood et al. (1979)	Comparative with small group therapy; matched with a similar group who did not do psychodrama	Comrey Personality Scales	More trust*, emotional stability*, and activity*
		Mini Mult (short form of MMPI, Minnesota Multiphasic Personality Inventory)	More defensive** and controlled** (p<0.01 (better than p<0.05))
		State-Trait Anxiety Inventory (A-State Scale)	Statistically not significant (n.s.)
Crawford (1989)	Naturalistic, post; follow-up (2 years)	Questionnaire	Great satisfaction with psychodrama led to good alcohol/drug status*
Waniczek et al. (2005)	Naturalistic; retrospective follow-up (1–4 years); comparison group	EBIS-A-sheet (EinrichtungsBezogenes Information System); SEDOS-inquiry-sheet (Stationäres Einrichtungsbezogenes DokumentationsSystem)	Abstinence rate of 72.9%, high general satisfaction of life**

Table 20.2 ICD-10 F20–F29 schizophrenia, schizotypal and delusional disorders

Study	Research method	Measure	Findings
Sturm and Stuart (1974)	Randomized clinical trial; psychodrama-based role retraining and remotivation group; self-created control group (treatment early terminators); pre-test	Tape recordings, observers; Inpatient Presentableness Scale, raters	No changes in feelings, happiness, thoughts, plans of the five most regressed patients on each unit
Peters and Jones (1951)	Controlled trial	Porteus Maze Test Ages	Difference in the post scores of qualitative errors**
		Mirror-Tracing Test	Improvement
		Rorschach	No report
		Draw-a-Person Test	No report
		Gardner Behavior Chart	No report
Jones and Peters (1952)	Controlled trial	Qualitative Maze scores	Ratio of between groups variance to within groups variance**
		Mirror Tracing Test	Improvement*
		Gardner Behavior Chart	Improvement*
		Rorschach Test	N.s.
		Draw-a-Man Test	In favour of the control group
		Picture Sorting Test	Increase of affective reactions
Harrow (1952)	Controlled trial, post	Role (action) test	Scale of realism*
		Rorschach Test	Improvement
		MAPS (Make-a-Picture Story Test)	Improvement
Parrish (1959)	Naturalistic	Ward observed and rated the behavior	Improvement
		Counted the amount of patients ready to leave hospital	Improvement

Table 20.3 ICD-10 F30–F39 mood (affective) disorders

Study	Research method	Measure	Findings
Pour Rezaeian et al. (1997a)	Randomized clinical trial	BDI (Beck Depression Inventory)	Better than a psychiatric group**; not different from a combination group
		MMPI	No report
Pour Rezaeian et al. (1997b)	Controlled trial	SLSCT (Sentence Completion Test)	Better than the psychiatric group**; equal with the combination group
Ernst et al. (1980)	Naturalistic	Questionnaire	Sociometric choices increased**; well-being improved

Comment

Mood (affective) disorders are effectively treated with psychodrama therapy, as shown by three statistically significant results. More studies need to be done to emphasize the scientific effectiveness. It is worth noting that Pour Rezaeian *et al.* (1997a, b) investigated only mild depression and Ernst *et al.* (1980) was not focused in particular on the kind of disorder.

Neurotic, stress-related and somatoform disorders (ICD-10 F40–F48)

In a total of ten studies, more positive than negative results are reported (see Table 20.4).

Comment

Neurotic, stress-related and somatoform disorders are the best validated area for psychodrama therapy, with 23 positive statistical significances. Under mixed groups of disorders, you will find neurosis as well, especially in Bender *et al.* (1979, 1981).

Behavioral syndromes associated with physiological disturbances and physical factors (ICD-10 F50–F59)

To date, no studies have been reviewed.

Disorders of adult personality and behavior (ICD-10 F60–F69)

To date, no studies have been reviewed.

Mental retardation (ICD-10 F70–F79)

Two studies report positive results but are more a kind of social pedagogical psychodrama (see Table 20.5).

Comment

Psychodrama has beneficial effects for people with mental retardation, but more studies have to be done to emphasize the scientific effectiveness of psychodrama psychotherapy.

Disorders of psychological development (ICD-10 F80–F89)

To date, no studies have been reviewed.

Table 20.4 ICD-10 F40–F48 neurotic, stress-related and somatoform disorders

Study	Research method	Measure	Findings
Lapierre et al. (1973)	Randomized clinical trial; double-blind (researchers do not know if the patient gets psychotherapy or not. Even the patients do not know. Placebo is, for example, a talking group without a psychotherapeutic aim); matched	Wittenborn Rating Scale; Eysenck Personality Inventory; Ad-hoc scale	Mesoridazine (drug) group as compared with the placebo group had less pronounced affective involvement in psychodrama psychotherapy*
Kipper and Giladi (1978)	Randomized clinical trial	STABS (Suinn Test Anxiety Behavior Scale)	Improvement*** (p<0.001); equally effective as systematic desensitization
		EPI-N scale (Neuroticism Scale of Eysenck Personality Inventory)	N.s. (normal range from the beginning)
		Background information form	
Bendorf et al. (1976)	Controlled trial, follow-up (3–6 months)	FPI (Freiburg Personality Inventory)	Nervousness**, depression**, sociability**, self-consciousness**, extraversion*, emotional unstableness* and masculinity*
		Well Being Scale (Zerssen)	A normal population (post)
		Interview, rating scale	
Arn et al. (1989)	Controlled trial, pre-post, follow-up (three months, three years)	Symptom questionnaire	Decrease of worry and tension*
Eibach (1980)	Naturalistic; qualitative case study	Questionnaire	After two years no further somatization in the whole group

continues overleaf

Table 20.4 Continued

Study	Research method	Measure	Findings
Newburger (1987)	Naturalistic; follow-up (7 months)	Therapist rating	All ten patients symptom free (post); Eight of ten symptom free (follow-up)
Schneider-Düker (1989)	Naturalistic, comparative	SYMLOG (System for the Multiple Level Observation of Groups)	More difficult for psychotherapy groups to enrich the role repertoires
Theorell et al. (1998)	Naturalistic; pre-post; follow-up (half year, four years)	Self rating	In art therapy, anxiety-depression improved
		General Health Questionnaire	Improved*
		Blood test in serum uric acid	Psychodrama worse than other kind of art therapy*
Hudgins et al. (2000)	Naturalistic; single case study; follow-up (six weeks)	Videotape, evaluator	Improvement**
		DES (Dissociative Experience Scale)	Improvement**
		TSI (Trauma Symptom Inventory)	Improvement*
		BDI	Improvement*
		BSQ (Body Sensation Questionnaire)	No report
		Narrative writing	
Lind et al. (2006)	Naturalistic; psychodrama and psychodynamic imaginative trauma therapy; pre-post, follow-up	BSI	Decrease in symptoms**; GSI pre-post g = 2.2, pre-follow-up g = 2.28 (very strong effect)
		Emotional and Behavioural Changes in Psychotherapy Questionnaire (VEV)	Improvement***

Table 20.5 ICD-10 F70–F79 mental retardation

Study	Research method	Measure	Findings
Strain (1975)	Naturalistic	Observer, raters	Sociodrama led to more engagement in social play afterwards
Amesberger et al. (1993)	Naturalistic	Observer	Improvements in personality development and conflict solution

Table 20.6 ICD-10 F90–F98 behavioral emotional disorders with onset usually occurring in childhood or adolescence

Study	Research method	Measure	Findings
Gelcer (1978)	Randomized clinical trial	RTT (Role Taking Task)	Improvement with role play**
		BSAG-School (Bristol Social Adjustments Guide)	Improvement*
Dequine and Pearson-Davis (1983)	Controlled trial	Norwicki-Strickland Personal Reaction Survey; interview	With drama therapy, more internal control*

Behavioral emotional disorders with onset usually occurring in childhood or adolescence (ICD-10 F90–F98)

Two studies report positive results with techniques related to psychodrama psychotherapy (see Table 20.6).

Comment

Behavioral emotional disorders with onset usually occurring in childhood or adolescence are effectively treated with role play and drama therapy (techniques related to psychodrama), as shown by three statistical significances. More studies have to be done to emphasize the scientific effectiveness of psychodrama psychotherapy.

Mixed groups of disorders

Ten studies report more positive results, and two additional studies report effectiveness in individual modality. Steffan (2000) compares psychodrama psychotherapy with integrative psychotherapy, Anbeh and Tschuschke (2001) with group analysis and Tschuschke and Anbeh (2000) with eclectic psychotherapy (see Table 20.7).

Comment

In psychotherapeutic practice, most patients have mixed disorders and not just one. That is why it is important to report results in this field of research. The effectiveness of psychodrama psychotherapy is shown by 20 positive statistical significances.

Area of disorder unknown

Seventeen studies were included with more positive results. Three investigated the psychodramatic double technique. Petzold (1979) is concerned with elderly people, and two other studies deal with youths (see Table 20.8).

Comment

A lot of controlled and naturalistic studies are a kind of basic research. Due to length restriction, there will be no detailed description in this paper.

Conclusion

In the area of organic, including symptomatic, mental disorders (F0), behavioral syndromes associated with physiological disturbances (F5), disorders of adult personality and behavior (F6), and disorders of psychological development (F8), there is still a need for basic research into the effectiveness of psychodrama therapy (see Table 20.9).

In the studies described above, there is a wide variety of measurement techniques. However, it should be noticed that some of those tests were written 50 years ago, and different ways of measuring may be in use today. There is a strong need for a consensus on the kind of measurement instruments that apply best to psychodrama, which would allow us to compare psychodrama studies with each other and even with other psychotherapeutic methods. This is a key task of the psychodrama research group of the International Association of Group Psychotherapy (IAGP), which is working to improve the quality of psychodrama research. Kellar *et al.* (2002), Kipper and Hundal (2005) and Christoforou and Kipper (2006) have developed instruments to measure spontaneity which investigate an important part of psychodrama theory. Independent of a psychotherapeutic method, the Brief Symptom Inventory (BSI, Derogatis 1993) is used in different languages.

Table 20.7 Mixed groups of disorders

Study	Research method	Measure	Findings
Bender et al. (1979)	Randomized clinical trial; follow-up (9, 10, 22 weeks)	AMDP (Working Group for Methods and Documentation in Psychiatry)	Decrease pre-post*
		MMPI	Paranoia and schizoid*
		SAF (Social Adjustment Questionnaire)	In the whole and in the scale leisure*
		EWL (Adjective List)	Emotional irritation*
		Giessen Questionnaire	Social power (for neurosis)
Carpenter and Sandberg (1985)	Controlled trial	Jessness Asocial Index	Reduction between and within subjects**
		High School Personality Questionnaire	Ego strength between subjects and pre to post-test**
		I-E (Introversion-Extraversion) Scale	Became more introverted**
Bender et al. (1981)	Naturalistic; comparative, pre-post; process, follow-up (three months)	MMPI	N.s.
		EWL	Well-being* (neurotics); worsening* (psychotics)
		Bf-S (Well-Being Scale)	N.s.
		SAF (Social Adjustment Questionnaire)	N.s.
		Giessen Questionnaire	Amenability*
		FPI	N.s.
		AMDP 3	Psychopathology*
		Goal Attainment Scoring (100mm line)	N.s.
		Therapy Assessment Scale	N.s.
		Video-recording and questionnaire	Protagonist improvement*

continues overleaf

Table 20.7 Continued

Study	Research method	Measure	Findings
Herfurth (1999)	Naturalistic; follow-up (one to three years)	Problem-centred interview Questionnaire Context journal Role play	Improvement Transfer problems Goals of the clinic attained No report
Lemke (1999)	Naturalistic; follow-up	Problem-centred interview	Improvement in therapy success (coping strategies, competency in perception, broadening the room for action)
Petzold et al. (n.d.)	Naturalistic; pre-post, process; follow-up (six months)	GSI-SCL-90R (Global Severity Index – Symptom Check List) IIP-C (Inventory of Interpersonal Problems, short form) Therapist questionnaire Therapy assessment scale Client questionnaire Relations questionnaire Session questionnaire	ES=0.63 ES=0.11 Improvement Improvement Improvement Improvement No report
Steffan (2000)	Naturalistic; comparative, pre-post process follow-up (six months)	Therapist questionnaire Client questionnaire GSI-SCL-90R IIP-C Therapy assessment scale Relations questionnaire Session questionnaire	Improvement Improvement ES=0.39 ES=0.52 Improvement Improvement No report

Tschuschke and Anbeh (2000)	Naturalistic; comparative, pre-post	IIP	N.s., ES=0.22
		GSI-SCL-90R	Improvements, ES=0.2
		Therapy Goal Attainment Scale	Improvements, ES=0.9
		GAF (Global Assessment of Functioning Scale)	Improvements, ES=0.44
Anbeh and Tschuschke (2001)	Naturalistic; comparative, pre-post	IIP	ES=0.57*** (p<0.0001)
		GSI-SCL-90R	ES=0.66***
		Therapy Goal Attainment Scale	ES=2.32***
		GAF	ES=1.28***
Tschuschke and Anbeh (2004)	Naturalistic; pre-post	IIP	ES=0.47***
		GSI-SCL-90R	ES=0.55***
		Therapy Goal Attainment Scale	ES=1.55***
		GAF	ES=1.18***
			Mean ES=0.94

Table 20.8 Area of disorder unknown

Study	Research method	Measure	Findings
Kipper and Ben-Ely (1979)	Randomized clinical trial	Modified Accurate Empathic Scale	After a role-playing procedure, differences***
Hudgins and Kiesler (1987)	Randomized clinical trial	IMI (Impact Message Inventory)	Effects***, positive impacts; higher level in revealingness**
		RI (Relationship Inventory)	Higher empathic understanding**; interviewer statements got more accurate*
		REV (Revealingness Scale)	Higher scores**
Culbertson (1957) Schönke (1975) Petzold (1979) Schramski et al. (1984) Joyce et al. (n.d.)	Controlled trial		
Toeman (1948) O'Connell and Hanson (1970) Ploeger et al. (1972) Enke (1984) Schmidt (1980) Ernst (1989) Geßmann (1994, 1995) Baim et al. (1999)	Naturalistic		

Acknowledgements

A related paper was presented at the Fifteenth and Sixteenth International Congresses of the International Association of Group Psychotherapy and Group Processes (Wieser 2003, 2006b), the Fourth Asia Pacific Conference on Psychotherapy (Wieser 2005) and published in German (Wieser 2004). I would like to acknowledge M. St. Martínez, C. Baim and K. Tudor for revising this text, and the comments of A. Blatner, P. Fontaine, P. F. N. Kellermann, R. Oudijk and J. L. Pio Abreu.

Table 20.9 Overview: studies on treatment effects of psychodrama psychotherapy

ICD-10	Method			Findings		
	RCT	CT	Naturalistic	Negative	Equal	Positive
F00–09						
F10–19		2	2		1	8
F20–29	1	3	1		9	5
F30–39	1	1	1		3	3
F40–48	2	2	6	1	4	23
F50–59						
F60–69						
F70–79	2				2	
F80–89						
F90–98	1	1				3
Mixed	1	1	8		11	20

Note: RCT = randomized clinical trial; CT = controlled trial

References

Amesberger, G., Fritsch, B., Gisinger, E., Siebert, W., Sotzko, V. and Weber, M. (1993) 'Tätigkeitsbericht Projekt, Hütte – Gemeinschaft – Natur 1992/1993' [Project report cottage – community – nature 1992/1993], unpublished paper, Vienna.

Anbeh, T. and Tschuschke, V. (2001) 'Effekte ambulanter Gruppenpsychotherapie-Behandlung in Deutschland – Zwischenergebnisse der PAGE-Studie' [Effects of outpatient group psychotherapy in Germany – interim results of the PAGE Study], in D. Mattke, G. Hertel, S. Büsing and K. Schreiber-Willnow (eds) Störungsspezifische Konzepte und Behandlung in der Psychosomatik [Disorder-specific Concepts and Treatment in Psychosomatics], Frankfurt: VAS.

Arn, I., Theorell, T., Uvnäs-Moberg, K. and Jonsson, C. O. (1989) 'Psychodrama group therapy for patients with functional gastrointestinal disorders – a controlled long-term follow-up study', Psychotherapy and Psychosomatics, 51: 113–119.

Baim, C., Allam, J., Eames, T., Dunford, S. and Hunt, S. (1999) 'The use of psychodrama to enhance victim empathy in sex offenders: an evaluation', Journal of Sexual Aggression 4, 1: 4–14.

Bender, W., Detter, G., Eibl-Eibesfeld, B., Engel-Sittenfeld, P., Gmelin, B., Wolf, R. et al. (1979) 'Psychodrama-versus-Freizeitgruppe: Effekte einer 25stündigen Gruppenpsychotherapie bei psychiatrischen Patienten' [Psychodrama versus patient club activity (leisure group): effects of a 25-hour group psychotherapy with psychiatric patients], Fortschritte Neurologie Psychiatrie, 47: 641–658.

Bender, W., Eibl-Eibesfeld, B., Lerchl-Wanie, G. and Zander, K. J. (1981) 'Psychodramatherapie mit Neurose – und Psychosepatienten unter Einsatz von Video-Feedback' [Psychodramatherapy with neurotics and psychotics using video-feedback], Psychother. Med. Psychologie, 31: 125–131.

Bendorf, G., Doubrawa, R. and Klaffki, E. L. (1976) 'Therapeutisches Spiel als klinische Gruppenkurztherapie in der rehabilitativen und präventiven Inneren Medizin' [Therapeutic play as clinical short-term group therapy in rehabilitative and preventive internal medicine], *Psychother. Med. Psychologie*, 26: 158–163.

Burmeister, J., Leutz, G. and Diebels, E. (eds) (n.d.) *Psychodramatherapie. Dokumentation zur Anerkennung als wissenschaftlich anerkannte psychotherapeutische Behandlungsmethode* [*Psychodrama Therapy. Documentation to get Accreditation as a Scientific Psychotherapeutic Treatment*], W. l.: Deutscher Fachverband für Psychodrama DFP.

Carpenter, P. and Sandberg, S. (1985) 'Further psychodrama with delinquent adolescents', *Adolescence*, 20: 599–604.

Christoforou, A. and Kipper, D. A. (2006) 'The Spontaneity Assessment Inventory (SAI), anxiety, obsessive-compulsive tendency, and temporal orientation', *Journal of Group Psychotherapy, Psychodrama & Sociometry*, 59: 23–34.

Crawford, R. J. M. (1989) 'Follow up of alcohol and other drug dependents treated with psychodrama', *New Zealand Medical Journal*, 102, 866: 199.

Culbertson, F. M. (1957) 'Modification of an emotionally held attitude through role playing', *Journal of Abnormal and Social Psychology*, 54: 230–233.

Dequine, E. R. and Pearson-Davis, S. (1983) 'Videotaped improvisational drama with emotionally disturbed adolescents', *Arts in Psychotherapy*, 10: 15–21.

Derogatis, L. R. (1993) *Brief Symptom Inventory (BSI)* (3rd edn), Minneapolis: National Computer Services.

Eibach, H. (1980) 'Der Einsatz des Psychodramas bei Psychosomatikern in Bezug auf die Kriterien der analytischen Kurztherapie' [The application of psychodrama with psychosomatic patients with respect to the criteria of analytic short term therapy], *Gruppenpsychother. Gruppendynamik*, 15: 315–329.

Elliott, R., Greenberg, L. S. and Lietaer, G. (2004) 'Research on experiential psychotherapies', in M. J. Lambert (ed.) *Bergin and Garfield's Handbook of Psychotherapy and Behavior Change* (5th edn), New York: Wiley.

Enke, H. (1984) 'Empirische Gruppenpsychotherapieforschung' [Empirical group psychotherapy research], in A. Heigl-Evers (ed.) *Kindlers Psychologie des 20. Jahrhunderts* [*Kindlers Psychology of the 20th Century*], Vol. 2, Weinheim: Beltz.

Ernst, M. (1989) 'Interactions of the protagonists and their auxiliary egos in psychodrama – process analyses and comparisons using the SYMLOG interaction scoring', *International Journal of Small Group Research*, 5, 1: 89–118.

Ernst, M., Wiertz, A. and Sabel, B. A. (1980) 'Veränderungen im soziometrischen Wahl- und Wahrnehmungsverhalten in einer Psychodramagruppe psychiatrischer Patienten. Eine Erkundungsstudie' [Changes in sociometric choice and perception acting in a psychodrama group of psychiatric patients. An investigation], *Sozialpsychiatrische Informationen. Psychodrama*, March: 20–52.

Gelcer, E. (1978) 'Social decentration: its measurement and training in emotionally disturbed institutionalized children', in R. Weizmann, R. Brown, P. Levinson and P. Taylor (eds) *Piagetian Theory and Its Implications for the Helping Professions*, Los Angeles: University Park Press.

Geßmann, H. W. (1994) 'Über die Wirksamkeit psychodramatischer Wochenendseminare auf die im Freiburger Persönlichkeitsinventar erfaßten Merkmale und auf das Aggressionsverhalten gemessen mit dem Rosenzweig-Picture-Frustration-Test' [The effects of psychodrama weekend seminars on personality and aggression], in H. W. Geßmann (ed.) *Humanistisches Psychodrama 1 [Humanistic Psychodrama 1]*, Bergerhausen: Verlag des Psychotherapeutischen Instituts.

—— (1995) 'Empirische Untersuchung der therapeutischen Wirksamkeit der Doppelmethode im Humanistischen Psychodrama' [An empirical study on the therapeutic effectiveness of the double method in humanistic psychodrama], *Internationale Zeitschrift für Humanistisches Psychodrama*, 2, 1: 5–23.

Grawe, K., Donati, R. and Bernauer, F. (1994) *Psychotherapie im Wandel. Von der Konfession zur Profession* [Psychotherapy Changing from Confession to Profession], Göttingen: Hogrefe.

Greenberg, L., Elliott, R. and Lietaer, G. (1994) 'Research on experiential psychotherapy', in A. E. Bergin and S. L. Garfield (eds) *Handbook of Psychotherapy and Behavior Change*, New York: Wiley.

Harrow, G. (1952) 'Psychodrama group therapy: its effects upon the role behaviour of schizophrenic patients', *Group Psychotherapy*, 5: 120–172.

Herfurth, C. (1999) 'Bin ich auf dem richtigen Weg? Psychosomatische Patienten nach stationärer Psychodramatherapie – eine qualitative Studie über subjektiv erlebte Veränderungen' [Am I on the right path? Psychosomatic patients after inpatient psychodrama therapy – a qualitative study on subjective experienced changes], unpublished Masters thesis, Technische Universität Berlin.

Hudgins, M. K. and Kiesler, D. J. (1987) 'Individual experiential psychotherapy: an analogue validation of the intervention module of psychodramatic doubling', *Psychotherapy*, 24, 2: 245–255.

Hudgins, M. K., Drucker, K. and Metcalf, K. (2000) 'The "containing double": a clinically effective psychodrama intervention for PTSD', *British Journal of Psychodrama and Sociometry*, 15: 58–77.

Jones, F. and Peters, H. (1952) 'An experimental evaluation of group psychotherapy', *Journal of Consulting Psychology*, 18: 345–353.

Joyce, A. S., Dyck, R. J., Prazoff, M., Shen, F. and Azim H. F. A. (n.d.) 'Short-term group psychotherapy versus brief psychodrama in an outpatient facility', unpublished paper, Edmonton.

Kellar, H., Treadwell, T., Kumar, V. K. and Leach, E. S. (2002) 'The Personal Attitude Scale-II: a revised measure of spontaneity', *International Journal of Action Methods. Psychodrama, Skill Training, and Role Playing*, 55, 1: 35–46.

Kellermann, P. F. (1987) 'Outcome research in classical psychodrama', *Small Group Behavior*, 18, 4: 459–469.

Kipper, D. A. (1978) 'Trends in the research on the effectiveness of psychodrama: retrospect and prospect', *Group Psychotherapy, Psychodrama & Sociometry*, 31: 5–18.

Kipper, D. A. and Ben-Ely, Z. (1979) 'The effectiveness of the psychodramatic double method, the reflection method, and lecturing in the training of empathy', *Journal of Clinical Psychology*, 35, 2: 370–375.

Kipper, D. A. and Giladi, D. (1978) 'Effectiveness of structured psychodrama and systematic desensitization in reducing test anxiety', *Journal of Counseling Psychology*, 25: 499–505.

Kipper, D. A. and Hundal, J. (2003) 'A survey of clinical reports on the application of psychodrama', *Journal of Group Psychotherapy, Psychodrama and Sociometry*, 55: 141–157.

—— (2005) 'The Spontaneity Assessment Inventory (SAI): the relationship between spontaneity and non-spontaneity', *Journal of Group Psychotherapy, Psychodrama and Sociometry*, 58: 119–129.

Kipper, D. A. and Ritchie, T. D. (2003) 'The effectiveness of psychodramatic techniques: a meta-analysis', *Group Dynamics: Theory, Research, and Practice*, 7, 1: 13–25.

Lapierre, Y. D., Lavallée, J. and Tétreault, L. (1973) 'Simultaneous mesoridazine and psychodrama in neurotics', *International Journal of Clinical Pharmacology*, 7: 62–66.

Lemke, B. (1999) 'Umsetzung psychotherapeutischen Erfahrungswissens in den Alltag' [Transfer of psychotherapeutic experiential knowledge to everyday life], unpublished Masters thesis, Technische Universität Berlin.

Lind, M., Renner, W. and Ottomeyer, K. (2006) 'Die Wirksamkeit psycho- dramatischer Gruppentherapie bei traumatisierten Migrantinnen – eine Pilotstudie' [The effectiveness of psychodramatic group therapy with traumatized female immigrants – a clinical study], *Zeitschrift für Psychotraumatologie und Psychologische Medizin*, 4: 75–90.

Mann, L. and Janis, I. L. (1968) 'A follow-up study on the long-term effects of emotional role playing', *Journal of Personality and Social Psychology*, 8: 339–342.

Newburger, H. M. (1987) 'The covert psychodrama of phobias', *Journal of Group Psychotherapy, Psychodrama and Sociometry*, 40: 33–36.

O'Connell, W. E. and Hanson, P. G. (1970) 'Patients' cognitive changes in human relations training', *Journal of Individual Psychology*, 26: 57–63.

Ottomeyer, K. and Wieser, M. (1996) 'Dokumentation – Informationspapier über die methodenspezifische Ausrichtung des Psychodramas, Rollenspiels und der Soziometrie. Einleitung A. Schigutt' [Documentation – information paper on the modality of psychodrama, role play and sociometry. Introduction by A. Schigutt], *Psychodrama. Zeitschrift für Theorie und Praxis*, 9: 185–222.

Parrish, M. M. (1959) 'The effect of short-term psychodrama on chronic schizo- phrenic patients', *Group Psychotherapy*, 12: 15–26.

Peters, H. N. and Jones, F. D. (1951) 'Evaluation of group psychotherapy by means of performance test', *Journal of Consulting and Clinical Psychology*, 15: 363–367.

Petzold, H. (1979) 'Zur Veränderung der sozialen Mikrostruktur im Alter – eine Untersuchung von 40 sozialen Atomen alter Menschen' [Changes in the social microstructure in aging – a study of 40 social atoms of old people], *Integrative Therapie*, 4, 1–2: 51–78.

Petzold, H., Märtens, M., Steffan, A. and Zdunek, K. (n.d.) 'Psychodrama in der Praxis. Erste Ergebnisse einer Evaluationsstudie im ambulanten Setting' [Psychodrama in practice. Preliminary results of an effectiveness study on outpatients], unpublished paper, Düsseldorf.

Pintér, G. (2001) 'Psychodrama training: a way to become a psychotherapist in Hungary', in P. Fontaine (ed.) *Psychodrama Training: A European View* (2nd edn), Leuven: FEPTO Publications.

Ploeger, A., Seelbach, G. and Steinmeyer, E. (1972) 'Änderung der sozialen Wahrnehmung und der Gruppenstruktur im Verlaufe einer ambulanten Gruppenpsychotherapie – Soziometrische Analysen' [Changes in the social perception and group structure in the course of ambulant group psychotherapy], *Z. Psychoth. Med. Psychol.*, 22: 112–116.

Pour Rezaeian, M., Sen, A. K. and Sen Mazumdar, D. P. (1997a) 'The usefulness of psychodrama in the treatment of depressed patients', *Indian Journal of Clinical Psychology*, 24, 1: 82–88.

Pour Rezaeian, M., Sen Mazumdar, D. P. and Sen, A. K. (1997b) 'The effectiveness of psychodrama in changing the attitudes among depressed patients', *The Journal of Personality and Clinical Studies*, 13, 1–2: 19–23.

Schmidt, B. (1980) 'Empirische Untersuchungen differentieller Wirkungen des Psychodramas' [Empirical investigation of differential effects of psychodrama], *Gruppendynamik*, 11, 1: 122–141.

Schneider-Düker, M. (1989) 'Rollenwahl und Gruppenentwicklung im Psychodrama' [Choice of role and group development in psychodrama], *Gruppendynamik*, 20, 3: 259–272.

Schönke, M. (1975) 'Psychodrama in Schule und Hochschule – eine empirische Untersuchung' [Psychodrama in school and university – an empirical investigation], *Gruppendynamik*, 6, 2: 109–116.

Schramski, T. G., Feldman, C. A., Harvey, D. R. and Holiman, M. (1984) 'A comparative evaluation of group treatments in an adult correctional facility', *Journal of Group Psychotherapy, Psychodrama & Sociometry*, 36: 133–147.

Schramski, T. G. and Harvey, D. R. (1983) 'The impact of psychodrama and role playing in the correctional environment', *International Journal of Offender Therapy and Comparative Criminology*, 27: 243–254.

Steffan, A. (2000) 'Intermethodenvergleich Integrative Therapie und Psychodrama in der Praxis – Ergebnisse einer Evaluationsstudie im ambulanten Setting' [Comparison of integrative therapy and psychodrama in practice – results of an effectiveness study in outpatient setting], unpublished paper, Düsseldorf.

Strain, P. (1975) 'Increasing social play of severely retarded preschoolers with sociodramatic activities', *Mental Retardation*, 13: 7–9.

Sturm, I. E. and Stuart, B. R. (1974) 'Effects of remotivation and role re-training on inpatient interview presentableness', *Newsletter for Research in Mental Health and Behavioral Sciences*, 16: 15–19.

Theorell, T., Konarski, K., Westerlund, H., Burell, A.-M., Engström, R., Lagercrantz, A.-M., Teszary, J. and Thulin, K. (1998) 'Treatment of patients with chronic somatic symptoms by means of art psychotherapy: a process description', *Psychother-Psychosom.*, 67, 1: 50–56.

Toeman, Z. (1948) 'The double situation in psychodrama', *Sociatry*, 1, 4: 436–446.

Tschuschke, V. and Anbeh, T. (2000) 'Early treatment effects of long-term outpatient group. First preliminary results', *Group Analysis*, 33, 3: 397–411.

—— (2004) 'Therapieeffekte ambulanter Psychodrama-Gruppenbehandlung – Ergebnisse der PAGE-Studie' [Effects of outpatient group psychotherapy – results of the PAGE Study], *Zeitschrift für Psychodrama und Soziometrie*, 1, 85–94.

Waniczek, S. Harter, K.-E. and Wieser, M. (2005) 'Evaluation von Psychodramatherapie bei Abhängigkeitsstörungen' [Effects of psychodrama therapy with addicts], *Psychotherapie Forum*, 13, 1: 12–16.

Wieser, M. (2003) 'Studies in treatment effects of psychodrama therapy', in International Association of Group Psychotherapy (ed.) *Crossroads of Culture: Where Groups Converge*, Istanbul: IAGP.

—— (2004) 'Wirksamkeitsnachweise für die Psychodrama-Therapie' [Evidence for the effects of psychodrama therapy], in J. Fürst, K. Ottomeyer and H. Pruckner (eds) *Psychodrama-Therapie. Ein Handbuch* [*Psychodrama Therapy. A Handbook*], Vienna: Facultas.

—— (2005) 'Studies in treatment effects of psychodrama therapy ordered on basis of ICD-10. Preliminary results and conclusion', in International Association of Group Psychotherapy & International Federation of Psychotherapy (eds) *Containment with Courage in a Century of Challenges. 7th Pacific Rim Regional Congress of Group Psychotherapy & 4th Asia Pacific Conference on Psychotherapy, September 24 to 28 in Taipei*, Taipei: Chinese Association of Group Psychotherapy & Taiwan Association of Psychotherapy.

—— (2006a) 'Die Meta-Analyse zur Psychodrama-Psychotherapie in "Psychotherapie im Wandel" von Grawe, Donati und Bernauer' [The meta-analysis of psychodrama psychotherapy in 'Psychotherapie im Wandel' by Grawe, Donati, and Bernauer], *Psychotherapie Forum*, 14: 47–53.

—— (2006b) 'Studies on treatment effects of psychodrama psychotherapy ordered on the basis of ICD-10', in International Association of Group Psychotherapy and Group Processes (ed.) *Groups: Connecting Individuals, Communities and Cultures. XVI International Congress of Group Psychotherapy*, Sao Paulo/Brazil: IAGP.

—— <https://www2.uni-klu.ac.at/claroline/160321/> Documents/treatment effects.

Wieser, M., Fontaine, P., Tauvon, L. and Teszary, J. (2005) 'Scientific validation of psychodrama therapy. Fifteen replies to European Association of Psychotherapy (EAP) statements', unpublished paper, Klagenfurt.

Wood, D., Del Nuovo, A., Bucky, S. F., Schein, S. and Michalik, M. (1979) 'Psychodrama with an alcohol abuser population', *Group Psychotherapy, Psychodrama, Sociometry*, 32: 75–88.

World Health Organization (1992) *The ICD-10 Classification of Mental and Behavioural Disorders: Clinical Descriptions and Diagnostic Guidelines*, Geneva: WHO.

Moreno's basic concepts

Adam Blatner and Rosa Cukier

Introduction

Dr. J. L. Moreno developed a wealth of concepts associated with his method of psychodrama, and these are discussed at greater length in other books (Blatner 2000) as well as in this volume. Serving only as a foundation, in this appendix we select, organize, and describe Moreno's most basic concepts.

The first point is that, although the focus of this book is on the application of psychodrama in psychotherapy, in fact Moreno's vision was much broader. At a general philosophical level, Moreno's basic concepts spring from his thoughts about how the dynamics of creativity and spontaneity express the way God operates throughout the Cosmos. At the level of the social problems of humanity, Moreno developed ideas about sociometry (in the broadest sense), the place of drama and the arts in culture, and role theory. At the specific level of method, psychodrama functions as a complex of tools for integrating these elements in the service of group problem solving, and at an even more specific level, Moreno elaborated a variety of ways in which psychodrama could serve as a type of psychotherapy. Moreno envisioned this method and its derivatives – role playing, role training, sociodrama and the like – to have applications not only for healing, but also beyond the clinical context, in schools, churches, businesses, community affairs and so forth. This appendix is organized so that the concepts will proceed from the broader principles of philosophy and social psychology to the more specific theoretical constructs involved in psychodrama itself.

Moreno's philosophy

As a young man, Jacob L. Moreno was filled with religious idealism and fueled by ideas from many sources, including various philosophers, Christian and Asian sages as well as from his own Jewish heritage (Blatner 2005). He had a strong intuition that *creativity* was a fundamental way God acts in the cosmos, and that divine creativity is expressed in human relations to the degree that humanity can interact with greater freedom, spontaneity, and authenticity.

Creativity

The various other concepts to be described may be understood as serving the ideal of helping people to keep themselves, their relations and their world in a process of ongoing revision, seeking to create a better world. Moreno also imagined God acting through the creativity of each person (Blatner 2000: 73).

Moreno (1972: 49) viewed the desire for creativity as a basic motivation, and contrasted this with the dominant psychological theory at the time, Freud's idea that all behaviors were derivatives of libido. Instead, Moreno proposed that spontaneity and creativity are primary drives and positive phenomena. He wanted to promote the use of impromptu techniques in group settings, believing that this would increase spontaneity and develop an anti-mechanical attitude towards our times (Moreno 1972: 31).

Cultural conserve

This is Moreno's term for the category of that which has already been created. Moreno gave a name to this phenomenon because people tend to unthinkingly accept tradition as 'the way things are,' and this habit of mind stifles creativity. Identifying and naming a pattern helps people to think more clearly about it (Moreno 1972: 205). He conceded that the conserve itself has value – much of civilization is built on it (1972: 106) – but saw as the problem the *tendency to rely on* the conserve, whether it be a book (sacred or scientific), a technical device, or even a child's toy (Moreno 1978: 602–603). The point was not to inhibit our creativity in the present moment. We need to re-evaluate, continue to use that which is still helpful, and dare to revise or even abandon that which has become sterile or counterproductive.

Spontaneity

Spontaneity is a mixture of attitude, ability, and behavior, a readiness to improvise, to re-create as needed, responding to the needs of the moment. One of Moreno's chief insights and contributions was that the best way to promote creativity is through spontaneity. Instead of sitting and contemplating, more often creative breakthroughs come from a process of becoming holistically involved in the task, which opens the mind to intuitive and imaginative inspirations from the creative sources of the subconscious (Blatner 2000: 80).

A corollary is that, according to Moreno (1978: 47), a great deal of psycho- and socio-pathology can be ascribed to the underdevelopment and fear of spontaneity (*sponte*, free will) and a kind of addictive clinging to old solutions, as if they represent safeguards for the rest of our lives. Again, Moreno prescribes spontaneity training as a way to exercise our ability to respond adequately to new situations and learn new responses to old situations.

Warming up

This term refers to the process of gradually increasing degrees of spontaneity being exercised in a given situation, and cannot be directly willed. Spontaneity is a dynamic psycho-physical state that involves a number of variables, including the promotion of supportive interpersonal relations, a context of relative safety or play, and the reduction of sources of anxiety. Moreno noted that psychodrama grew out of the principle of play:

> play as a principle of cure, as a form of spontaneity, as a form of therapy and as a form of catharsis; play, not only as an epiphenomenon accompanying and supporting biological aims but as a phenomenon 'sui generis,' a positive factor linked with spontaneity and creativity.
>
> (Moreno 1950: 1–2)

Moreno felt that a deeper type of learning was associated with the greater degrees of warming up, because the spontaneity dynamic establishes special associations (1978: 540). Just as warming up is necessary for the body before vigorous exercise, so too the mind needs to warm up in order to engage in the creative activities that require a significant measure of spontaneity. In the process of psychodrama, everyone – protagonist, audience (group), auxiliary egos, and director – needs to warm up (Moreno 1972: xii, 1978: 61).

Encounter

Moreno applied the principle of spontaneity in interpersonal relations through his ideal of encounter. This involves an authentic willingness to engage others directly and to deeply consider their viewpoints. The Jewish theologian Martin Buber popularized a similar ideal, calling it the 'I–Thou' relationship. Interestingly, Waldl (2005) has observed that Buber was in fact influenced by Moreno.[1] (The concept of encounter is also related to the technique of role reversal, to be discussed further on.)

The theater of spontaneity

Moreno's interest in spontaneity may be rooted in his storytelling with children in the parks around Vienna. As a young man, he encouraged the youngsters to enact the stories he told. He was struck by the spontaneity they exhibited when they were given the freedom to improvise. Later, as a medical student, he became disenchanted with what he felt were tendencies towards stagnation in theatre practices, and felt that the introduction of more improvised elements would bring a measure of vitality and relevance back to the drama.

In the early 1920s, Moreno organized perhaps the first improvisational theatre troupe and conducted events in which the actors interacted with the audience (Moreno 1973: 28). Beyond the form of theatre, though, this principle applies also to the value of promoting more improvisational activities in other arts and activities.

Social psychology

After Moreno's most general thinking about philosophy, his next broadest theoretical complex of ideas is about aspects of social psychology. Sometimes he used the term 'sociometry' to include many other ideas, including role theory and concepts such as the social atom, interpersonal relations and group psychotherapy.

Sociometry

This term should be recognized as having two senses. First, it is the general category of ideas and practices that are aimed at promoting the spirit of spontaneity in human relations. It seeks to help people to feel able to exercise their preferences in selecting those with whom they want to affiliate in various interpersonal and group contexts. The second, narrower sense of the term sociometry refers to a variety of techniques for identifying, organizing, and giving feedback on the interpersonal preferences people have. Its classic approach involves asking people in a group to indicate who they would prefer to be with regard to a specific criterion. This might be done through paper-and-pencil questionnaires, the answers tabulated, and the presentation being in the form of a large map-like diagram. Other variations include the making of different kinds of diagrams, such as the social atom (see below), allowing the group to choose who will be the protagonist in a psychodrama, and so forth. In all sociometric processes, it is essential to consider the mutuality of the identified relationships. Sociometry became a minor but significant method for a while in the field of sociology, but its fullest potential has yet to be developed and applied.

Tele

This is Moreno's term for what is measured by sociometry, those patterns of reciprocated interpersonal preference. There can be neutral, indifferent, and negative forms of tele, as well as mildly and strongly positive connections. (Blatner suggests that using the term 'rapport' would more effectively communicate the idea to a wider range of people.) When tele is strongly positive, it seems to be associated with telepathic-like phenomena (Blatner 1994).

Interpersonal relations

At a time when psychoanalysts and academic psychologists were focusing on the individual, Moreno was a pioneer in viewing the person as embedded in a social field. He noted the still unappreciated idea that relationships can be problematic even if the people involved are not in themselves diagnosable as disordered. Similarly, people can seem dysfunctional in one group, but among a different set of relationships they may thrive. Thus, it is useful to apply sociometric principles in helping people in organizations and society to find their most congenial setting.

Social atom

This is Moreno's term for an individual's primary social networks. The term is also used for a diagram drawn of these networks so as to consider these dynamics. A variety of networks may be portrayed and reviewed: a network in the past, a hoped for social atom, one's cultural roles, inner role repertoire, affiliations with various groups, and so forth. Moreno notes that people have a dynamic social atom that begins before and at a person's birth. First containing mother and child, it slowly expands to include all individuals toward whom the child is emotionally related (Moreno 1974: 3). Prior to the emergence of object relations theory in psychoanalysis, Moreno (1978: 705) suggested that an individual is tied to his social atom as closely as he is to his body.

Group psychotherapy

Moreno was also one of the first proponents of the idea that people could help each other without the constant intervention of the expert (Moreno 1978: xv). He promoted the use not only of a more interactive group psychotherapy, but also milieu therapy in hospitals, self-help groups, and group work of all kinds. Moreno claimed that making full use of the potential of group therapy – and beyond the clinical context, other kinds of more democratic and interactive groups – would constitute the 'third psychiatric revolution.' (This numbering was based on a then prevalent tradition in psychiatry that the first psychiatric revolution involved the freeing of the insane from their chains, around 1793; the second revolution was the invention of psychoanalysis and other psychodynamic psychotherapies, in the first part of the twentieth century. Moreno did not anticipate the revolution brought by new medicines, which others have now called the third psychiatric revolution. Meanwhile, as group methods for learning together advance throughout the culture, his vision might yet constitute a 'fourth' revolution.)

Role theory

In the 1930s, drawing on his view of the dramaturgical foundation for psychosocial interaction, Moreno employed role theory as a bridge to social psychology, thus becoming one of the pioneers of this uniquely American approach to sociology, field theory, and so forth (Biddle and Thomas 1966). The role concept offers an accessible language for better understanding individuals and interpersonal and group situations. Of course, the role concept is the natural base metaphor for role-playing and psychodrama.

Moreno thought concepts such as 'self' or 'ego' were too vague (1978: 75), and that considering the individual as a dynamic interplay of roles was more useful. Some role theory principles include the idea that every individual has a range of roles and faces a series of counter-roles. These roles can be observed, developed, trained, extinguished, etc. At a given point in time, the various roles are in different levels of development and they tend to form clusters that influence each other (Moreno 1972: 175). Moreno wrote: 'Role is the functioning form the individual assumes in the specific moment he reacts to a specific situation' (1972: iv). We human beings are role players, blending private and collective elements in our outward behavior (1953: 75–88). This explains why everyone is capable of experiencing the role process on the stage (1972: 389). We are also expected to live up to our official (expected) role in life, and this can undermine our cravings to embody far more roles or more varieties within the same role. This usually produces some sort of anxiety (1978: 535).

The roles develop following the growth of the infant, starting with the psychosomatic roles (role of the eater, for instance) and then social roles (the parent) and psychodramatic roles (the god) (1972: 73). If everything runs normally, the child will gradually increase his abilities to include role taking, role playing, doubling, reversing roles (1972: 62–63) and role creating, achieving higher levels of spontaneity and freedom (1978: 503).

Role analysis

Systematic methods for examining roles – a practical extension of role theory – may be applicable in organizational analysis, in business, and so forth – as well as in therapy. Role analysis is synergistic with other approaches such as sociometry. Role analysis helps to examine role dynamics at the intrapsychic, interpersonal, group, and even socio-cultural levels of interactions.

Psychodrama

Like sociometry, psychodrama should also be thought of in a broader and narrower sense. Broadly, it refers to the general field that includes all of Moreno's work – sociometry, role theory, sociodrama, role playing in the schools, as well as psychodrama in therapy. Also, psychodramatic methods and related techniques are often integrated into many different kinds of therapy. In the narrower sense, psychodrama is a complex of principles and techniques that can be applied as a form of psychotherapy, most commonly in a group setting. There is also use of psychodramatic methods with families, couples, and individuals.

In enacting the protagonist's experience, psychodrama explores that person's phenomenological 'truth,' using dramatic methods to bring into the open the more subtle nuances. In addition to psychodrama being a magnification of reality into a drama, the replaying an event in light of present consciousness and a therapeutic context generates 'a second chance' to free people from the oppressive characteristics of reality and help reconstruct real life (Moreno and Moreno 1975a: 98).

Role playing

In the service of seeking solutions, problems, instead of just being discussed verbally, are enacted as if they were a scene in a dramatic play. In psychodrama, the person whose problem is being explored (the protagonist) generally takes the role, initially, of himself or herself, rather than playing the role of some fictional character. Psychodrama also has value as a holistic vehicle for analysis, rehearsal or even celebration. Moreno used role playing as a diagnostic method, as a training method, and also as a kind of 'role therapy' to improve relationships between the members of a group (1978: 503). Another feature of role playing is that it expands the role repertoire, helping people to be more able to respond to situations with a greater range of options. This offers not only more mental flexibility, but also a richer range of experiences. The surplus reality represented by the acting can in itself help people find new possible behaviors and expand the way they understand each other.

Here-and-now

Drama involves enactment as if it were in the present moment, even if the situation being explored in fact occurred in the past, or is an anticipated scene in the future. Attention is also given to heightening awareness in the present, and making new decisions in the present moment. Moreno used the Latin words, 'hic et nunc,' meaning the here (this place) and now (this moment) (Moreno and Moreno 1975a: 226), and this emphasis suggested Moreno's existentialist background. After all, the past and future are only remembered or anticipated – only the now exists.

Director

When facilitating a psychodramatic enactment, therapists become more active. Like the conductor of an orchestra, the director observes, supervises, interviews, and facilitates the interactions among the protagonist, auxiliaries, audience group, and so forth (Moreno and Moreno 1975a: 321). Moreno (1972) noted three functions of the therapist-director: therapeutic agent, co-investigator of social dynamics, and producer of the drama. Kellermann (1992) describes other role components and functions of the director, such as warming-up the all the participants, suggesting the use of various psychodramatic techniques, and moving the action forward.

Auxiliary ego

Moreno introduced the idea of having other people in the group play various roles in the enactment, such as the protagonist's spouse, parent, child, as well as surplus reality roles such as the double or 'higher self.' Fritz Perls' adaptation of psychodrama's empty chair technique in his method of Gestalt therapy avoided the use of the auxiliary, seeking to preserve the purity of the client's projections. Thus, he used a modified monodrama technique, though he hardly acknowledged Moreno's influence. Yet there are many situations in which the presence of another person who responds in direct interaction can evoke powerful responses and action insights that go beyond what monodrama can achieve. Moreno (1972: 242, 316) criticized the tendency in psychoanalysis of making the therapist the sole agent of healing, and instead affirmed that other people in the group and the group-as-a-whole might be helped to marshal a great proportion of the required healing factors.

Direct interaction

In the service of the principle of encounter, protagonists are helped to shift from a tendency to talk *about* their problems and instead to express their feelings and thoughts by (through role playing) directly speaking to the other person, whether that person is actually present, played by an auxiliary ego, or imagined to be sitting in an empty chair. Moreno (1972: x) notes the value of physical action, expressing feelings nonverbally as well as verbally in the here and now in such an encounter, as well as the insight-promoting presence of the group.

The stage

Moreno built an actual stage designed just for psychodrama, but even if it is only an area in a room designated for enactment, the point is to separate the role playing from the ordinary interactions among the group members (1972: 162–276). The stage concretizes the idea that certain behaviors are meant to be understood as exploratory, 'as-if,' dramas rather than final conclusions.

Psychodramatic techniques

There are scores of more commonly used techniques, such as asides, soliloquy, replay, the mirror, doubling, and hundreds of variations or refinements. These are designed to bring forth those ideas and feelings that operate just at the edge of explicit consciousness. Other techniques, such as future projection, help to evoke the protagonist's imagination, rehearse various activities, and so forth (Blatner 2000: 227–255).

With the scientific spirit of exploration, psychodramatic techniques might examine a situation using a variety of novel approaches in order to generate more creative perspectives (Moreno 1978: 42). The director might suggest that the protagonist try another person's role, try out a different physical position, or respond in the enactment to some coaching (1972: 138–139). The surprise element erodes more habitual and ordinary ways of solving problems, and challenges the protagonist to exercise a greater level of spontaneity to find a more satisfactory response (1972: 47).

Sharing

After a psychodramatic enactment, instead of mere interpretation and discussion, the protagonist is helped more by re-establishing a connection with and feeling supported by the group. The director says to the group: 'How has this drama been like something in your own life?' Moreno and Moreno (1975b: 237) called the post-action sharing by the group the third portion of a psychodramatic session. The director asks all the participants to share the feelings, emotions, and thoughts elicited through the dramatic work with the protagonist. Special care is taken in order to avoid criticism or intellectual analysis, since the protagonist is in a vulnerable position at the end of a psychodrama session, and needs support.

Role reversal

This is both a technique and a principle, promoting the exercise of empathy and moving beyond egocentricity in interpersonal relations. The path to understanding is aided by taking and playing the role of the other person in a situation, which builds trust and opens the imagination to understanding.

The activity of helping a protagonist role reverse with the significant other may be one of the more important techniques in a psychodramatic exploration. Role reversal is a key technique for helping people to develop empathy, and Moreno considered role reversal to be a major technique of socialization and self-integration, essential for couples (Moreno 1950: 142; Moreno and Moreno 1975b: 84–132), optimal group dynamics, parenting, teaching, and healthy child development (Moreno and Moreno 1975a: 155–157).

Act hunger

Moreno recognized that people need to feel themselves physically enacting their feelings, beyond mere verbal expression. He appreciated the somatic, holistic nature of experience, and the essential need for experience as part of healing. By naming this need 'act hunger,' it lends validity to the integration of activity and experience in psychotherapy. Moreno and Moreno (1975a: 156–157) note that the memory of the child is in his act as much if not more than in his purely mental dynamics. Since our body constitutes our first instrument and memory stock, it too desires expression: the body itself has 'act hunger' (Moreno 1978: 717).

Improvisation

Carrying on the philosophical theme of spontaneity, Moreno wove the principle of role playing as an improvisational rather than scripted activity. The experience of discovering in action what words and actions come up has its own therapeutic benefits, as it sensitizes the protagonist and group members to the potential insights that can come through this means, thus fostering increasing trust in the method.

Self-expression

Moreno found in drama a number of associated principles that could be used in the healing of patients. Better than talking with one person was having a group to act as audience, because the group offered the opportunity for the patient/protagonist to share their feelings with a number of people and have those people share their own feelings in return. Better than talking was acting, because dramatizing the feelings of the response made it more authentic, felt more true to the depth of the protagonist's experience, and also more readily touched the feelings of the audience who were associating this problem with events in their own lives. The use of art, music, dance or poetry might further facilitate the expression of the fullness of one's experience.

Catharsis

Catharsis was recognized by Freud, and described in ancient times by Aristotle, and Moreno noted that the flow and intensity of psychodrama often led to a flood of feelings which, when expressed, generated a sense of emotional release and a sometimes dramatic relief of symptoms. (Similar findings were observed in wartime: shell-shocked soldiers under short acting barbiturates, when helped to tell their stories, were able to relieve some of their psychosomatic symptoms.) Moreno noted that when people could fully express their feelings, there was a relief of psychic tension. He also observed that protagonists in psychodramas experienced an even more healing relief when they could enact a feeling or behavior that could be integrated into their lives. Moreno offered the guiding principle that every catharsis of abreaction should be followed by a catharsis of integration.

In a larger sense, there is a subtle catharsis that accompanies the 'aha' moment that occurs in every type of learning (Moreno 1978: 546). This can happen in self-realization as well as in conflict resolution, and, especially with more integrative types of catharsis, as an expression of deep peace as well as emotional release and relief.

Surplus reality

This is Moreno's term for the bringing into manifest form (through enactment) those situations that cannot happen in ordinary reality, such as an encounter with an unborn infant or a dead parent. It recognizes the phenomenological validity of 'psychological truth.' As Moreno wrote:

> It can well be said that the psychodrama provides the subject with a new and more extensive experience of reality, a 'surplus reality,' a gain which at least in part justifies the sacrifice he made by working through a psychodramatic production.
>
> (Moreno 1978: 85)

Axiodrama

In addition to exploring socio-cultural roles through sociodrama, it is also possible to engage in axiodrama, a type of psychodrama in which the protagonist explores his or her understanding of his own more abstract ideals or principles, matters of ethics, values, and 'eternal truths' such as justice, beauty, truth, perfection, eternity, peace, and so forth (Moreno 1978: xxvi, 61). For example, a protagonist might imagine the form taken by a spiritual entity, such as democracy, heaven, Nature, God, and so forth, and then use the 'empty chair' technique and role reversal, encountering them in a dialog (Blatner 2002). Other variations are possible, such as having auxiliaries play designated archetypal figures and interacting with them in different ways.

Beyond the clinical context

Moreno's vision was broad, attending to a range of applications for his ideas far beyond the realm of psychotherapy. His ideas beyond the clinic included the following.

Sociatry

This is another of Moreno's coined words, a play on the word 'psychiatry,' suggesting that treatment methods should be applied to help the larger society to resolve its conflicts and become healthier. The term expresses the idea that all of the aforementioned concepts and techniques may be applied, separately or integrated, in the service of 'therapy' not just for people in the sick role, but to help larger groups, communities, and the culture as a whole. For example, Moreno experimented with sociometry in school classrooms, and wrote about applications in business and religion. His open sessions in New York City also expressed this ideal, and doubtless supported the continued emergence in the theatre of improvisation and interactivity between actors and audiences.

Sociodrama

While psychodrama involves the role playing of the various specific roles associated with an individual, sociodrama addresses the predicaments and depth associated with more general roles. This approach is more appropriate for exploring collective concerns. Many of the techniques used are similar to psychodrama. This approach has wide applications in business, education, and other settings. 'Bibliodrama' is a type of sociodrama that explores the issues associated with certain widely known stories, such as from fairytales or the Bible.

Moreno felt his complex of methods might be utilized universally. Indeed, his objective was helping the whole of mankind (Moreno 1978: 3). Using sociometry, sociodrama and related approaches, he attempted to begin to engage in research regarding such issues as: group identity (Moreno 1972: 364–365); racial problems (Moreno 1978: 410, 560, 701); envy between groups (1978: 563), and other social issues.

Summary

One of the needed advances in theory is the development of some consensus as to definitions, meanings, and implications of key concepts in the field. However, we are aware that some might think other principles should deserve inclusion, and also that the various concepts should be presented in different words or with a different meaning. We, the authors, have presented the basic concepts of psychodrama, first in our own words, in light of modern language and concepts, but also to some extent in Moreno's more traditional language. Rosa Cukier (2002) has written a compilation of the innovator's writings, with the title (in Portugese) *The Words of Jacob Levy Moreno: Vocabulary of Quotations from Psychodrama, Group Psychotherapy, Sociodrama and Sociometry.* Her purpose has been to preserve Moreno's words so that everyone can understand in their own way what Moreno said.

Since the field is growing, we need to rely on more than Moreno's own writings. We can recognize his writings as a cultural conserve that can and should be transcended. We need a collaborative effort to rethink and redefine a number of terms. Such an ongoing creative process would also contribute to the continuing professional development of our field.

Note

1 Ed: In correspondence related to the present volume, Zerka Moreno adds:

> Robert Waldl, a psychotherapist and student of philosophy in Vienna, has discovered that it was Moreno's publications in Vienna, from 1914 until the early 1920s, concerning the significance of The Encounter, which pre-dated and influenced Martin Buber in his *I and Thou*. While Buber enlarged this idea and made it his singular contribution to philosophy, theology and psychotherapy, the elements underlying his labors point directly to the nine-years-younger J. L. Moreno, including Moreno's particular use of the German language. A handwritten letter from Moreno to Buber, dated 26 September 1918, has recently been found by Moreno's nephew, Joe Moreno, and sent to me. Moreno published a contribution by Buber in Moreno's expressionistic literary magazine *Neue Daimon* in 1919. That paper of Buber's dealt with Chassidism and contained no reference to the living encounter in the sense of Moreno. Buber's book appeared in 1923. The letter confirmed receipt of the manuscript. In addition, the magazine *Daimon* in 1918 carried

an announcement of Moreno's *Einladung Zu Einer Begegnung* [Invitation to an Encounter] – directly above that of Buber's forthcoming piece. There is no doubt that they were in direct contact. These facts contradict the written opinion of some years ago that it was Buber who influenced Moreno. But equally significant is that Moreno accompanied his *Invitation* in 1914 with his postal address and instructed that only those who actually intended to meet him there should answer him. No other letter was going to be taken seriously. That invitation is certainly unique.

References

Biddle, B. J. and Thomas, E. J. (eds) (1966) *Role Theory: Concepts and Research*, New York: Wiley.

Blatner, A. (1994) 'Tele: the dynamics of interpersonal preference', in P. Holmes, M. Karp and M. Watson (eds) *Psychodrama Since Moreno*, London: Tavistock/ Routledge (also accessible at www.blatner.com).

—— (2000) *Foundations of Psychodrama: History, Theory, and Practice* (4th edn), New York: Springer.

—— (2002) 'Enacted dialogue'. Retrieved from www.blatner.com

—— (2005) 'Role theory, archetypes, and Moreno's philosophy, illuminated by the kabbalistic "Tree of Life"', *Journal of Group Psychotherapy, Psychodrama & Sociometry*, 58, 1: 3–14.

Cukier, R. (2002) *The Words of Jacob Levy Moreno: Vocabulary of Quotations from Psychodrama, Group Psychotherapy, Sociodrama and Sociometry*, São Paulo: Agora. (Published in Portuguese and Spanish, as yet unpublished in English.)

Kellermann, P. F. (1992) *Focus on Psychodrama*, London: Jessica Kingsley Publishers.

Moreno, J. L. (1950) 'Hypnodrama and psychodrama', in *Psychodrama Monographs No. 27*, Beacon, NY: Beacon House.

—— (1972) *Psychodrama, Volume One*, Beacon, NY: Beacon House. (Originally published 1946.)

—— (1973) *The Theatre of Spontaneity*, Beacon, NY: Beacon House.

—— (1974) 'Psychodramatic shock therapy: a sociometric approach to the problem of mental disorders', *Group Psychotherapy and Psychodrama*, 27: 2–30.

—— (1978) *Who Shall Survive? Foundations of Sociometry, Group Psychotherapy and Sociodrama* (2nd edn), Beacon, NY: Beacon House.

Moreno J. L. and Moreno, Z. T. (1975a) *Psychodrama, Volume Two: Foundations of Psychotherapy*, Beacon, NY: Beacon House. (Originally published 1959.)

—— (1975b) *Psychodrama, Volume Three: Action Therapy and Principles of Practice*, Beacon, NY: Beacon House. (Originally published 1969.)

Waldl, R. (2005) 'J. L. Moreno's Einfluss auf Martin Buber's Ich und Du' ['J. L. Moreno's Influence on Martin Buber's "I and Thou"'], *Zeitschrift für Psychodrama und Soziometrie*, 4, 1: 175–191.

Author index

Subject index

abuse, 47, 76, 87, 90, 154, 161, 176, 177, 185, 193, 205, 206, 239, 240, 243–5
drug, 249–50
substance, 23, 249–50, 274, 275
act hunger, 102, 103, 105, 231, 232, 249, 302
action, 21, 25, 33, 34, 44, 47, 56, 60, 69, 70, 71, 84 *see also* experiential reintegration action therapy
insight, 34, 147
phases, 22–5, 36
representation, 233, 236
research, 140, 141, 143–4, 145, 148, 216
techniques, 8, 119, 121, 198
theory, 21, 22
addictions, 6, 37, 180, 193, 227
Adler, A., 5
affect regulation, 211, 228, 230
Allen, W., 262
all-identity, 88, 90
alter-image, 113, 114, 120, 121
amygdala, 229, 230, 232, 233, 234, 236 *see also* brain
anniversary syndrome, 157, 159–60, 164, 166
antithesis, 115, 116, 117, 120
anxiety, 24, 25, 29, 31, 35, 45, 116, 118, 119, 122, 123, 161, 180, 181, 228, 229, 230, 232, 249, 251–3, 254, 255, 279, 295, 298
Aristotle, 267, 303
art, 17, 63, 148, 195, 303
therapy, 165, 279
assessment, 8, 17, 44, 203, 244, 248
attachment, 129, 178, 211, 228, 240, 241, 243, 245, 246
theory, 152, 153, 175, 178, 239

attentional system, 231–2, 236
audience, 53, 56, 102, 104, 107, 127, 128, 135, 136, 206, 212, 217, 254, 267, 295, 296, 300, 302, 303 *see also* double, roles
auxiliary/ies, 49, 88, 89, 102, 103, 104, 106, 107, 108, 109, 145, 169, 195, 205, 220, 256, 300, 304
ego/s, 31, 35–36, 84, 85, 89, 90, 102, 129, 130, 217, 257, 258, 265–6, 300, 301 *see also* group
world, 255
axiodrama, 7, 304

Bateson, G., 67
Berne, E., 11
bibliodrama, 304
body, 6, 7, 13, 72, 73, 83, 84, 85, 129, 130, 132, 134, 164, 165, 166, 169, 170, 171, 177–8, 179, 181, 182, 193, 198, 227, 228, 230, 231, 232, 235, 236, 240, 241, 250, 253, 254, 255, 295, 297, 302
double, 176, 180, 182–3, 185
image, 83, 84, 85
language, 84, 134, 253
theatre of the, 235
Boyden, D., 16
brain, 6, 42, 136, 165, 171, 177, 184, 192, 227, 228, 229, 230, 233, 234, 240, 245 *see also* amygdala, corpus collosum, hippocampus, memory
executive, 235
left (hemisphere), 183, 184, 204, 211, 228, 230, 231, 232, 233, 234, 235, 236
limbic 164, 229
meta-representational, 235